379.15

Wakefield Libraries & Information Services

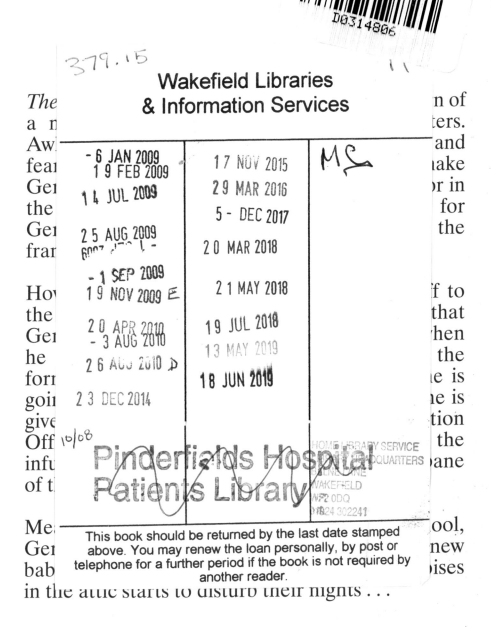

- 6 JAN 2009
1 9 FEB 2009
1 4 JUL 2009
2 5 AUG 2009
6007
- 1 SEP 2009
1 9 NOV 2009 E
2 0 APR 2010
- 3 AUG 2010
2 6 AUG 2010 D
2 3 DEC 2014

1 7 NOV 2015
2 9 MAR 2016
5 - DEC 2017
2 0 MAR 2018
2 1 MAY 2018
1 9 JUL 2018
13 MAY 2019
1 8 JUN 2019

M S

10/08

Pinderfields Hospital Patients Library

HOME LIBRARY SERVICE
HEADQUARTERS
BALNE LANE
WAKEFIELD
WF2 0DQ
01924 302241

This book should be returned by the last date stamped above. You may renew the loan personally, by post or telephone for a further period if the book is not required by another reader.

The ... n of
a ... ters.
Aw... and
fea... ake
Ge... r in
the ... for
Ge... the
fra...

Ho... f to
the ... that
Ge... hen
he ... the
for... e is
goi... e is
give... tion
Off... the
inf... ane
of t...

Me... ool,
Ge... new
bab... ises
in the attic starts to disturb their nights . . .

THE HEART OF THE DALES

Gervase Phinn

WINDSOR
PARAGON

First published 2007
by
Michael Joseph
This Large Print edition published 2007
by
BBC Audiobooks Ltd by arrangement with
Penguin Books Ltd

Hardcover ISBN: 978 1 405 61832 8
Softcover   ISBN: 978 1 405 61833 5

Copyright © Gervase Phinn, 2007

The moral right of the author has been asserted

All rights reserved.

British Library Cataloguing in Publication Data available

Printed and bound in Great Britain by
Antony Rowe Ltd., Chippenham, Wiltshire

For
Harry John Gervase Phinn,
my first grandchild

ACKNOWLEDGEMENTS

The author would like to thank Child's Play (International) Ltd for permission to use the extract from *Little Snail's BIG Surprise*, copyright © Carla Dijs, 1999.

The poem 'A Dalesman to His Son' on page 473 is based on the poem 'Mother to Son' by the American poet, Langston Hughes.

Remembering Mr Firth

So—
You are curious to know
What sort of man he was,
What kind of teacher?
Some, I guess, would say that he was unpredictable
    and loud,
Heavy-handed, hard-headed, proud,
A fiery figure with his froth of wild white hair
And bright all-seeing eyes,
That he talked too much
And listened too little.

Well—
I'll tell you.
He was a teacher
Who lifted history from the dusty page,
Re-fought battles on a chalky wooden board,
A storyteller who painted pictures of the past in
    vivid colour,
An enthusiast who, with bursts of energy
And eyes gleaming with a quick impassioned fire,
Resurrected shadowy characters of a bygone age:
Fabled kings and tragic queens, pale-faced martyrs
    and holy monks,
Princes and peasants, tyrants and warriors.
He brought history to life.

I recall
One cold November day,
In a hushed classroom
When he told the story of the sorrowful Scottish

    queen
Who climbed the scaffold stiffly,
Clad in a gown the colour of dried blood
To meet her fate at Fortheringhay,
And I felt that I was there.

So—
You are curious to know
What sort of man he was,
What kind of teacher?
He was the best.

CHAPTER ONE

David Pritchard, the inspector for Mathematics, PE and Games, was in rare good mood that Friday morning. It was during the schools' summer holidays and the two of us had been busily occupied for a good couple of hours packing up all our belongings in our old place of work, ready to take to the school inspectors' new office downstairs. We were having a break from our exertions, much of which entailed sorting through old files and putting papers no longer needed into rubbish bags—in the sure knowledge that we would require something we had thrown away within the first week of term. David, perched on the edge of a desk, was entertaining me with some amusing anecdotes related to his visits to the county's schools the previous term.

'There was the occasion,' he said, smiling widely at the memory of the incident, 'when the teacher, in an effort to test the children in their numeracy skills of addition, asked his class of nine-year-olds: "Now, children, if I laid eight eggs over here and nine eggs over there, what would I have?" "A bloody miracle," had come a muttered voice from the back of the room.'

I hooted with laughter—I just loved the things these young 'innocents' came out with.

'Another time,' David continued, 'a teacher was reprimanding a child who hadn't used a ruler and had drawn a very wobbly line freehand across his exercise book. "Don't you know what the word 'straight' means?" the teacher asked crossly. "Yes, miss," had come the reply, "without water".'

David and I were both laughing uproariously when a figure appeared at the door to the office.

Mrs Brenda Savage, Personal Assistant to Dr Gore, the Chief Education Officer, stood framed in the doorway with the usual haughty expression on her carefully made-up face. She was dressed in a tailored grey tweed jacket, tight pencil skirt, cream silk blouse with filigree lace collar, black patent leather shoes and, as was her wont, was garlanded in an assortment of expensive-looking jewellery. She looked for the entire world as if she were about to enter the set of one of those glamorous American soap operas. There was not a crease, not a hair out of place. She remained there regarding us with a self-important expression on her face.

'May I help you, Mrs Savage?' asked my colleague, staring over his spectacles.

'Mr Pritchard,' she said slowly and deliberately and giving him a decidedly chilly look, 'I had assumed that by this time the school inspectors would have relocated themselves to the office downstairs.'

'My dear Mrs Savage,' said David calmly, 'I have no desire to be impolite, much less disobliging, but we are in the very process of moving.'

'Well, as far as I can see, Mr Pritchard,' continued Mrs Savage, surveying the room, 'you haven't got very far. It is now Friday and you have to vacate these premises by today at the very latest so that Mr Reid and the Social Services team can move in at the beginning of next week. It's on my schedule here.' She tapped a long scarlet-painted fingernail on the clipboard she held in front of her.

Mrs Savage paused a moment, waiting for a reply but when one was not forthcoming she continued, her voice dripping with condescension. 'It appears to me that very little has been done.'

'I am fully aware of what day it is and what needs to be done, Mrs Savage,' replied David, giving her a thin smile that conveyed little more than feigned interest. 'I will be out of here by the end of the day, you can be quite certain of that. Come Monday, the area of the office which at present I occupy will be as empty as the North York Moors in December.'

'I did send a memorandum,' Mrs Savage persisted, 'stating quite clearly that it was imperative that the school inspectors' office be cleared in good time so that Mr Reid and the Social Services team are able to occupy it at the beginning of next week.'

'Indeed you did, Mrs Savage, and I read your memorandum with immense interest, as I always do when I receive one of your missives. I will vacate the office by the end of the day.' He replaced his glasses and returned to sorting through some papers on his desk.

The CEO's Personal Assistant was as unrelenting as a starving bulldog with a juicy bone and remained at the door standing stiff and straight, looking back at David with a stern expression. Since starting my job as a school inspector some four years before, I had found Mrs Savage, as had my three colleagues, extremely prickly and sometimes downright objectionable. This dramatically good-looking widow of indeterminate age, always immaculately turned out and dressed in the most expensive and elegant of outfits, sadly did not have a personality to match. She could be by turns rude and deferential, depending on the status and position of the person to whom she was talking. And it was patently clear she did not like talking to the school inspectors who she felt had far too much clout and influence. Her dislike of us was obvious and she seemed to go out of her way to be the most irritating, ill-mannered and petty member of the Education Department. Mrs Savage had a frightening reputation, an acid manner and a penchant for burdening us with a snowstorm of memoranda on every conceivable subject.

Getting no further response from David, she now turned her frosty eye in my direction and arched a carefully plucked eyebrow. 'Mr Phinn.'

'Mrs Savage?' I said.

'May I have *your* assurance that this office will be cleared and available for Mr Reid and the Social Services team by Monday morning?'

'You have my assurance, Mrs Savage,' I told her. 'The day is yet young. All will be removed by the end of this afternoon.'

'It's just that there appears to be still so much in here to pack,' she said, glancing around the room and pulling a face as if there were a bad smell. 'That corner area looks as if it hasn't been touched at all.'

'That's because it hasn't,' said David airily, without looking up from his papers. 'That's Mr Clamp's domain.'

'And where—' Mrs Savage began.

'And he's away in Italy,' added David.

'Away in Italy!' she exclaimed.

'On his holidays,' said David.

'On his holidays!' repeated Mrs Savage.

'Even school inspectors have holidays, Mrs Savage,' said David, looking up. 'As the inspector for Visual and Creative Arts, he is spending two *creative* weeks in Venice, Florence and Rome, where he is collecting material for next term's art courses. Then he is spending a third week in Sorrento.'

'But this is a *most* inconvenient time for him to decide to take a holiday,' she growled.

'Mrs Savage,' said David, 'you must understand that we school inspectors can only take our holidays when the teachers and pupils take theirs and not in term time.' He blinked up at her through his spectacles.

'But Mr Clamp should have kept this week free,' she said peevishly. 'My memorandum specifically earmarked this week for the office to be cleared prior to the move next week,' she continued, relentlessly pursuing her theme. 'When it was agreed by Dr Gore that the school inspectors should have larger premises downstairs— something about which I had strong reservations, I have to admit—I indicated in a first memorandum that the move would take place during the schools' summer holidays.'

'But not exactly when,' I commented.

'I beg your pardon?' She gave me a disdainful glance.

'You never gave an exact date when you required us to move.'

'I stated the date specifically in the second memorandum,' said Mrs Savage sharply, tapping at her clipboard again. 'It was all carefully planned. I said it in my memorandum quite distinctly, the one that Mr Clamp has clearly ignored.'

David began shuffling papers with more noise than was necessary. I stared out of the window.

'And when will Mr Clamp be back, may I ask?' she enquired. 'Perhaps you can—'

'Mrs Savage,' sighed David, raising his hand and, in the process, stopping her mid sentence, 'I am not my colleague's keeper. What he does and where he goes is entirely his own concern. Knowing Mr Clamp, as we all do, you will be well aware that, like many a creative person, he is somewhat elusive, unconventional and unpredictable and is certainly not one to be easily directed by others. He is one of the world's individuals, a maverick.'

'Well, we will have to see what Dr Gore has to say about it,' she replied, her face flushing with annoyance.

'It's not Mr Clamp's fault,' I told her. 'I'm afraid your second memorandum with the dates of the move must have arrived on our desks after Mr Clamp had departed for Italy.'

'I think not!' she snapped. 'I sent that memorandum out a good three weeks ago. It is typical of Mr Clamp to ignore my memoranda. I have had occasion to speak to him about it before.'

'Well, whatever,' said David dismissively, 'he's not here and no doubt at this very moment he's lying on the beach in Sorrento.'

'But what about all his files and folders, his cabinets and cupboards, all these pictures and posters, papers and boxes?' Mrs Savage asked. 'They can't remain here.'

'Don't worry, Mrs Savage,' I said, 'we'll move his things for him.'

David gave a hollow laugh. '*We* most certainly will not!' he cried, emphasising the first word. 'I do not intend moving them. I've got quite enough of my own stuff without lugging all Sidney's rubbish down two flights of stairs. Not with my bad back, I'm not.'

'Well, this is most unsatisfactory,' said Mrs Savage. 'It is imperative that this room is cleared today for—'

'Mr Reid and the Social Services team to move in on Monday,' interrupted David. 'Yes, Mrs Savage, so you keep saying.' Then he added mischievously, 'Perhaps you could arrange for someone to pack Mr Clamp's stuff? What about Derek from the Post Room?'

'Certainly not!' she snapped. 'I am far too busy to arrange anything of the sort. I have a major conference for Dr Gore to organise, quite apart from all my other urgent administrative duties within the department.'

'My, my, what a busy bee you are, Mrs Savage,' observed David.

She ignored the sarcasm. 'And, in any case,' she continued, 'it is the inspectors' responsibility to move their own files and materials and to clear their desks.' She glanced at the only area of the room that was empty of everything apart from the cleared desk. 'It's a pity that all the inspectors aren't as efficient and well organised as Dr Mullarkey. I notice that she has moved everything of hers.'

'We can't all be as efficient and well organised as the inspector for Science and Technology,' said David.

'More's the pity,' she muttered.

'Mrs Savage—' began David in a voice threatening to brim over with fury.

'Don't worry, Mrs Savage,' I interrupted, 'the room will be cleared by the end of the day.'

'I sincerely hope so,' she said, her mouth drawn together.

'Is there anything else, Mrs Savage?' asked David. 'It's just that we are rather busy at the moment and we do wish to make a start moving into our new offices downstairs.' He peered over his glasses. 'We certainly wouldn't want Mr Reid and the Social Services team to be inconvenienced, now, would we?'

Mrs Savage gave him a look like the sweep of a scythe and made a loud clucking noise with her tongue. 'I shall be having words with Dr Gore,' she threatened.

'Please do that,' Mrs Savage,' said David. 'In fact, perhaps *he* might like to give us a hand moving.'

The Personal Assistant of the Chief Education Officer departed angrily in a whiff of Chanel Number 5.

'In all my years in education,' said David, removing his spectacles, 'I have never, never met such a pettifogging, tactless, infuriating and interfering person as Mrs Savage. Who does she think she is, swanning over here, speaking to us like an infants headteacher telling off some naughty children? It's a pity she hasn't anything better to do with her time. "I have a major conference for Dr Gore to organise," she says. Who does she think she's kidding? When was the last time the CEO held a conference?'

'She just likes to appear important,' I said. 'You

8

shouldn't let her wind you up so much. You'll give yourself a coronary getting so angry.'

'Gervase,' said David, 'if the woman had, like any normal person given the job of organising an office move, enquired in a pleasant and good-humoured way how things were going, I wouldn't have got all wound up. Goodness knows how such a tactless, talentless and tyrannical person like Mrs Savage has managed to get the position she has, and how in heaven's name Dr Gore puts up with her is beyond belief.'

'She does have some abilities,' I said. 'She's quite efficient in her own way. It's just her manner.'

'The only ability that virago is blessed with,' said David, 'is to appear very busy whilst actually avoiding work of any kind. "Major conference for Dr Gore", my foot! And what are all these urgent administrative duties within the department? She delegates everything she's given. I don't recall seeing Mrs Savage in her tight skirt and high heels ever risk breaking her nails taking so much as a pile of files from her office to one of the committee rooms. I've a good mind—'

David's diatribe was interrupted by the appearance at the door of Julie, the inspectors' secretary. 'Has she gone?' she asked in hushed voice.

'She has,' I told her.

'Thank goodness for that,' she sighed. 'I just couldn't face she of the joyless countenance and the viper's tongue this morning. Mrs Savage has that wonderful effect of brightening up the room by leaving it.'

David grunted, shook his head and muttered

9

something inaudible. He was obviously still simmering.

'What did she want at half past ten on a Friday morning?' Julie asked.

'To see if we'd cleared the office,' I told her.

'Well, what's it got to do with her?' asked Julie.

'She's been put in charge of the move,' I told her, 'and she was checking up.'

'As you well know, Julie,' said David, 'everything in the Education Department has to do with the meddlesome Brenda. She has her long red-nailed fingers in every pie. Well, if she thinks that pestering me will make me vacate this office any quicker, she's got another think coming. I shall move out in my own good time. And there's no way I'm shifting all Sidney's stuff downstairs.'

'Don't worry about that, ' said Julie. 'I'll sort it out later.'

'You can't possibly do all that on your own,' said David.

'We'll do it together, Julie,' I said, 'when I've finished moving my own things.'

'OK,' she said smiling. 'Now, who's for a cup of coffee?'

'I'll have a large strong sweet mug of caffeinated coffee, please,' I said. 'I have an idea that it's going to be a long long day.'

'I could do with a double brandy after that encounter,' David remarked. He picked up a large cardboard box full of files. 'I'll dispense with the coffee, thank you, Julie, and make a start re-homing this little lot downstairs. I want to pick a spot well away from Sidney. When he's in the office, I never get anything done.'

'I'll get the coffee and then I'll give you a hand,'

10

Julie told me.

'And, despite what I told the wicked witch of County Hall,' said David, 'I suppose I shall reluctantly have to help you move all Sidney's stuff or I'll never hear the last of it.' He shook his head like a terrier. 'Not that I wish to agree with Mrs Savage, but it is damned inconvenient for Sidney to be away just now. Typical, of course. That man could fall into a mound of steaming manure and emerge smelling of roses.'

'I'll put the kettle on,' said Julie, laughing, and headed for the door.

If the man in the street were to describe what he imagined a school inspectors' secretary might look like, I guess he would picture a small, serious-minded and quietly efficient woman with grey hair scraped into a neat little bun at the back of her head. She would be dressed soberly with sensible flat-heeled shoes and a few bits of plain jewellery. She would be deferential, inconspicuous and innocuous. Well, Julie could not have been more different. She wore ridiculously short skirts, tight-fitting jumpers and outrageously high heels, and had thick bubbly dyed-blonde hair. Heads turned whenever this young woman with the hourglass figure and swinging hips sashayed down the marbled corridors of County Hall.

Everyone in the inspectors' office loved Julie and relied heavily upon her. She had the qualities of many a Yorkshire lass; she was funny, excessively talkative, outspoken and big-hearted but also possessed the sterling qualities of the really good secretary. Julie was industrious, highly organised and entirely loyal. She was also very discreet when it came to anything within the

11

inspectors' office but she had a useful network of contacts within County Hall who supplied her with all the latest gossip, which was relayed to us at regular intervals.

That morning, Julie was wearing a body-hugging turtleneck jumper of shocking pink, a black pelmet of a skirt, treacherously high red leather stiletto shoes and a pair of large pendulous silver earrings. It was not the sort of outfit best suited for someone who would be spending the day moving everything down two flights of stairs from one office to another.

A few minutes later she arrived back with two steaming mugs, which she set down on Dr Mullarkey's desk, the only one with an area left uncovered.

'So how was your holiday?' I asked, reaching for the coffee.

'Never again!' she exclaimed, perching on the edge of the desk, crossing her long legs and throwing her head back like a model posing for a photograph.

'Not too good then?' I hazarded.

She uncrossed her legs and sat up straight. 'I went camping in France with my boyfriend and his mum and dad. For the last three years we've been on holiday with Paul's parents, and I should know better by now. Well, this is definitely the last time I'm going with them. After that disastrous time in Spain three years ago when Paul fell asleep in the sun and woke up like a lobster with an attitude problem and a face full of blisters the size of balloons, we decided to stay in England the next year and go to Skegness in his auntie's caravan. I think I told you it rained for the full two weeks except for the one fine day when Paul broke his ankle jumping off the sea wall. I spent most days at the hospital and most nights wide awake listening to Paul's father snoring like a hippopotamus with sinus trouble.'

'Yes, I remember you regaling me with the Skegness saga. So what happened in France?'

'It was worse,' she said. 'We were squashed in two leaking tents near a stagnant, mosquito-infested lake, the showers packed up, Paul's mum moaned about the food the entire time, and his dad got into an argument with the site manager when he told him that the French were pretty quick to surrender to the Nazis in the last war and if it wasn't for the British Army bailing them out, he'd be wearing great jackboots and speaking German.'

'Oh dear,' I said, smiling.

'Then Paul got food poisoning from a plateful of prawns, the car broke down just as we were driving onto the ferry and all the French lorry drivers we held up behind us hurled abuse at us. When we did finally manage to get across the Channel, the Customs men found and confiscated the extra bottles of duty free that Paul's mother had hidden under her coat, and she never stopped whingeing all the way back to Yorkshire.'

'Yes, it was certainly eventful,' I said.

'Never again,' sighed Julie, shaking her blonde curls. She took a sip of coffee. 'Have you been to France?'

'I went to Paris with the school when I was fifteen and I can't say it was a great success,' I told her, remembering the miserable time I had had in a dark and spartan hostel on the outskirts of the

13

city, sleeping in a dormitory colder than death, on a bunk bed as hard as nails. 'It came as quite a shock,' I told Julie, 'that all the French I had been learning for years and years at school was completely incomprehensible to the Parisians. People just laughed when I opened my mouth.'

'Well, it'll be the last time I go to France, I can tell you,' said Julie.

'Oh, I shall go again one day,' I said. 'Of course, it helps having a wife who can speak the language. Christine spent a year there as part of her French course at college so I won't make a fool of myself the next time. I'll let her do all the talking. When the baby gets older, we intend to go camping in Brittany.'

'So where did you go for your holidays this summer then?' Julie asked.

'We stayed in Yorkshire,' I told her, recalling the wonderful two weeks Christine and our baby son Richard had spent in a guesthouse in Robin Hood's Bay on the east coast.

The weather had been gloriously bright and rain-free, and we had enjoyed many a happy hour sitting on the beach in the sunshine making sand castles—I claimed I had to get in practice for when Richard was older—collecting shells, searching for crabs in the rock pools, walking along the cliff top with the baby strapped to my back, and exploring the little snickleways between the cottages in the village. Each evening, when the baby was safely tucked up in his cot, Christine and I would sit in the guesthouse's conservatory that overlooked the great sweep of the bay. What a scene it was: the looming cliffs rising from a placid sea turned pink and gold by the setting sun, the jutting outcrops of

14

dark purple rocks reaching out like gnarled fingers. I had been so happy.

Tricky Dicky, as we called him, had not lived up to his nickname; he had been far from demanding. In fact, he had not been an ounce of trouble, feeding happily, sleeping soundly and crying rarely. He was such a contented child that we really couldn't believe our good fortune in having such a model baby.

'So was it good?' asked Julie.

'It was super,' I told her. 'We had a great time.'

'Well,' she said, stretching, 'I'm glad somebody did. You had better finish your coffee. We have work to do.'

By the end of the afternoon, the small cramped room that had been my place of work for four years was clear of everything. David, Julie and I had made journey after journey up and down the narrow stairs, struggling with boxes full of reports and guidelines, balancing armfuls of files and folders, carting books and journals. The worst stuff to carry down was, of course, everything that belonged to Sidney. By five o'clock, all that remained in the office was the furniture that was not coming with us—the four heavy oak desks with their brass-handled drawers, the ancient wooden swivel chairs, and the now-empty grey metal filing cabinets and dark heavy bookcases.

David, Julie and I surveyed the room, hot, tired and ready for home.

'Well, that's a job well done,' I said.

'I shall miss this room, you know,' said David. 'Even though we complained over the years about the lack of space, the icy draughts in winter and the unbearable heat in summer—'

15

'The creaking floor and threadbare bit of carpet,' added Julie.

'And the uncomfortable chairs and the fact that we couldn't find anything amidst the clutter, but it did have character,' said David. He ran his hand across a desktop. 'I shall miss my old desk.'

'Although I, too, feel rather sorry having to leave the place,' I said, 'we shall be able to spread out in the new office with its modern furniture, and we won't have those stairs to climb every day.'

At that very moment we heard heavy footsteps on the selfsame stairs, accompanied by a loud and discordant voice giving a rendering of 'Come Back to Sorrento'.

'Tell me I am imagining things,' whispered David.

'No,' said Julie, 'it's Mr Clamp all right.'

The great bearded figure with the deep-set, earnest eyes appeared at the door like a pantomime villain. Sidney stopped singing, removed a large fedora hat in a flourish and beamed at us. Then he stared beyond us and around the empty office.

'Sweet angels of mercy!' he cried. 'Where is everything? The place is as bare as Old Mother Hubbard's cupboard.' We stood looking at him, stony-faced and silent. 'Whatever is the matter with you three?' he asked. 'You look like some strange Eastern statues. From the look on your faces, it appears that I am intruding on some private grief.'

David breathed in noisily, raised his eyes heavenwards but said nothing.

'Hello, Sidney,' I said.

'Did you forget, Mr Clamp,' asked Julie, 'that

16

we were moving into the new office this week and that we had to clear everything out from here to there?'

'Aaaaah,' groaned Sidney smacking his forehead dramatically with the flat of his hand. 'The move, the move! Of course, we're relocating to the new office this term, aren't we?'

'We are,' I said.

'I only popped in to collect my mail,' he said. He tapped his chin thoughtfully. 'Was it this week we were supposed to be moving?'

'It was,' I said.

'We have to be out of here by the end of the day so Social Services can come in on Monday,' added Julie. 'The three of us have had to take all your stuff downstairs to the new office for you.'

'We assumed you weren't coming in today,' I told him.

'How awfully decent of you to move my bits and bobs,' said Sidney. Then his face clouded over. 'I say, I do hope that you have taken great care with my things. There were a lot of valuable artefacts amongst my possessions. Dear God,' he said, his eyes roving round the almost empty room, 'what have you done with Aphrodite?'

Sidney had a fairly ghastly white plaster model of the Goddess of Love, which he used in his drawing classes.

'Aphrodite is safe and well in the new office,' replied David who, amidst loud complaining, had carried the scantily clad female downstairs.

'I trust you haven't been heavy handed with the portfolios and not damaged any of the artwork,' Sidney continued. 'I know how maladroit you can sometimes be, David.' He strode across to what had been his desk, and wrenched open the top drawer. 'Oh heavens, there were some most important documents in this drawer. What's happened to them?'

'Don't panic,' I said, 'I've locked them away in your new desk downstairs.'

The telephone sitting on Sidney's desk suddenly rang, echoing round the almost empty room. Julie, standing nearest it, picked it up.

'Inspectors' office,' she said. She listened for a moment, nodded her blonde head, and then replaced the receiver. 'That was Mr Reid of Social Services. He said that we shouldn't rush as they are somewhat behind schedule and won't be ready to move up here until Tuesday at the earliest.'

'Open the window, Gervase,' said David, slowly and quietly, 'I am about to jump out.'

CHAPTER TWO

Thursday morning of the first week of the new autumn term found me at Ugglemattersby County Junior School to undertake what I imagined to be a morning's routine follow-up inspection. The building, unlike many of the Dales village schools in Yorkshire, was entirely without character: a featureless, squat, grey stone structure with long, metal-framed windows, blue slate roof and a heavy black door. It was dwarfed by the neighbouring boarded-up, red-brick Masonic Hall on one side and a down-at-the-mouth public house on the other.

I had visited the school some two years earlier

on a bleak and blustery morning in late April. Setting off from the Inspectors' Division of the Education Department in the bustling market town of Fettlesham, I had driven through a desolate, rain-soaked landscape of rolling grey moors to reach the school in the large sprawling village of Ugglemattersby.

On that occasion, I had not been impressed with the standard of education provided and my largely critical report had led to the enforced early retirement of the headteacher. Mr Sharples, a dour man, with the smile of a martyr about to be burnt at the stake, had rattled on in wearisome detail about the stresses and strains, pressures and problems, difficulties and disappointments he had to face day after day. He had bemoaned the awkward parents, interfering governors, disillusioned teachers, lazy cleaners and wilful children, and now critical school inspectors had appeared on the scene to depress him even more.

'I feel like jumping off Hopton Crags,' he had told me disconsolately, 'or down a pothole at Grimstone Gill, I really do.'

In actual fact, he had jumped—jumped at the chance, when offered a generous package, to retire early and the last I had heard of him he was running a health-food shop in Whitby, happily selling dried fruit, cashew nuts and wholemeal flour.

A new headteacher, Mr Harrison, was appointed. I had sat on the interview panel and had been impressed with this youthful, bright-eyed deputy headteacher from a large multi-racial school in inner-city London, who had performed extremely well, impressing the panel with his

19

enthusiasm, good humour and by the vivid description of how he would set about changing things for the better were he to be appointed.

Sadly on this September morning, if the initial impressions I had were anything to go by, the new headteacher had not come up to expectations, for little appeared to have altered since my last visit. What I thought would be a meeting of ten or fifteen minutes before classes started, turned out to be quite different.

'It's been difficult, Mr Phinn,' Mr Harrison told me sadly, tugging nervously at his small moustache. 'I rather imagined that moving north to such a lovely part of the country, to become the headteacher of a village school in rural Yorkshire, would be idyllic and certainly less challenging and stressful than at my last school in the inner city. I little imagined the problems I would have to face.' He sounded unnervingly like his predecessor and, indeed, was beginning to take on Mr Sharples' appearance, too.

The headteacher seemed to have aged considerably since our last meeting at his interview. As I sat in his cramped office that morning, I was concerned at the change I saw in him after so short a time. Gone were the broad and winning smile, the bright eyes, the bubbly enthusiasm and the confident manner. He looked ashen and deeply uncomfortable and stared at me with the doleful eyes of a sick spaniel.

'Perhaps you would like to tell me about it,' I said, realising that what I imagined would be a pleasant, uneventful routine visit was turning into something likely to be far more problematic.

'Well, this is a very different world from the one

I knew in London,' Mr Harrison continued. He interlaced his fingers slowly and rested them beneath his chin in the attitude of a child at prayer, and then took a deep audible breath. 'I came from a large multi-cultural and very vibrant inner-city school where the staff worked hard and pulled together. The children were challenging and, yes, perhaps a little too lively at times. We had our fair share of problems, but it was a very positive and productive environment. Ugglemattersby is completely different. In terms of discipline, the children are biddable enough, though rather blunt, but everything is so—how can I put it—laid back. Your report on Mr Sharples' regime quite rightly mentioned the lack of rigour and creativity in the curriculum and, since starting, I have attempted to change things but, sadly, with little apparent success. People in this part of the world seem very resistant to change. The parents on the surface are friendly—well, most of them—and, like their children, they too certainly speak their minds, but I can't say I've been accepted. I think you have to live in the area for upwards of three centuries to lose the tag of "off-comed-un".'

'I know what you mean,' I replied. 'I've only been in this part of the county for four years myself and, despite being Yorkshire born and bred, I am definitely still in the category of the alien foreigner.'

'If I may say so, Mr Phinn, it's hardly the same for you.' The headteacher rose from his chair and stood looking pensively out of the small window, his hands clasped behind him. 'School inspectors travel around and are not confined to live and work every day in the heart of a closed, parochial

21

community where everyone knows everybody else's business. My wife and I bought our dream house in the centre of the village, a little stone cottage with beams and a flagstone floor and a stream at the bottom of the garden, which, with hindsight, was a mistake. My wife can't walk down the street in Ugglemattersby without a curtain moving, she can't say anything in the post office without it being broadcast around the whole neighbourhood and she can't purchase an item from the village shop without all and sundry knowing what we are having for tea. I get stopped by parents all the time, wishing to discuss their children's education.' He turned away from the window, bit his lip momentarily and began tugging nervously at his moustache once again. 'It's so very claustrophobic!'

'I see.' He should have considered all this, I thought to myself, before he had accepted the position, but I kept this observation to myself and changed the subject. 'Does Mrs Braddock-Smith at the Infant School have this problem?' I asked.

'Ugglemattersby Infant School,' Mr Harrison told me, sitting down again at his desk, 'is in a much better position than mine. For a start, Mrs Braddock-Smith's school is not in the centre of the village, sandwiched between the noisy pub and a derelict building, like we are. The people who live on the new estate of executive houses send their children to the Infant School. From what I have heard, they are very supportive and have great expectations for their children. Staff at the Infant School are keen, hard-working and ambitious, and the headteacher very sensibly lives outside the catchment area.'

I had visited Ugglemattersby Infant School just after I had started as a school inspector and remembered it as a modern, spacious building with endless views across the ever-changing moors. When, a number of years earlier, the village had begun to increase and the pupil population accordingly, it had been decided to split the Juniors from the Infants, then currently in the one school, and the new school had been built on a large open site just outside the village. I also recalled the extremely confident and effusive headteacher who spent most of our meeting singing the praises of her wonderful school.

'Well,' I said to the obviously unhappy headteacher, 'perhaps you ought to consider moving.'

'To be honest, I have been looking for other jobs.'

'I meant moving house,' I said quickly.

'Oh, I see. To be frank, it's not the fact that I live in the village that's the real problem,' Mr Harrison continued disconsolately, resting his hands on his desk. 'I can just about cope with the twitching curtains and the lack of any privacy. It's the people I work with.' He shook his head again, took a deep breath and lowered his voice. His gullet rose and fell like a frog's. 'The two teachers I inherited are not exactly incompetent but, my goodness, they can be difficult. They do the very minimum, and are not the most enthusiastic or accommodating of colleagues, either. In fact, they spend most of the day complaining, as you will no doubt discover. Mrs Battersby, who teaches the top Juniors, has been here all her teaching career. Not only that, she attended the school herself as a child, went to school with most of the grandparents and taught most of the children's mothers and fathers. She's part of the furniture. In fact, the wing-backed armchair she sits in in the staff room, she brought from home. Her husband, another former pupil, owns an antique shop in the village. He's a parish councillor, churchwarden, treasurer of the Pigeon Fanciers Society, a stalwart of the community. He knows everything and everybody. Mrs Battersby leaves school two seconds after the bell to help her husband in the shop. You would think from her reaction when I suggested that she might like to produce the school play or attend an additional parents' meeting that I was making some grossly improper advance.

'The other teacher, Mrs Sidebottom—which she prefers to be pronounced Siddybothome—well, I don't know where to start with her. She, too, has been here many years and is far far pricklier. It's like dancing through a minefield every time I speak to her. We never hit it off from the start after I mentioned that I felt her manner with the children was rather sharp. Of course, as soon as I took over as the headteacher, I followed your recommendations to send them both on courses but it was wishful thinking to imagine that a couple of days of in-service training at the Staff Development Centre was going to change the habits of a lifetime. They came back saying what a complete waste of time it had been and I later discovered the science guidelines, recommendations and notes given by Dr Mullarkey, the tutor, had been deposited in a wastepaper basket. Again, as you suggested in the report, I did insist that they planned their lessons more carefully, which they now do—more or less, anyway—and to mark the children's work more thoroughly, which they have done with something of a vengeance, but I have got nowhere with my requests that they should contribute rather more to the life and work of the school. Mention out-of-school activities and they look fit to faint. They are forever reminding me that it is not in their contract. I am sorry to say that many of my efforts have fallen on stony ground.'

'Perhaps you should have contacted the Education Office before this,' I said. 'The situation sounds serious.'

'I did think of doing just that, but a newly-appointed headteacher running to the Education Office before he's got his legs under the table, complaining and saying he was having problems, would not have gone down very well, now, would it?' He paused, tugged nervously at his moustache again, then looked straight at me. 'Actually, Mr Phinn,' he continued, 'I had rather thought that you would have called in to see how I was getting on. In your report, you did say that you would be making a visit to check on how things were progressing. I rather expected that you would have got in touch before now. At my last school in London, the school inspectors were regular visitors and I always welcomed their support and advice.'

He had been right, of course. I had promised to return to the school and monitor progress but I had failed to do so. 'Yes,' I replied now, rather sheepishly, 'I did. I'm afraid I've been so very busy and I assumed, quite wrongly as it turns out, that things were improving. It was remiss of me.' Then I added defensively, 'Of course, Yorkshire is the biggest county in the country—the size of Israel, I've been told—and there are so many schools to visit by a relatively small team of inspectors.'

'I'm not blaming you, Mr Phinn,' the headteacher told me. 'I am responsible for the effective running of the school and it is down to me to implement your recommendations and make the necessary changes.'

Nevertheless, I thought to myself, I should have followed things up.

'I assumed,' Mr Harrison continued, 'that once I had settled in and gained the confidence of the governors, parents and, hopefully, my teaching colleagues, I could develop so many new and interesting initiatives and move the school forward. Sadly, I have not been very successful. Many parents of the children at the Infant School don't want their children educated at Ugglemattersby Juniors and opt for other schools when their offspring reach seven, rather than sending them here. Over the last few years, there's been a steady haemorrhaging of children from this school and I've not been able to stem the flow. Ugglemattersby used to have four classes ten years ago but now we're down to three and we lost our brightest pupil in the top class last week. She's gone on to a preparatory school in Ribsdyke. It's all very depressing.'

'Well, I think we may have to consider competency here, Mr Harrison,' I said.

'Mr Phinn!' Mr Harrison burst out. 'I have tried, I really have and—'

'No, no, not your competency but that of your teaching staff,' I hastily assured him. 'I assume the governors are aware of your concerns?'

'In some part, yes, but there lies another difficulty. I get little support from the present governing body. The governors who appointed me and were keen on the changes I suggested at my interview, unfortunately resigned—albeit for perfectly valid reasons—before I took up my position. They were replaced by Councillor Sidebottom, who is now the chairman of the board, assisted by the parish council nominee and that's Mr Battersby. The clerk to the governing body is the school secretary and she's Mrs Battersby's sister-in-law. Even the caretaker is a relative. They are all as thick as thieves. It's all terribly incestuous.'

'Then the Education Office must assist you to grasp this particular nettle,' I told him. Whilst I felt sorry for the man, I did not relish such an unpleasant business, particularly at the beginning of the new term, but I knew it was likely to be the only course of action. 'I've not seen the two teachers since my last visit when, as you are aware, I was not impressed. But if, as you describe, things have not improved, then we have to go down the road of competency proceedings, which may lead to their dismissal. I will put the wheels in motion.'

'You imagine that it might come to that?' Mr Harrison asked, clasping his hands tightly in front of him and resting them on the desk.

'Children only have the one chance at education,' I told him. 'They deserve enthusiastic, optimistic, committed teachers who have high expectations of the pupils in their care. From what you have told me, the children in this school are getting a poor deal.' I stopped for a moment. I seemed to be repeating the selfsame words as I had done when I had visited the school just over two years before and had delivered my report. Clearly my own efforts had produced little effect either.

'It's not going to be easy,' the headteacher told me sadly, tugging at his long-suffering moustache once more. 'No, it's not going to be easy.' He looked completely defeated and weary.

'On the positive side,' I told him, attempting to sound cheerful, 'the state of the buildings has certainly improved since I was last here, on the inside at any rate. It looks a whole lot brighter and more welcoming and it's good to see the children's efforts displayed to such good effect on the walls. I noticed coming in that you now have a small library and it seems well stocked with some appropriate books. This is certainly an improvement.'

'I do try,' he said unhappily, 'but I sometimes wish I had never left London. Being a big fish in a little pool does not have as many merits as I hoped for.'

*   *   *

Following the depressing conversation with the headteacher, I spent the next part of the morning observing the lower Juniors, a class of seven- to nine-year-olds and their prickly teacher.

Mrs Sidebottom, tall and thin with a pale, melancholy, beaked face, was like a heron in her prim white blouse buttoned up to the neck and tight grey skirt from which protruded skeletal legs. Her thick white hair was twisted up untidily on her head and speared with what looked like wooden

28

meat skewers. When I entered her classroom, she fingered the cameo brooch at her throat, drew her lips together into a tight little line and stared at me with Gorgon ferocity.

'Good morning,' I said heartily.

'Good morning,' Mrs Sidebottom replied, with cool immutable gravity in her voice.

'Good morning, children,' I said, turning to the class that sat in serried rows behind old-fashioned wooden desks.

'Good mo-or-ning, Hinspector Phinn,' they chorused.

'We were expecting you, Mr Phinn,' the teacher said in a coldly formal and superior voice. Her eyes refused to meet mine. 'I rather assumed that you would be here at the very start of the lesson.' She glanced theatrically at her wristwatch. 'I suppose the roads from Fettlesham were busy at this time in the morning.' There was a quiet sarcasm in the tone of her reply.

'I was with the headteacher,' I explained, 'and have been since I arrived at the school at eight thirty.' I was minded to add, 'before you arrived' but I resisted the temptation.

'I see.' She gave me a little smile—but still wouldn't look directly at me; it was not a very pleasant smile. 'Well, now you are here, I'll explain a little of what we are about.'

'Perhaps one of the children could tell me.'

'Very well,' the teacher said, bristling a little. 'Simone, could you explain to Mr Phinn what we do on Thursday mornings?'

'We're learnin' 'ow to speyk proper,' a large healthy-looking girl with cheeks as round and as red as a polished apple informed me in her strong

Yorkshire accent. 'All on us in t'class 'ave to—'

'I am endeavouring, Mr Phinn,' the teacher cut in sharply, 'to encourage the children to speak clearly, expressively and accurately with distinct articulation so that they can be understood by those with whom they converse. Most of the children come from the immediate locality and it is so difficult sometimes to understand what they are saying.' She gave the unpleasant little smile again. 'Mr Harrison, being a southerner, has experienced quite a deal of trouble deciphering the children's speech. Their accents do tend to be—'

'An' on Thursday mornin', all of us in t'class, we 'ave to—' Simone started to say.

'One moment, Simone,' the teacher intervened, quickly and irritably, 'it's rude to interrupt when someone else is speaking.' It had been, of course, exactly what she herself had done. 'Put down your hand and sit up properly.' She turned in my direction again and this time our eyes met and I discerned in hers a flash of defiance. 'I don't suppose in this politically-correct world of ours it is the "done thing" to improve children's speech and teach them correct pronunciation but I consider it to be of the utmost importance. One hears such slovenly use of the English language these days, doesn't one, the dreadful jargon, colloquial vulgarisms, sloppy expressions and awful slang, much of it gleaned from the television, I should add. So, once a week, we do a little work on our spoken English.'

'I see,' I said, my heart beginning to plummet.

'So, if you would like to take a chair,' Mrs Sidebottom instructed, 'we shall continue.' She gestured at a wooden straight-backed chair in the corner of the room. 'You might care to see my lesson plan a little later,' she added pointedly. 'Now,' the teacher said, turning to face the class, 'when everyone is looking this way—and that does include you, David Scrimshaw—we can resume. Where were we?'

'Page forty-seven, miss,' the class chorused.

'Ah yes,' the teacher said. 'Exercise one on page forty-seven. Off you go.'

The children then proceeded to chant half-heartedly various elocutionary exercises.

'Gertie Gordon from Glasgow grew a gross of gaudy gay gladioli.'

'Good!' the teacher snapped out. 'And the next.'

'Careful Katy from Colchester cut and cooked a crisp and crunchy cabbage.'

'Good! Next.'

'They thought they had fought to defeat the fort but they found they had fought for naught.'

'Good! Next.'

'Wendy and William walked wearily down the wet and winding way to the water-swelled weir.'

'Miss, what's that word?' a small pixie-faced girl sitting at the front enquired.

'What word?' the teacher asked.

'T'last un, miss.'

Mrs Sidebottom scrutinised the page before informing her, 'Weir.'

'Theer,' the child replied, stabbing the book with a small finger.

The teacher sighed. 'A weir is a low dam built across a river to raise the level of the water.'

'Tha can trap fish in a weir, miss,' a child at the back of the classroom volunteered.

'I'm sure you can,' the teacher replied. 'Let's

31

continue.'

Exercise four caused some problems for the children who, I guessed, had all been raised in the heart of the Yorkshire Dales.

'Enery 'All 'ops on 'is 'eels.
What an odd 'abit.
'Ow 'orrid hit feels.
'Oppin' on 'is 'eels
Hisn't 'oppin' at all.
So why not 'op properly, 'Enery 'All?

There was a long deep audible exhalation from Mrs Sidebottom. 'No, no, no!' she cried, shaking her head so vigorously that a strand of white hair escaped and fell over her forehead. 'How many *more* times do I have to tell you not to drop your aitches?' She then demonstrated how the poem should be recited, over-enunciating every syllable. '*H*enry *H*all *h*ops on *h*is *h*eels . . .'.

When she had finished huffing, the teacher looked up from the textbook. 'Now, children, let us try again.'

Despite several more attempts the children continued to drop every aitch possible and add the letter where none was required.

'Let's try exercise number five,' Mrs Sidebottom said, sighing again and colouring slightly. 'First, listen carefully to how it should be said.' She declaimed another piece of doggerel.

Down the paaath and across the graaas,
The little children run,
To see the bird baaath by the bower
And the tall trees in the sun.

And so the lesson dragged on for a further wearisome and pleasure-destroying quarter of an hour until the teacher told the children to write out the exercises neatly and carefully in their books and to learn them at home for another practice the following Thursday morning. This gave me a chance to look at the dull and hurriedly displayed work on the walls and to examine the children's books as, heads down, the class applied itself quietly to copy out the silly exercises.

The door suddenly flew open and a boy with long black hair tied back in a pony tail and prominent, very white front teeth, burst in. 'Sorry I'm late, missis,' he said breathlessly in a pronounced Irish brogue, 'but the 'osses got out again and I 'ad to 'elp mi da get 'em back. It was the divvil's own job rounding 'em up.'

'Come in, Niall,' the teacher said. She stared at the boy as a rattlesnake might stare at a rat. 'Now you've arrived, sit down quickly and get on with your work.'

'Yes, missis,' he said, heading for a desk at the back near to where I was sitting. He gave me a crooked smile when he caught sight of me.

'We are copying out the exercises on page forty-seven in your textbook, *The Road to Effective Speaking*,' she told him and then adding, 'To be practised at home.'

Mrs Sidebottom sidled over to me at this point and informed me *sotto voce* that the boy was from a travellers' family, 'tinkers to be more precise', and that he missed more time at school than he attended, but that fortunately he wouldn't be with her for much longer. She went on to tell me that he could just about read and write and that his number work was extremely poor.

'In my day, they were called gypsies,' she told me quietly, 'but now, of course, we have to refer to them as travellers, tinkers, Romanies, whatever the "in" word happens to be. To my mind, this is another silly example of political correctness. After the Appleby Horse Fair in June, a gaggle of them always sets up camp near here for the summer, parking on the soft verges, disrupting the whole community, dropping litter, and making a general nuisance of themselves until they leave about now to travel south to some other horse fair. My husband, County Councillor Sidebottom, is trying to stop them coming here but to date, unfortunately, it has been to no avail. Have you met my husband, by the way?' she asked.

'No, I haven't,' I replied.

'He's recently been elected to the County Council,' Mrs Sidebottom informed me, 'and is a colleague of Councillor Peterson, who, as you are no doubt aware, is very influential on the Education Committee. My husband has a particular interest in schools and teaching and hopes to be elected to the Education Committee in due course.'

I detected a veiled threat in her voice. 'Well, I haven't met him,' I said, somewhat dismissively.

'I'm sure you will,' she told me. I had an uneasy feeling that the meeting with County Councillor Sidebottom would be sooner rather than later.

'You were telling me about the traveller children,' I said.

She shook her head and another strand of hair escaped. 'It really is very inconvenient. The

34

children arrive one minute and leave the next so I hope you are not expecting to see a great deal in Niall's book.' Before I had a chance to reply, she continued. 'I would be very interested to hear what suggestions *you* have in helping me to teach the child.'

Her voice was persistently filled with quiet sarcasm. I was certain that any suggestions I might proffer to this teacher would fall on stony ground and any guidelines I gave her would be consigned to the bin.

'I think we are running a course on that very subject next term,' I told her gleefully. 'I'll send you all the information and reserve you a place, if you wish.'

When Mrs Sidebottom returned to her desk at the front of the classroom, I approached the boy who had been the topic of the conversation.

'Hello,' I said, pulling up the hard wooden chair to sit beside him.

'How are ya?' he asked, with nonchalant confidence. He was a handsome lad with a tanned skin and a ready smile.

'I'm fine.'

'So am I, but I'm a bit knackered, so I am, after chasing the bloody 'osses. By Jaysus, they gave us a run for us money. Still, we got 'em all back.'

'May I look at your book?' I asked.

'Now, who would ya be?'

'An inspector,' I replied.

'Ah, ya do have a look of the polis about ya,' he remarked, screwing round to peer up at me closely.

'A school inspector.'

'So what do ya do?'

'I visit schools to hear children read and look at

their work,' I told him.

'Well now, that sounds like a great number to be on, spending your days listening to kids read. Now, how would ya be getting a job like that?'

'By working hard at school,' I told him, reaching for his exercise book.

He placed his hand on mine. 'Now, don't yous be expecting much in there,' he said. 'I'm not one for the reading and the writing and the mental arithmetics. I just can't get my head around this fraction and percentages business.'

'You need to know about fractions and percentages, Niall,' I told him.

'And why is that now?'

'Because if you don't know about fractions and percentages, people might cheat you.'

'They won't be cheating *me*,' he said vehemently, banging his fist on the desk as he reached the word 'me'. 'Just let 'em try!'

'What do you want to do when you leave school?' I asked the boy.

'I want to do what my da does.'

'And what does he do?'

'He collects scrap metal and sells it.'

'And what's the sort of scrap that is best to collect and resell, that gives you the greatest profit?'

'Oil drums,' he answered after a moment's thought. 'There's a good market for used oil drums.'

'Now suppose someone told you he'd got a hundred oil drums and he said that he would sell you a quarter of them—that's twenty-five per cent of them. Because you don't know about fractions and percentages, you wouldn't know, would you, if

36

he sold you the right amount? He could be cheating you. He could sell you ten or fifteen rather than the twenty-five because you wouldn't know what a quarter of a hundred is. So you see, you need to understand about fractions and percentages.'

'No one would dare cheat me,' the boy insisted, in a hard determined voice.

'But you wouldn't know whether he was or not,' I persisted.

Niall considered what I had said for a moment, rubbed his chin and then nodded. 'He wouldn't cheat me because if he said you can have a quarter of them there oil drums, I'd say to him, "I'll have the lot or none at all."'

There was little chance, I thought, of anyone cheating one so canny.

As I looked through the boy's book, red-cheeked Simone piped up, 'Miss, I can't find mi readin' book. I don't know weer I've gone an' putten it.'

'I cannot find my reading book,' the teacher repeated slowly and precisely, 'because I do not know where I have put it.'

'That's wor I just said, miss. I've gorran putten it down someweer an' I don't know weer I've putten it.'

'I have put it down somewhere, Simone,' corrected Mrs Sidebottom, 'but I do not know where I have put it.'

'Have ya, miss?' the child asked innocently. 'Did *you* 'ave mi book, then?'

'No, *you* have put it down,' the teacher said, drawing a deep exasperated breath.

'I know, miss, that's wor I just said,' the girl

answered, screwing up her nose.

'There is no such word, Simone, as "putten",' the teacher explained. 'The word is "put". "I have put down my book" and not "I have putten down my book."'

'Miss!' another child piped up. 'She's gone an' putten it on *my* desk. It's 'ere.'

'Put, William, put,' the teacher corrected sharply. Mrs Sidebottom sighed dramatically. 'You know, Mr Phinn,' she said, 'sometimes I really ask myself why I bother.' I asked myself the selfsame question. 'I think I am fighting a losing battle,' she continued, 'trying to get the children to speak properly.' I was certain she was right in that as well.

Just before morning break, the teacher wrote a sentence in large white letters on the blackboard: 'I have putten my book on the teacher's desk.'

'Now, children,' she said, facing the class. 'Look this way, please. On the blackboard I have written a sentence. Who can tell me what is wrong with it?'

Young William waved his hand backwards and forwards in the air like a lupin in a strong wind. 'I know, miss!' he shouted out.

'Come along then, William, what is wrong with the sentence, "I have putten my book on the teacher's desk"?'

'Miss,' the boy replied, 'tha's gone and putten "putten" when tha should 'ave putten "put".'

CHAPTER THREE

I had only been in the school for just over two hours, had had a revealing conversation with the unhappy headteacher, had sat in on a distinctly dull and unnecessary lesson, and had looked at a range of children's workbooks, most of which I judged to be unsatisfactory. I was dismayed to find that the various major recommendations about the teaching contained in my previous report seemed to have been largely ignored.

During the break, therefore, I found a secluded area in the small school library. I was keen to make some notes while my concerns were still fresh in my mind. I was just starting to jot down my observations about the conversation with Mr Harrison when I was aware of a figure standing a few feet away.

He was a small wiry lad of about ten or eleven with an earnest, purposeful face, wild tufty ginger hair sprouting up from his head like a clump of dry grass, a scattering of freckles around his nose and bright intelligent eyes. His small hands were placed firmly on his hips, his legs apart. He looked like a miniature admiral on the quarterdeck facing a mutinous crew and demanding who the ringleader was.

He thrust his face into mine, stuck out his chin and demanded, 'So, what are you for?'

I smiled and shook my head. 'What am I for?' I repeated, chuckling.

'Aye,' he said quickly, 'what are you for?'

'I'm a school inspector,' I told him, continuing

to smile.

'I knows that,' he sighed, screwing up his nose. 'Mester 'Arrison, our 'eadteacher, 'e telled us that you were a school inspector and you'd be comin' in today. Mester 'Arrison, 'e said we 'ad this important visitor this mornin' an' for us to be on us best behaviour, mek sure we watches us manners, an' answer yer questions and 'e telled us 'ow all on us 'ad to look 'appy an' interested—but what I wants to know is what are you *for*?'

A large girl with a pale moon face, large owl eyes and two big bunches of thick straw-coloured hair tied with crimson ribbons, appeared from behind a shelf of books and stared at me impassively. She was sporting a tight pink T-shirt with 'LITTLE MISS SUNSHINE' emblazoned across the front in large glittery uneven letters. I smiled at her but she stared back at me as if I were some strange and rather unpleasant exhibit displayed in a museum case. She then proceeded to explore her nose with her index finger. A little green bubble emptied and filled in the other crusty nostril.

'Well,' I said to the boy, 'I go into schools and see what children are doing.'

'Why?' the child asked brusquely, tilting his head to one side.

'Because that is what I do for a living.'

'Well, dunt you 'ave a proper job, like?'

I laughed. 'I think it *is* a proper job,' I told him. This question had been put to me a good few times before by inquisitive pupils, so I was well used to hearing it and answering it.

The large girl was now examining the contents of her nose critically. Then she wiped her finger on

40

her T-shirt, sniffed loudly to remove the bubble of mucus, ran a small finger across the base of her nose and departed. I hoped the boy might depart too but he remained resolutely rooted to the spot in front of me, his arms still akimbo.

'Dooan't mind 'Yacinth,' he informed me, confidentially. He tapped the side of his nose knowingly. 'She's got what they calls especial needs, tha knaas.'

'Thank you for telling me,' I said. I noticed his use of 'tha'. The children of the Dales tended to drift in and out of the local dialect.

'She lives up on t'tops at Ferntop Farm and foots it to t'schoil every day—all two mile on it. 'Yacinth's not much cop at yer writin' an' yer readin' an' yer addin' up an' such, but by the 'ell, she can't 'arf arm wrestle. Champion at conkers an' all, an' good at footie in t'goal. Aye, she's a gret feighter is 'Yacinth. Nob'dy messes around wi' 'er.'

'I'll bear that in mind,' I said.

This pupil interrogation, interesting though I was finding it, was becoming rather time consuming and I was keen to get on with writing down in my notebook some initial thoughts on the morning's events. There was much to record and I wanted to get on with it while things were fresh in my mind.

'So what do you actually *do*, then?' said the ginger-headed boy, thrusting his freckled face even closer to mine. 'What are you *for*?'

'I visit schools and I hear children read,' I informed him patiently. 'I look at their books and examine the work, see how well they write, if they can spell words, use punctuation and then I talk to the teachers to see that everything is all right.'

41

'Why?'

'Because I have to make sure that all in the school is as it should be.'

'Is that abaat it, then?' he asked.

'Just about, but I then suggest ways that we can make the education in the school even better.'

'Well, if tha asks me,' confided the boy, 'I think tha's got a reight job on 'ere.'

'Really?'

'Oh aye.'

When visiting schools, I often ask the children questions about how satisfied they are with their education, but without singling out particular teachers and lessons. I now asked the boy, 'So, if you had a magic wand and could change things in this school, what would you change?'

He puffed out his cheeks and exhaled noisily. ' 'Ow long 'as tha got?' he asked.

'All right,' I said. 'What is the best part of your day in this school?'

'Goin' 'ome,' he replied, without pause for thought.

'I see.'

'Are tha gunna write it down in that little black book o' yourn?'

'Not at the moment,' I told him.

'So, tha'r a sooart of expert on education then, are tha?' he observed.

'Yes, I suppose I am.'

The boy blew out noisily again through pursed lips. His expression was one of exaggerated disdain. 'Mi dad 'ates hexperts,' he told me, screwing up his face. His eyes gleamed with an impish delight. 'Oh aye, no time for 'em at all. He 'ates inspectors, an' all. 'E don't see point to

42

inspectors, mi dad. 'E dunt know what they're for. We 'ave inspectors from t'Ministry comin' up to our farm checkin' up on t'beeasts, watchin' what we're gerrin up to, askin' questions, writin' stuff down. Mi dad says they're a bloody nuisance and it's a reight pity they've got nowt else berrer to do wi' their time than interferin' in other people's lives. Any road, that's what 'e says. 'E says they're abaat as much use as a chocolate fireguard, allus pokin' their noses into other people's business.' The boy nodded soberly and set his chin a little harder.

I had been the County Inspector for English and Drama in Yorkshire now for four years and had become well used to the plain, outspoken and disarming pupils I had met in the course of my work. I had found the young children of the Dales in particular to be amusing, forthright, inquisitive and sharply observant and, on some occasions, like this lad, possessing the tenacity of a Yorkshire terrier and the bluntness of a sledgehammer.

I thought it an opportune moment to curtail the conversation with my critical young chatterer. 'Isn't it morning break?' I asked pleasantly.

'Tha'r not wrong theer,' he replied.

'So shouldn't you be out in the playground getting some fresh air and exercise?'

'I'd like to be,' he told me, grimacing, 'but I've been kept in. We 'ave to sit in t'corridor if we're in trouble. It's called detention.'

'So you're in trouble then?' I asked.

'Missis Battersby, she's my teacher, she said I 'ad to stop in 'cos I've been chatterin' too much this mornin' an' not gerrin on wi' mi work.'

I could see the teacher's point of view.

He stabbed a small finger in the direction of my lap. 'Can I see what tha's writ down in that little black notebook o' yourn?'

'I'm afraid not.'

'Why?'

'Because it's private,' I told him.

'Well, *you* look at *our* work.'

'It's a bit different,' I said, attempting to extricate myself from a difficult position. 'This is confidential.'

'Aye, all reight,' he said. 'Suit thissen. I'll no doubt see thee later. *I've* got work to do so I can't stand 'ere blatherin' all day.'

'Goodbye then,' I said, greatly relieved. I flicked open the cover of my notebook and got ready to put down my thoughts but the boy remained where he was, watching my every movement.

'Yes?' I asked. 'Is there something else?'

'I'm writin' about what I did on Sat'day,' he told me.

'Really?' I snapped the notebook shut. I could see that I was in for another long conversation.

'Missis Battersby 'as gor us to write abaat summat interestin' we did ovver t'weekend.'

'So what did you—' I began.

The boy was in full flight and continued without seeming to draw breath. 'I know what Missis Battersby's been doin' ovver t'weekend,' he said with a knowing wink. 'She's gone an' putten that display up theer on t'yonder wall in t'corridor outside 'er classroom. She never puts owt much up out theer but she's gone to town wi' this 'un. It's all abaat t'Gret Fire o' London so tha berrer tek a look at it or she'll not be best pleased. Sometimes she gets in a real paddy an' starts shoutin' at us but

44

I reckon they'll not be much o' that when tha'r in wi' us. She's as nice as pie if we 'ave visitors. It's been purrup special like, that display.'

'It's very impressive,' I said.

'Aye,' he replied, nodding sagely.

'So what can you tell me about the Great Fire of London?' I asked.

'Nowt.'

'I thought you'd been studying it.'

'Nay, I dint say we'd been studyin' it. Last 'istory topic we did were on t'Vikings. We did 'em wi' Missis Sidebottom last year and we did 'em ageean wi' Missis Battersby. I'm sick o' t'Vikings. I can tell thee owt abaat t'Vikings if tha wants but I know nowt about t'Gret Fire o' London. Class what she 'ad some year back did all t'writin' and all t'pictures were done by Missis Battersby. None of us write that neat or paint like that.'

'I see.'

'Mi dad passed schoil on Sunday neet and all t'lights were still on. It were like Blackpool Hilluminations, mi dad said. 'Appen t'teachers were markin' t'books and tidyin' up and mekkin' things shit-shape for thy visit.'

'Ship-shape,' I corrected. 'It's ship-shape.'

'What is?'

'The school.'

'Aye, it looks a lot berrer than it usually does. There's never much on t'walls usually 'cept what Mester 'Arrison puts up. He's all reight, Mester 'Arrison. 'E's from t'south, tha knaas. Reight difficult to know what 'e's on abaat sometimes though. 'E's not from these parts.'

The boy made a move but then he stopped in his tracks to add with a broad smile. 'I think

Missis Battersby's really looking forward to thy visit.'

'Really?' I doubted that very much.

'Aye. I 'eard 'er telling Missis Sidebottom that tha were comin' in today. She said that was all she needed. 'Appen that's why she's 'ad 'er 'air done special.'

'Before you go,' I said, 'you might like to tell me your name.'

'Well, mi mam an' dad calls me Charlie but mi teacher, she calls me Charles.'

'And what shall I call you?'

'Tha can suit thissen,' he said. 'I'll answer to owther.'

'Tell me, Charlie, what is your account about?'

'Tha what?'

'The piece of writing you are finishing, about what you did over the weekend. What is it about?'

'Oh, that. Me an' mi brother 'elped mi dad castrate three bullocks.' With a cheerful wave, the boy returned to his desk leaving the Inspector of Schools with open mouth and completely lost for words.

*　　　*　　　*

Following the break, I joined Mrs Battersby's class and met young Charlie again.

'Hey up, Mester Phinn,' he said as I entered the classroom.

'Hello, Charlie,' I replied.

'It's Mester Phinn, miss,' Charlie informed her enthusiastically, pointing at me. 'I've met 'im.'

'I do have eyes, Charles,' said the teacher. 'It's nice to see you, Mr Phinn,' she said unconvincingly.

It was clear by her demeanour that Mrs Battersby was far from happy to see me. My report of her lesson on the last visit had been critical so I could hardly expect to be received like the Prodigal Son, and was therefore prepared for the tight-lipped and solemn countenance.

'Sit down, Charles,' instructed the teacher. 'You're jumping up and down like a jack-in-the-box with fleas.' There was a slight tremble in her voice.

'Good morning, children,' I said brightly.

'Mornin', Mester Phinn,' they replied in unison.

'So you've met Charles,' said the teacher, raising a hand to her throat where a small red nervous rash was appearing. 'Quite a little character, isn't he?'

'Yes, we've had an interesting conversation.'

She glanced at the boy disapprovingly and looked quite disconcerted. 'Really?'

'Yes, we were having a little chatter at break time,' I said.

'When he should have been completing his work,' said the teacher. 'Charles has a great deal to say for himself, Mr Phinn, as I imagine you discovered. He does so like to chatter.' She emphasised the final word. 'I hope that he behaved himself and didn't speak out of turn.'

'Oh no, he was very polite,' I told her. Charlie's face broke into a wide smile and there was a hint of mischief in his bright eyes. 'We were talking about the Great Fire of London and I was admiring your display.'

Mrs Battersby's face coloured a little and she gave a thin smile. 'I'm pleased to hear it,' she said.

'Sometimes children tend to say the wrong thing. I always say to their parents that if they don't believe everything their children say about me then I won't believe everything that their children say about them.' She gave a small agitated laugh.

Mrs Battersby was a dumpy, sharp-eyed woman of indeterminate age, and wearing a bright pink turtleneck jumper and heavy grey shapeless skirt. To complete the ensemble she sported a large rope of amber beads and heavy brown brogues. I smiled inwardly when I caught sight of the carefully permed hair and recalled the conversation shortly before with young Charlie.

During the lesson, the children worked quietly, copying up their accounts of their weekend activities. Mrs Battersby sat at her desk and a small queue of readers formed to read to her from their books. As I wandered around the classroom talking to the children and examining their work, the teacher constantly looked up and watched my progress with small black suspicious eyes.

The first child to whom I spoke, a stout girl called Ruby, was only too pleased to show me her book. It was neat and contained some interesting stories, poems and language exercises but the teacher had been very heavy-handed with the marking pen. There was so much red on it that it looked as if someone with a nosebleed had leaned over the page.

'We usually have the Leprosy Hour every Thursday after break,' she told me confidentially, 'but we've got to finish our account of what we did over the weekend.'

'Whatever is the Leprosy Hour?' I asked mystified.

'It's really called the Literacy Hour,' the girl told me, 'but miss calls it the Leprosy Hour because she hates it. When Mr Harrison came, he said we all had to do an hour of English and maths every morning because we needed to get better at writing and number work. We have the Innumeracy Hour as well.'

'I see. So what is your account about?' I asked, pulling her exercise book towards me.

'Well,' replied the girl, swivelling around to face me, 'I'm writing about what I did on Saturday.'

'And what did you do on Saturday?' I asked.

'I helped my Grandpa Morrison build a drystone wall.'

'Really? That sounds very interesting.'

'Do you know anything about drystone walling?' she asked.

'I do, as a matter of fact,' I told her. 'At the cottage in Hawksrill where I live I had a drystone wall built at the bottom of the garden. The man who built it for me—'

'Who was it?' interrupted the child.

'His name was Tom Fields.'

'I'll ask my Grandpa Morrison if he knows him,' she said. 'He knows most of the wallers around here. Go on, then.'

'Pardon?'

'You were telling me about your drystone wall.'

'Well, Tom told me a little bit about how drystone walls are built. For example, how the fields around where I live were all walled at one time but when they fall down, the farmers usually replace the wall with fencing. Sometimes they use bits of the old wall to patch somewhere else.'

'That's true enough,' agreed the girl. 'So how

49

high is your wall, because they vary, you know.'

'Tom told me it would be high enough to keep out the sheep and low enough not to spoil my lovely view. I suppose it must be about four feet high.'

'We usually work in metres these days,' Ruby told me in the manner of a teacher correcting a child who had answered a question wrongly. 'So how long is it?'

'I'm supposed to be looking at your work, Ruby,' I said pleasantly, and then I winked. 'And I'm usually the one who asks the questions.'

The child's account was clear and detailed. She described how at six thirty on the Saturday morning she had got 'kitted out' in old jeans, woollen jacket, boots (with metal toe caps) and a large pair of leather gloves, and had set off with her grandfather and two of his friends in the Land Rover to repair a hundred-year-old wall on the estate of Lord Marrick. First she had helped when the men dug a trench, pulling out the roots. They had then neatly stacked the small stones called 'heartings' that would be used later to pack the centre of the wall. The base of the wall, she wrote, was usually twice the width of the top layer otherwise the whole lot would collapse. 'If the wall is built properly, it will last for 150 years.' She described how the heavy stones had been put in place first and finally the copestones had been packed tightly on the top which gave the finished wall added strength and height—'but they were too heavy for me to lift up that high,' she wrote.

'It's really like doing a big jigsaw puzzle,' she told me. 'If my Grandpa Morrison can't get a stone just right, he sometimes pushes it in really hard

50

and says, "Get in, tha bugger!" and then says, "Pardon mi French."' She giggled. 'My Grandpa Morrison says that drystone walls make cosy homes for all sorts of creatures—voles, wizzles, lizards, slow-worms, hedgepigs, toads, spiders and bees—so they're very important. You also get mosses and foxgloves and wrens and wheatears. Did you know that?'

'I didn't,' I said. What a confident girl I thought and what an amazing account.

After Ruby, I headed for another desk but was cut off by Charlie. 'Mester Phinn, come an' 'ave a look at mi book. I've just finished.'

I was not particularly interested to read about the boy's morning spent castrating bullocks so I told him I would look later. He would not, however, let me get away so lightly.

'I'm gerrin a book for mi birthday next week,' he told me. 'A big un. I'm mad on books.'

'I'm very pleased to hear it,' I said. 'So am I.'

'Are tha?'

'I am,' I told him. 'There's nothing better than a book.'

'Tha's reight theer, Mester Phinn.'

I arrived at another desk but Charlie followed me and thrust his face into mine.

'Mi dad says I can go wi' 'im and choose one for missen.'

'So how many books have you got already?' I asked.

'None.'

'None?'

'It's mi first,' announced the boy. ' 'As tha any books then, Mester Phinn?'

'Lots and lots of them. My house is full of them.'

51

'Do yer keep 'em in tha 'ouse?' He looked astonished by this revelation.

'I do, yes. I have a special room where I keep all my books.'

'How many 'as tha got?'

'Hundreds.'

' 'Undreds! Gerron!'

'Yes, I have.'

'Where do you pur 'em all?'

'On the shelves.'

The boy threw back his head and laughed. 'I've just cottoned on,' he said. 'Tha talkin' about books what you read, aren't tha?'

'Yes,' I replied.

'Well, I'm on abaat bucks what ya breed—male rabbits!'

I shook my head and laughed too.

'Something appears to have amused you both.' Mrs Battersby had materialised at our side with an expression like the wicked fairy at the christening feast.

'We were just discussin' bucks, miss,' Charlie told her.

'Well, you can fetch your book now, Charles, because it's your turn to read to me.' Mrs Battersby turned to me. 'Charles's reading leaves a lot to be desired, I'm afraid, Mr Phinn. Too much television, I shouldn't wonder.'

I felt like saying something but I bit my lip. It would wait until later.

I found Hyacinth poring over a large picture book at her desk.

'Hello,' I said.

The girl wiped her nose with the back of a finger and eyed me apprehensively.

'Let's see what you are doing, shall we?' She didn't object as I slid her reading book across the desk and started to examine it.

'Is it a good book?' I asked.

She eyed me suspiciously but didn't answer.

'Would you like to read a little of your book to me?' I asked.

She shook her head, gazing at me now with unabashed intensity. She wiped her nose on her finger again and then told me in a loud voice, 'I'm special needs.' Perhaps she thought that this revelation might convince me to leave her in peace. When I didn't move, she added, 'Don't you know? I'm special needs.'

'I do, but what do you think it means, special needs?'

'If you know what it means, why are you askin'?'

It was a fair question. 'So, will you read to me?'

'Are you the infector?' she asked.

'Inspector,' I replied.

'What's t'difference?'

I thought of the earlier comment from Ruby about the Leprosy Hour. I reckoned her teacher would not have considered that there was much difference between the two words.

The girl reluctantly read to me, slowly and with fierce concentration on her face, her finger following each word on the page. There was no expression in her voice and not once did she pause for breath but read on, determined to get the ordeal over and done with.

'Hyacinth,' I said, when she snapped the book shut, 'that was very good, but what do you do when you come to a full stop?'

'What?'

'When you get to a full stop, what do you do?'

She eyed me like an expert in the presence of an ignoramus. 'You gerroff t'bus,' she replied.

I chuckled. 'Of course you do,' I said.

She shook her head again and I saw a slight tremble on her bottom lip. 'Are you goin' to put me in a special school?'

'No, I'm not,' I told her.

'I don't want to go in no special school.'

'Don't worry,' I reassured her. 'I'm just here to look at your book, to hear you read and to see how you are getting on.'

'Oh,' she said. Then, after a moment's thought she sniffed noisily, ran the full length of her index finger across the bottom of her nose and asked me, 'So, what are you for?'

*　　　*　　　*

Before I left the school at the end of the morning, I spoke to both the teachers, one after the other, before seeing the headteacher. Incomprehension crept across Mrs Battersby's face when I gave her the feedback on her lesson and my assessment of the work in the pupils' books. This soon turned to a wary resentful look.

'Goodness knows, I try my best,' she told me, shuffling uncomfortably in her wing-backed armchair. 'And let's be fair. You can't expect a lot from these children. I can't be expected to make silk purses out of pigs' ears. I mean, they're not going to end up brain surgeons or nuclear scientists, are they now? They're country children and all they're interested in are sheep, cattle, pigs and farming. All they want to do when they leave

54

their senior school is work on their parents' farms and that's all their parents want them to do as well. It's a losing battle getting them to write about anything other than about farm animals.'

'That is my point, Mrs Battersby,' I told her. 'I think your expectation of these children is too low and the work they are expected to do lacks challenge and variety.'

She gave me a brief hostile glance. 'I believe in discipline, Mr Phinn,' she informed me brusquely. 'Give them an inch, and they take a mile. Some of these children can be very difficult. They were well behaved because you were in today and they know how to turn it on for visitors. Take Charles, for instance. He can be a real nuisance at times.' The teacher was now looking decidedly resentful. 'And another thing, I don't know how you can judge anything after seeing just one lesson and talking to a few children.'

I reminded her that I had observed her teaching before and explained that I had examined the children's books and looked at their test results, and had also spoken to the headteacher who had expressed his concern about her work. I told her that I therefore felt my comments were valid.

'Well,' she said, with a slight smirk, 'and I make no bones about it when I tell you, everybody thinks it was a mistake to have appointed Mr Harrison. He's a southerner and doesn't understand our ways.'

The reaction of Mrs Battersby's colleague to my comments was aggressively defiant. Mrs Sidebottom sat before me tight-lipped, straight-backed and steely-eyed with her thin hands clasped on her lap and her thin legs clamped together. As diplomatically as possible, I told her that, in my opinion, it was misguided to try and change the children's natural way of speaking with one lesson a week in which they chanted doggerel. Children, I informed her, should not be expected to leave the language of the home at the wrought-iron gates of the school and speak some kind of artificial argot.

'There is a widely held misconception,' I said, 'that dialect is a corrupt form of what people imagine to be normal English. Far from being a deviation of the standard form of the language, dialect is an earlier form of English and has its own vocabulary, syntax and grammar. Children do need to learn standard forms of English but trying to change their accents is undesirable.'

She gave me a glance like broken glass. 'Mr Phinn,' she said with slow deliberation in her voice, 'I do not intend to sit here and listen to a lecture on the English language. I am of the considered opinion, formed over many years, I have to say, that it is my job to eradicate the slovenly, lazy and inaccurate way the children speak. You may call it dialect if you wish. I call it bad English.'

I then ceased to be tactful and told her straight that I was surprised and, indeed, very disappointed that very few of my recommendations contained in my last report had been addressed, and that I was not impressed with what I had seen that morning.

The teacher's eyes bulged in indignation and her lips drooped in obvious displeasure. I rather expected a spirited defence of her teaching but Mrs Sidebottom glanced up at the clock on the wall and, with an air of ingrained disapproval, informed me that it was her lunch hour and it was in her contract that she should have a one-hour

56

break in the middle of the day.

As I saw her head for the door, I knew it would prove very difficult to dismiss such a teacher. The more I thought about it, the more I was reminded of the words of Mr Nelson, the headmaster of King Henry's College in Brindcliffe. When, the previous year, I broached the possibility of instituting disciplinary proceedings against a member of his staff, he had leaned back in his chair and remarked: 'As you will be well aware, it is very difficult to do anything about a teacher in terms of disciplinary action unless he runs off with a sixth-form girl or steals the dinner money.'

Following the acrimonious interviews, I promised Mr Harrison that I would return before half-term, accompanied by my colleagues, to undertake a more thorough inspection. In the interim, I told him, I would see the Chief Inspector of Schools and discuss with her the possibility of starting competency proceedings. I advised the headteacher to keep a careful and thorough record of all incidents, infringements, conversations and refusals to carry out instructions on the part of the two teachers. I agreed with him that it would prove difficult to dismiss either of them, particularly since both teachers were so established and well connected locally. Neither lesson I had observed was disastrous but neither was good. The teachers were not incompetent: they prepared their lessons, albeit scantily, marked the work, albeit over-zealously, they were punctual, had few absences and had good discipline. It was just that their teaching was lacklustre and short of challenge and they both had an unfortunate manner with the children.

'I should point out, Mr Phinn,' said Mr Harrison, as I made a move to leave, 'you made similar comments in your last report, before my time, of course, and you promised to return to the school to see if progress had been made, that your recommendations had been implemented and to offer support and advice.'

'I did, yes,' I replied, feeling decidedly guilty. 'It's just that there were quite a few pressing matters and—'

'And you never got around to it.'

'No, I never got around to it,' I repeated. 'I should have followed things up.'

'It's just that had you done as you had promised,' said the headteacher, 'things might not have turned out quite as badly as they have.'

'Well, I can assure you, Mr Harrison,' I told him, 'that I will follow things up this time.'

'I hope so,' he murmured. 'I do hope so.'

When I reached the gates of the school I found two boys sitting on the steps, their elbows on their knees and their heads cupped in their hands. It was Charlie and the lad from Mrs Sidebottom's class called William. I stood behind them and eavesdropped.

'I'll tell thee what, our Charlie, I can't get mi 'ead round all this stuff abaat speykin' proper what we're a-doin wi' Missis faffing Sitheebum. We say "path", she says "paath". We say "grass" and she says "graas". We say "luck" and she says "loook". We say "buck" and she says "boook". It's reight confusin'.'

'Tha dooan't wants to tek no notice, our Billy. I 'ad all that carry-on when I were in Missis Sitheebum's class, and she nivver changed me,' his companion told him.

'Nay, we've got to practise it for t'next week. Dust thy know then, our Charlie, dust tha say "eether" or dust tha say "ayether"?'

The elder boy thought for a moment before replying. 'Dunt mek no difference 'ow tha says it, our Billy. Tha can say owther on 'em.'

CHAPTER FOUR

I arrived at Ugglemattersby Infant School, the other side of the village, just as the bell was sounding for the end of lunchtime. I watched for a moment from the gate as the small children, who had been running and jumping, chasing and chattering, skipping and playing games, suddenly lined up obediently in the playground at the shrill sound of a whistle. Dressed identically in their bright red jumpers, white shirts and grey shorts or skirts, they resembled a miniature army as they marched smartly into school behind their teachers, swinging their arms backwards and forwards. This looked a happy and well-ordered school.

'Did you want something?'

I was jotting down a few first impressions in my notebook, and the loud and strident voice behind me made me jump.

I swivelled around to be confronted by a hawk-faced woman in an ankle-length fluorescent yellow coat, black peaked cap pulled down over her eyes and substantial leather gauntlets. With one hand she was wielding, like a weapon, a large red and yellow lollipop sign with 'STOP!' painted across it.

The other hand was resting on her hip.

'I beg your pardon,' I began, 'I didn't quite—'

'I asked you if you wanted something?' demanded the stout harridan in luminous yellow. 'Because I've been watching you watching the kiddies and writing things down.'

'Ah, I see,' I said. 'Let me explain. I'm a school inspector.'

'You're a what?' she snapped.

'Would you mind awfully not pushing your lollipop in my face,' I said. 'I am a school inspector, here to visit the school.'

'And I could be the Queen of Sheba, for all you know.' I couldn't quite see the relevance of this retort but there was not the slightest chance of this woman being mistaken for the Queen of Sheba. 'Where's your identification?' she asked sharply.

I reached into the inside pocket of my suit and produced my official card with photograph and details of my profession. It was plucked unceremoniously from my hand and scrutinised in detail, the woman screwing up her eyes and running a gloved finger over it.

'Mmmmmm,' she hummed.

'All right?' I asked pleasantly.

'Yes, well, you have to be very careful these days where kiddies are concerned. I'm always on the look-out for strange men standing at the school gates taking an unnatural interest in children. We've been told to be very viligent for weirdos and perverts and paediatrics.'

'Well, you have most certainly been very *viligent*,' I told her, smiling at her inventive use of the language, 'and I can assure you that I am not a weirdo, pervert or, for that matter, a paediatric.'

'I mean,' the woman informed me, still eyeing me suspiciously, 'they don't all come in dirty raincoats, you know.' She inspected what I was wearing. 'Some of them come in suits.'

'I'm sure they do.' I was minded to say that some may very well come in long fluorescent yellow coats and peaked hats but I resisted the temptation to do so. 'And now, if you will excuse me,' I told her, 'I have an appointment with the headteacher.'

With that I left the belligerent old woman and proceeded at a swift pace up the path. At the entrance I turned. She was still standing stubbornly at the gate like a sentinel, watching. I waved and smiled theatrically but she remained stiff and static, clutching her lollipop like a halberd.

Because I had spent most of the last hour talking to Mr Harrison at the Junior School, I had had no time for lunch and was conscious of my grumbling stomach.

In contrast to the Junior School, Ugglemattersby Infant School was a modern, attractive and spacious building constructed in warm red brick with an orange pantile roof and large picture windows. It was set amongst open fields, enclosed by silvered limestone walls, with views stretching to the nearby moors that rose to purple heather-clad domes. A coloured mural depicting rows of happy children, arranged as if posing for a school photograph, had been painted on one exterior wall and a great coloured sign above it proclaimed: 'We learn to love and we love to learn.' It was a cheerful, welcoming environment with trees and shrubs, flowerbeds, bird tables and benches. Everything about the school looked clean and well tended.

The headteacher, Mrs Braddock-Smith, a young woman in a very stylish black suit and elaborately frilly white blouse, took me on a tour of the school, proudly telling me about the interesting work the children were undertaking and their apparently considerable achievements. She bubbled with enthusiasm as she tripped along a corridor resplendent with the pupils' paintings, sketches, drawings, poems and stories, all of which were carefully double-mounted and clearly labelled. Shelves held glossy-backed picture books, small tables had vases of bright flowers, corners had little easy chairs and large fat cushions where children could relax and read. Each child we passed said, 'Hello, miss,' cheerfully, and in all the classrooms I could see busy little people hard at work. What a difference, I thought, from the Junior School!

I explained to Mrs Braddock-Smith that I wished to spend the first part of the afternoon with the top Infants listening to them read, looking through their exercise books and asking them a few questions about their work. Then I would join the youngest children for the remainder of the day, meeting with her after school to report back.

'Certainly,' trilled the headteacher. 'I think you will be very impressed with what you see and hear, Mr Phinn. Our standards are extremely high, even if I do say so myself, and this last couple of years have been so very successful that we have attracted a growing number of "G and T" children.'

'"G and T" children?' I repeated. Did she mean gin and tonic? Was this some kind of description of children from middle-class homes?

'Gifted and talented,' the headteacher explained before babbling on. 'An increasing number of parents from the professional classes have moved into the executive houses on the new development at Waterfield on the edge of the village, and we have had an influx of very bright and interested children with most supportive and ambitious parents. We're getting quite a reputation. Indeed, there's a long waiting list for places for children who live outside the catchment area. Perhaps I shouldn't blow our own trumpet but we do very well here, very well indeed.'

'It's a most impressive building,' I said, thinking of the dark brooding grey stone school down the road.

'We are very lucky,' said the headteacher. 'The PTA has raised quite a substantial amount of money, while the library has been sponsored and paid for by a parent-governor, and it was his company that built the new housing development. Of course, this being a church school, we get so much help from the vicar. You will be meeting our chairman of governors, Archdeacon Richards, later today. He's calling in to take the assembly.' She didn't pause to take breath or give me the opportunity to get a word in edgeways. 'I have to say, Mr Phinn,' she warbled, 'we are so very fortunate here to be blessed with the lovely building, dedicated staff, supportive parents, interested governors and delightful children.' Her enthusiasm was overpowering.

There were twenty bright-eyed six-year-old pupils in the top Infants, in the charge of a plump, red-faced teacher called Mrs Hartley. They listened attentively to her as she finished reading the fairy story of 'The Princess and the Pea'. She then set them to write about the story she had read them, and to draw pictures to illustrate their work. I sat in the small reading corner and, in the course of the first hour, heard one child after another read to me from his or her own reading book. The headteacher's proud boasts were certainly not unfounded since all the infants read clearly and accurately and answered my questions politely and with enthusiasm.

When it came to Joshua's turn, he scurried over to sit down next to me, clearly eager to demonstrate his ability. Before I could open my mouth he informed me that he was a 'free reader' and that he was not on a reading scheme book like the other children in the class.

'Mrs Hartley lets me choose my own books,' he informed me immediately.

'Really?'

'I'm between books at the moment so haven't brought one to read to you.'

'Don't worry,' I said, 'we'll pick one from the shelf.'

'I've just finished a novel.'

'Have you?'

'It was by Enid Blyton.'

'I remember reading Enid Blyton when I was young and I always—'

'I'm top of the top table, you know,' interrupted the child enthusiastically.

'My goodness!'

'I could read before I came to school.'

'Could you really?'

'I didn't bother with phonics and reading scheme books.'

'Really?'

'And I know all my times tables.'

'Good gracious!'

'Do you want me to do the eleven times table? I can if you want.'

'Not at the moment,' I told him. 'I would like you to read to me.'

I had become quite accustomed to precocious young children on my travels around the county schools. I was tickled by their serious humour, impressed by their exuding confidence, intrigued by their responses to my questions and amused by their sharp observations on life. But on a few rare occasions, like this one, I was somewhat lost for words. Clearly here was one of the headteacher's 'G and T' pupils.

'Now, let's see,' I said, 'what we have on the shelf, shall we?'

'I'd rather not have a fairy tale, if you don't mind. I've read all those and I don't like stories about princes and princesses. I think they're very soppy and you always know how they are going to end. Everyone always lives happily ever after.'

The boy started busily rummaging through the bookcase behind him in search of a book to his liking. 'May I have this one with the snail on the front?' he asked. 'I like snails.'

He presented me with a brightly coloured pop-up picture book called *Little Snail's BIG Surprise.*

'This looks interesting,' I said.

'Snails are called gastropods, you know,' he told me seriously. 'That's a sort of mollusc with a shell. I learnt that at the Natural History Museum in London. I went there with my father during the summer holidays.'

The boy opened the book and began to read with gusto. '"Sandy Snail lived in a beautiful garden filled with delicious plants. One day Daddy Snail said, 'Go to your Mother. She has a big surprise for you! Go straight there. Look both ways. And don't talk to strangers!"' You're not supposed to start a sentence with "and", are you, Mr Phinn?' he asked, looking up at me with wide, inquisitive eyes behind the glasses.

'Some writers do,' I told him.

'Mrs Hartley told us never to start a sentence with "and",' he persisted.

'Would you like to continue, Joshua?' I said, not wishing to engage in a debate about the technicalities of the English language with a six-year-old.

The boy read on: 'Sandy raced off. Let's follow his tracks.' He stopped again, his finger beneath the sentence he had just read. 'Mr Phinn, snails can't race. They're very slow creatures.'

'It's supposed to be funny,' I told him. 'The writer knows snails move slowly and has used "raced" to make us smile.'

'Oh,' said Joshua, his small brow furrowing. He was clearly not amused. He shrugged and continued reading: ' "Good morning, Mrs Dragonfly. I can't stop now. I'm so excited! Mother has a big surprise for me!" "Lucky you!" whirred the Dragonfly. "Maybe it's a munchy mosquito." ' Joshua paused again. 'This writer uses a lot of exclamation marks, doesn't he, Mr Phinn?'

'He does,' I agreed.

'Mrs Hartley says we shouldn't use too many exclamation marks.'

'Does she? Well, let's not worry too much about that at the moment, Joshua. Shall we get on with the story?'

And so the saga of Sandy Snail continued with our little slimy friend meeting a whole host of interesting mini-beast characters in the course of his travels, including Mr Caterpillar who chomped his way through the juicy cabbage leaf, and Mrs Bee who had a liking for poppy flowers filled with nectar.

'I don't think bees like poppies that much,' said Joshua, looking up from the book. 'They much prefer foxgloves.'

'I wonder what creature Sandy will meet next?' I asked, anxious to change the subject. I wasn't very informed about bees.

'It better not be a Frenchman,' he said.

I was intrigued. 'Why not a Frenchman?' I asked.

He looked at me as if I were simple-minded. 'Because they *eat* snails,' he said, shaking his head. 'Didn't you know that? When we went to a *gîte* in France last year, my father ate some snails. They're called *escargots* in French. Disgusting!'

The child read on until he came to the final page where Sandy Snail meets his mother. ' "Here I am. Where's my BIG surprise? Can I have it now, please? I'm so excited!" "See if you can find it!" said Mother Snail. Two little snails, one with a blue shell and the other with a pink shell, popped up from behind a leaf. "We're your big surprise, your new brother and sister!" '

Joshua snapped shut the book and shook his head.

'You read that very well, Joshua,' I told the boy. 'You're an excellent reader. And wasn't it a delightful story?'

He scowled. 'I didn't think much of it.'

'Why is that?' I asked.

'Well, for a start, snails don't have blue and pink shells. They are more of a greeny-brown colour. And for another thing, snails and those other creatures can't talk.'

'No, but then neither can Peter Rabbit, nor Mole and Ratty in *The Wind in the Willows*, or Mickey Mouse or some of Enid Blyton's animals. It's only a story.'

'And another thing,' said Joshua, not really listening to me, 'you can't have boy and girl snails.'

'Why not?' I asked innocently.

'Because everyone knows that snails are hermaphrodites,' he said.

I smiled but said nothing; I thought of the words of Oscar Wilde who once observed that a child 'has a disgusting appetite for facts'.

At afternoon break, the teacher told me that Joshua was a mine of information on natural history. 'Of course, you would expect as much,' she told me, 'his father being a professor of biology.'

*　　　*　　　*

The Chairman of the School Governors, Archdeacon Richards, a cheerful little cleric with a round red face and white bushy eyebrows which curled like question marks below a shiny pate, was in the headteacher's room when I arrived there at afternoon break.

'I believe you know Mr Phinn, Archdeacon,' said the headteacher as I entered the room.

'Yes, indeed,' chortled the Chairman of the School Governors, extending a small plump hand. 'We met at Manston Hall a few years ago, did we not, Mr Phinn?' He turned to the headteacher to explain. 'We were on a planning committee chaired by Lord Marrick, set up to organise the event to mark the five hundred years of the establishment of the Feoffees.' The archdeacon spoke with the same lilting, birdlike trill as the headteacher.

'Freebies?' exclaimed Mrs Braddock-Smith, her eyes lighting up at the thought, no doubt, of more funding that might come her way. 'Did you say freebies?'

'No, no, Barbara,' chuckled the cleric. 'The Feoffees. I won't bore you with the details but suffice it to say that the Feoffees are of ancient provenance, founded in the reign of Henry VII, the first of the Tudor monarchs, to maintain law and order.'

'I can't say that I have ever heard of them,' said the headteacher, making a small dismissive gesture.

'They were very important in their day,' announced the archdeacon, preparing to do the very thing he proclaimed he would not do—bore us with the details. 'The Feoffees were typically composed of a group of local gentry, important landowners and civic worthies, men who held high rank or—'

Mrs Braddock-Smith interrupted the archdeacon. 'Well, I can't say that I have ever heard of them,' she said.

The archdeacon faltered momentarily but then continued. 'I am a Feoffee myself,' he said proudly and proceeded to give us the full benefit of his knowledge of this arcane institution.

The headteacher was patient for about a minute then she gently interrupted the archdeacon a second time. 'Perhaps you could tell me all about it another time. In fact, we could discuss it at the next governors' meeting, Archdeacon,' she said. 'I think the school is a very worthy cause, and if the Feoffees are a charitable group, perhaps they could send a bit of money our way. Some extra funding for the new play area we have planned would be very welcome.'

'Maybe,' Archdeacon Richards replied and swiftly changed the subject. 'And what do you make of our school, then, Mr Phinn?'

'I've only been in the building for a little over an hour,' I told him, 'but I am impressed with what I have seen so far.'

'I hope you feel the same after my assembly,' said the clergyman. 'I must own that I do feel a trifle nervous at the thought of a school inspector sitting at the back of the hall with his little black book.'

'Oh, I feel certain that Mr Phinn will not find anything amiss,' the headteacher said quickly. 'I was telling him about our outstanding results. I don't think he'll find better readers in the whole county and I should hazard to say that the written work is well above that of children in many schools.'

'It is true we are justifiably proud,' said the archdeacon softly.

'Mr Phinn visited the Junior School this morning,' observed Mrs Braddock-Smith, giving the chairman of governors a knowing look. I had suspected that it would not be long before the situation at Ugglemattersby Juniors was raised.

'Really?' said the archdeacon.

'Yes, I did,' I replied simply.

'And how is Mr Harrison?' he asked in the most solicitous of voices.

'He's very well,' I lied. There's no way, I thought to myself, that I was going to discuss the problems of the headteacher of another school with Mrs Braddock-Smith and her chairman of governors, particularly in a village where the jungle telegraph was so obviously finely developed.

'I don't know Mr Harrison that well,' continued the clergyman. 'He's of the Methodist persuasion, you know, so we don't see him in church although he does hold the school's harvest service at St Mary's. Speaking of the harvest service, Barbara,' he began, 'I thought that this year—'

The headteacher clearly did not wish to be diverted from the subject in hand. 'He does try so hard, Mr Harrison,' she said in an overly sad and sympathetic voice. 'He must feel so very disappointed that so many of our parents chose to send their children on to other schools rather than his.' She looked at me expectantly. I could tell there was another agenda going on here but I was determined not to be a part of it.

'I am sure he does,' I replied.

'It's quite a mystery really, isn't it?' said the headteacher.

It was no mystery. All three of us knew why so many parents opted to send their children elsewhere. Mrs Braddock-Smith was waiting for me to make a comment but I remained silent.

'And how is Mrs Battersby?' asked the archdeacon. 'Her husband is one of my churchwardens, you know, a man of—er—strong views which he is not afraid of expressing.'

'She's very well, too,' I replied and before they

could ask about the other teacher, I added, 'and so is Mrs Sidebottom.'

'Well, that's good, isn't it?' said the archdeacon, realising at last that I would not be any more forthcoming on the question of Ugglemattersby Junior School. He glanced at his watch. 'Nearly time for assembly, I think.'

When the bell sounded for the end of afternoon playtime, the Infants filed into the hall to a stirring tune, hammered out on the piano with great vigour by Mrs Hartley, and sat down cross-legged on the floor. I had gone to the back but was ushered forward to the front by the headteacher to a seat next to hers and the archdeacon's. I faced the sea of red. In the very front row, sitting straight-backed and serious-faced and with his arms folded tightly over his chest, was Joshua.

'Good afternoon, children,' said Mrs Braddock-Smith when silence had fallen.

'Good a-f-t-e-r-n-o-o-n, Mrs Braddock-Smith,' they chanted.

'This afternoon in our assembly we have got not one but two very important visitors with us,' said the headteacher. All eyes looked at the archdeacon and me. 'You all know Archdeacon Richards, who is our special friend and comes to see us often, but some of you will not yet have met our other important visitor. His name is Mr Phinn and he is a school inspector. Mr Phinn is here to see all your wonderful work and hear you read. Shall we all say a good afternoon to our visitors?'

'Good a-f-t-e-r-n-o-o-n, Archdeacon Richards, good a-f-t-e-r-n-o-o-n, Mr Phinn, good a-f-t-e-r-n-o-o-n, everybody,' the infants chanted.

'Good afternoon, children,' I replied.

72

'Good afternoon, children,' repeated the archdeacon.

'You know, Mr Phinn,' continued the headteacher, waving an expansive hand at the rows before her, 'not only are these children such remarkable readers and excellent writers, they are also wonderful singers as well, aren't you?'

'Yes, Mrs Braddock-Smith,' the whole school said in unison.

'And I am sure Mr Phinn would like to hear you sing, wouldn't you, Mr Phinn.'

'Yes, I would,' I said loudly and wishing she would get on with the assembly. I had heard quite enough about how wonderful the children were for one day.

'Well, let us all stand up nice and smartly,' said the headteacher, 'fill those lungs and raise the roof.'

Very soon the hall was filled with the singing, which was sadly drowned by the over-zealous playing of Mrs Hartley.

'Did you enjoy that, Mr Phinn?' asked the headteacher when the children had finished the hymn.

'Very much,' I said.

'Now, please sit down, children, legs crossed, arms folded, and nice straight backs. The archdeacon would like to say a few words.'

Far from being 'a few words', the archdeacon spoke at length to the children, who shuffled and fidgeted and yawned and found it increasingly difficult to concentrate. The clergyman droned on about how the seasons change and how autumn—'the season of mists and mellow fruitfulness'—was fast approaching. 'The crops in the fields are nearly all gathered in,' he said, 'the fruits ripe on the boughs are being picked and the vegetables collected and stored for the winter. And what is the word which means the gathering in of the crops?' he asked.

'Digging up,' suggested a child.

'Well, the produce would be dug up, yes,' said the archdeacon smiling, 'but this word begins with the letter "H" and we have a very special festival in church.'

'Halloween!' shouted out another child.

'No,' said the vicar, attempting to keep his composure, 'not Halloween.'

'Holiday!' suggested another.

'No, not holiday.'

'Helicopter!' shouted a third child.

'Now we're being silly,' said the archdeacon. 'No, children, the word I was thinking of is "harvest", the gathering in of all the fruit and vegetables and crops from the fields, and each year in church we have a Harvest Festival to thank God for all His wonderful gifts to us.'

'I like Halloween,' called out one infant. 'I can dress up as a witch and go "trick-or-treating" with my brother.'

'Well, that's something very different,' said the archdeacon, his face colouring up. 'Now, I think we'll have our last hymn, if you please, Mrs Hartley.'

Accompanied by more spirited martial music from the piano, the children then marched back to their classrooms, followed by Mrs Braddock-Smith and the other teachers. The archdeacon and I remained—along with one small and very distressed girl standing alone in the middle of the hall, wailing piteously. A little puddle could be seen on the floor beneath her. Her tiny face was flushed with great anxiety and I could see that her eyes were filling with tears.

'Oh dear,' said the archdeacon sympathetically.

'I've wet myself,' moaned the child, her cheeks smeared where her hands had tried to wipe away the tears.

'Don't worry, my dear,' he said.

'I've wet myself,' repeated the child.

'Accidents do happen,' said the clergyman, now standing in front of her. 'It's nothing to get all upset about.'

'I've wet myself,' said the child again.

'Why didn't you put your hand up?' asked the archdeacon.

'I did,' replied the child, sniffing noisily, 'but it trickled through my fingers.'

CHAPTER FIVE

After my visit to the Ugglemattersby schools I decided, rather than go straight home, to return to the office and write up my report while things were fresh in my mind.

Little did I expect to find Sidney and David at their desks and I was even more surprised to find Geraldine there, too.

'Ah!' cried Sidney as I entered the room, 'a full complement! What a rarity. We must celebrate— all in the office at the same time. We shall retire to the local hostelry for a little drinkie and catch up on what we did over the summer.'

'Not for me, Sidney,' said Geraldine hastily. 'I must be going in a minute. I have a little boy to get home to. The child minder will want to get away.'

'And I've a meeting at the Golf Club at seven,' said David, 'so you can count me out.'

'Well, that just leaves us, Gervase,' said Sidney. 'Fancy a pint, old boy?'

'No thanks, Sidney,' I told him. 'I have this report to write up.'

'Pish!' he exclaimed. 'It can wait until tomorrow.'

'Not this one,' I said.

'Oh dear,' said David, 'that sounds serious. I detect something dark and troubling in our young colleague's eyes. Would you like to tell us about it?'

'How long have you got?' I asked, placing my briefcase on my desk and flopping into a chair. 'No, I'll tell you another time.'

'Gerry was telling us about her holiday to the Emerald Isle this summer,' David told me.

'Yes, it was memorable,' said Geraldine. 'I know it sounds clichéd, but I don't think I've ever seen anything more beautiful than the sun setting over Galway Bay at Oranmore, and the pale moon rising over the grey mountains.'

'Oh sure and beggora,' said Sidney, adopting a mock-Irish accent, 'don't I just feel one of my mawkish Irish melodies a-comin' on, to be sure.' He then began to sing, 'If you ever go across the sea to Ireland, be certain at the closing of the day—'

'Behave yourself, Sidney,' interrupted Geraldine, laughing.

'The Welsh have a great deal in common with

76

the Irish, you know,' said David.

'Here we go,' mumbled Sidney.

'And, of course,' continued David blithely, 'the shared Celtic heritage explains why both races have such a love of and talent in music and poetry.'

'I will grant you that the Welsh and the Irish do have something in common when it comes to language,' said Sidney, 'and that is their inability to shut up. Get a group of you Celts together and nobody can get a word in. It's like throwing a bone to ravening dogs. Yap! Yap! Yap!'

I smiled. 'Well, it is a fact that the Irish and the Welsh do like to use words and have a lot to say for themselves,' I said.

'Thank you, Gervase,' said Sidney. 'That is exactly my point.'

'But I have to say that the Irish and Welsh are often better users of English than the English themselves,' I said. 'They embroider the language, make it more colourful, more inventive. Oscar Wilde once said that if only the English knew how to talk and the Irish how to listen. "The Saxon took our lands from us," he said, "and left us desolate. We took their language and added new beauties to it." In Wales, I think it's called "talking tidy" and in Irish it's "a touch of the blarney".'

'Well I call it verbal diarrhoea,' said Sidney dismissively.

'When I hear you expounding thus, Sidney,' said David, 'three words come to mind: "kettle", "pot" and "black".'

'Speaking of pots,' said Sidney, going off on one of his tangents, 'have any of you seen my ceramic vase which was on the windowsill in the old office? I've searched high and low for it and it seems to

77

have disappeared into thin air.'

David and I exchanged glances.

'Ceramic pot?' said David innocently.

'The one that was on the windowsill. It was a very good example of a finely-glazed earthenware vase,' said Sidney. 'I made it on my pottery course last term.'

'I've not seen it,' said Geraldine. 'Have you asked Julie?'

'Yes, and she doesn't know where it's gone, either,' replied Sidney. He looked at David and me. 'Do either of you know where it is?'

David and I did indeed know where it was. The remains of the finely-glazed earthenware vase were in the skip at the back of County Hall where I had deposited them. The item in question, an ugly brown specimen, had slipped from my hands when, during the office move, I was negotiating the narrow stairs. I had thought it prudent not to tell my colleague.

'It was a lustrous piece of pottery,' said Sidney, 'and I was very attached to it. It's a mystery where it's gone. Mind you, there are a lot of things I can't find since you two took it upon yourselves to move all my stuff. Folders and important files have gone walkabout, I am missing a number of books, and now my unique finely-glazed lustrous earthenware vase has gone, goodness knows where.'

'I'm sure it will turn up, Sidney,' said David, knowing full well that it would not. 'Well, I shall have to be going.' He rose from his chair and stretched. 'Goodnight, Gervase. Don't stay too late. Come along, Sidney, let's leave the man to finish his report.'

'And I must be away, too,' said Geraldine, giving

me a small wave.

'I'll see you all tomorrow at the meeting,' I said.

'Ah, yes, I can ask our esteemed boss if she knows where my vase has gone,' persisted Sidney, following his two colleagues. 'Bye, Gervase.'

The three of them departed noisily and in the silence of the office I thought back to my previous visit to the Ugglemattersby Junior School, when I had presented such a critical report. I had, as Mr Harrison had pointed out, promised to return to ensure that my recommendations for improvement had been implemented—and I hadn't done so. I had been too busy with the affairs of other schools, and my mind had been occupied with more pressing matters. These, I knew, were feeble excuses. I should have followed things up. I had convinced myself that Mr Harrison, the new headteacher, keen, experienced and confident, would quickly sort things out but this clearly had not been the case. I had not even bothered to ring him up and check that he had settled in and that the situation in the school was improving. Now I had to face Miss de la Mare, the Chief Inspector, and explain myself. I supposed my report would have to be a bit colourful and inventive. With a sigh, I finally got around to putting pen to paper.

*   *   *

I arrived home to my cottage in the pretty little Dales village of Hawksrill on that wet and windy evening with Ugglemattersby still on my mind. I parked the car on the narrow track that ran along the side of the cottage, turned off the engine and sat for a while in the silent darkness. I thought

79

about the depressing day I had had, considered what I needed to do next and then I rehearsed mentally just what I would say to the Chief Inspector when I saw her at the inspectors' meeting the following day. I suppose I could try to shift the blame by telling her that I had assumed, quite wrongly as it had turned out, that if things had not been going well at the school after his appointment, the headteacher would have contacted me to ask for support and advice. I could argue that I had so many schools to visit and so many courses to run, conferences to organise and a whole raft of other important jobs to do, that I had put Ugglemattersby to the back of my mind. But these excuses sounded unconvincing. I would just have to face the music.

I was usually keen to get home from work to my dream cottage and my family. We would bath the baby together and kiss him goodnight before putting him in his cot in the little bedroom under the eaves. Then I would snuggle up with Christine on the old sofa in front of the open fire, and share my day with her and hear what she had been doing, while the smell of supper cooking wafted through from the kitchen. Through the car window now, the cottage looked cheerful and welcoming, and I knew the two people I loved most in the world would be waiting for me.

Christine and I had wanted Peewit Cottage in the village of Hawksrill as soon as we had set eyes upon it. Colleagues at work thought we had taken leave of our senses, cobbling together every penny we had to buy this rundown, dark stone barn of a building with its sagging roof, old-fashioned kitchen and cold damp rooms, but, standing in the overgrown garden, we had fallen hopelessly in love with the magnificent views. We had stood on the tussocky lawn with its bare patches and mole hills, surrounded by waist-high weeds, tangled brambles and rampant rose bushes, and gazed across a panorama of green undulating fields criss-crossed with silvered limestone walls that rose to the craggy fell-tops, and we had marvelled. We knew we could transform this old cottage into our dream home.

Our 'dream home', in fact, turned out to be something of a house of horrors. We soon discovered that we had an expanding family of woodworm in the quaint beams, persistent dry rot in the cosy little sitting room and rising damp in the dining room, cracked walls in the bedrooms, a leaking roof and broken guttering and nearly every conceivable problem that could face the home-owner. But we had been optimistic and cheerful and now, after nearly two years, we were getting somewhere. Having spent most of our spare time renovating and repairing, refurbishing and decorating, Peewit Cottage was beginning to take shape.

There was a rap on the side of the car, which made me jump. Outside, peering through the car window, was a wide-boned, weathered face I immediately recognised. It was our nearest neighbour, Harry Cotton, a man whose long beak of a nose was invariably poking in everyone else's business. Harry was a man of strong opinions, most of which were usually complaints, pieces of unwanted advice and unhelpful observations. He was the world's greatest prophet of doom and the incarnation of the good old Yorkshire motto:

'Ear all, see all, say nowt;
Eayt up, sup all, pay nowt;
An' if ever tha does owt fer nowt,
Do it for thissen!

I wound down the window. 'Hello, Harry,' I said wearily.

'I thowt it were thee,' he said, scratching the impressive shock of white hair.

'How are you?' I asked.

'Nobbut middlin',' he replied. 'I were badly last week. 'Appen summat I'd etten. I 'ad tripe an' onions an' I reckon it dint agree wi' me. Any road, what's tha doin' out 'ere, sittin' in t'dark by thissen?'

'Just thinking,' I told him.

'I thowt tha were deead or summat, just sittin' theer. I was tekkin' Buster out for 'is constitutional an' I saw thee.' Buster was Harry's wiry-haired Border terrier that now barked excitedly at the mention of his name, and jumped up at the door of the car. 'Get down, Buster!' ordered Harry. 'Sit down!' He turned his attention back to me. 'I thowt for a minit that tha'd 'ad an 'eart attack or summat an' were deead at t'wheel. 'As tha 'ad a bit of a barney wi' t'missis, then?' he asked. 'Been kicked out, 'as tha?'

'No, no, nothing like that,' I replied. 'I'm just a bit tired after a long day and a lot of driving.'

'How long 'as tha been wed now then?' he asked. 'Is it two year?'

'Not quite,' I said, reaching over to the back seat for my briefcase. The last thing I wanted at that moment was Harry Cotton and his potted philosophy.

'Aye, when t'honeymoon's ovver, first flush of living together wears off. I've seen it time an' time ageean. Once a woman's got that ring on 'er finger, things change and they don't change for t'better. I'm glad I nivver got wed. Too much trouble. Tek my sister, Bertha.' He chuckled. 'I bet my brother-in-law would like somebody to tek her. Talk abaat bein' under t'thumb. Soon as 'e walks in through t'dooer she's at 'im to do this an' do that an' when 'e does do it, nowt 'e does is reight. Comes in from work, 'e does, and just as 'e sits dahn she's at 'im. "Are yer gunna sit theer all neet? That winder wants fixin' an' cooal wants fetchin' in an' yer can peel t'taties if tha's nowt better to do." She's nobbut five foot two an' as thin as a lat but, by the heck, she's gor a gob on 'er. Two year into t'marriage and—'

'Harry,' I said, attempting to get out of the car, 'Christine and I have not had any barney, as you put it. We are very very happy and everything at home is fine. I've just had a bit of a bad day, that's all.'

'Tell me abaat it,' he said and then, without waiting, started to describe his own 'dreadful' day.

Finally, I managed to extricate myself from the car and headed for the cottage, but Harry and his still yapping dog followed me up the path. 'By the way, I've had a word with thy missis about yon garden,' he called after me. 'It needs sooarting out. I mean your missus can't be expected to do all that diggin' and prunin' and plantin' what wi' a young bairn to tek care on, now can she, and it's t'time o' year when it wants fettlin'.'

'I'll see to it,' I told him shortly.

83

'Tha wants to,' he told me, stubbornly pursuing his theme. 'I was telling 'Ezekiah Longton last neet ovver a pint o' mild at t'Royal Oak. His garden's a picture, like summat out o' one o' these glossy 'orticultural magazines. Cooarse, it would be, what wi' 'im bein' Lord Marrick's head gard'ner for nigh on fotty year. Any road, I were tellin' 'im what a jungle your garden were and 'e says that tha can 'ave some on 'is 'ardy perennials if tha wants.'

'That's very kind of him,' I said.

'An' that allotment of yourn needs a bit o' work on it an' all. It's goin' dahn t'nick, by looks on it. George Hemmings, on t'Allotment Committee, were only mentionin' it to me last week in t'Oak. Now, if it was up to me—'

'I'll see to it, Harry,' I said wearily, my hand on the back door latch.

'An' I'll tell thee summat else an' all,' he persisted. 'That new landlord at t'Oak is goin' down like a dose o' sheep flu. Tha wants to see what 'e's gone an' done to t'old place.'

'Goodnight, Harry,' I said, going into the cottage and closing the door behind me.

'Goodnight,' he called from the step. 'Come on, Buster.'

Christine was in the kitchen preparing supper. The cottage was as cheerful and welcoming as I knew it would be, and I could see that a lazy fire burned in the sitting room grate. It was good to be home.

'You're late,' said Christine as I wrapped my arms around her and gave her a kiss on the cheek.

'Yes,' I sighed, burying my face in her neck.

'You don't sound full of the joys of spring.'

'It's autumn,' I replied holding her close, 'and I

84

need a strong drink and some TLC.'

'Hard day?' Christine returned to the sink where she was peeling potatoes in a bowl.

'Dreadful!' I said, bending over Richard's carrycot. He looked washed and scrubbed and was gurgling away contentedly.

'Oh dear.'

'I don't want to talk about it,' I said.

'As bad as that, is it?' she asked.

'As bad as that,' I repeated.

Of course I needed to talk about it so, as I sat at the kitchen table nursing a dark brown whisky, Christine had to endure a detailed account of my day. She was, as always, a sympathetic listener and full of good advice and by the time supper was ready, I felt slightly better.

'Would you take Richard up, then we can eat,' she said.

When I came downstairs, having tucked the sleepy baby into his cot, supper was on the table.

'Harry Cotton's been round today,' Christine said, heaping beef stew onto my plate.

'So I hear. He told me he'd had a word with you.'

'Was that who I heard you talking to before you came in?'

'Yes, he was practically lying in wait for me outside,' I told her. 'I had to endure five minutes of his blather before I could get rid of him. Once he gets started there's no stopping him, and he's always got the weight of the world on his shoulders. The last thing I wanted tonight was a dose of Harry's words of wisdom.'

'He's not that bad,' said Christine. 'Harry's quite endearing, really, and it's good to have a neighbour who keeps an eye on things. He told me he's a bit down in the dumps at the moment because of the new landlord at the pub. Apparently, the man's causing a few waves, upsetting the regulars by changing things.'

'He told me,' I said. 'Harry doesn't like change and that's for sure. If it was up to him, we'd still live in the dark ages. He's always harping on about the good old days when bobbies walked the beat, nobody dropped litter and children did as they were told.'

'Well, in my opinion, the Royal Oak wants changing,' Christine said. 'It's a smelly, run-down place at the best of times. Only the old villagers go there.'

'It's not that bad,' I said. 'It's got character, although I must admit it could do with a lick of paint and some new furniture.'

'It'll take more than a lick of paint and new furniture,' she said. 'It's very old-fashioned. People nowadays want a more cheerful place in which to drink.'

'Harry also mentioned the garden,' I said.

'Yes, he did to me as well,' said Christine, 'and he wondered if we might be interested in his—er, brother's grandson, I think, tidying it up a bit. I'm too busy at the moment trying to get the spare bedroom sorted, and Richard takes so much of my time, and I know you're not up to it.'

'It's not that I'm not up to it,' I replied, a little annoyed by the comment. 'It's just that I'm up to my eyes at work and have so much on my plate at the moment.' I must have sounded like a petulant schoolboy.

'Don't be so touchy,' said Christine, stretching

86

out her hand to mine. 'What I meant was that you're far too busy and that you haven't the time. Anyway, Harry's brother's grandson, Andy, leaves school next summer and could do with some extra money. He's working up at Ted Poskitt's farm at the weekends but it's not a regular job and he's trying to save enough to put himself through Askham Bryan Agricultural College near York. From what Harry says, he seems a willing enough lad and would be a real help with the digging and weeding and doing a few repairs. What do you think?'

'So long as it doesn't cost us too much,' I said, 'it sounds like a good idea.'

'I thought you'd say that,' said Christine, 'so I've asked Andy to come up and see you. Now, what about the washing up?'

*   *   *

I just could not sleep that night. My thoughts kept returning again and again to the situation at Ugglemattersby Junior School and what I would say to Miss de la Mare when I faced her the next morning. In the bright light of day, problems always seem far less important than they do in the dead of night. When you're in bed surrounded by the silence and the darkness with your mind going over things again and again, it is then you imagine the worst possible scenario.

Finally I drifted off into a fretful sleep but was soon wide awake again, with Christine jabbing me in the back.

'Gervase! Wake up!' she whispered.

'What is it?' I mumbled.

'Can you hear it?' Christine asked in a hushed voice.

'Hear what?'

'That noise.'

I rubbed my eyes and sat up. 'What noise? I can't hear anything. Is it Richard?' I asked. 'He probably wants feeding. Shall I get him?'

'It's not the baby!' hissed Christine sharply. 'It's a sort of scratching noise, coming from the loft. There's something up there, moving about.'

'Somebody in the house?'

'Not some *body*, some *thing*.'

'A ghost?'

'Don't be silly,' she said. 'It's some sort of animal.'

'Oh no,' I said, sitting up and gazing up at the ceiling, 'I bet we've got mice.'

'Don't say that!' exclaimed Christine, clamping her arms around me. 'You know I hate mice. If I thought there was—' She stopped mid-sentence. 'There it is again. Can you hear it?'

There was certainly something moving about above us, a sort of scraping noise then a skittering sound obviously made by some small creature. 'Yes, I can hear it,' I said.

'You don't think it's a rat, do you?' asked Christine shuddering.

'No, no, of course not,' I told her in a matter-of fact tone of voice, as much to reassure myself as my wife. 'Rats don't make that noise and, anyway, they wouldn't be up in a loft. They don't like heights. It's probably a little field mouse come in out of the cold.'

'It's a pretty big field mouse that makes that sort of noise. It sounds huge.'

88

'It just sounds loud, that's all,' I said.

'Go and look,' Christine told me, getting out of bed and putting on her slippers and dressing gown.

'Go and look?' I repeated. 'What, now? At this time of night?'

'I can't sleep with a rat in the house. I'm moving the baby in with us until you find it. The thought of a rat scuttling about in the cottage makes me feel ill.'

'I've told you,' I said, 'it's not a rat, but I suppose I'd better take a look.'

'And be careful,' Christine said. 'Cornered rats are said to go for the jugular.'

'Thanks very much,' I said. 'That makes me feel a whole lot better,' and I plodded downstairs to fetch a ladder.

I poked my head up through the hatch but I saw nothing in the torch's beam except the black water tank and a few large cardboard boxes that we used for storage. The rest of the loft was dark and dusty. I hardly expected the creature, whatever it was, to be waiting to wave at me. It was probably in some dark corner, watching me at that very moment, but not moving an inch.

After my unsuccessful sortie, I found Christine sitting in the kitchen, feeding Richard. 'Well?' she asked nervously.

'I can't see anything,' I told her, 'but I'll have another look in the morning when it's light.'

'What about giving Mr Hinderwell a call?' suggested Christine.

Maurice Hinderwell was the County Pest Control Officer whom I had met the previous year when visiting one of the county's schools. He was a strange little man, not unlike the rodents he caught and killed, with dark inquisitive eyes, small pointed nose, protuberant white teeth and glossy black hair bristling on his scalp. The school had had a nest of rats, which he had disposed of in quick time and with a great degree of relish. When rats appeared in the garden of Peewit Cottage, I had called on his services and since then not a rat had been seen. Now, it seemed, there was a strong possibility that a rat had returned and was in the house.

'I'll call him in the morning,' I said.

As soon as I was back in bed with Christine snuggled up beside me and the baby in his carrycot beside us, the noise started again in earnest. Added to the scratching and scraping, there was now the noise of tiny feet racing up and down above us.

'Sounds as though he is preparing for the Rat Olympics,' I commented unwisely.

Christine gave a muffled shriek. 'I'm going to my parents in the morning,' she said, 'and not coming back until you've got rid of it.'

As soon as it was light, I climbed the ladder to the loft, armed with a poker. I pushed my head charily through the hatch and saw our nocturnal visitor. Sitting on its haunches and staring at me with large black eyes was a grey squirrel. I could also see how it had got into the loft—light was coming through a hole in the corner where a slate had come loose.

'It's a squirrel,' I called down to Christine. 'A cute, little bushy-tailed squirrel. He's getting in through a hole under the eaves.'

I could hear the relief in Christine's voice. 'Well, I'm glad it's not a rat,' she said, 'but I still don't want a squirrel, however cute, taking up residence.'

A moment later, I came down from the loft. 'Well, he'll not be back,' I said. 'I've blocked up his entrance and that should stop him getting in. That's the end of our little visitor.'

Would that had been the case! As it turned out, the squirrel became yet another item on my list of problems.

CHAPTER SIX

The following day, Friday, was the day of the first meeting of the new autumn term of the team of inspectors. I wanted to get to the Staff Development Centre before my colleagues to discuss the situation at Ugglemattersby Junior School with Winifred de la Mare, the Chief Inspector.

I had been so looking forward to the start of the new term and little expected that in the very first school that I would visit there would be a problem, and what was likely to be a major one at that. After we had moved downstairs to our new office we had had a week before schools went back, during which time I had planned all my forthcoming courses, worked out a timetable of school visits, and had organised support materials for teachers, and had then sat back in my chair the Friday before the start of the new school year feeling rather smug. I should have recalled the cautionary advice of one of my colleagues.

David Pritchard, the small, good-humoured Welshman responsible for Mathematics, PE and Games, had once warned me against the danger of becoming too complacent. In his sonorous, lugubrious Welsh valley voice he had told me that when things seem to be going swimmingly, disaster generally strikes—like someone poking a great stick through the spokes of your bicycle when you are least expecting it, with the result that you are over the handlebars and flat on your face. After my visit to Ugglemattersby Junior School I felt decidedly prone.

The child's innocent question at that school, 'What are you for?' had stayed firmly in my mind. What *was* I for? It was clear to me that my function was to help improve the education of the young in the county by observing, recording, reporting and advising headteachers and teachers. It appeared I had not been very successful in the case of the Junior School and I guessed that the Chief Inspector would have something pretty sharp to say when she found out.

Winifred de la Mare had only been in post for a term, having taken over from the previous Senior Inspector, Dr Harold Yeats, an easy-going, tolerant, gentle giant of a man. Harold, ever optimistic, phlegmatic and of a kindly disposition, avoided confrontation and had been a delight to work with. Our new boss was a very different character altogether: extremely efficient, clear-sighted, frighteningly intelligent and, for anyone foolish enough to take her on, a formidable adversary. She did not suffer fools gladly and expected the highest professional standards and a great deal of hard work from her colleagues. Years of experience as a highly-respected and senior member of Her Majesty's Inspectorate of Schools, had prepared her well for the ups and downs of this new appointment and she was fully equipped to deal with difficult headteachers, unpredictable colleagues, well-meaning Chief Education Officers who liked to delegate, and demanding and frequently interfering elected members of the Education Committee on the County Council.

When that Committee had proposed the closure of a number of small schools, two of which were not only greatly valued by the small communities they served but also produced more than adequate results, Miss de la Mare had marshalled the facts, come out fighting and had persuaded the councillors to scrap the idea. I was greatly relieved and very grateful to her for one of the schools on the list for closure had been Hawksrill, the school which my own child would one day attend. Miss de la Mare spoke her mind, fought her corner and got things done but she was also good humoured, supportive and was someone for whom we inspectors had a great deal of respect.

Since she had taken up her post at the beginning of the previous term, there had been many changes and all for the better. A month after she had arrived, Miss de la Mare had emerged from the Chief Education Officer's room at County Hall with the new title of Chief Inspector and the promise that all the inspectors' salary scales would be re-negotiated. Julie, the inspectors' clerk, had soon after been promoted and re-designated inspectors' secretary: that was no change so far as we were concerned since we had always called her 'secretary'. She had now been promised extra clerical help. She would no longer have to type all the school reports, which had occupied so much of her time, but send them to the central typing pool at County Hall. But the major change, of course, had been the move downstairs of the inspectors' office. No longer were the four of us in a cramped and cluttered office, but in a much more spacious and newly refurbished area on the ground floor, formerly occupied by the school psychologists. Julie had been upgraded from her broom cupboard to a still small but light and airy room. Yes, indeed, Miss Winifred de la Mare had certainly got things done. As I drove into the Staff Development Centre that September morning I wondered just what she would do about me.

The Staff Development Centre, where all the courses and conferences for teachers and most of the staff meetings and interviews took place, had once been a secondary modern school. The former playground area was now the car park, the biggest classrooms and the hall had been adapted for lectures and courses, and the smaller rooms had been converted into meeting rooms and resource centres. There was a small staff room, reference library, well-equipped kitchen, spacious lounge area and office. The SDC was as a good school should be—bright, cheerful and welcoming and, above all, spotlessly clean and orderly. This was as a result of the industry and devotion of the caretaker, Connie, who kept the building, inside and out, immaculate.

Connie was a colourful and assertive character—a warm-hearted, down-to-earth Yorkshire woman who had no understanding whatsoever of rank, status or social standing in the world. She was severally known by Sidney Clamp as 'that virago with the feather duster', 'the tyrant with the teapot', 'the caretaker from hell', 'the termagant in pink', 'the despot with the stepladders' and various other assorted cognomens. Everyone who drove through the gates or crossed the threshold of her domain, be it Dr Brian Gore, our esteemed Chief Education Officer, or the humble man who arrived to empty the dustbins, was greeted with the same uncompromising forthright manner, usually with the words, 'I hope you've parked your vehicle in the correct specificated areas and not blocked my entrance.'

Connie had a delightfully eccentric command of the English language. She was a mistress of the malapropism and a skilled practitioner of the *non sequitur*. For Connie, English was not a dull and dreary business, it was something to twist and play with, distort, invent and re-interpret. She could mangle words like a mincer shredding meat.

She had a somewhat explosive relationship with Sidney who, being loud, expressive, untidy and larger than life, was a person guaranteed to cross swords with her. She once vowed 'to take the bull between the horns' and tackle Sidney (who she described as 'a wolf in cheap clothing') once and for all. 'The mess that man leaves behind,' she frequently complained, 'with all his artificated courses. I'm sick and tired of clearing up after him. He leaves a trail of debris and destruction wherever he goes.' Once when she had returned to work after being 'in bed with her back'—the result of moving large bags of clay Sidney had left after his pottery course—Connie had announced that because of Mr Clamp she had been 'under a psychopath for a week'.

On another occasion, when some teachers

complained that they couldn't hear one of the speakers who was delivering a lecture in the main hall, she agreed that the 'agnostics' were not too good in that particular room.

Such a character, positioned at the entrance to the Centre, with her copper-coloured perm, attired in a brilliant pink nylon overall and holding a feather duster like a field marshal with his baton ready to do battle, could be quite unnerving for visitors. Teachers attending courses at the SDC, seeing Connie's set expression, which could freeze soup in cans, and the small sharp eyes watching their every movement, would creep past her like naughty schoolchildren. After the coffee break they would dutifully return their cups to the serving hatch under Connie's watchful stare, and they'd leave the cloakrooms in the pristine condition in which they had found them. At the end of their lectures, visiting speakers would ensure that the equipment they had used was neatly put away, the chairs carefully stacked, the rooms left in an orderly fashion, litter placed in the appropriate receptacles and all crockery returned to the kitchen. She had been known to pursue offenders into the car park and berate them if they did not leave the room exactly as they had found it.

On this damp, dreary September morning, Connie was standing at the entrance in her familiar pose as I entered the Centre. Under her scrutinising eye, I thoroughly wiped my feet on the mat and closed the door without banging it.

'Oh, it's you, is it?' she said. No 'Good morning, Mr Phinn, have you had a nice holiday?' No, 'Hello, and how are you?' Just 'Oh, it's you, is it?' was all I was going to get.

'Good morning, Connie,' I replied, trying to sound cheerful.

'You're early. The meeting doesn't start till eight thirty. I've only just put the tea urn on.'

'I was hoping to see Miss de la Mare before the start,' I told her. 'Has she arrived yet?'

'She's in Meeting Room One, rootling through a pile of papers,' Connie replied. 'The amount of paperwork you lot get through! Acres of Amazon rainforests must get chopped down every week to keep you inspectors in paper. There's such a thing as conservatism, you know. I suppose you'll be wanting a cup of coffee?'

'That would be splendid,' I said.

'I've only got the ordinary kind,' she said, staring at me fiercely as if expecting some sort of confrontation. 'Not that decaffeinicated stuff.'

'That's fine,' I replied.

'I had a headteacher in here last term asking for "proper" coffee. "And what's proper coffee when it's at home?" I asked her. "Proper ground coffee," she said, "that you get in one of those caf . . . er, cath . . . um, catheters."'

'Cafetière,' I murmured.

'What?'

'Nothing.'

'Any road, I said to her, "I don't serve anything fancy, just ordinary instant coffee out of a jar not out of an er . . . um . . . and you can like it or lump it."'

'Well, I would like it, Connie,' I told her, 'just so long as it's hot and wet.'

'Just as well,' she told me, mollified, 'because that's all I've got. I'll go and put the kettle on. Oh, before I go, I've told Miss de la Mare that we've

97

got painters and decorators in the Centre next week and to remind you inspectors at your meeting that some of the rooms will be unavailable and there'll be a lot of wet paint about. If Mr Clamp thinks he can swan into the Centre without a by-your-leave and arrange courses without booking a room, as he's accustomised to do, then he's got another think coming.'

'I'll remind them,' I told her.

'The last thing I want is decorators messing the place up, leaving paint all over the floor, putting marks on my walls, moving my stepladders. I shall be keeping a close eye on them, you can be sure of that.'

Oh yes, I thought to myself, as she strode off in the direction of the kitchen, flicking her feather duster along the walls and across the top of the bookshelves as she went, I can be sure of that and no mistake.

I found Miss de la Mare at a large table in the meeting room scribbling some notes on a vast pad of paper. The whole of the surface around her was covered in papers and booklets, folders and files. Dressed in a substantial and rather loud red and green tweed suit, she looked more like the Madam Chairman of the Yorkshire Countrywomen's Association than the Chief Inspector of Schools.

'Good morning,' I said, feeling my stomach churning.

'Oh, good morning, Gervase,' she replied, looking over the top of her rimless half-moon spectacles. 'You're bright and early.'

'Yes,' I said. 'I was hoping to have a word with you before the meeting.'

'That's a coincidence,' she replied, putting her

pen down, removing her spectacles and turning to face me. 'I was hoping to have a word with you, too.'

'Really?'

'Yes, about something—how shall I put it—of a somewhat delicate nature.'

'That sounds ominous,' I said.

'Well, it might blow up into something very serious if it's not handled carefully. Dr Gore has asked for it to be dealt with as a matter of some urgency.'

'And it concerns me?' I asked.

'Yes, it does,' she replied.

'I had better sit down.'

'This is not something that is going to take a few minutes, Gervase,' she told me. 'I need to speak to you at some length about this particular matter. It concerns a school report you wrote some time ago.' My heart sank into my shoes. Surely no one could have spoken to her about Ugglemattersby Junior School so soon. Then I recalled Mrs Sidebottom's words that her husband was a colleague of Councillor Peterson, an important member of the Education Committee and Mr Sidebottom had probably been on the phone to his chum who, in turn, had most surely been on to Dr Gore straight after my visit the day before.

'So,' said Miss de la Mare, 'are you able to remain behind after the meeting?'

'Yes, of course,' I said, feeling the stirrings of tension and dread building up inside of me. 'My first appointment this afternoon is at one thirty.'

'Well, you may have to cancel that,' she said, placing the spectacles back on her nose and picking up her pen. 'Now, if you'll excuse me, I really don't wish to appear rude but I have to finish the agenda for this morning's meeting. There is quite a deal for us to get through.'

I joined Connie in the kitchen.

'There's no Garibaldis,' she said bluntly, pouring boiling water into a mug. 'It might be a pigment of my imagination but I could swear blind there was a full two packets of biscuits at the beginning of this week. They consume Garibaldis in this place like there's no tomorrow. I've an idea it's Mr Clamp who's the culprit. He's always got his hands in my biscuit barrel, nibbling away like a half-starved squirrel.'

'Don't mention squirrels,' I said.

'Why, what's wrong with squirrels?'

'Don't ask,' I told her.

'Anyway,' said Connie, 'there are only custard creams and a couple of ginger nuts, though I dare say it's a bit early for biscuits.'

'Did you have a nice holiday?' I asked, trying to take my mind off the impending interview with the Chief Inspector.

'No, I didn't!' she replied, pulling open the fridge door and taking out a jug of milk. She swirled it around and then sniffed at it. 'You know, that new milkman must think I was born yesterday trying to palm me off with old milk. I always order three bottles, all semi-skimmed. This morning I gets two full cream and neither are fresh.' She slid the jug across to me. 'I could swear it's on the turn.'

'What was wrong with your holiday?' I asked, pouring some milk in my coffee and perching on a stool. 'I thought you usually take your grandchildren to your caravan.'

I knew from experience that once I moved the conversation on to the topic of her grandchildren, Connie's apparently sharp and offhand manner would immediately evaporate for she doted on little Damien and Lucy. At the mention of them, the thin line of her mouth would disappear, the arms that had been tightly folded under her bosom would relax and her eyes would sparkle. There was nothing she liked better than talking about her grandchildren.

'We did take them on holiday with us,' Connie told me, 'but it rained cats and dogs for most of the week. Torrential it was and the winds were wicked and nearly blew us into the bay. We hardly got on the beach. Poor little mites were as good as gold-dust but we never had a chance to build sandcastles or go on the donkeys or take a stroll along the prom. We did go out on a boat trip but if I vomited once I vomited five times. Up and down went that boat like a fiddler's elbow. We spent most of the holiday in a caff on the front or in the amusements.'

'So, what—' I began.

'Our little Damien was no trouble at all but then he went and lost his purse with all his holiday money in it. At the police station, the sergeant was about as much use as a grave robber at a crematorium. "Can you remember where you lost it, sonny?" he asks him. I said, "If he knew where he lost it we'd be there looking for it, wouldn't we, and not wasting police time?" People say the daftest things. Anyway we never did find the purse. I said to Ted, I said, "Well, we can kiss that down the drain." I bought him a stick of rock to cheer him up—Damien, that is, not Ted—and he went

101

and dropped that in a puddle and roared his little eyes out for the rest of the day. No, Mr Phinn, the holiday was not a success. It was catastrophical.'

'You ought to be on the stage Connie,' I said, laughing. I was feeling much better already.

'What's that supposed to mean?' she asked.

'Just that you can tell a very entertaining story. Anyway, your grandchildren are back at school this week.' I took a sip of the coffee and pulled a face. The milk was indeed sour. 'I do think this milk—' I started.

Connie was now in full flight and, once on the topic of her grandchildren, was not to be diverted. 'Keen as mustard to get back to school, they were. You should have seen the school report from their headteacher what they brought home at the end of last term. At the confrontation meeting, Miss Pilkington told my daughter that they are a delight to teach and both doing really well. As sharp as buttons they are and very good little readers. Top table material, she said. I wouldn't say they were child progenies or anything like that but they certainly weren't at the back of the queue when the brains was given out.'

'I'm glad they like reading,' I said. 'You know, if every parent in the country read with their children every night for just half an hour it would make so much difference.'

'Oh, they get a story every night and when they're on their own they never have their noses out of a book,' said Connie. 'It was our Damien's birthday over the summer and his granddad bought him this picture book about a crocodile, which came with a glove puppet. I said to Ted that I thought it was a bit frightening myself. Big green thing this puppet was, with huge yellow eyes and rubber teeth and a long scaly tail. Put the wind up me, I don't mind saying. Ted, daft as a brush, kept chasing me round the bedroom with this crocodile. I don't know what the neighbours must have thought hearing me shouting at him, "Put it away, it's horrible." Anyhow, he got Damien on his knee and kept snapping the creature's jaws together. There were these two pieces of wood under the fabric and they clacked really loudly every time he snapped them together.'

'It's just the sort of thing children love,' I said.

'Any road,' continued Connie, 'in the crocodile's mouth was a small fish, little coloured plastic thing. Ted opened the jaws wide and asked young Damien, "Would you like to take the fish out of the crocodile's mouth?" He looks up at his granddad with these big eyes and do you know what he replied?'

I shook my head. 'You tell me, Connie.'

'He said, "Dream on!"' Connie laughed, and repeated, '"Dream on!" Can you beat it!' Then her smile went. 'But, if you was to ask me, I think that my daughter—Tricia, that is—tends to spoil Lucy when it comes to food. Damien eats like there's no tomorrow. Damien Dustbin his granddad calls him but Lucy's very fernickity. She wants all this fancy stuff, wholemeal bread and high-fibre cereals. Won't touch butter. Has to have this margarine with that monoglutinous sodomite. I told her, I said that when I was a girl, I'd have given my right arm for a bit of butter and you ate what you were given. There was no choice and if you didn't clean your plate then there was no pudding. I said there are lots of people starving in Africa who would be glad of what she's turning her nose up at. There were no burgers and chips and chicken nuggets and ice creams and sweets when I was a girl. None of this decaffeinicated coffee and orgasmic vegetables. They were lean years in the nineteen-thirties and forties, and you ate what you got. I remember my mother boiling up a sheep's head to make soup and it lasted for a fortnight. We went berserk at the sight of an orange, and I remember my first banana. You couldn't get them during the war, unless you was pregnant, which of course I wasn't.'

I glanced surreptitiously at my watch and wished I had never started this conversation. 'Well, I had better make a move,' I said.

'To be honest, it came as a bit of a surprise that first banana,' she said, smiling at the memory.

I was now intrigued. 'In what way?' I asked.

'Well, I don't know whether I should tell you,' she said, still smiling.

'Go on,' I coaxed.

'No, I'll tell you another time,' she said. 'They'll be here for the meeting in a minute.' Connie picked up the jug of milk, sniffed it again, harrumphed and poured the contents down the sink. 'I thought this milk had gone off. It'll be dried milk or black coffee for you inspectors this morning.'

I was now desperate to know. 'I'm not moving until you tell me.'

'Tell you what?'

'About the bananas.'

'Well, Ted and me were on our first date. I've probably told you that my father was very strict with us girls. I had to tell him where I was going and who I was meeting and how I was getting home. I had to be in by a certain time or there'd be fireworks. Once I was only down the road at my friend's house and Dad came and collected me. I was sixteen and felt so embarrassed. I don't know what he thought I would be getting up to. I was very naïve. I mean, I didn't even know what a homosexual was until I met Ted.'

'What's this got to do with the bananas?' I asked, stifling my laughter.

'I'm coming to that. My mother was like my father and was forever warning me about boys and what they would like to get up to.' She lowered her voice in case there was anyone in the vicinity eavesdropping, and mouthed. 'You know, hokey-pokey—that sort of carry on. She'd say, "Boys are only after one thing, Constance. Just remember that your name means faithful and dependable so don't go sitting on a boy's knee but if you do find yourself in that position always have a telephone directory between the pair of you." I don't for the life of me know where you'd get hold of a telephone directory at a dance.' Connie vigorously wiped down the already pristine stainless steel draining board. 'She wouldn't let me wear patent leather shoes in case they reflected my knickers. Anyway, Dad wanted to meet Ted to give him the once over and warn him to watch his step. He was very protectionist was my father. He insisted Ted should see me back home after the film, ten thirty at the latest. I mean, you'd laugh about it now when youngsters stay out all hours and get up to all sorts. And it wasn't as if I was a slip of girl or anything, I was getting on for thirty when Ted first took me out. In those days the Tivoli Cinema—we

105

called it the flea pit—in the High Street had these double seats at the back for courting couples where it's all dark and secluded. There were no arm rests separating so some of them were having a right old kiss and canoodle and a whole lot more if truth be told.'

'And the bananas?' I prompted.

'I'm about to tell you,' said Connie. 'We were halfway through *Brief Encounter* and Ted had his arm around me, as they do, and he says, "I've got a surprise for you." Oooh, I thought, a box of chocolates or a pair of silk stockings or something of that sort. Then Ted thrusts this banana into my hand. Course, it was pitch black so I couldn't see what it was. "Here you are," he whispers, "get hold of that." I screamed blue murder, the film stopped, the manager came running down the aisle and we were asked to leave the cinema.'

'Connie!' I said in a mock-outraged voice. 'I'm shocked!'

'Go on with you! You're a married man with a kiddie. Mind you, I'd been married for twenty-five years before I told Dad about it. How he laughed. I remember the tears rolling down his cheeks. And I always remembers that time if anyone mentions bananas.'

CHAPTER SEVEN

Following my chat with Connie, I was certainly feeling a whole lot better than I had been when, ten minutes later, two of my colleagues arrived for the meeting. David Pritchard and Sidney Clamp were arguing as usual as they entered the building.

'The Welsh are not stand-offish at all, Sidney,' David was saying angrily. I could hear him down the corridor.

'As soon as you go into a shop in Wales they all stop talking English and break into that spluttery incomprehensible language of yours,' Sidney replied. 'They do it deliberately. I find it infuriating.'

They arrived at the hatch to the kitchen and I moved out of the kitchen to meet them. 'Good morning,' I said.

'Gervase,' said Sidney, not returning my greeting, 'is it not a fact that the Welsh are less than friendly, in particular when it comes to the English?'

'Not at all,' I replied. 'I have always found the Welsh a most agreeable race. Most of the masters when I was at school were Welsh, and they were very friendly and pleasant.'

'You see,' said David, 'Gervase agrees with me. The Welsh are the world's greatest teachers and preachers, and the Land of my Fathers is a most hospitable nation, despite what the English have done to it over the centuries, repressing our way of life, trying to ban our mellifluous language and stamp out the culture.'

'Oh please, I beg you,' pleaded Sidney, pressing his hands together as if in prayer, 'don't let's go down the road of the English oppression of the Welsh again, the heroism of Glendower and the decline of the Druids.'

'It's a fact,' said David. 'My dear grandmother had to wear the Welsh Knot at school for daring to speak her native language.'

'The what?' I asked.

'It was a sort of noose,' explained David, 'which the teacher placed around a child's neck as a punishment for speaking Welsh. The English tried to suppress our native language, you see. If a teacher heard a child speaking Welsh, the language of his home and his forefathers, he or she was made to wear this noose as a punishment. Barbaric it was. My poor grandmother never forgot that humiliation.'

'From what I have heard of your Welsh grandmother, this Welsh Knot had little effect,' said Sidney. 'She never stopped talking or missed an opportunity of proffering her homely advice.'

'Cruel it was,' said David, 'putting a noose around a child's neck. But despite the tyranny of the English over the centuries, we Welsh have remained a very generous and welcoming nation. Perhaps, Sidney, it is because of your loud and aggressive manner that people react to you in the way they do.'

'Loud and aggressive!' spluttered his colleague. '*Moi?*'

Connie poked her head through the hatch and glowered. 'It's like a Punch and Judy show out there,' she said. 'Will you keep your voices down?'

'Morning, Connie,' said David.

'Do you two want coffee?'

'Ah, Connie,' said Sidney, 'what a delight to see your happy, smiling countenance, brightening up my sad and sorry life on such a wet, windy and incredibly inhospitable morning.'

Connie grimaced and thrust two large mugs of black coffee through the hatch.

'And perchance I might crave a *soupçon* of milk,'

suggested Sidney.

'It's off!' snapped Connie slamming the hatch cover with a bang and missing Sidney's fingers by an inch.

'You know, I can see the efficacy of this Welsh Knot,' said Sidney thoughtfully. 'I wonder if Connie might be prevailed upon to wear the English equivalent.'

The three of us retired to the small staff room. Sidney put down his coffee before flopping in a chair and looking at his watch. 'So, are our loins fully girded up for the onslaught of the new term and our meeting with the wonderful Winnie?'

'Sshh! Don't let the boss hear you call her that,' I warned him.

When the Chief Inspector, Miss Winifred de la Mare, had started at the beginning of the previous term, none of us had known how to address her. We had been sitting in the same staff room before the first inspectors' meeting of the term, much as we were doing now.

'What are we going to call our esteemed leader?' Sidney had asked. 'Winifred is such an awful name,' he'd said, tipping back in his chair, 'and Miss de la Mare is a terrible mouthful.'

'I had an aunt called Winifred,' David had said. 'Dreadful old crone she was, always moaning and groaning and—' He had stopped abruptly when a large figure loomed in the doorway.

'Good morning, gentlemen,' the lady in question had boomed as we had all shot to our feet. 'I quite agree about the name—and don't even think about shortening it to Winnie, which is what I had to suffer all through my school days. "Winnie the Pooh", some of the other girls would call me. My close friends called me Della and I suggest that is what you do.' She had beamed at us, but then added quickly, 'But only when we are working together, mind. At any public event, I should be grateful if you would please revert to Miss de la Mare, just to keep up appearances.' We had all mumbled our agreement, and that was how it had been.

Sidney now looked up at the clock on the wall. 'If Geraldine doesn't get her skates on, she'll be late for the meeting. Incidentally, do you know—'

Whatever knowledge Sidney was going to impart came to an abrupt halt as the door opened and Miss de la Mare put her head round.

'Good morning, gentlemen. Could you bear to wait just a bit longer? I am having a word with Geraldine at the moment, but we'll be through in five minutes.'

'I wonder why she is having a word with Geraldine?' mused David when Miss de la Mare had gone.

'I suppose the only time she can manage to see our elusive colleague is at our meetings,' observed Sidney. 'It was quite a surprise to see her in the office yesterday, having friendly chit-chat. She was like a ghostly presence for most of last year.'

Dr Geraldine Mullarkey, the inspector in charge of Science and Technology, was the most recently appointed member of our team and tended to keep very much to herself.

'She has her small child to see to,' David reminded his colleague. 'It can't be all that easy, a single parent bringing up a lively toddler and holding down a demanding job. I should think that the last thing she wants is badinage and friendly

110

chit-chat with you.'

'You don't need to jump to her defence, my Welsh friend,' said Sidney. 'I wasn't being critical of the woman. I was merely observing that she is not one to fraternise or join us for witty conversation.'

'Witty!' spluttered David. 'Is that what you call it?'

'I've been called a shining wit, I'll have you know,' said Sidney, winking at me.

'Well, that's what you thought you heard someone say about you,' I commented. 'I reckon you misheard, Sidney. You have heard of a spoonerism, I take it?'

'I shall ignore that cruel and cutting comment,' said my colleague. 'It's nearly eight thirty, so I suppose we had better be making a move.'

'I must say,' said David getting to his feet, 'that since our Winifred arrived, we get through business like a dose of salts. Meetings went on interminably with Harold, largely because he was unable to shut you up, Sidney.'

'I strongly object to that slur,' began his colleague. 'If there is anyone with verbal diarrhoea, *il mio amico piccolo*, it's you. Bring back the good old Welsh Knot, that's what I say.'

'Come along, you two,' I said. 'We'd better return our cups to the kitchen before we start, or we'll have Connie after us.'

'Something I positively do not wish to experience,' groaned Sidney, picking up his mug.

Geraldine Mullarkey was chatting to Miss de la Mare when the three of us arrived in the meeting room. She was a pretty young woman with short black hair, a pale, delicately-boned face and great

111

blue long-lashed Irish eyes. Gerry was clever, personable and very efficient but was an exceptionally private person who, when she wasn't visiting schools, tended to work away from the office, preferring either the SDC or her own home. She kept her life outside the job strictly to herself and was something of a mystery. Soon after she joined the inspectorate, we had learned, by accident, that she had a small son, Jamie. Despite Sidney's interrogation, Gerry would reveal nothing about her past life, whether or not she had been married, or who the father of her child was. Sidney had once brought up the matter of her little boy's parentage and received a curt response.

'My private life is my private life, Sidney,' Geraldine had told him sharply. 'I do not wish to discuss it.'

In Meeting Room One, Miss de la Mare sat at the head of the table surrounded by her papers. We took our places around her. 'Good morning,' she said cheerfully. 'All present and correct and on time, and I hope all bright-eyed and bushy-tailed and ready for a challenging term.' The squirrel in the loft immediately flashed into my mind. 'Now, we have a lot to get through this morning,' continued the Chief Inspector, 'but before I start—'

Miss de la Mare's introduction was cut short when Connie poked her head around the door. 'I'm sorry to disturb your deliberations, Miss de la Mare,' she said, 'but I have an urgent message for Mr Phinn. His wife's phoned and said to tell him that the squirrel has returned.'

'How very intriguing,' said Sidney at once.

'Thanks, Connie,' I said. 'I'm sorry about this,

112

Della.'

'All she said,' continued Connie, 'was, "the squirrel has returned".'

'You're not some secret agent are you, Gervase?' asked Sidney. 'This is not some sort of coded message: "The eagle has landed", "The lion is on the loose", "The squirrel has returned"?'

'We have a squirrel in the loft,' I told him.

'They come in our garden regular,' added Connie. 'Some of them are quite tame. I found one in the kitchen once, large as life.'

'Actually, squirrels are fascinating little creatures,' added Geraldine. 'I attended a conference on environmental education recently and the speaker said that grey squirrel predation is a growing threat to other wildlife, particularly birds whose eggs they eat. It's the indigenous red squirrel that has all but been wiped out by the foreign grey squirrel.'

'A sort of "off-comed-un" squirrel,' said Sidney, sniggering at his little joke.

'Apparently, the North American grey squirrel has been particularly clever at adapting to the British environment,' continued Geraldine, 'and there is a very wide range of food it will eat compared to the vegetarian red. It is a little-known fact—'

'Colleagues,' interrupted the Chief Inspector, 'I think we have said quite enough about squirrels for one day. Thank you, Geraldine, for that fascinating insight, but we really must proceed. Gervase will deal with his squirrel when he gets home tonight.' She caught sight of Connie still standing by the door. 'Was there something else, Connie?' she asked.

'Will you remind them about the painters?'

'Painters!' exclaimed Sidney. 'And what painters pray are these?'

'Not your sort,' said Connie. 'Painters and decorators. They'll be in the Centre next week so I suggest you all give it a wide berth.'

'But I am running an art course next week!' exclaimed Sidney.

Miss de la Mare now looked decidedly annoyed by the prolonged interruption to the meeting. 'Perhaps you might like to discuss the matter with Connie after the meeting, Sidney,' she said firmly. 'We really must get on. Thank you once again, Connie.'

Connie departed, mumbling something under her breath.

'Now, as I was saying,' continued the Chief Inspector, 'the term ahead promises to be very challenging but I have every confidence that we will all rise to that challenge.' She picked up a large red folder and placed it before her. 'The main business of the morning concerns re-organisation.'

'Oh no,' sighed Sidney, leaning back precariously on his chair. 'Not more change.'

'I'm afraid so,' said Miss de la Mare. 'The numbers of children attending the county schools has declined quite considerably over the last few years, which will mean changes in staffing and, with that, redeployments, retirements, redundancies and, I'm afraid to say, some school closures.' I looked up sharply. 'Don't look so worried, Gervase,' she added, 'this won't involve Hawksrill, where the numbers are looking very healthy and are on the increase.'

'Very fecund lot in Hawksrill,' murmured Sidney

114

beside me.

'I *beg* your pardon?' I whispered crossly.

Miss de la Mare gave Sidney a withering look before continuing. 'As you are all aware, I fought long and hard to stop the closures of some schools last year, schools that I felt were viable and doing well, but I'm afraid I've had to bow to the inevitable with those schools that are less successful. Massive savings have to be made in the educational budget and, sadly, this means that some schools have to close. Accompanying this, of course, will be the interminable public meetings and, no doubt, strong objections from parents and governors.' She picked up a paper. 'Now, I have here a rather convoluted memorandum from Dr Gore, confidential, of course.'

'Written by Mrs Savage, no doubt,' added David, 'in her usual incomprehensible style.'

'Now there's a case of predation if ever there was one,' said Sidney. 'Predatory would be too kind a word to describe Mrs Savage. She's been a growing threat to everyone in the Education Department since she was promoted way beyond her meagre capabilities.'

'I have to say,' said the Chief Inspector, 'that the CEO's Personal Assistant does have an excessively wordy way of saying things. I have an idea this style of writing is called galimatias—rather confused and full of somewhat meaningless jargon. Is that the right word, Gervase?'

'I've no idea,' I said.

'I've another name for it,' said David. 'Twaddle!'

'Well, let me read it,' said Miss de la Mare. '"The Education Department, as part of the rigorous ongoing process of consolidating and

115

developing its educational provision and in the light of the increasing pupil shortfall in the county and in concert with the Education Sub-Committee Staffing and Resources, will be instituting a thorough, effective and consultative initiative in which the school inspectorate will take a leading strategic part. The Chief Education Officer is looking for an ongoing 360 degree feedback before the necessary re-engineering, restructuring and realigning of the educational provision takes place."'

'Give me strength,' sighed David. 'And what is that gobbledegook supposed to mean?'

'What it means,' explained the Chief Inspector, 'is that we, the inspectors, will be responsible for consulting interested parties and then seeing through the closures.'

'I don't like the sound of that,' observed David, giving a deprecatory shrug.

'We will be about as popular with schools as King Herod at a playgroup,' said Sidney.

'If I may continue,' said Miss de la Mare, allowing herself a slight smile at Sidney's witticism, 'an initial selection of the five schools has already been made by Mrs Savage, based on a number of factors, or as she likes to term them, "triggers": where the pupil population is declining most rapidly, where there is another school in reasonable travelling distance or where two schools might amalgamate, where the teaching staff are nearing retirement age and might favourably consider a redundancy package, and where the standards in the schools, based on your reports, are deemed unsatisfactory.'

'Mrs Savage has been a busy bee over the

summer and no mistake,' said David. 'Just the sort of job she would like—closing schools and putting people out of jobs.'

'Predatory,' murmured Sidney.

'I have to say that you are rather hard on Mrs Savage,' said the Chief Inspector. 'I appreciate that she's not the most personable and co-operative of people and at times can be a little tactless, but I have always found her very professional and one who takes her duties seriously.'

Geraldine raised an eyebrow in wordless contradiction but said nothing.

'With respect, Della,' said David witheringly, 'you have not worked with her as long as we have. She can be the most infuriating, interfering and domineering person with whom it has been my misfortune to come into contact.'

'I rarely agree with my Welsh colleague,' said Sidney, 'but on this one I am with him all the way. The purpose of the woman's life is a warning to others. She needs one of these Welsh Knots around that swan-like neck of hers. Let me give you an instance of why she can be so disagreeable. Once, when—'

'I'd rather you didn't, Sidney,' said Miss de la Mare, cutting him off. 'We are not here to discuss Mrs Savage and I do think it is in rather bad taste to talk about strangling her. She's not really that bad. Let's move on. Each of us,' continued the Chief Inspector, 'will take one of these schools, make a visit, explain things to the headteacher and the respective governing body, address the parents' meeting, attend the consultative discussions, and submit a report for Dr Gore to take to the Education Sub-Committee. Then, when all things have been considered, final decisions will be made. I am sure I do not need to stress that this is likely to be an extremely sensitive issue, bearing in mind what happened last time when it was suggested some schools should close, so it requires a great deal of diplomacy and discretion.'

It was a depressing meeting but near the end the Chief Inspector attempted to raise our spirits and conclude on a positive note. 'Before we go on our way, colleagues,' she said, 'I should like to thank you all for the sterling work and great efforts you put in during the last academic year, and most especially for all your support since I took up my present position. The comments from headteachers and teachers speak for themselves.' Miss de la Mare picked up a letter and held it before her. 'For example, David, Miss Bronson, the headmistress of Lady Cavendish High School for Girls, has written to Dr Gore who has passed the letter on to me. She wishes to place on record her gratitude to you for your, and I quote, "quite superb support and advice with the 'A' level students last year". I believe you did a series of masterclass workshops with the sixth form.'

'I did indeed,' replied David, looking extremely pleased at the praise, 'and very well received they were, too.'

'Well, the results in mathematics at 'A' level,' continued Miss de la Mare, 'were the best ever and every applicant that went on to university to read mathematics was successful. Indeed, the school has seen its highest number of students accepted to read mathematics at Oxbridge.'

'Very gratifying,' said David.

'So, well done,' added Miss de la Mare.

118

'It's very nice to know that one's efforts have been appreciated, Della,' said David, plucking his spectacles from his nose, which he then proceeded to clean with a large coloured handkerchief. He breathed noisily on the lenses, vigorously polishing and holding them up to the light to look for smears. 'Yes, very gratifying,' he said, smiling beatifically.

'In addition, I received only yesterday a very complimentary letter from the Schools Athletic Association also commending your work.'

'My, my,' remarked Sidney, once more leaning back dangerously in his chair, 'we shall have to erect a blue plaque in his honour.' Then he added, 'In Welsh, of course.'

'And congratulations I think are in order for you, too, Sidney,' said the Chief Inspector.

'Really?' No one looked more surprised than he did.

'The Arts Week you organised during the summer was a great success, and I hear on the grapevine that you are going to have an exhibition of your paintings—in a gallery in York, I believe?'

'You kept very quiet about that,' I said. 'Congratulations.'

'Well done, Sidney,' said Geraldine, 'that's brilliant.'

'They aren't those awful red and black splodges, splotches, splashes, smears and daubs fancifully called abstract art which any infant could paint, are they?' asked David.

'Never use one word, my dear fellow, when four will suffice,' replied Sidney. 'Actually the exhibition will include some portraits that I have done during the last few years and several landscapes of the

119

Yorkshire Dales. My agent tells me that the latter should sell for a not insubstantial amount.'

'Well, it's very good for the county to have such a talented artist on the team,' said Miss de la Mare. 'Well done.'

'Your good wishes are gratefully received, Della,' said Sidney, sitting up in his chair and bowing his head.

'We certainly seem to have had a good last term,' Miss de la Mare said, turning to Geraldine. 'The teachers' evaluation forms for your courses, Geraldine, which I have just been looking through, were, without exception, excellent. Many of the delegates said how very practical, interesting and varied your in-service training has been. So, well done to you, too.'

Now all eyes seemed to be trained on me for my plaudit.

'And Gervase,' began the Chief Inspector, looking me straight in the eyes.

'Yes,' I looked back at her expectantly.

'You won't forget that I want to speak to you after this meeting, will you?'

*   *   *

'I have had a serious complaint,' said Miss de la Mare.

The other inspectors had gone about their business and I was alone, with dry mouth and beating heart, facing the Chief Inspector for the dreaded meeting.

'And it's about one of my reports?' I asked hesitantly.

'Yes, it does concern one of your reports,' she

120

said. 'I had Mrs Savage on the telephone yesterday just as I was on my way home, and I had to drop everything and go and see the CEO.'

'It's that serious, then?' I asked.

'I'm afraid it very well might be,' replied Miss de la Mare. 'County Councillor Peterson is on the war path.'

As I suspected, Councillor Sidebottom hadn't wasted any time in getting in touch with his pal on the Education Committee. He had probably got on the telephone to County Hall just as soon as his wife had got home that afternoon to complain about my visit. I recalled her pointed observation about her husband having a particular interest in education and that he had aspirations to be appointed to the Education Committee alongside Councillor Peterson. Of course, it was no surprise that it hadn't been long before *that* councillor was poking his fat finger into this particular pie.

County Councillor George Peterson was an insufferably garrulous and self-opinionated man who, on the several occasions we had met, had always succeeded in really irritating me with his sarcastic comments, tasteless observations and vacuous views. If I saw his barrel-bodied figure striding down the top corridor at County Hall, or if I caught sight of the ponderous, fleshy face, the huge bull neck with folds which overlapped the top of his collar and the mop of unnaturally black hair appearing around a corner in Fettlesham High Street or if I heard his unmistakably bombastic voice issuing forth from one of the committee rooms, I did a fast disappearing act.

We had had a number of skirmishes, the most significant of which was when, as a member of an

121

Education Committee, he had been in the vanguard in trying to close Hawksrill Primary School. Christine had been extremely active with the pressure group to stop the closure and had tackled Councillor Peterson at the various consultation meetings. Councillor Peterson had collared me at County Hall and had warned me: 'You should per'aps 'ave a quiet word with your wife and tell 'er to go easy'—advice which I had diligently ignored. So the name Phinn was not one for which he had a great deal of time. Now, as I guessed, he would eventually have his sights firmly trained on me.

'Councillor Peterson?' I said. 'So he's involved, is he?'

'Yes, I'm afraid he has seen fit to take up the matter,' Miss de la Mare replied, shaking her head. 'Now,' she said, reaching for a substantial file, 'I do not intend to take any sort of action until I am acquainted with all the facts. I have the school report here and need to check on a few things.' I prepared myself for the worst. 'So what can you tell me about Mr Hornchurch at Tarncliffe Primary School?' she asked.

'Tarncliffe!' I exclaimed. 'Is this about Tarncliffe?'

'Yes, it is,' the Chief Inspector replied, appearing startled by my outburst. 'There has been a serious complaint about a teacher at the school called Mr Hornchurch. I believe you have seen this young man teach on a number of occasions, a teacher whom you rate, according to this report, very highly.'

I had geared myself up to discuss Ugglemattersby and was so taken by surprise that I was lost for words. Another of David's *bons mots* suddenly came to mind. 'In this job,' he told me when I had first started as a school inspector, 'you expect a bullet from one direction, you steel yourself for the impact, mentally prepare for it, and then, out of the blue, it comes up from behind and hits you smack in the back.'

'Gervase?'

'Ah yes,' I said. 'Er—er—Mr Hornchurch?'

'What can you tell me about him?' asked Miss de la Mare.

'Well, let's see,' I said, trying to re-focus my thoughts. 'Um—he's an unusual man in many ways, but a real enthusiast. He's keen, hard-working, spends many hours outside school time, organises trips, coaches the football team, conducts the choir, runs an astronomy club, quite apart from being a very good practitioner. I think you'll find details of the outstanding results his class achieves in my report. He's just a bit unconventional, that's all. I did have occasion to see Dr Yeats about him because he's, well, rather different from your run-of-the-mill teacher.'

'And what did Dr Yeats say?' asked Miss de la Mare.

'As I recall, I think he said Mr Hornchurch was a successful deviant—deviant in the sense of diverging from accepted standards of behaviour—and that education would be a dull business if teachers were all the same. He said there is a place in education for the teacher who is a bit out of kilter and that the teachers we tend to remember most from our own schooldays were the ones who were rather different.'

'And how is Mr Hornchurch different?' enquired

123

Miss de la Mare, staring at me intently.

'He's idiosyncratic,' I said. 'He's untidy, dresses like a down-at-heel student and his classroom looks as if a hurricane has hit it.' As I said this, I recalled the man in question—tall, pale-faced, with an explosion of wild, woolly hair and a permanently startled expression, dressed in faded denim jeans, old trainers and a T-shirt with 'PEACE' splashed across the front.

I decided not to tell the Chief Inspector about Mr Hornchurch's unique teaching methods that I had witnessed on that specific visit. He had sat cross-legged on his desk, with a cardboard box on his head. His face peered out of a large hole in the front, and this was, he explained, to simulate a television set. He then proceeded to tell the children a story, and I have rarely seen a class of children so engrossed.

'When I visited Tarncliffe, I found his lesson plans were disorganised, his planning virtually non-existent and the record system was so incomprehensible a code-cracker wouldn't have stood a chance. But I must add that the quality of the pupils' work was of the very best, the progress the children made under him was excellent and his teaching was first class.'

'The proof of the pudding,' murmured Miss de la Mare.

'In fact,' I said, 'he seemed to me to be the sort of teacher you once described when you were HMI, speaking at a meeting in this very room. If my memory serves me right, you said that what all outstanding teachers had in common was their enthusiasm for learning and a desire to help their students appreciate and explore the subjects they taught more profoundly. I think Mr Hornchurch does just this.'

'And his relationship with the children?' she asked.

'Very good,' I replied. 'So what's this all about?'

Miss de la Mare stared out of the window and thought for a moment and then glanced down at a sheet of paper before her. 'A parent of a child in Mr Hornchurch's class has complained to Councillor Peterson that his daughter's teacher uses bad language in the classroom. The parent owns a building firm, NBG Construction, on which Councillor Peterson is a non-executive director, and he mentioned it to him.'

'Bad language?' I repeated.

'Yes,' replied the Chief Inspector. 'But there is more to it than that. This parent was in a public house and was apparently telling all and sundry about this long-haired, hippy person who teaches his daughter, who swore like a trooper and how he had made a formal complaint. As chance would have it, a reporter from the *Fettlesham Gazette* overheard the conversation, and is writing an article based upon this overheard discussion about the decline in standards in schools, teachers using bad language and so forth, which will appear in next Friday's newspaper. The Editor of the *Gazette* contacted Dr Gore yesterday for a comment, hence the panic at County Hall. The Chief Education Officer, understandably, does not like negative publicity, particularly when there is a strong possibility that the county will shortly be getting a visit from the Minister for Education and Science.'

'And what were these words that Mr

125

Hornchurch has supposedly used?' I asked.

'I don't know,' replied Miss de la Mare, 'but I am led to believe that they were extremely vulgar and offensive. Of course, Councillor Peterson hurried down the top corridor of County Hall to see Dr Gore, demanding action.'

'As one might expect,' I observed.

'Have you ever heard this teacher use any bad language or say anything inappropriate in front of his class?' asked Miss de la Mare.

'No, I haven't,' I replied, 'and it seems to me that it would be so out of character for him to do so. He has a very gentle, positive and encouraging manner with the children. It's certainly not like him to swear in front of them. He might look a bit of an odd-ball but he's extremely professional.'

'Very well,' said Miss de la Mare. 'I would like you to telephone Tarncliffe's headteacher, and arrange to go into the school this afternoon. Report back to me first thing on Monday morning. I don't want anything heavy-handed, you understand. I suggest a quiet word with both the headteacher and Mr Hornchurch would be in order. Then we shall have to report back to Dr Gore and prepare a carefully-worded statement for the newspaper. Hopefully, the matter will be sorted out before it goes to press next week.'

'Right,' I said, getting up from my chair, 'I had better cancel this afternoon's appointments and get straight on to it.'

'Before you go, wasn't there something you wished to discuss with me?' asked the Chief Inspector.

'Oh that,' I said. 'That can wait.'

126

CHAPTER EIGHT

As soon as I got back to the office, I telephoned Miss Drayton, the headteacher of Tarncliffe Primary School, to arrange the visit for the afternoon. I then called Maurice Hinderwell.

'A squirrel, eh?' he said in that familiar thin nasal voice of his. 'Oh dear.'

'I'd like to get rid of it,' I told him.

'Of course you would,' he replied. 'It'll be a grey squirrel, of course, *Sciurus carolinensis*, brown tinge along the centre of his back, white belly and grey bushy tail.'

'Well, I didn't get that good a look as it was dark in the loft,' I told him.

'Oh dear, oh dear,' he sighed, in a prophet of doom voice. 'It was in your loft, was it?'

'I caught sight of it in the torch's beam.'

'Sure it wasn't a rat? They are far more active than squirrels at night. Clever devils are rats.'

'No, no, it was definitely a squirrel.'

'You see, Mr Phinn, your grey squirrel is most lively at dawn and dusk, not in the middle of the night,' said Mr Hinderwell. 'That's when they forage for food. He's a cheeky little devil, is this one.'

'Well, I want to get rid of it,' I said. 'It's disturbing our sleep, and my wife's getting into a bit of a state about it.'

He gave a hollow little laugh. 'I can understand that. Disturbing your sleep is not all it'll be doing. It'll be chewing and gnawing with its incisors, and scratching and scraping away with its sharp claws, if I know squirrels. They can cause untold damage can squirrels, stripping your trees, biting through your electric cables, nibbling your woodwork, defecating all over the place. They might look pretty and appealing but they can be bloody pests, can grey squirrels. They take food from bird tables, raid birds' nests and eat the eggs and even the very young chicks. And, of course, they are responsible for the decline of *Sciurus vulgaris.*'

'I beg your pardon?'

'The red squirrel,' he told me. 'The indigenous species. All but wiped them out.'

'So, can you help me?' I asked.

'That is what I do, Mr Phinn, help people with a pest problem. I'm the County Pest Control Officer, known affectionately as the Verminator. If there's a pest, Maurice Hinderwell is the man to contact. Now, your squirrel is a rodent like the rat but not quite as elusive and as clever as your average Samuel Whiskers. He's a wily and very agile little rascal, but have no fear, I'll tell you how to get him.'

'I should be very much obliged,' I said, greatly relieved.

'It's not a good idea to try and poison him.'

'No, I wouldn't want to do that,' I said.

'If you put poisoned nuts out, the birds will eat them and you don't want a garden full of dead bluetits, now, do you?'

'Not at all.'

'Do you know anyone who has a gun?'

'Mr Hinderwell, I really would rather not kill him.'

'Not kill him!' exclaimed Mr Hinderwell. 'It's no use being sentimental about squirrels, Mr Phinn, leastwise your grey variety. They're as verminous and destructive as your common or garden rat.'

'All the same, Mr Hinderwell,' I said, 'is there some other way? I just want to catch him.'

'Well, you could use a trap, I suppose,' he said. 'I could drop one off at the Education Office next week. I used it recently in a school where squirrels had chewed through a window frame and caused a great deal of damage. I caught three of them. Told the kiddies they were going to a squirrel refuge since I didn't want to upset them. Course, when I got hold of them, I—'

'I'm very grateful, Mr Hinderwell,' I interrupted, not wishing to know the fate of the little creatures.

'Just put some peanuts in the trap and place it in a secluded spot in the garden, and you'll have your squirrel,' he told me. 'Then you can do what you want with it—or them.'

*　　　*　　　*

I arrived at Tarncliffe at the very end of the lunch hour, having negotiated an empty grey ribbon of a road, which seemed to twist and turn interminably across an immense landscape of dark fields, where sheep and cattle sheltered in the lee of the old limestone walls. There was a squally wind and the noisy rooks circled and flapped high above the blustery trees like scraps of black paper.

The small primary school, which faced the village green, was a typical Dales stone building, with porch and mullioned windows. I noticed that the impressive solid black door sported a highly-polished brass plate bearing the words: 'WELCOME TO OUR SCHOOL'. This was new from my last visit and I suspected it had been added because, for all the world, the school looked like a private dwelling at first glance. On one side was the village shop, on the other the grey brick Primitive Methodist Chapel.

The headteacher, Miss Drayton, was an optimistic and cheerful person whom nothing and no one seemed to dishearten or discourage, but when I informed her of the reason for my impromptu visit her face fell.

'Bad language!' she exclaimed. 'Mr Hornchurch? That's ridiculous! There must be some mistake. As you know, the school comprises one large room divided by a partition between the infants and the juniors. I can hear virtually everything that is said next door to me and I would know if he had used any offensive words.' Then she thought for a moment. 'Mind you, I've had a supply teacher in for the odd day or two over the past few weeks when I have had to attend regional headteachers' meetings, but she didn't mention she'd heard anything untoward. No, I'm certain Mr Hornchurch would never use any kind of inappropriate language with his class. He's very professional, if a little unorthodox, and extremely well liked by the children and the parents. Who made the complaint?'

'A Mr Gaskell,' I told her.

'Oh well, that explains a great deal!' The headteacher blew out noisily through pursed lips. 'I hate to say it, but Mr Gaskell is a most disagreeable man. He bought the old manor house next to the church last March, and he thinks he owns the village already. The first thing he did was try and stop the church clock chiming during the night because it disturbed his sleep. Then he tried to get planning permission for the manor's old orchard, so his building company could erect some unsightly executive houses there. He's a man with more money than sense. His daughter only started school last term and already he's been in complaining about this, that and the other—that we don't give his Miranda hard enough books to read at home and that we spend too much time on art, poetry and music, which he considers largely a waste of time. And he is always at great pains to tell me how one of the directors of his company is a councillor on the Education Committee and that he agrees with his views.'

'That would be Councillor Peterson, would it not?' I asked.

'It would indeed,' replied Miss Drayton.

'It was Councillor Peterson who brought the matter to the attention of the Chief Education Officer.'

'Was it indeed?' said Miss Drayton, bristling. 'And isn't Councillor Peterson's wife a teacher?'

'Yes, she's the headteacher at Highcopse County Primary School,' I said.

'Well, Councillor Peterson ought to know better then, agreeing with this man,' said Miss Drayton angrily. 'Mr Gaskell's daughter, when she started, was a frightened little thing and hardly said a word—and stuttered when she did. Mr Hornchurch brought her out of her shell. He's amusing, mild-mannered and, as I have said before, highly professional. The very idea of him using bad language is inconceivable. I suspect that Mr Gaskell took against him from the start when he tried to get the parents to agree for Miranda to see a speech therapist about her impediment. Mrs Gaskell had no objection but her husband resolutely resisted, saying that the child would grow out of it. His discussion with Mr Hornchurch, I'm afraid, got a bit heated.' Miss Drayton paused for breath and sighed again. 'Anyway, Mr Phinn, I suppose you had better have a word with Mr Hornchurch and sort this out. Since it is Friday, we don't have an afternoon break but go straight through until three thirty so I suggest I take both the infants and the juniors while you speak to him.'

'I would prefer it, Miss Drayton,' I said, 'if you were present. I really feel you need to be there when this interview takes place.'

'As a witness to what is said?' she asked.

'I think it would be wise. Obviously, I don't wish to spend the whole of the afternoon in Mr Hornchurch's class. Perhaps I could join you and the infants for the first part of the afternoon, observe Mr Hornchurch for the remainder and then speak to you both after school.'

'Very well,' she agreed. 'Perhaps it would be better if I were present.' She looked extremely angry. 'I should have thought, Mr Phinn, that you have far more important things to do than waste your time looking into some ridiculous allegation.'

'I am certain it's a storm in a teacup,' I reassured her, 'but I am sure that you understand that I do have to investigate it.'

'Very well then,' she said, 'we will leave it until after school when we will get to the bottom of this. In fact, Mr Gaskell usually collects Miranda on Fridays so we can hear about this complaint straight from the horse's mouth. I cannot for the life of me understand why he never mentioned the

132

matter to me, going to County Hall instead.'

Miss Drayton was clearly furious and I could just imagine what her reaction would be when she learned from me later that Tarncliffe School might very well be on the front page in the *Fettlesham Gazette* the following week.

*   *   *

When I entered the infants' class, my mind was on the forthcoming—and what I guessed would prove to be contentious—meeting that would take place at the end of the school day. While Miss Drayton settled the children down, I wandered around the room looking at the colourful displays on the walls and the range of books in the small bookcase. I could hear Mr Hornchurch quite clearly behind the partition dividing the room, explaining to his class what they were to do that afternoon. The headteacher's claim that she could hear virtually everything that was said next door was absolutely right.

Miss Drayton approached and gave me a selection of the children's workbooks to look at while she marked the register.

'You might care to browse through these, Mr Phinn,' she said. 'As you will see, children do very well in this school.' I could tell she was making a point.

I sat in the corner of the classroom in the small carpeted reading area adjacent to the partition to examine them, but placed them on the nearest chair and strained my ears to eavesdrop on the lesson going on next door. Mr Hornchurch was telling the children about the effects of pollution

133

on the environment in a clear and interesting manner.

I was so engrossed in his account that I didn't see the girl who had appeared at my side. She tugged at my sleeve.

'Hello,' she said.

'Hello,' I replied.

She was a small child with sparkling intelligent eyes and corkscrew curls, and was dressed in a blue-and-yellow gingham skirt and a white shirt as crisp as a wafer. She stared at me intently. I smiled.

'You were daydreaming,' she told me with all the precocious confidence of a six-year-old.

'I suppose I was,' I said.

'Who are you?' she asked.

'Mr Phinn,' I answered.

'I'm Rhiannon.'

'Are you?'

'It's a Welsh name.'

'Yes, I know.'

'Can you speak Welsh?'

'No, I can't.'

'My mummy and daddy can and I know some words.'

'Really.'

'Yes, big words. I know a lot of four-letter words.'

'Do you really?' I must have sounded very impressed.

'And some five-letter ones too. *Cwtch*—that means cuddle,' explained the child. 'I have a *cwtch* every night when I have my story. We'll be having a story this afternoon, after we've finished our poems.'

'And what are your poems about?' I asked.

'We're writing poems about excuses.'

'Are you?' My mind immediately thought of the excuses I might give to Miss de la Mare about my mishandling of the situation at Ugglemattersby and what Mr Hornchurch might proffer if, indeed, he had used some inappropriate language.

'Yes,' said the child.

'And what is your poem called?'

'It's called, "Excuses, Excuses!"' she told me. 'We have to think of lots of reasons for coming late to school.'

'Like, the dog ate my homework,' I said.

'I don't have a dog,' she said pertly, 'and we don't have homework. We will when we go in the juniors but we don't have homework in the infants.'

'I see. And what excuses have you thought of so far?' I asked.

'The alarm clock didn't go off,' the child told me, 'the car wouldn't start, I forgot my PE kit and had to go back home to get it, and Mummy thought it was a Saturday so didn't bring me to school.'

'Those are very good excuses,' I told her.

'I've got another one, too,' she said. 'A really good one because it really happened when I came to school late once,' the child informed me, nodding her little head.

'And what's that?' I asked.

'Our electric gates wouldn't open,' she told me.

With that, she took off, sat at her table, took out her book and pencil from her bag and got on with her poem.

I have had so many conversations like this with young children and have so often been brought out of a black mood by their innocent and intriguing chatter. Small children are a delight. Everything in the world to them is new and exciting. They are fascinated by people, and are wonderfully self-assured and forthcoming in their talk. It's not like that with older children and adults. With age, one tends to become far more self-conscious and reticent, perhaps more suspicious of others. One only has to travel in a lift with a group of adults: they stare at the ceiling, examine their shoes, look fixedly over your shoulder, anywhere as long as their eyes don't meet yours. If a child is in the lift, it is a different matter. He or she will stare intently at you, taking everything in, and then very often make a comment such as: 'I have my Mickey Mouse knickers on', or *'I'm* going to the pet department, where're *you* going?'

Rhiannon, like all young children, had no problem confronting adults, asking uncompromisingly forthright questions whilst staring them straight in the eye. What is also endearing about small children is that they have no conception of race, background, status, religion and class; smile at a little one and the smile is always returned. They are confident and not afraid of asking questions of adults, or of making blunt observations that sometimes cause their parents to redden with embarrassment: 'Is that fat lady going to have a baby?' 'Grandma, who will fetch the fish and chips when you're dead?' 'My daddy says Granny is well past her sell-by date.' Such things are said without any malice; they are just the innocent observations of the very young.

I recalled a Dales sheep farmer once telling me about his four-year-old son who went with him to the hospital in Skipton to see his new baby sister. In the maternity ward, the child was far more interested in the smiling black woman in the next bed than he was in his baby sibling. He had obviously never seen a black person before and was fascinated. The little boy couldn't take his eyes off her.

'Stop staring, John,' his father said in a hushed voice, 'it's very rude to stare.'

The child continued to stare, his eyes, as we say in Yorkshire, 'as wide as chapel hat pegs'.

The woman smiled and wiggled her fingers at him but he continued to stare. Eventually she got out of bed, put on an attractive white dressing gown and snow-white fluffy slippers and left the ward to feed her own baby, who was in the adjoining room. As she headed for the door, the child pointed after her and announced loudly to his father, 'Suffolk!' at which his father could not contain his laughter. The Suffolk sheep, as he explained to me later, are a very distinctive breed: long white woolly bodies and black wool-free face and legs.

I was brought out of my reverie by Miss Drayton. 'Mr Phinn?' she said.

'Yes?'

'I was wondering if you might like to tell the children a story. We always have storytime at this point in the day and I thought, since you are here, it would be nice to make use of you. Some of the children rarely hear a man telling a story.'

'Of course,' I said. I hadn't expected to take part in the lesson but was happy to acquiesce.

'I was about to start the traditional tale of *The Three Billy Goats Gruff*,' she said, handing me

137

a book open at the start of the story. 'While you are telling them the story, I'll take the opportunity of making a phone call.' She lowered her voice. 'I think it might be prudent for me to have a word with someone in my professional association and seek some advice on the situation. It may appear to be a storm in a teacup to you, Mr Phinn, but in my experience, these things tend to have a habit of developing into hot potatoes. If accusations are being made, Mr Hornchurch might need to have his union representative present.'

'I really don't think, Miss Drayton—' I began.

'I am sure you'll be all right with the class by yourself, won't you?' enquired the headteacher, giving me little chance of arguing with her. She clapped her hands loudly to gain the children's attention. 'We are very lucky, children,' she announced, 'to have Mr Phinn, a very special visitor, with us this afternoon and he has asked if he might tell today's story. He's really good at telling stories and I know'—at this point she stared intently at a small boy with a shock of ginger hair and his two front teeth missing—'that we will all be on our very best behaviour, won't we?'

'Yes, Miss Drayton,' chanted the class obediently.

'And you will be very good, won't you, Jack?' warned the headteacher, continuing to give the boy with the ginger hair and the missing teeth a long and knowing look.

'Yes, Miss Drayton,' the boy shouted.

Without any bidding, the children gathered around me on the carpet in the reading area, and sat with crossed legs and folded arms, their faces staring up at me expectantly. Miss Drayton quietly left the room.

Anyone who thinks that handling a group of twenty infant children, all of whom have their own little personalities, is an easy job, should have a go. It demands a great deal of skill, expertise and patience, as I was soon to discover.

'Good afternoon, children,' I said cheerfully.

'Good afternoon, Mr Thin,' they all chorused.

'Good afternoon, everybody.'

'Is that your real name?' asked ginger-haired Jack. He had a small green candle of mucus appearing from his nose. He sniffed it away noisily but it re-emerged immediately. 'Because you're not very thin, are you?'

'It's Mr Phinn,' I said. 'Like on the back of a shark.'

'I like sharks,' said the boy.

'I don't,' said a tiny, elfin-faced child with long black plaits and impressive pink-framed glasses. 'I'm frightened of sharks.'

'I'm frightened of spiders,' said another.

'I'm frightened of snakes,' added a third.

'Well, this story isn't about sharks, spiders or snakes,' I told the class, smiling. 'It's about three goats.'

'I don't like goats,' said the girl.

'These are very nice goats,' I reassured her. 'They're called the Billy Goats Gruff.'

'They don't sound like nice goats,' said the girl.

'Goats have horns,' volunteered Rhiannon.

'Yes, that's correct,' I said.

'And they butt,' she added.

Jack immediately began to butt the girl next to him.

'Don't do that,' I said. 'It's not very nice to butt

other people, is it?' The boy pulled a face but stopped. 'So, children,' I said, continuing, 'this is a famous story called *The Three Billy Goats Gruff*.'

'I've heard it before,' announced Jack, sniffing loudly.

I knew from experience that I would have to keep a close eye on this little character. 'And what's your name?' I asked.

'James Oliver Jonathan Ormerod,' he replied. 'My granddad calls me Jo-Jo but my dad calls me Jack.'

'Well, Jack,' I said pleasantly, 'you're going to hear the story again.'

'But I know what happens,' he replied.

'So do I,' said another.

'And I do,' added a third.

'Well, it's always good to hear a story again,' I told them.

'Why?' asked Rhiannon.

'Well, because it is,' I replied feebly. 'And you haven't heard *me* tell it, have you?'

'My grandpa's read it to me,' said Rhiannon. 'He's got the book with pictures in it and he's really good at reading stories.'

'Have you got the book with pictures in it?' asked the child who was afraid of sharks.

'No, I haven't,' I replied, wondering just what I had let myself in for.

'And he pulls faces and makes noises as well,' added Rhiannon.

'Does he?'

'Are you going to pull faces and make noises?' asked Jack.

'No, I'm not,' I said sharply. 'Now, let us all sit up nice and straight, children, ready to listen, otherwise we won't hear the story.'

'I know what happens,' said Jack, turning to face the rest of the class.

Undeterred, I began. 'Once upon a time there were three Billy Goats Gruff. There was the father, Big Billy Goat Gruff; the mother, Medium-Sized Billy Goat Gruff; and—'

'Little Billy Goat Gruff,' cut in Jack.

'Little goats are called kids,' added Rhiannon.

'And Little Billy Goat Gruff,' I repeated, fixing Jack with an eagle eye. 'They lived in a valley in the cold cold winter to keep warm, but when spring came they climbed up to the rich green meadow on the hillside—'

'And crossed a bridge,' interrupted Jack, before wiping his nose on the sleeve of his jersey. 'They have to cross a bridge.'

'We've not got to the bridge yet,' I told him, and continued. 'They climbed up to the meadow on the hillside to eat the fresh green grass that grew there. Each morning, when the sun shone high in the sky, they would run across the fields and, as Jack has already told us all, they would cross the rickety-rackety old wooden bridge that spanned the river.'

'I wouldn't like to go over a rickety-rackety old wooden bridge,' said the child who was afraid of sharks. 'It sounds dangerous.'

'Well, the Billy Goats Gruff were very careful when they went over the bridge,' I told her.

'And there's this troll under it,' said Jack, pulling a gruesome face and growling. 'Grrr! Grrr!'

'Yes, I know there is,' I said, 'and we haven't got to the troll yet. Now, be a good boy, Jack, and listen to the story. You're spoiling it for everyone else.' I proceeded. 'Every day, the billy goats liked

141

to cross the rickety-rackety old wooden bridge which went over the river, to get to the fresh green grass on the other side.'

'You've told us that,' said Rhiannon.

'Now, in the darkness under the bridge there lived a mean and ugly troll, with eyes as big as saucers, ears as sharp as knives and a nose as long as a poker.'

'He can't help being like that,' announced Rhiannon.

'No, I don't suppose he could,' I said.

'My grandpa says that people can't help the way they look.'

'Oh dear,' I sighed. 'Now this troll—'

'I told you there was the troll,' mumbled Jack.

'This troll,' I continued quickly, 'was very bad-tempered and unfriendly.'

'Like my granny,' said the child frightened of spiders. 'She's very bad-tempered and unfriendly.'

I moved on hurriedly. 'The troll was always hungry and slept for most of the time.'

'Like my granny,' said the child. 'She's always hungry and sleeps for most of the time.'

I sighed, and continued: 'And the ugly troll waited under the bridge for creatures to cross, and then he gobbled them up.'

'With great sharp teeth and claws,' added Jack.

'That's right,' I said, 'and—'

'I know what I'd do if an ugly troll with sharp teeth and claws jumped out on me,' said Jack.

'And what would you do, Jack?' I asked wearily.

'I'd shit myself!'

'Perhaps we ought to have another story,' I suggested, reaching over to the bookcase.

CHAPTER NINE

Mr Hornchurch greeted me enthusiastically when I entered his classroom later that afternoon, shaking my hand vigorously and telling the children what a pleasure it was to have such a distinguished visitor in their midst. I feared that this warm welcome was going to make my meeting with him later in the afternoon all the more difficult.

At first glance, the teacher seemed to have followed the recommendations in my last report since his classroom was now a whole lot tidier. On my first visit, the mass of clutter and colour that I had walked into would have been the perfect set for a film version of *The Old Curiosity Shop*. Huge posters, book jackets and long lists of difficult and awkward words had covered every wall, revolving mobiles had hung from the ceiling, boxes of every conceivable shape and size had been stacked in a corner along with piles of books and a basket of footballs and cricket equipment. On two large trestle tables there had been old tins and strangely-shaped bottles, bleached skulls and old bird feathers, shards of pottery and clay models. Now it looked more like the conventional classroom, far better organised and neater but, I guessed for the children, a great deal less interesting.

Mr Hornchurch's appearance had undergone a change, too. He was now dressed more conservatively in a pair of baggy blue corduroy trousers, shapeless tweed jacket, white shirt, and a loud kipper tie. However, he still had the wild and woolly head of mousy hair surrounding his long pale face.

Having wished me good afternoon, the junior class resumed their activities. One group of children was gathered round the teacher as he conducted an experiment involving a tank of water and various objects. They were predicting whether various objects would sink or float, and I listened for a while to a fascinating and impressive discussion. It was explained to me by one of the pupils that the class was to visit the Science Museum in London the following weekend, and they were undertaking some preparatory work. Another group was busy writing a play the class would perform at the end of term, while a third group was writing stories. The classroom was a hive of creative activity and not once did the teacher have to tell any child to get on with his or her work.

'May I look?' I asked a blond-haired boy with large ears who was poring over an exercise book.

'Sure,' he replied, sliding the book across the desk. I sat next to him and examined his work. He watched me for a moment before telling me, 'I'm writing a newspaper article about the effects of pollution on the marine environment. We went on a trip with Mr Hornchurch to an aquarium last Saturday and we learnt all about oil tanker leaks and the rubbish that gets dumped in the oceans of the world, so I've got lots of facts and figures.'

It was an excellent piece of work—clear, well structured and neatly written. I glanced though his exercise book and was struck by the quality of the other pieces of writing. His work was unusually accurate and well presented for one so young.

'You're a fine writer,' I told the boy.

'Thanks,' he said. 'I want to be a journalist like my mum when I leave school.'

'And you seem to be a very good speller,' I said. 'How old are you?'

'Eleven,' he replied.

'I don't think I've ever met an eleven-year-old as good at spelling as you.'

The boy smiled broadly. 'Cheers, mate!' he said, nudging my arm with his elbow.

'Is everyone in the class as good as you?' I asked.

'Mostly,' he told me. 'You see, we do quite a bit on spellings with Mr Hornchurch.'

'And what do you do to become so good?' I asked.

'Well,' replied the boy, 'we do rules for a start.'

'Such as?'

'There's "i" before "e" except after "c". Of course, it doesn't always work. Mr Hornchurch says that where there's a rule, there's generally an exception.'

'He's right there,' I agreed. 'At school I learnt the little poem:

It is "i" before "e",
Except after "c",
Or when it is "eigh",
As in "neighbour" and "weigh".'

'That rule works with me,' the boy continued, 'because I'm called Kieran but it doesn't work with my mum, she's called Sheila, and it doesn't work with my dad, he's called Keith. They're what's called "irregulars". We list any irregulars in our spelling book.' The boy reached into the drawer beneath his table and produced a notebook. On each page was a different spelling rule neatly written out in large black letters. 'So you see,' he explained, 'under the irregulars for this rule we have: "weigh" and "weight", "freight" and "height", "heir", "heifer", "beige", "feign", "weir" and loads of others. Mr Hornchurch says the English spelling system is really confusing, specially to those trying to learn the language. He says that foreigners have to learn the language three times: first its meaning, then how to pronounce it and then how to spell it.'

'I see,' I said, extremely impressed. I thought at that moment of Mrs Sidebottom and tried to imagine the fun foreigners would have attempting to pronounce her name.

'When Mr Hornchurch was at university, he studied languages and taught foreign students over the summer holidays. He used to ask each of them to read a sentence at the end of the course. Hold on a minute, I've got it written down in my jotter.' The boy reached into the drawer again and produced another book. 'This is the sentence: "A rough-coated, dough-faced, tough-looking thoughtful ploughman strode through the streets of Scarborough, and after falling into a slough by the side of a lough, he coughed and hiccoughed and went on his way."'

'That's very good,' I said, chuckling.

'Mr Hornchurch said that if the students could pronounce all the words correctly at the end of the course, they had just about mastered the English language and they had been taught well.'

'You don't seem to have a problem with the English language, Kieran,' I told the boy, 'and Mr Hornchurch appears to have taught you very well indeed.'

'He's a good teacher is Mr Hornchurch. He makes the lessons interesting, and likes a laugh—but he sometimes comes out with things.'

'Does he?' I said, my thoughts returning fast to the principal reason for my visit to the school. I wondered just what the 'things' were that the teacher came out with.

'He uses unusual words and expressions. He says, "English is a real can of worms, as slippery as a snake in olive oil, like walking blindfolded through a minefield." He's full of expressions like that.'

'Well, you seem to be pretty knowledgeable about the English language,' I told him and I meant it.

'Look at this word for example,' said the boy, picking up a pencil and a scrap of paper and scribbling something. 'Look at that word—"GHOTI". How would you pronounce that, then?'

I had come across George Bernard Shaw's capricious spelling before. I often used this word on my English courses to demonstrate what I grandly called 'the orthographic irregularities' in the English language. However, I decided with young Kieran to play dumb. 'I've never heard of it,' I said, 'but I suppose I would say "goaty".'

'It says "fish",' the boy informed me. 'You have "gh" as in "laugh", "o" as in "women" and "ti" as in "station". Mr Hornchurch said he was shown this by a famous writer called George Bernard Shaw—probably a friend of Mr Hornchurch's.'

'Well, I don't think your teacher has actually met George Bernard Shaw,' I said, 'but I do know that that particular writer was very keen on making spelling easier for people.'

147

'But we don't just do rules,' the boy continued. 'We learn what Mr Hornchurch calls "little wrinkles".'

'Go on,' I said, intrigued.

'Say if you want to learn a particular word like "necessary". We learn a "little wrinkle"—"one coffee and two sugars"—then you remember it has one letter "c" and two letter "s"s. "Accommodation" is another difficult word—"two cottages and two mansions"—and you remember the two "c"s and two "m"s.'

'That's very good,' I said, laughing.

'Mr Hornchurch's got loads of "little wrinkles" and we also work out our own.'

'I must try myself,' I told him.

'Then we do mnemonics,' said the boy.

' "Richard Of York Gave Battle In Vain",' I said.

'Pardon?'

'That's a mnemonic,' I told him, 'to help remember the colours of the rainbow in sequence: red, orange, yellow, green, blue, indigo and violet. If you want to learn the order of the planets you learn: "My Very Easy Method Just Speeds Up Naming Planets" for Mercury, Venus, Earth, Mars, Jupiter, Saturn, Uranus, Neptune and Pluto.'

'It's good that,' said the boy. 'I'm going to write that down in my jotter. Mr Hornchurch says that if we come across something interesting, or an unusual word or phrase or an old expression, we should write it down because it may come in useful later on when we are doing our writing.'

'That's a very sensible idea,' I said, and watched the boy begin to write the two mnemonics I had given him. 'Well, thank you for talking to me, Kieran,' I said, standing and getting ready to see what the other children in the class were doing.

'Don't go yet,' he pleaded. 'I've not explained what mnemonics we use to help us remember how to spell difficult words.'

'Very well,' I said, sitting down again.

'As I was telling you, we work out mnemonics for difficult words. Take "because"—"big elephants can always understand small elephants"; "rhythm"—"rejoice heartily, your teacher has measles". Then there's "embarrass"—"every mother's boy acts rather rudely after some sausages". You can work out a mnemonic for any difficult spelling.'

As the boy spoke I was reminded of the word that was almost consistently misspelt in letters I received from parents when I was a teacher. The word was 'diarrhoea'. One very inventive parent wrote to me saying that, 'Debbie is off with dire rear', another that his son was absent with 'diahr, dihia, diahrh,' with all three attempts crossed out and then the phrase, 'the shits' written after it.

'See if you can work out a mnemonic for "diarrhoea". Do you know how to spell that?'

The boy shook his blond head.

'Look the word up in the dictionary, and then see if you can think of a sentence to help you remember how to spell it.'

'I'll have a go,' he said and off he went to find a dictionary.

I turned my attention now to two girls working together on the next table, which was covered with brochures and booklets.

'Once you get Kieran started,' the first girl told me confidentially, 'you can't shut him up. Mr Hornchurch says he talks like a Gatling gun,

149

whatever one of those is.'

'May I ask what you're doing?'

'Me and Miranda—I'm Rowena, by the way—' said the girl, 'are writing a guide for the aquarium of the future. We all visited the aquarium last Saturday and—'

'I d-didn't,' interrupted her partner, a mousy little girl with large glasses.

'Well, no, Miranda, you didn't go but the rest of the class did,' continued Rowena.

'My f-father wouldn't l-let me g-go,' stuttered Miranda, 'H-he said I had to s-stay at h-home to p-practise my p-piano. He d-doesn't believe in s-school trips. He s-says they're a waste of t-time.'

'Well, perhaps he'll take you to the aquarium himself one day,' I said.

'N-no, he w-won't. He's always too b-busy,' said the child, firmly.

Undoubtedly, this diffident girl with the pronounced stutter, large sad eyes and small pinched face was the child who had innocently been the cause of all the upset.

'Anyhow,' said Rowena, 'we visited this brilliant aquarium and we had a talk from this woman fish expert—she's called a piscatologist or something— who says there are hundreds of species of fish no one ever sees because they are so deep down in the ocean where no divers can go.'

'Why can't the deep-sea divers see them?' I asked. Very often inspectors ask pseudo-questions. They know the answers and are merely testing to see if the children know. I always found it refreshing to ask a real question.

'Because the water pressure is too great right at the bottom of the sea,' the child told me. 'But

Mr Hornchurch says eventually we will be able to see them when scientists have invented special breathing apparatus.'

'I see.'

'Mr Hornchurch says the deep ocean is the greatest frontier of discovery.'

'So what have you written so far?' I asked.

The girl shuffled through the papers. 'This is our second draft. We've just got it back from Mr Hornchurch with ideas on how we can improve it.'

'Would you like to read it to me?' I asked.

Rowena gave a dry little cough. 'Hem-hem.' Then she read. ' "Eleven thousand fathoms down in a dark, dark world where man has never been, there are sorts of alien life forms. There are snails, molluscs, octopuses, squids, eels and crustaceans." ' She stopped and giggled. 'I didn't know what the last word was or how to spell it so I wrote "crushed Asians". Mr Hornchurch said it was a very good attempt.' She read on. ' "There's a big variety of very strange fish at the bottom of the deep black sea. There's gaper eels with big eyes at the front of their heads, vampire squids with flappy ears like Dumbo and white jaws and blood red eyes, there's angler fish, headlight fish, sea stars and dragon fish which light up their prey before gobbling them up." '

'It sounds a very interesting and unusual world,' I said, turning to the other girl.

'And s-scary,' added Miranda.

'Yes, it does sound a bit frightening,' I agreed. 'And how are you getting on at school then, Miranda?'

She nodded. 'I l-like it here. It's much b-better

151

than my l-last school.'

'Good,' I said, but before I could question her further, Kieran was at my side.

'Diarrhoea!' he announced loudly and spelt out the word slowly and deliberately: 'D-I-A-R-R-H-O-E-A.' Then he recited his very inventive mnemonic: ' "Died in a Rolls Royce having over-eaten again".'

'Very good,' I said, clapping my hands.

'There's more,' he said. ' "Did I actually really run home on energy alone?" '

'Excellent!' I said.

'There's more,' he said.

'That's fine,' I said, holding up a hand, 'I think that's quite enough of mnemonics for one day, Kieran.'

'No, no, this is the best,' he told me with a cheeky grin on his face. ' "Dash in a real rush, help or exploding arse!" '

Biting my bottom lip to stifle my laughter, I suggested that perhaps he might like to tweak the ending a little bit, so it became: ' "Dash in a real rush, help or else accident".'

Miranda, who had been privy to this lively exchange, turned her little face in my direction and screwed up her nose. Perhaps another word would be added to her father's list when she got home that afternoon.

Towards the end of the lesson, my thoughts inevitably returned to the dreaded meeting that would take place after school but they were interrupted by Kieran who had seen me glancing at my watch and getting ready to depart.

'Mr Hornchurch,' he shouted out, 'can we give Mr Phinn the spelling test?'

152

'I don't think so, Kieran,' replied Mr Hornchurch. 'I think Mr Phinn needs to be away. He's probably got an important meeting to attend.' If only he knew, I thought.

'Oh, go on, sir,' pleaded the boy. 'It's only a bit of fun and Mr Phinn's really interested in spelling, aren't you, Mr Phinn?'

I could see the pit opening before me, ready for me to fall in headlong. I could just imagine the sort of credibility I would have in schools as the school inspector for English who couldn't spell. 'Well, er, I am, er, but . . .' I stumbled.

'Perhaps another time,' said the teacher, kindly coming to my assistance.

But the boy continued obstinately. 'You don't mind, do you, Mr Phinn?' he asked.

'Well,' I said charily, 'what sort of test is it?'

'You had better explain, Kieran,' said the teacher.

'Mr Hornchurch says people get really angry when it comes to spelling and they get on their high horses. Spelling's important but not as important as what you are trying to say.'

'Come along, Kieran,' prompted the teacher, 'Mr Phinn's got to be away soon.'

The boy continued. 'And a lot of really brainy people have problems with their spelling and this famous Prime Minister—er, I can't remember his name.'

'Lord Palmerston,' prompted Mr Hornchurch. 'He was a bit of a stickler for correct spelling.'

'Yes, him. Well, he was sick and tired of all his— what do you call them, sir?'

'The members of his Cabinet, his eleven ministers,' said the teacher.

'Yes, them. Well, he was so sick and tired of all his ministers sending him letters full of spelling mistakes that he gave them all a test.'

Oh dear, I thought to myself, this is going to be tricky. Mr Hornchurch clearly saw the expression of anxiety which had come over my face but rather than revel in my discomfiture, as some teachers might have done with a school inspector in their midst, he very generously helped me out.

'Don't be bullied by Kieran, Mr Phinn,' he said. 'I know you're in a hurry to be away.'

'And none of Lord Palmerston's Cabinet ministers got all the spellings right,' piped up Rowena gleefully from the back.

'Come along, then,' I said bravely. 'In for a penny, in for a pound.'

'That's one of Mr Hornchurch's expressions,' Kieran told me.

'Let's have this test of yours,' I said.

As Kieran dictated the sentence from his jotter, I wrote it down slowly and clearly on the blackboard in large block capitals: 'It is disagreeable to witness the embarrassment of a harassed pedlar gauging the symmetry of a peeled potato.'

There was a loud cheer from the children. Much to my relief, I had spelt every word correctly.

I was rather elated as I left the classroom that afternoon clutching a small tin badge that had been presented to me and which said to the world: 'STAR SPELLER'.

*   *   *

The elation was short lived for, some minutes

later, after school had broken up, I stood by the window in the headteacher's study-cum-office-cum-storeroom listening as Miss Drayton explained to Mr Hornchurch the real reason for my visit that afternoon. To my surprise, the man did not look at all concerned. He sat with his legs crossed and one hand in a jacket pocket, appearing neither angry nor upset as he listened patiently until the headteacher asked for his comments.

He smiled and shook his head. 'I assure you,' he said, 'that I have never used any inappropriate language in front of the children, and there must be some sort of misunderstanding.'

After questioning him in more detail, Miss Drayton seemed satisfied that her colleague had nothing for which to answer, and I have to say I agreed with her. She turned in my direction, but then looked past me and out of the window. 'Ah, here comes Mr Gaskell,' she said, rising from her chair. 'Now we will get to the bottom of this matter.' She shot out of the room and into the little lobby, leaving the door open for us to see what was going on.

'May I have a word with you, Mr Gaskell?' she said as he headed for the classroom to collect his daughter.

'I'm in a hurry, Miss Drayton,' he replied, not stopping. 'I'm late for a meeting already.' He sounded an ill-mannered individual.

'It is important,' she said stiffly, 'very important. I should be grateful if you would step into my room for a moment. Miranda has been told to wait in the classroom until we are finished.'

'Well, you'll have to be quick,' he said, looking at his watch but retracing his steps. 'As I say, I've got an important meeting.'

Miss Drayton returned to the room, accompanied by the parent who was a stout man with a florid face and precious little hair. Mr Hornchurch immediately got to his feet, but while Mr Gaskell eyed me suspiciously, he did not acknowledge the teacher in any way.

'What's it about, then?' he asked brusquely.

Miss Drayton sat down on the edge of her chair behind her desk, as stiff as a snooker cue. 'Do take a seat, Mr Gaskell,' she said, gesturing to the chair where Mr Hornchurch had been sitting. 'This will hopefully only take a moment.' Her tone of voice was glacial.

The parent, however, remained standing by the door, arms folded. 'I've not got a moment, Miss Drayton,' he told her irritably. 'I told you that I have a meeting and I'm running late.'

'This gentleman, by the window, Mr Gaskell,' said the headteacher, maintaining her meticulous coldness, 'is Mr Phinn, the County Inspector for English and Drama.'

'Oh yes,' said the parent, not looking at me but glancing again at a very flashy gold wristwatch. 'So what's this all about?'

The headteacher stiffened further, her face rigid. 'Mr Gaskell,' she said slowly, 'the sooner you sit down and listen, the sooner you will know what it's all about, and the quicker you will be away.'

He flopped in the chair and breathed noisily. 'What is it, then?'

'Mr Phinn has been sent from the Education Department at County Hall regarding a complaint you have made, a serious complaint. I believe you have had reason to contact County Councillor

156

Peterson about Mr Hornchurch,' she said.

The parent coloured up. 'Yes, I—er—did mention something to Councillor Peterson,' he said.

'Could I ask why?' asked the headteacher sharply.

'Because I was unhappy about Miranda coming out with some of the words Mr Hornchurch had used in his lesson.' The man puffed himself up like a huge turkey.

'And might I ask why you did not bring this complaint to me,' asked the headteacher, 'rather than taking it to a county councillor?'

'I've complained about things at the school before, Miss Drayton, as you well know,' said the parent defensively, 'and nothing's been done.'

'Your other complaints were curricular matters, Mr Gaskell,' said the headteacher, 'concerning reading books and homework and how, in your opinion, we spend too much time on what you call the "fripperies" of art and music. As I explained to you, I do not seek to tell you how to build houses and asked you not to tell me how to run a school.'

'Yes, well as a parent—'

'And now,' continued Miss Drayton, ignoring his response, 'you are unhappy about something Mr Hornchurch is alleged to have said—some words. Perhaps you would like to explain.'

The parent bristled. 'Yes, words,' he said, 'vulgar words, swear words.'

'Would you like to tell us what these words were that Mr Hornchurch has supposedly used?' she asked.

'I don't like repeating them,' he said, sticking out his chin. 'As I say, they're rude.'

'You are a man of the world, Mr Gaskell,' said Miss Drayton, 'and I am sure that on your building site you have heard and, perhaps used yourself, some colourful language.'

'Not in front of children, I haven't!' he retorted swiftly.

'Maybe you could tell us then what letters these words begin with?'

'There was the "b" word,' he said.

'The "b" word,' mused Miss Drayton, raising an eyebrow. She gave a dry little cough. 'There are quite a few of those.'

'Look, Miss Drayton,' he said, getting to his feet, 'I've an emergency site meeting going on at the moment and people are waiting for me.'

'And the sooner you stop beating about the bush and tell me what words were supposedly used,' replied the headteacher, 'the sooner you will be able to attend your site meeting.'

'Balls!' said the parent.

'I beg your pardon,' said Miss Drayton.

'Balls!' repeated the parent, sitting down again. 'That's the word he used and I'll tell you this, when my Miranda came out with it, I couldn't believe my ears.'

'Is it not possible that your daughter could have heard this word from someone on your building site?' asked Miss Drayton.

'No, she couldn't!' exclaimed the parent. 'I asked her where she had heard it and she said in the classroom from Mr Hornchurch. I was having my breakfast and she came out with it. I nearly choked. "It's cold enough to freeze the balls of a brass monkey this morning," she said, and then later she asked me if there'd been a "cock-up"

158

when I told her I was collecting her from school and not her mother. This is not the sort of thing you expect your child to learn at school and to hear from a teacher.'

Miss Drayton turned to the accused. 'Mr Hornchurch?'

'I did indeed use these expressions,' he admitted.

I saw the headteacher close her eyes momentarily and take a short breath.

'You see!' blustered the parent. 'He admits it!'

'But the expressions are in no way vulgar, Mr Gaskell,' explained Mr Hornchurch, who still appeared quite unruffled.

'They are in my book!' the parent snapped.

'Well, they are not vulgar in the *Oxford English Dictionary*,' said the teacher, 'which is the world authority on the use of the English language and where you will find the origins and the meanings of these old expressions. If I might elucidate?'

'What?' asked the parent.

'You see,' enthused Mr Hornchurch, clasping his hands together in front of him, 'we are doing a history topic in class on Admiral Lord Nelson and I was explaining to the children that some of the expressions in common parlance today such as "swinging the lead", "spick and span", "fagged out", to be a "loose cannon", to be in "at the bitter end"—all these date back centuries and often have nautical origins. For example, I have been quite "taken aback" by your comments. "Taken aback"—to be surprised, astounded—referred originally to a sailing ship caught by a powerful gust of headwind. I appear to have "fallen foul" of you, Mr Gaskell. This term too comes from the language of the sea where a ship's rope is a "foul" when it becomes entangled.'

'I am not here to listen to a lecture about seaside expressions,' said the parent.

'You see, the old expressions to which you have referred,' continued Mr Hornchurch undeterred, 'contrary to popular belief, are in no way vulgar. Something done badly or inefficiently is known as a "cock-up" and the expression has a long provenance. The "cock" is the firing lever of the pistol, which can be raised to release the trigger. If the cock is up too far, the gun will not fire, hence the old expression a "cock-up". I imagine you were thinking of something else.' He gave a small smile. 'As to "freezing the balls of a brass monkey", this is an old and familiar naval expression dating back to before Trafalgar. I was describing to the children the scene at the famous battle and what could happen if the sailors were not prepared. The "monkey" was a brass rack on which the cannonballs were stored. In very cold weather this monkey contracted thus ejecting the balls. The expression actually is "cold enough to freeze the balls off"—and not "of"—"a brass monkey".'

'It sounds very far-fetched to me,' mumbled Mr Gaskell.

'Would you like to see the *Oxford English Dictionary*?' asked the teacher, stretching down to a bookcase beside the headteacher's desk.

'No, I wouldn't,' said the parent aggressively.

'You see, English is a rich and poetic language,' continued Mr Hornchurch, 'full of interesting idioms and proverbs, age-old adages and maxims, colourful expressions and pithy sayings, which I think children should know about, and always seem to enjoy. I think if you had listened to Miranda she might have explained things.'

'Or taken the time to have a word with me about it,' added the headteacher.

'Well, I wasn't aware that's what these expressions meant,' said Mr Gaskell, beginning to rise from his chair, 'and now I've got this meeting to go to.'

'Do sit down, Mr Gaskell,' said the headteacher like a school ma'am correcting a recalcitrant pupil, 'I haven't quite finished with this matter yet.'

The plump man sat down again. 'It's just a bit of a misunderstanding, that's all,' he said.

'Mr Gaskell,' said the headteacher quietly and distinctly, but fixing him with a cobra stare, 'you have made a serious allegation against a member of my staff, a false and malicious accusation which might very well have damaged his reputation and that of the school. I mean, a busy school inspector has been sent from County Hall to investigate, not to congratulate me on the school's excellent results or the awards we have won, but to investigate an unsubstantiated accusation.'

'All I said—' began Mr Gaskell, now crimson-faced.

'Let me finish,' interrupted Miss Drayton. 'An unsubstantiated accusation that has stirred up a veritable hornets' nest. I am sure you are aware of the term "slander"—a false and defamatory spoken statement.' The parent's face drained of colour. 'You made these unfounded claims before me, an officer of the Education Authority, a county councillor and various other people who have better things to do with their time than go on a wild-goose chase. Further to that, it appears that

161

you have repeated these unfounded allegations in a public house and now a newspaper article is to appear, so I hope you know the meaning of the word "libel", too. It seems to me, Mr Gaskell, you are in very hot water indeed.'

'Well, I wasn't to know,' he whined. 'I thought— as most people do, I reckon—that these—er—'

'Expressions.' Mr Hornchurch came to his aid.

'Yes, that these expressions were rude.' He squirmed in the chair like a large slug sprinkled with salt.

The headteacher nodded towards me. 'This is Mr Phinn, as I informed you, Mr Gaskell, the County Inspector for English and Drama. Had you or Councillor Peterson contacted him, he too could have cleared up the matter, being fully aware of the origins of the expressions.' I nodded knowingly, but kept quiet. I had had no idea from where the expressions had originated. I too had thought they were rather vulgar phrases. 'Have you anything to add, Mr Phinn?' asked the headteacher.

'I think Mr Gaskell should contact the *Fettlesham Gazette* and explain it was all a misunderstanding,' I said.

'That goes without question,' said Miss Drayton, 'and I shall most certainly be getting in touch with the Editor because the reputation of the school could very well have been tarnished by such accusations.' She turned to her colleague. 'Have you anything to add, Mr Hornchurch?' she asked.

'It's just a misunderstanding,' he said. 'Let's forget all about it. I've got more important things to think about at the moment. I'm taking the children on a trip to the Science Museum next

162

Saturday and I've still got lots to do.' Mr Gaskell continued to stare at the carpet. 'It would be very nice if your Miranda could come after all.'

'I don't know about that,' he replied quietly, without looking up.

'School trips are a very important part of the curriculum,' said the headteacher.

'Miranda is doing very well, you know,' said Mr Hornchurch.

The parent stood up. 'Well, I must be off.'

'Yes,' said Miss Drayton, rising from her chair and giving Mr Gaskell a tight little smile of dismissal. 'I think your daughter is waiting to be taken home. I suggest we conclude this very unfortunate meeting.'

'Yes,' said Mr Gaskell, heading for the door. 'Good afternoon.'

'But before you go, Mr Gaskell,' said Miss Drayton, 'I rather think you have something to say to Mr Hornchurch.'

'Something to say?'

'An apology?'

The man coughed nervously. 'Yes, well ... er ... I'm sorry for the ... er ... trouble, I'm sure,' he mumbled. 'And ... er ... I'll let you know about Miranda and the trip.' And with that, he lumbered from the room.

'One expression from this rich and poetic language of ours,' I observed, 'which comes to my mind is being "taken down a peg or two".'

'Ah yes,' said Mr Hornchurch. 'Now that's another very interesting nautical expression.' It was as if I had wound him up like a clockwork toy. 'At the time of Nelson, there was a strict hierarchy at sea displayed by the position of the ship's

163

colours after they had been raised. The greatest honour was conferred by the flags flown at the masthead. To be "taken down a peg or two" was to receive a reduction in the honour shown to you. Of course, nowadays, it has come to mean taking the conceit from a boastful person, rather like "taking the wind out of one's sails". Now there's another expression which—'

'I think we have had enough expressions for one day, thank you,' said Miss Drayton, laughing. 'Well,' she said, 'I think that was very generous of you, Mr Hornchurch. I don't think I would have been quite so understanding.' Her brow creased a fraction, 'You *were* quite right about those particular expressions, weren't you?'

Mr Hornchurch stretched out a hand towards the bookcase. 'Would you like me to get the *OED*?' he asked.

'No, that won't be necessary,' said the headteacher. 'Off you go, then, but I do think it might be wise to modify the range of idioms that you discuss with the children.'

Mr Hornchurch nodded and then, with a mischievous grin on his face, made a mock-naval salute, and said, 'Aye, aye, sir!' With that, the most eccentric teacher it has been my pleasure to meet strode for the door, leaving us both laughing.

CHAPTER TEN

I was at the office early on the Monday morning, eager to report back to Miss de la Mare about 'the storm in the teacup' at Tarncliffe, and also determined to broach the question of Ugglemattersby once and for all.

Julie was already tapping away noisily at the typewriter in the adjoining office when I arrived and she shouted down the corridor: 'Morning, Mr Phinn.'

'How do you know it's me?' I called back.

Julie appeared at the door of the inspectors' office. 'Mr Pritchard is running a course this morning,' she said, 'and Mr Clamp is never in this early at the start of the week and Dr Mullarkey is at a meeting in York. Anyway, Miss de la Mare has you in her appointment book for eight o'clock.'

'How do you know that?' I asked.

'Because she rang through just before you came in,' she replied, 'and told me you had an appointment with her this morning. She asked me to tell you she's running a bit late and she'll ring when she's ready for you. She's likely to be held up because she has to see venomous Brenda, the black widow of County Hall—something to do with the school closures.'

There was no love lost between our secretary and the Chief Education Officer's PA. In fact, there was a mutual dislike bordering on hostility between the two of them, and a long-running history of disputes and disagreements. Any mention of Mrs Savage to Julie was guaranteed to wind her up.

'It might not have been me coming into the office,' I said. 'It could have been the Personal Assistant from hell checking up on us again,' I said.

'If it was Mrs Savage,' Julie retorted, 'I'd have heard her a mile off. With all that jewellery she wears, she sounds like a wind chime in a gale

165

whenever she moves. Mind you, it's more difficult in the new offices to be warned of her arrival since she doesn't have to come up the two flights of stairs any more. She was always huffing and puffing by the time she got to the second floor.'

It was true. Mrs Savage did like to adorn herself in expensive and heavy jewellery. It was a wonder that her neck, hands and wrists were capable of supporting so many chains, rings, necklaces and bracelets that hung from her like Christmas tree baubles.

'So I have an extra ten minutes, good,' I said.

'Well, there's plenty of work for you on your desk to be getting on with, and there're some calls to make from Friday afternoon.'

'No peace for the wicked,' I said, looking through the pile of papers on my desk.

'So, how's that little squirrel of yours, then?' she asked.

'Who told you about the squirrel?' I asked.

'Mr Clamp, who else?' She perched herself on the end of my desk and straightened her strip of emerald-green skirt. 'We were having a laugh about it on Friday when he was in the office. He told us about two little boys at one of the schools he was visiting. When they saw a squirrel outside the classroom window, one of them said, "Ooh, look at that squirrel in the tree. Let's tell miss." "Shurrup, Gavin," said the other, "she'll make us write about it."' Julie laughed. 'I get no work done when Mr Clamp is around.'

'Well, I can tell you that Christine and I aren't laughing at the moment. We keep being woken up in the dead of night by its wretched scratching and scraping and scuttling about in the loft. It is driving

166

us mad. In fact, I'm expecting Mr Hinderwell to deliver a squirrel trap today or tomorrow. Keep an eye out for it, will you?'

'Certainly. I'll put it by your desk when it arrives.' Julie adopted a pose of a squirrel begging, with her hands held up in front of her substantial chest. 'I played a squirrel once in the infant nativity play,' she said. 'I was burning hot in that grey woollen costume under all the stage lights, and it smelt revolting, too—of smelly socks and sweat and toilets. I couldn't see properly through the eyeholes and kept banging into things. I knocked the frankincense off the stage and tripped over the manger.'

'I wasn't aware that they had squirrels in the stable at Bethlehem?' I said, smiling at the thought of the mayhem.

'There was in our version. In fact, there were all sorts of assorted animals. I think the costumes were left over from when the juniors did *The Wind in the Willows*. It was a real laugh, that Nativity. Maureen Broadbent was a mole and stole the show by biting one of the angels. Jimmy Parker walked on stage in a white sheet with cardboard wings and a halo shouting, "Shift thissen. It's t'Angel o' Lord 'ere. Move out of t'way!" and then he trod on Maureen's paw—they were really her fingers, of course. So she bit him!'

'It sounds great,' I chuckled, 'a real barrel of laughs.'

'The best part was when we presented Baby Jesus with His presents,' Julie told me. 'After the Three Wise Men had given their gifts, all the animals gave theirs. Well, I went on stage without mine and Mrs Proctor, my teacher, brought the

167

house down by shouting out from the wings of the stage, "Squirrel, get back here, you've forgotten your nuts!" So why does the boss want to see you so early on a Monday morning?' asked Julie, suddenly changing the subject.

'It's about a school with a problem,' I told her. 'Well, it was supposed to be a problem but, as it turned out, it was all a fuss about nothing, a storm in a teacup. I had better things to do with my time last Friday afternoon I can tell you than go on a wild-goose chase for Councillor Peterson.'

'Marlene, who works on the switchboard, was telling me about Councillor Peterson's latest gaffe. Joyce, who takes the Education Committee minutes, was telling her how she overheard Councillor Peterson telling another councillor about it. Marlene nearly wet herself laughing. Listen to this! The Ministry of Education and Science asked for an elected member to represent the county at a Regional Race Committee meeting in York. It was all to do with equal opportunities, multi-racial matters, making sure that people of different races and cultures are not discriminated against.'

'Well, that's a good idea,' I said. 'It's about time some notice was taken of that.'

'Anyway,' she continued, 'who should put himself forward but Councillor Peterson.'

'I would have thought he was the very last person to represent the Authority on racial awareness,' I said, 'but, of course, he does like to have his fat fingers in every pie.'

'Let me finish,' said Julie. 'So off he goes to this Race Committee meeting in York, and comes back and reports that he'd thought it was all about horse racing! He thought he was all set for a slap-up meal and a day at York Races. He was dressed for the part as well, in his tweeds and trilby hat and with a pair of binoculars round his neck—or so Joyce said she'd heard him say, and that's what she told Marlene who told me.'

'Typical of him,' I said. 'And speaking of meetings, could you ring County Hall and see if Miss de la Mare wants to see me yet?'

'Well, I thought it was very funny,' said Julie, presumably stung because I hadn't laughed. 'And I'm not going to ring County Hall because, if you remember, I told you she would ring over when she's ready for you.' And with that, she tottered back to her office on her bright green high heels.

Oh dear, I realised I had now upset Julie. I was definitely on edge about the forthcoming meeting with the Chief Inspector.

A moment later, she popped her head around the door. 'I meant to say, will you *please* give that double-barrelled woman with the fancy name a call before your meeting? I've left a note with her number on your desk. I couldn't get her off the line on Friday and I don't want a repeat.' She then adopted what she considered a frightfully upper-class accent. 'I hev to speak to Mr Phinn abite something very himportant. It's abslewtly hessential he rings me, *tout de suite*.'

The urgent call was from Mrs Cleaver-Canning, or should I say the Honourable Margot Cleaver-Canning. I had met this impressively large and formidable woman a couple of years before when I had been inveigled by her into speaking at the Christmas dinner of the Totterdale and Clearwell Golf Club when she was the Lady Captain. Prior to being formally invited, she had summoned me to her elegant house so she could vet me and make sure I would be suitable. Here I had met this vision with purple-tinted bouffant hair, large grey eyes and scarlet bow of a mouth, and her long-suffering husband, Winco—Wing Commander Norman Cleaver-Canning (Rtd) DFC. Some time later, the honourable lady had dragooned me into taking a minor part in an amateur production of *The Sound of Music*. Perhaps 'memorable' is not the right word to describe the last performance. 'Traumatic' might be more fitting. As the curtain had fallen, I had been informed that Christine had been rushed into hospital to have our first child who had decided to arrive a bit earlier than expected. There had been no time to change out of our costumes. Winco, resplendent in a heavily be-medalled German admiral's uniform, had driven me in his Mercedes at breakneck speed to Fettlesham Royal Infirmary with the Mother Abbess, (Mrs Cleaver-Canning), with an inch of stage make-up on her face, directing proceedings from the passenger seat. I had arrived just in time to see my son being born.

I made the call.

'Gervase, how are you?' came a loud and high-pitched voice down the line.

'I'm fine, thank you, Mrs Cleaver-Canning,' I replied.

'I do wish you would call me Margot.'

'Well, I'm fine, thank you, Margot, and how are you?'

'Top notch. And how is that dear little child of yours?'

'He's thriving.'

'Good. And your charming wife?'

'She's very well, too.'

'I am so glad to hear it,' she said. 'It was quite an experience, wasn't it, the evening your little boy came into the world? A performance to remember.'

'It was indeed,' I replied.

'Now, I am sure you will have ascertained that I am not telephoning you merely to exchange pleasantries.'

'No, I guessed there would be something else,' I said, with a sinking feeling.

'I'll come straight to the point. I am desperate for a man again.'

'Oh, no, no, Mrs Cleaver-Canning—er, Margot. I really cannot. I'm afraid—' I started.

'Now, before you turn me down,' she interrupted, 'please hear me out. It's a truly wonderful play and everyone is so excited about performing it, but the sticking point is that there are nine parts for men and we have only secured eight. It's not a big part and you would only make a short entrance at the very end, just as you did when you gave that barnstorming performance as the SS lieutenant in *The Sound of Music*. The way you strutted on the stage in the last act and delivered your four words was quite masterful.' Flatterer, I thought. 'So please don't turn me down. There would be minimal attendance at rehearsals and you wouldn't need to be there on the nights of the performance until well into the second half.'

'I'm up to my eyes at the moment and—' I began again.

'It's called *The Dame of Sark* by William Douglas-Home,' Mrs Cleaver-Canning continued

171

blithely. 'A magnificently patriotic and poignant piece set in one of the Channel Islands at the time of the last war and the German Occupation. I will be playing the lead part of Sybil, the fiercely determined and courageous Dame of Sark, who comes to respect and even like Colonel von Schmettau, the Commander of the German forces. Winco will be playing him.'

'It's just that—'

'You would take the part of Colonel Graham who liberates the island in the last scene. It's a little gem of a part, a mere eighteen lines, a perfect cameo, and you're just ideal for it. As Raymond, our producer, said, the part could have been written for you. It is your *métier.* Winco will drop a copy of the play off and you can peruse it at your leisure.'

'That's just the point, Margot,' I said, trying to sound forceful. 'I don't seem to have any leisure at the moment. As I mentioned, I am up to my eyes—'

'All the more need for a hobby outside work,' she interrupted. 'You know what they say about all work and no play.'

'Mrs Cleaver-Canning, Margot,' I said. There was a touch of desperation in my voice. 'I really am so very busy. There's work and the baby and the garden and so much to do in the cottage.'

'Oh *please,* Gervase,' she said in a high pleading voice. '*Please* don't disappoint me. The whole production depends upon you.' And then she played her trump card. 'And you do owe me a favour. I mean, if it hadn't been for Winco driving you to the hospital . . .'

I thought for a moment. 'The least I can do is

look at the play,' I said feebly.

'Thank you *so* much,' oozed Mrs Cleaver-Canning, who never ever took No for an answer.

Of course I knew, and so did Mrs Cleaver-Canning, that in effect I had agreed to take the part. I couldn't very well look through the playscript, build up her hopes and then refuse to do it. When I thought about it later, I was quite pleased I had agreed. I had enjoyed the badinage at the rehearsals, meeting people outside the world of education and talking about things other than schools and teachers. I had also enjoyed my few brief moments in the spotlight and, to be honest, taking part hadn't involved a great deal of time and effort. And, as Mrs C-C had reminded me, I did owe her a favour. However, despite all these positives, I decided to pick the right moment to tell Christine.

*   *   *

Miss de la Mare's office was on the top corridor of County Hall. When she had taken up her appointment the term before, the Chief Inspector had wasted little time in relocating to a spacious and modern office near to Dr Gore's. I recall well when she had first seen the office previously occupied by her predecessor, Harold Yeats—that cluttered and cramped room, with its row of ugly olive-green metal filing cabinets, heavy bookcases, square of threadbare carpet and Harold's vast ancient oak desk. She had shaken her head and said to no one in particular, 'This just will not do.' Within the month she had moved.

County Hall was an imposing building,

magnificently ornate and sturdy, dominating the market town of Fettlesham and standing in extensive and well-tended formal gardens. The interior was equally impressive: endless corridors, high ornate ceilings, great brass chandeliers, heavy velvet drapes, and walls full of gilt-framed portraits of former worthies. I always felt rather intimidated when I entered the huge oak doors that led into the great entrance hall.

The meeting with the Chief Inspector was not quite the ordeal I had expected. I presented a full written report on Tarncliffe School and explained to her how the confusion had arisen.

'And if the parent in question had taken the trouble to contact the headteacher in the first place,' I told her, 'instead of telephoning one of his cronies at County Hall, all this could have been avoided.'

'Maybe,' Miss de la Mare said, 'but to be fair to the parent, and indeed Councillor Peterson, the two expressions that caused all the contention really do sound rather vulgar. I shouldn't think that many people—apart from English specialists like you—are aware of their origins or what they actually mean. Personally, they are not expressions I would use, or I suspect that you would either. Perhaps Mr Hornchurch should have pointed this out to the children. However, to use a more familiar expression, "that's all water under the bridge now".' Thank you for dealing with it, Gervase. I shall read your report with interest and explain matters to Dr Gore and Councillor Peterson when I meet with them later this morning. I will also ring the Editor of the *Gazette* to make sure that article doesn't go ahead. Now, I

174

am sure that you, like I, have a very busy day ahead of you so I won't detain you further.'

I took a deep breath. 'There was another matter I wanted to speak to you about,' I said, placing a second report on her desk and sliding it across. 'Ugglemattersby Junior School.'

The Chief Inspector gave a slight smile and stared down at the report. 'Go on,' she said.

Miss de la Mare listened patiently as I explained how I had visited the school and had been unhappy with what I had seen and heard. I admitted that I had been at fault for not having followed through the last report, which I had written just over two years before, by returning to the school to check on progress. I told her that I hadn't even telephoned the headteacher to see how he was getting on. I accepted it had been my responsibility to ensure that the recommendations in my report had been addressed, and I had failed in that regard.

There was what I felt to be an interminable silence before the Chief Inspector spoke. 'You are right,' she said at last, 'you should have followed things up. It's all very well writing critical reports on schools but if nothing is done about them it is a pointless exercise.'

'I see that,' I said quietly.

'Having said that, there are several hundred schools in the county and we are a small team and it is to be expected that things, at times, slip through the net. The headteacher and indeed the governors should have been more proactive, of course, and sought help.'

'I don't think the governors and the headteacher exactly see eye to eye,' I told her.

175

'I see.'

'To be fair to him, the headteacher did try and implement some of the recommendations and there have been changes for the better but I think you need to read the whole report to get the full picture.'

'Since it wasn't just English in which the children were under-achieving, your colleagues too should have been into the school with support and advice. I take it you acquainted them with your concerns?'

'Yes, I did.'

'And did they go in?'

'I'm not sure,' I replied feebly.

'You're not sure?'

'No.'

'You didn't think to check?'

'No, I didn't.'

'Well, I think there are a number of people who are at fault here.' I felt a little better after that remark until she added, 'Having said that, Gervase, it was really down to you to have dealt with the situation since you instigated it.'

The words of Mr Hornchurch suddenly came to mind. I had certainly 'cocked-up' this time.

'I know it's a case of closing the stable door after the horse has bolted,' I said, 'but I've suggested in this current report that the team undertakes a full inspection of the school and that competency proceedings be considered with regard to the two teachers.'

'That might not be necessary,' said the Chief Inspector. 'You see, Ugglemattersby Junior is on the list of five schools we are thinking of closing.'

'Closing!' I exclaimed.

'We have it in mind to amalgamate the Junior and the Infant Schools,' she told me. 'Numbers in the Juniors are declining and the Infant School is on a spacious site which could be further developed to accommodate the older children. It seems the best course of action in the present circumstances.'

'I see,' I murmured.

'Quite fortuitous really, isn't it, Gervase?' said the Chief Inspector, giving a small enigmatic smile.

*   *   *

On my way back down the top corridor I literally bumped into Mrs Savage at the top of the great staircase. My mind was on the surprising news that Miss de la Mare had just divulged about Ugglemattersby Juniors and, hurriedly turning the corner, I collided with the CEO's Personal Assistant, knocking the files she was carrying out of her hands.

'For goodness' sake!' she snapped. 'Watch where you are going!' There was no mistaking that sharp, disapproving voice.

'So sorry, Mrs Savage,' I said.

'Oh it's you,' she replied, her eyes bright with indignation. She drew her lips together into a tight little line.

I bent to retrieve the files. 'I apologise,' I said, 'I wasn't looking where I was going.'

'No, you were not!' she exclaimed. 'Coming down the corridor at that speed. I could have been seriously injured. I might have suffered whiplash.'

'Yes, I'm sorry,' I said again.

'And now I shall have to sort out all these files,'

she said crossly. She meant, of course, that a clerical assistant would have to sort them out. There was no way she would concern herself with such a menial task. 'Actually, Mr Phinn, I'm glad to have this opportunity of having a word with you.'

'I'm in rather a rush,' I replied. 'I've got a school appointment this morning.'

'This will only take a moment of your time,' she said frostily.

'Very well.'

'It has come to my attention that the school inspectors are parking their vehicles in the designated bays outside County Hall. I noticed this morning, for example, as I was looking out of my office window, that you yourself have parked your car in an area specially allocated and marked off for the use of County Councillor Morrison.'

'I should hardly think that Councillor Morrison is likely to be at County Hall this early in the morning,' I told her.

'That is neither here nor there,' replied Mrs Savage. 'I should like to point out to you, and perhaps you will convey this to your colleagues, that the bays are reserved exclusively, I repeat exclusively, for the elected members, chief officers and senior members of staff, and not for other people, particularly those who have their own specified parking spaces near their place of work.'

'Sometimes, Mrs Savage,' I said, 'we have to collect a report or deliver a document and we just stay for a few minutes, or when we attend a meeting with Miss de la Mare or Dr Gore.'

'Mr Phinn,' she said, stiffening, 'I don't think I have made myself entirely clear. There is no excuse for parking in the designated bays be it for

178

the full day or for a few minutes. The *modus operandi* at County Hall will only be successful if everyone abides by the rules. To be frank, the inspectors believe they are a law unto themselves. I have had occasion to speak to Miss de la Mare about the failure of some of your colleagues to send in their weekly programmes on time and—'

'I thought this was about parking,' I commented.

'It is,' she replied. 'Your office is but a short distance from County Hall and it is not that onerous, I am sure, for the inspectors to walk. The biggest offender is Mr Clamp who appears to think he can park that large and unsightly estate car of his wherever he pleases. It was in Councillor Peterson's bay last week. Councillor Peterson was not best pleased and he raised the matter with Dr Gore who, of course, asked me to deal with it.'

'I will pass your message on,' I told her, 'and, now, if you will excuse me.'

'Those who illegally park will have their vehicle immobilised,' she continued. 'Instructions have been given to Security that there will be no exceptions. I shall be sending a memorandum over to the inspectors' office later this week reminding you all of the parking regulations and informing you that any offender in future will be clamped.'

'It will be read with interest, as we do all your memos,' I told her, 'and now if you—'

'I haven't finished yet, 'she said sharply. 'There is another matter.'

'Yes,' I sighed.

'It has also come to my attention that some of the inspectors appear to be making personal calls from their office telephones. This has got to stop. County Council regulations dictate that no personal calls of any kind, except in the most severe emergencies, may be made in work time and from office telephones. I have raised the matter with Miss de la Mare, and my staff will be keeping a close check on all calls. You might acquaint your colleagues with the fact that—'

'I suggest you put it in a memo, Mrs Savage,' along with all the other complaints,' I interrupted and, brushing past, I hurried down the stairs. 'Frightful woman!' I said under my breath.

CHAPTER ELEVEN

Andy was a large pink-faced bear of a boy, with coarse bristly brown hair and enormous ears. I had just come down to the kitchen on Saturday morning the following week in my old towelling dressing gown, and was making an early morning cup of tea, when his great beaming face appeared at the window.

'You must be Andy?' I said as I let him into the kitchen.

'That's reight, Mester Phinn,' he said. 'Up wi' t'lark and rarin' to go.'

'Well, it's very early and I've just—' I began.

'Is that a pot o' tea tha brewin'?' the boy asked, eyeing the teapot on the stove.

'It is. Would you like a cup?' I asked.

'Cup o' tea gus down a treat this time o' t'mornin',' he said, seating himself at the kitchen table. 'Mi Uncle 'Arry 'appen told thee I'd be comin' up this mornin', did 'e?'

'Yes, he did,' I replied, 'but not quite this early.

It's only eight o'clock.'

'Well, tha sees,' he said, leaning back on a chair, 'there's things to do. After I've sooarted thy garden out, I'm down to owld Missis Poskitt's to paint 'er iron yats, then Mester Umpleby 'as need o' me to do a bit o' muckin' out an' 'elp fotherin' 'osses. Then I've got sheep to fettle and beeasts to feed an' toneet I'm goin' to Young Farmers pea and pie supper.'

I passed the boy a mug from the dresser. 'Busy man,' I said. 'Help yourself.'

'Can't complain,' he replied, getting up and reaching for the teapot and pouring himself a mugful. 'I'm tryin' to save a bit o' money, tha sees, to get me through college. When I leave school next year, I'm 'opin' to go to Askham Bryan Agricultural College, best college in t'north, but there's fees an' such.'

'So I hear. It's a very good college,' I told him. 'My wife's cousin lectures at Askham Bryan—Dr Iain Bentley. He's a specialist in horticulture. You might come across him.'

'Sheep are my specialism,' said Andy, before putting some milk and two heaped teaspoonfuls of sugar in his mug and stirring the tea vigorously. 'Though I'm all reight wi' plants an' I can turn mi 'and to owt. I like pigs an' all an' I 'ave a few goats. Thing is wi' beeasts is that a dog looks up to you, a cat looks down on you but a pig looks you straight in t'eye. Tha knaas where thy are wi' pigs. Not like that wi' most fowk, is it? As mi Uncle 'Arry says, "There's nowt as queer as folk. They're all on 'em queer, bar thee and me—an' sometimes ah'm not that sure abaat thee."' He laughed. 'I can't wait to leave school. Can't see t'point missen o' doin' halgebra an' geometry an' leaarnin' French an' writin' soppy poetry.'

'You'd be surprised how it comes in useful in later life,' I told him, sounding like his teacher.

'What, poetry?' He laughed loudly. 'It's all la-di-da and bloody daffodils.'

'I'll tell you something, Andy,' I said, 'and you must never tell Mrs Phinn I told you, but poetry is the very best way to get a girlfriend. A little love poem, I have found, works wonders on the female heart.'

'Nay, nay Mester Phinn,' he spluttered, shaking his head vigorously, 'I'm not into that sooart o' thing at t'moment. There's plenty time fer that later on. There's this big lass at t'Young Farmers called Bianca, wi' red hair an' spots, who's set her cap fer me but I'm not hinterested. I just want to leave school and do summat worth doing.'

'Well,' I said, 'school and passing your exams are important.'

'I can't see how what tha does at school'l 'elp me wi' sheep. I'd be better leaarnin' 'ow to repair a drystone wall, dig a dyke, chain 'arrow, lamb a yow, milk a cow an' 'andle a collie. Can't see how workin' out circumference of a circle or writin' abaat flowers and fairies is gunna 'elp me much in t'line o' work I wants to do.'

'Which school do you go to?' I asked him.

'West Challerton 'Igh. 'Eadmaster, Mester Pennington-Smith, is only bothered abaat bright kids an' them what are good at sports. Wunt know me from Adam.'

'Really?'

'I liked t'other 'eadmaster, Mester Blunt, better. Tha knew where tha were wi' 'im. Bit like what I

182

was sayin' abaat pigs.'

I decided not to probe any more. 'So,' I said, 'do you think you can sort out my garden?'

'Oh, I can fettle it all reight. I can see there's a fair bit o' work needs doin', mind. It's like a jungle out theer. Garden's full o' wickens.'

'Whatever are they?' I asked. They sounded as if they might be some sort of strange furry creature with sharp teeth.

'Weeds, Mester Phinn, weeds—dandillylions, twitch grass, nettles, docks, daisies, you name it, you've got it. An' I don't know when's last time tha mowed tha lawn.'

'I've not had much time to do it lately,' I said. 'I meant to make a start after we got back from our holidays but didn't and now autumn is here.'

'T'recent downpour's med it grow ageean,' said the boy. 'Nivver thee mind, Mester Phinn, I'll soon 'ave it fettled.'

'We haven't discussed your—' I started.

'I reckon I'll do your borders fust,' he told me, taking a great gulp of tea and smacking his lips noisily. 'Good tea, this. Mi grandma allus likes her tea strong enough to stand a spoon up in it. Proper Yorkshire tea. Just the ticket. Any rooad, I reckon I'll mek a start on t'lawn this mornin'. Needs mowin' an' rakin' an' spikin' and grass food purrin on. Then I'll do t'diggin' next week. Best to wait till next month to tackle yer trees. Lot o' prunin' needs doin' theer.'

'I can see you've done your homework,' I said.

'Aye, I've 'ad a quick look round.' He took another great gulp from the mug.

'About payment,' I said.

'We can sooart that out later,' he told me, 'when

183

tha's seen what I've done. I'll do a good job for thee, Mester Phinn. Tha'll not be disappointed.'

'Fair enough,' I said.

'Tha needs a compost 'eap, tha knaas,' the boy continued. 'I'll build thee one round t'side, if tha likes. Oh, and there's three panes o' glass wants replacin' in yer cold frame. I'll measure 'em up and tha can 'appen ger 'em for me for next week, an' some putty an' all, an' some black paint an' brushes.'

'Right,' I said, scribbling a note. 'Is that everything?'

'Yer gutterin' needs replacin' round t'side otherwise tha'll get watter comin' in. An' a couple of yer slates are loose. I'll fix 'em, an' all. I'll bring mi ladders next week. I could clean yer winders while I'm at it. Might as well, since I'm up theer anyway. They needs doin' by t'looks on 'em.'

Andy drained the mug and banged it down onto the kitchen table just as Christine came into the kitchen with the baby. She at least had dressed.

'You must be Andy,' she said.

'I am, missis,' he replied, standing up and extending a hand as large as a spade. 'Pleased to meet you.' He then pushed his large pink face close to the child. 'And this must be t'little un. Hey up, he's a bobby dazzler, in't 'e?" Andy tickled little Richard gently under his chin. 'Oochy coochy coo,' he burbled. 'Oochy coochy coo.'

The baby immediately started screaming.

'I allus 'ave that effect on kiddies,' Andy said laughing. 'I'm all reight wi' sheep an' beeasts but when it comes to babbies, they allus start a-rooarin when I look at 'em.'

'I think he's hungry,' Christine explained. 'Don't

take it personally, Andy.'

'I nivver do, missis,' said the boy, beaming. 'Life's too short to tek things personally.'

'So,' said Christine, rocking the baby in an attempt to quieten him, 'is everything arranged?'

'It appears so,' I said.

'So what's wi' t'squirrels, then?' Andy asked.

'Who told you about the squirrel?' I said.

'Well, I've seen 'em',' he replied.

'Them?' Christine and I asked in unison. 'There's more than one? Where?'

'There's a brace on 'em round back in a cage,' replied the boy, 'runnin' around as if somebody's put a firework up their backsides.'

As he had promised, Maurice Hinderwell had delivered a squirrel cage to the office at the beginning of the week. When I arrived home that evening, I had done as he had suggested and had positioned the rectangular wire cage with the trap door a short distance from the house in a corner of the back garden, secluded yet quite close to the squirrel's point of entry under the eaves. I stocked it with a handful of honey-coated peanuts. However, much to my dismay, our nocturnal visitor obviously had a liking for our roof, and my slumbers were greatly disturbed by the pitter-patter and scratching above me of a squirrel that didn't seem to need the sleep that I did, by a nervous wife who prodded me in the back whenever she was woken by the squirrel, not to mention a fractious baby who wanted feeding. Each morning, I would check the trap but it remained irritatingly empty. I was beginning to wonder if I would have to call in Maurice Hinderwell to help me.

185

'So we've caught *two* squirrels?' I asked Andy now.

'Big uns, an' all,' said the boy. 'Dust tha want to look at 'em?'

Christine picked a shawl out of the carrycot and gently covered Richard with it, then the Phinn family went out into the garden with Andy to view our bushy-tailed captives, which were cowering in the furthest corner of the cage.

'Ahh,' said Christine, 'aren't they sweet?'

'You didn't say that last night when they were scratching and scraping in the loft,' I grumbled. 'I'm black and blue with all that poking.' Andy gave me a strange look.

'They look rather scared,' said Christine, peering down into the cage, 'but at the same time very cute with their little furry faces and bushy tails. Just like in the picture books.'

'Tree rats,' said Andy bluntly. 'Does tha want me to get rid of 'em for you?'

'Not kill them!' exclaimed Christine, looking aghast. 'You don't mean to kill them, do you, Andy?'

'Best thing, missis,' replied the boy. 'They're vermin. 'Armful to game, crops, farm animals, vegetation, an' they carry disease an' all. Best thing to do is kill 'em. I'll just drop t'cage in your watter butt an' drown t'little devils.'

'No, no,' said Christine firmly, 'I won't let you do that.'

'They're no good as pets, if that's what yer thinkin', Missis Phinn,' he told her.

'I know that,' said Christine, 'but I don't want them killed. My husband will take them somewhere well away from here and set them

186

free.'

'Will I?' I asked.

'Yes, you will,' she said firmly.

'Suit thissen, missis,' said Andy, shrugging, 'but they'll be back. You mark my words. This is their territory an', sure as sixpence, they'll be back.'

'Not if I take them a good distance,' I said.

'Want to bet on it?' asked Andy. 'I'll wager thee a fiver to a penny they'll be back.'

'How will you know?' I asked. 'One squirrel looks pretty much like another.'

'I'll show thee,' said Andy, 'hang on a mo,' and he walked across to the back door where he had left an old hold-all, out of which poked various tools. He rifled through the contents and returned holding a spray can. 'I shall be using this rust-repellent undercoat on one of Missis Poskitt's yats later on. I'll put a touch on t'tails of these two critters and then we'll know whether or not it's t'same squirrels if we catch any more.'

Before I could argue with the boy, he liberally sprayed the tails of the two terrified creatures with the dark red-coloured paint. The squirrels went into a frenzy, squealing, scrabbling around the cage in circles and displaying sets of sharp, vicious-looking teeth.

'You were a bit heavy handed with that paint, Andy,' Christine observed. 'Their tails are totally coated.'

'Won't 'urt 'em, missis. Soon come off will that paint,' Andy said, winking at me. 'Now, if a couple o' grey squirrels wi' red tails are in your trap next week, we'll know I was reight, won't we, an' you, Mester Phinn, will be 'andin' ovver a fiver.'

Andy worked hard in the garden for the next three hours, and when he left to go down to paint Mrs Poskitt's gate, the place looked a whole lot better. The sun had come out, and it had turned into a glorious early autumn day. I suggested to Christine that we should load the squirrels into the car and take them up to the moors to release them.

So, with the caged creatures, which didn't seem any less lively with their red undercoat, safely in the boot of the car, baby Richard securely strapped in the back and Christine beside me, we set off for what I assumed would be an uneventful drive. I set off at a leisurely pace through Hawksrill village with its cluster of grey stone cottages, ancient Norman church and the little school.

As we passed the pub, the Royal Oak, Christine pointed out of the window. 'Look,' she said, 'it's been done up.' The window frames and door had been painted a bright green and there were two large stone troughs on either side planted with dahlias.

'It's the inside that Harry has been moaning about,' I said, driving on.

We were just out of the village when Christine tapped my arm. 'Pull over,' she said, 'there's Harry, waving at us.'

'Do I have to?'

'Yes, you do,' she said. 'He's been really helpful and I want to thank him for sending Andy up to sort out the garden.'

Reluctantly, I pulled over and wound down the window.

Harry was standing by a gate, beside a man who

could have been his twin. Buster, the Border terrier, was sitting at their feet. Both men had the same weather-reddened, craggy countenances, sharp noses and substantial outcrops of silver hair. They were attired in threadbare tweed working jackets, collarless white shirts, baggy blue serge trousers and heavy boots and both sported ancient brown flat caps.

'Good morning,' I said pleasantly.

'How do,' said Harry. His companion nodded.

'Beautiful day,' I said, looking through the windscreen at a seamless sky of eggshell blue.

'So far,' grunted Harry. 'Tha knaas what I allus says: "If rooks fly 'igh, t'weather will be dry. If rooks fly low, we're sure to 'ave a blow."'

'I haven't seen any rooks,' I said.

' 'Appen tha will.' He nodded in the direction of his companion. 'This is mi brother, Cyril.'

'Good morning,' I said. Cyril nodded. 'I'm sorry I was a bit short the last time I saw you, Harry. I'd had a busy day and was very tired.'

He nodded.

'Morning, Harry,' said Christine, leaning over me and giving him one of her disarming smiles.

'Mornin', missis,' he replied.

'Morning, Cyril,' said Christine. Harry's brother tapped the peak of his cap.

'Thank you for sending Andy up to do our garden,' I said. 'He's making a splendid job of it.'

'Does thy 'ear that, Cyril? Andy's doin' a good job up theer at Peewit Cottage.'

Harry's brother nodded but the expression remained unchanged on his craggy face.

'I've just been talkin' to our Andy,' Harry told me. 'Met 'im on 'is way to owld Mrs Poskitt's to paint 'er iron yats. 'E were tellin' me there's a fair bit to do up at Peewit Cottage. Course, there allus is with these owld cottages. Place were all but fallin' dahn when owld Mrs Olleranshaw 'ad it. I don't know why people bother doing 'em up, missen. Gimme me a modern 'ouse any time. You sooart one thing owt—dry rot, creepin' damp, woodworm, subsidence—and then there's another problem reight behind. T'squirrels are t'least o' your worries.'

'Andy told you about the squirrels then?' I asked.

'Aye, he said you'd 'ad an infestation.'

'Hardly that,' I said. 'Just a couple and I've caught them.'

'Weer there's two, there's likely more,' said Harry. 'They do breed tha knaas, do squirrels.'

'Bloody nuisances,' growled Cyril.

'They are that,' said Harry. He turned his attention back to me. 'And I 'ear that tha's set on letting 'em go?'

'We wouldn't like to kill them,' said Christine.

'Townsfolk!' explained Harry to his brother.

'Typical,' replied Cyril.

'Tree rats, that's what they are,' said Harry. 'Vermin.'

'They wants shootin',' said Cyril.

'Tha reight there,' agreed his brother. 'If I find any squirrels, I mek short work on 'em, I can tell thee that.'

As if on cue the squirrels in the boot began scrabbling and scratching in their cage.

'What's that?' asked Harry.

'Oh, just the baby,' I lied. 'Well, we must be making tracks.'

190

'Andy'll do it for thee if tha's a bit squeamish,' said Harry.

'Do what?'

'Dispose of your squirrels.'

'No, thank you,' I said, starting the car.

'Trouble with townsfolk,' said Harry, addressing his brother, 'is they don't understand abaat t'ways of t'country. Rabbits, foxes, squirrels, badgers, they get all sentimental about 'em and then start interferin' in our way o' life.'

'Bloody nuisances,' growled Cyril.

'Turn off t'engine a minute,' Harry told me, 'an' I'll tell thee abaat summat what 'appened up at your cottage when old Mrs Olleranshaw lived there.' I dutifully turned off the engine. 'I was passing t'gate of your cottage some year back an' a game bird dropped out o' t'blue in front of me. They was shootin' at t'time up on Lord Marrick's estate and this pheasant, which must 'ave bin clipped by one o' these chinless, cross-eyed aristocrats wi' a shotgun, fell out of t'sky an' landed smack bang in front of me. Manna from 'eaven, it were. Sunday lunch delivered at mi feet. Any road, I'd just picked t'pheasant up when these two ramblers walked by.'

'Bloody nuisances,' growled Cyril.

'They are that,' agreed his brother. 'Any road, these two ramblers must 'ave been seventy if they were a day, wi' great big boots an' bobble hats an' rucksacks an' fancy walkin' sticks. They stopped in their tracks when they saw me pickin' up this bird. "Ooo," says one, a woman wi' a face like one o' them gargoyles on t'church, "poor creature. Is it hurt?" Is it 'urt, I thowt to missen, its bloody wing's 'angin' off. Course it's 'urt. But it won't be 'urtin' in

191

a minute, I told missen. "Can you fix it?" she asks. "Oh, yes, missis," I says, "I can fix it all reight." Any road, when they were a bit down t'track I got hold of t'pheasant an' wi' one quick—'

'I don't want to hear,' said Christine quickly.

'See what I means, Cyril,' laughed Harry, 'over-bloody-sentimental, that's what townsfolk are.' He shook his head. 'They don't mind a bit o' meat on their plate but they don't like to think 'ow it got theer. An' next time I turn up on your doorstep, Mrs Phinn, wi' a nice plump pheasant for you under mi arm, I don't expect that you'll be askin' 'ow it met its end.'

'And how are you getting on with the new landlord of the Royal Oak?' I asked Harry mischievously.

'Don't you bloody start me off!' he exclaimed. 'He's another of yer "off-comed-uns", is that new landlord! Knows nowt about country ways. Knows nowt about tradition. Comes up from t'south wi' all his fancy ideas and pulls t'place apart. Tha wunt recognise it. Tekken all stuff off t'walls, pulled t'carpet up, changed furniture. Tha wunt recognise t'place now. We're gerrin a pertition up in t'village, so 'appen I'll be callin' round for thy signature.'

We left the two brothers standing at the gate discussing the pub's new landlord.

'You did that deliberately, didn't you?' said Christine.

'What?'

'Mention the new landlord of the pub. You were winding him up.'

'Well, I'm getting my own back on him for always going on and on about my neglected garden and the wretched overgrown allotment. I now know a sure-fire way of getting old Harry Cotton to change the subject—just mention the new landlord of the Royal Oak.'

We drove on for several miles, past pale green fields where flocks of black-faced sheep meandered between bleached limestone walls and sleepy-looking cattle, chewing the cud, stared impassively.

After about fifteen minutes, Christine said suddenly, 'What about there? You could release the squirrels in that little copse.'

Beyond a field was a clump of tall firs surrounded by thick bushes.

'It's right off the road,' I said. 'It would be easier if I put them out here.'

'It's not that far and, look, there's a track down the side of the field leading to it. We don't want to have brought them this far for them to get run over, do we?'

'All right,' I grumbled, 'but I can think of a lot better things to do on a Saturday than trekking across a field with a cage full of multicoloured squirrels.'

'Like digging the allotment?' said Christine impishly.

So, taking the cage with its contents from the boot, I set off down the track that led to the edge of the little covert. It took some time to persuade the wretched creatures to leave the cage. I shook it, tilted it, even lifted it up and tipped it upside down but they hung on to the wire in the corner of the cage, chattering angrily and refusing to move. Finally, I wedged open the door with a twig and waited. After what seemed an age, they left their prison and scampered off into the grass and up a tree where they flicked their red bushy tails before disappearing in the branches.

I had just set off back down the track when a loud voice sounded behind me. 'Hey, you there! What do you think you're doing?'

I stopped and turned to see that a figure had come round from the back of the trees. He was a small, sinister-looking man, wiry of frame and with a face as wrinkled and brown as an old russet apple. He was wearing leather gaiters and a green padded waistcoat and carried a shotgun under his arm.

I tried a conciliatory smile but to no effect. 'Good morning,' I croaked somewhat nervously.

He glowered at me in return and raised the shotgun. 'You're trespassing,' he told me in a deadpan voice.

'I'm sorry, I didn't realise,' I replied.

'This is Lord Marrick's estate,' he told me, eyeing the cage I was holding. 'What are you doing?'

'It sounds rather bizarre,' I started.

'Try me.'

'I was releasing some squirrels.'

The man curled a lip and lowered the gun. 'Releasing some squirrels?' he repeated very slowly, as if I had said something highly offensive. 'What do you mean "releasing some squirrels"?'

I attempted to explain. 'I had—er—caught a couple of squirrels and was letting them go.'

'Why did you want to catch them in the first place?' he asked.

It seemed, thank goodness, that he hadn't actually caught sight of my releasing the squirrels with their red tails. I could just imagine the difficulty in explaining that one. 'They decided to make their home in my cottage,' I told him. 'I managed to catch them and was just setting them free.'

'Setting them free?'

'Yes.'

'On Lord Marrick's land?'

'I wasn't aware that it was Lord Marrick's land.' Had I known, I thought, I certainly wouldn't have chosen it as the place to release the squirrels.

'Well, it is.'

'May I ask who you are?' I was becoming rather irritated by this interrogation.

'I'm Lord Marrick's gamekeeper,' he told me, 'and I spend most of my time killing vermin that eat the eggs of his lordship's game birds and seeing off poachers and trespassers.'

'I'm not a poacher!' I exclaimed. 'I wasn't trying to catch animals, just to free them.'

He ignored me and continued. 'So I spend my time killing vermin and you decide to dump it on Lord Marrick's estate.'

'I didn't see it quite like that,' I said lamely, 'but now that you have explained . . .'

The man narrowed his eyes and thrust his chin forward. He turned the shotgun, which was pointing towards the ground, restlessly in his hands. 'You do know that squirrels are vermin, don't you?'

'I've been told as much.'

'And are you aware of the damage they cause?' he asked.

'No, not really,' I replied.

'Well, let me tell you. Young saplings, which we plant in this woodland at great expense, are destroyed by your squirrels. They gnaw through the bark of the hardwood trees, the newly planted beech and sycamores, to get at the sap. They leave a raw scar, which encourages a fungus, which can kill or deform trees. Did you know that?'

'I wasn't aware of that, but—' I started.

'And I don't suppose that you were aware either that it is illegal to either keep or release grey squirrels unless you have a special licence from the Ministry of Agriculture. Have you such a licence?'

'No.' Personally, I thought the man was making a great fuss about something pretty trivial but I kept my thoughts to myself and kept my eyes on his shotgun. 'I'm sorry,' I said. 'I didn't realise.'

The gamekeeper sucked in his bottom lip and scratched his head. 'I'm minded to take you up to Manston Hall with me and get you to explain yourself to his Lordship.'

'I won't do it again.' I sounded like a naughty schoolboy caught in the act by an angry headteacher. The last thing I wanted was to be hauled up in front of Lord Marrick, who just happened to sit on the Education Committee and whom I had worked with on a number of occasions during the past few years.

'Well, make sure you don't. Now, take your bloody cage,' ordered the gamekeeper, 'get off this land and if I see you again, you'll get a backside full of buckshot.'

*   *   *

'You were a long time,' said Christine when I arrived, hot and flustered, back at the car. 'I was beginning to worry. Have you released them?'

'I have,' I said shortly. I was keen to be on our way.

'I think they'll be happy in that little wood, don't you?' she asked.

'Idyllically,' I replied and thinking of what awaited them if they so much as showed a glimpse of their red tails.

CHAPTER TWELVE

'Come along,' said Christine the following day before lunch. 'Get your coat. I'm taking you for a drink.'

'What's brought this on?' I asked. 'I thought you wanted me to dig the allotment this afternoon—'

'I was thinking about what Harry told us yesterday about the changes at the Royal Oak, and I think it's about time we met the new landlord,' she told me. 'He's obviously been treading on a lot of toes in the village with all the changes he's been making since he took over. I've heard other mutterings. I thought we'd pop in and have a look for ourselves.'

'Will your mother keep an eye on Richard?' I asked.

'Yes, and she's also offered to do the vegetables, so we've got an hour before lunch is ready.'

Chris's mother had come over to measure the armchair that she was going to re-cover for us, and now appeared in the kitchen, a tape measure round her neck. 'Go on out, you two. Take the chance while I'm here.'

'But if I have a pint now, I'll be no good for

digging the allotment after lunch.'

'Look,' said Christine, putting her hands on her hips, 'we have precious little time to go out together what with the baby, so when my mother agrees to look after him for an hour, we're going out. No arguments. Now come along, chop, chop.'

'I love it when you play the headteacher,' I said, laughing. 'You're like a dominatrix.'

'If you don't hurry up,' she said, 'I'll get my whip out.'

'OK, but do we have to go to the Royal Oak? You said yourself that it was a run-down, friendless place.'

'Yes, we do,' she said, handing me my jacket. 'I want to meet the new landlord and see what changes he's made. Despite what Harry says, there are some people in the village who will welcome the change. Anyone taking over the Royal Oak would be an improvement on the previous incumbent. That Mr Clarke was such an unpleasant man, running his poor little wife off her feet. It's a wonder people ever went in. Landlords are supposed to be hospitable and friendly, not downright rude. Anyway, it's about time that old pub was brought into the nineteenth century, never mind the twentieth.'

'I like it like that,' I said. 'It's rather quaint.'

'Quaint!' exclaimed Christine. 'Quaint! My understanding of the word "quaint" is "attractively old-fashioned". There is nothing attractive about the Royal Oak. What it needs is pulling down and rebuilding. It is—or, rather, was—smoky, dirty, noisy and uncomfortable. It's a wonder there weren't spittoons on the floor and holes in the ground for the lavatories. The place needed more

198

than a lick of paint, and the changes may not be that bad.'

'That olde-worlde atmosphere is what is so appealing about the place,' I told her. 'It would be a real pity if it has become like the Golden Ball, one of these dreadful modern pubs.'

'Let's just wait and see what has been done to it,' said Christine. 'It can't be worse than the last time we went in when you complained about the state of the bar and how the beer was off and how it took an age to be served. You didn't say it was quaint then, did you?'

'Yes, well, I still wouldn't like to see the old place being altered too much,' I said, wrapping my arms around her waist. 'It's part of the history of the village. It's all about tradition. But I will go out with you, Mrs Phinn, only if you promise to get your whip out later.'

*   *   *

Hawksrill had the two public houses, the Royal Oak and the Golden Ball. When we first came to live in the village, we had enjoyed going to the Golden Ball—or the Lacquered Knacker as locals used to call it. Although it was a more modern building than the Oak, it was a popular place, and we got to know many of the locals there. While we were busy working on getting the cottage habitable, we would often pop in for a pie and a pint of beer. However, when the landlord put in game machines and piped music—to encourage the younger generation, he said—some of the locals had shifted their allegiance to the village's other pub.

In contrast, the Royal Oak hadn't, until now, changed in years. Outside, a dilapidated wooden board, depicting a warlike be-wigged Charles II posing, one hand on his hip and the other holding high a sword, and standing regally beneath a huge oak tree in full leaf, had hung from a gallows-like structure to the front of the inn. Attached to the wall beside the heavy front door, with its flaking paint, had been a large faded wooden sign that read: 'Purveyors of fine ales, liquor and porter since 1714.'

The public bar had been dim and smoky, reeking of beer and tobacco and had been as hot as a sauna. There had been four ancient and sticky-topped trestle-style tables, a selection of rickety hard wooden chairs, a dusty inglenook, and a flagged and heavily-stained floor. The walls had been bare save for a few oddments: a pair of old bellows, a tarnished warming pan, various rusty farm implements including a vicious-looking man-trap, and a couple of antique shotguns. There had been no attempt to provide any kind of physical comfort for the customers. Walkers would enter and ask if food was served, to be told bluntly by the landlord, 'No, and close t'door on yer way out.' The other room, euphemistically called the Lounge, had had a threadbare red-patterned carpet and a further selection of dusty local memorabilia on the walls, a few round plastic-topped tables, a couple of Windsor chairs and an assortment of old armchairs, wing-backed chairs and stools.

The previous landlord, Tobias Clarke, known affectionately as Fat Toby, had bent down to lace up his boots one morning a couple or so months ago and had dropped down dead. He had been a lugubrious-faced individual of immense girth, a great barrel of a man with shoulders as broad as a barn door. He had been a man of few words and little humour and had liked nothing better than to sit in a high-backed grandfather chair at the side of the open fire in the public bar while his long-suffering wife served behind the bar. Mrs Clarke was a small, slight woman; she was never seen wearing anything other than black and as she scuttled about the inn she reminded me of an industrious little beetle. Her hair, silver-white and parted in the middle, was scraped back across her head and into a tight little bunch. Christine and I, on the few occasions that we had visited the pub, often wondered why she put up with such a lazy and disagreeable husband, whose face and manner clearly demonstrated his will to dominate the poor woman. When the pub had more than the usual handful of customers, he would rise slowly from his throne to assist her but he had never been in any rush. He would take an inordinate amount of time to serve you. On one occasion when I asked if he had forgotten about my order, he had sniffed noisily, closed his eyes for a moment and then enquired tetchily, 'Is there a fire?'

After his death, Mrs Clarke had promptly bought herself a new coat as red as a pillar box, had had her hair permed a pale purple and had put up the Royal Oak for sale. The pub had realised a surprisingly large sum of money; as Harry Cotton observed lugubriously, 'Ma Clarke were fair bow-legged wi' brass', and it was no surprise when she had booked herself onto a luxury P&O cruise to the Caribbean on the *Oriana*. Mrs Poskitt received

201

a postcard from the Bahamas from 'the Merry Widow', informing her that she had met a very nice elderly gentleman and was having a wonderful time. And that was the last we heard of her. The postcard showed a transformed Mrs Clarke with her ageing paramour, posing next to Captain Hamish Reid like a dowager duchess.

Much to the concern of the locals, things had soon started to change. The new landlord of the Royal Oak was 'nobbut better than t'landlord of t'Knacker' grumbled Harry Cotton. 'Dunt know what t'word "tradition" means.' On Thursday and Friday nights, it was the custom for Harry and three other worthies of the village to arrive at the Royal Oak and take their places at the corner table to play dominoes. The foursome comprised Harry, George Hemmings, Thomas Umpleby and Hezekiah Longton. Harry, George and Thomas were peas out of the same pod: all three had full heads of silver hair, thick bristling eyebrows, wide, weather-beaten faces and small shrewd eyes nestling in nests of wrinkles. They could have been brothers.

Mr Longton was very different. He was a tall, lean individual who, despite his advancing age, walked with a straight back and without the aid of a stick. He was one of those men whom it is difficult to imagine had ever been young, and yet, when this quietly-spoken man did venture an opinion, which was rare, it was clear to all that he had a lively, intelligent mind and a good command of the English language. Whereas Harry, Thomas and George would appear at the pub in their old working clothes, Mr Longton always made an effort to look smart. He was never seen in the village without a clean white collar and tie, a waistcoat (usually mustard in colour) with a heavy silver fob dangling across his chest, a finely-cut tweed jacket, green cord trousers and highly-polished brown boots. He looked incongruous amongst the company he kept, but he had never been known to miss his dominoes nights at the pub.

On Thursday and Friday evenings, the 'gang of four' would ensconce themselves in their corner at the Royal Oak, discuss the day's events and share an anecdote or two before settling down to their game, which they played in complete silence. When the serious business of the dominoes was over and tankards were filled with frothing ale, Harry would light his old black briar pipe and fill the room with evil-smelling smoke. Sometimes Thomas Umpleby could be persuaded to recite a poem. His *pièce de résistance* was 'The Wensley Lass', a wonderfully expressive dialect poem, which he would declaim loudly and passionately, hand on heart, in his rough, rich, racy native idiom.

I had heard this verse a number of times but always loved to hear the deep resonant voice bringing the Yorkshire dialect to life.

> Thou 'as nae need to worry, lass,
> There'll nivver be another fer me.
> Sin' time began, there's ne'er been man
> Who cud luv as I luv thee.
> As long as t'River Yore it flows
> Atween 'igh Wensley 'ills,
> An' bonny becks sing leetsomly
> Ower steeans in Wensley gills,
> So I will luv thee 'til I dee

An' from thee nivver part,
Fer thy are the bonny Wensley lass
Who stole away my 'eart.

I had first heard him recite the poem one evening the previous autumn, soon after the locals had migrated here from the Golden Ball. We had called in at the pub just before what we thought would be closing time and an hour later we were still there sitting on the hard chairs listening to Thomas Umpleby's recitations. I had told him how much I had enjoyed his verses and the following morning the man himself had arrived at my door with a copy of his poem dedicated 'For t'newlyweds—a long life and 'appiness'. It was neatly written in a large copperplate hand.

Harry later told me how Thomas had become quite a celebrity a few years before. A lecturer from Leeds University, together with a Norwegian academic who was undertaking research into the decline in European dialects, had called in for a drink at the Royal Oak as they were passing through the village. They were in search of authentic Yorkshire dialects and their attention was soon caught when they heard the elderly men at the corner table conversing in their thick regional accents. But when Thomas Umpleby, who rarely ventured out of the dale and spoke as his forefathers had spoken, opened his mouth, the two academics thought they had struck gold and quickly reached for their notebooks. Old Thomas's conversation, peppered with unusual and archaic words and phrases and delivered in an almost incomprehensible accent, completely flummoxed them. Finally, he had enquired of the two men, 'So weersa banner lig?'

'I beg your pardon?' the lecturer from Leeds University had asked, perplexed.

'I sais, weersa banner lig?'

The Norwegian had replied, 'We are staying at the Marrick Arms.'

His colleague had been astounded. 'How on earth did you understand what he was saying?' he had asked.

'He's a Viking,' the Norwegian had replied, 'and is speaking Old Norse. "Weersa banner lig?"— Where do you lay down your head?'

The university lecturer had tried to persuade Thomas to visit Leeds and be a case study in his research but Thomas had shaken his old head. 'Nay, nay, lad,' he had sighed. 'I'm too owld to gu gallivantin' to t'city. I'm champion as I am.'

When we arrived at the pub that Sunday morning we were expecting change but, even so, were surprised by the extent of it.

'I see that the Merry Monarch has been given his marching orders,' I said, looking up. The old inn sign had gone and in its place hung a brightly painted board with the outline of an oak tree and the lettering 'THE OAK'.

We put our heads into the lounge bar. The old armchairs had been replaced with banquettes and shiny tables. The tarnished horse brasses and dusty hunting horns, framed sepia photographs and faded paintings of rural scenes had disappeared; the walls had been painted white and were bare save for two minimalist paintings. There were only a few people in there, none of whom we knew, so we came out and went into the public bar.

Gone was the old stone-flagged floor; instead

205

there were polished anaemic-looking floorboards. The ancient and sticky-topped trestles and hard wooden chairs had been replaced by high round tubular steel stools and matching tables. In the fireplace, where there used to be a blazing log fire, blackened copper kettles and pans, a large wicker basket full of logs and a huge brass fireguard, there was now a modern electric unit with flickering false coal. Perched on the stools like strange and shabby birds sat three of the regulars looking far from happy. Mr Longton stood, rather self-consciously, holding his pint tankard.

'Hey up,' said Harry as we entered. 'It's t'schoil hinspector.'

'Hello,' I said cheerfully.

'Don't offen see thee in 'ere,' said George Hemmings and then, raising his hand in greeting, said, 'Mornin', Missis Phinn, looking as lovely as ever, I see.'

'Good morning,' replied Christine, giving him one of her stunning smiles.

'We've just called in to meet the new landlord,' I told the assembled company.

There were assorted snorts and sighs. 'Aye sithee, tha mun see him reight enough if thy 'as a mind,' said Thomas Umpleby, picking up his pint glass and grimacing.

'I was wantin' to speak to you, Mester Phinn,' said George Hemmings, 'about that allotment of yourn. It wants fettlin'.'

'Yes, I know,' I said wearily. 'Harry mentioned it. I've been rather busy lately and haven't had a moment to get down.'

'Way I see it,' said George, sucking in his lips, 'is them what takes on an allotment have to look after

206

it. It's all abaat 'ard work and commitment.'

'Tha right there,' agreed Harry.

I began to wish that we had never set foot in the pub. 'I thought I might ask your Andy to tidy it up a bit,' I said to Harry.

'He did a grand job at the cottage yesterday,' added Christine. 'He's a really hard worker.'

'He's a good lad, our Andrew,' said Harry. 'Not at front of queue when t'brains were given out, but not a bad worker.'

'I thowt thy young un were doin' summat wi' beasts,' said Thomas Umpleby.

'Aye, that's what 'e's gor 'is 'eart set on, workin' wi' sheep. Wants to gu to t'college in York next year and leaarn all about 'em. I towld 'im, 'e could leaarn them a thing or two.'

'I dunt 'ave no truck wi' eddication and book leaarnin' and t'like,' observed Thomas. 'Gives people ideas. Havin' prefixes after yer name dunt mean owt to me. All them fancy words an' such. I dooant knaa who said it but a cauliflower is nowt but a cabbage wi' a college education. An' as my owld mother used to say, "A 'andful of good life is better than a bushel o' leaarnin'." Experience is t'best teacher in my book. Now you tek 'Ezekiah 'ere.' Mr Longton smiled. 'It's not as if 'e needed any books and college diplomas an' susstificates to become best gardener in Yorkshire. In't that reight, 'Ezekiah? I'll tell thee what, Mester Phinn, tha wants to let 'im 'ave a look at thy hallotment and tell thee what to plant.'

'I'd be more than happy,' said Hezekiah. 'More than happy.'

'That's very kind of you, Mr Longton,' I said. 'I might very well take you up on that.' I was keen to move the conversation on from the discussion about my neglected allotment so, looking around me, commented, 'It certainly looks a great deal brighter in here.'

'Oh aye,' said Harry, 'it does that an' I'll tell thee summat else an' all, some of us dunt like it.'

'Nay,' agreed George, and shifted uncomfortably on the high stool. 'I gets vertigo up 'ere.'

'I 'ates and habbominates it,' growled Thomas Umpleby.

'Is somebody serving?' asked Christine, looking towards the empty bar.

'You 'ave to tinkle that little brass bell on t'bar to get attention now,' Harry scoffed. 'New chap'll be chattin' up customers in t'lounge, few that are theer.'

'Fancy London ways,' growled Thomas. 'Bloody bells now, what next?'

I rang the bell and a fresh-faced young man with a ready smile emerged from the back. His black brilliantined hair was slicked back from the forehead in one smooth wave, and he wore a brightly coloured open-necked shirt and sported a gold chain and a heavy gold ring.

'Good morning,' I said. 'A pint of your best bitter, please, and a glass of red wine.'

'Would you care to go into the lounge, sir?' He glanced in the direction of the four men in the corner. 'It's a bit more comfortable in there.'

'No, we're fine here,' I said. I was about to add that the public bar had more atmosphere but thought better of it.

'We have a selection of fine wines,' he told me. 'There's a particularly good Rioja, a couple of nice

French wines—a Fitou Reserve and a Rhône from a small vineyard—and, if you like Italian wine, a *gallo nero* Chianti.'

A selection of disapproving noises emanated from the stools.

'The house red will be fine,' said Christine.

The landlord began to pull the pint. 'Just passing through, are you?' he asked.

'That's what Winston Churchill asked this fancy American general during t'last war,' announced Harry in a loud voice. 'This Yank said to Winnie that in 'is opinion Britain was the asshole of Europe. "Just passing through?" asked Churchill.' This was followed by raucous laughter.

The landlord look extremely embarrassed. 'I'm sorry about that.'

'We're used to it,' I told him. 'We live here. We're locals.'

'In Peewit Cottage,' added Christine.

The young man stretched a hand across the bar, took hers and smiled. 'Ah, yes, the wife of the school inspector. I'm very pleased to meet you. I'm David Fidler, the new landlord. I do hope I'll be seeing a great deal more of you.'

'Oh, they dunt come in 'ere much,' said Harry, quite happy to involve himself in another's conversation. 'Yon Mester Phinn is far too busy inspectin' schools an' tryin' to close 'em down.'

'I was going to buy you a pint, Harry,' I said, 'but I've thought better of it now.'

'Gerron,' he said, 'I'm only pulling thee leg. We'll join thee in a drink, won't we, lads? Mi throat's as dry as a lime-burner's clog. Mild for me, please.'

'Very kind of you,' said Thomas Umpleby,

209

draining his pint glass.

'Don't mind if I do,' said George Hemmings, doing the same.

'And what about you, Mr Longton?' I asked.

'Thank you kindly,' said Hezekiah, raising his tankard.

'Four pints for the regulars, please,' I said.

'You've certainly made a big difference,' Christine told the landlord as he began to pull the pints.

He lowered his voice. 'Well, I have tried to brighten up the place to attract more customers. Modernise it. It was like going back hundreds of years when I first walked in. But as soon as I saw the place, I immediately saw the potential. As you know, the other pub in the village, the Golden Ball, is a bit of a dive. I think I can really make a go of this. With professional people like yourselves coming to live here and passing trade, it could be very good. I want to attract a better class of customer and eventually offer high-quality food—a fashionable new menu featuring home-cooked dishes. I was manager of a pub in Chiswick in London, which was very successful.'

'This is hardly Chiswick,' observed Christine.

'Oh, I know that,' said the landlord. He leaned over the bar. 'Quite frankly, I want to attract a rather better clientele. I have big plans for The Oak.'

'Well, I wish you luck,' I said, thinking that he would certainly need it. I carried the drinks over to the regulars, and the landlord returned to the lounge bar.

Thomas Umpleby raised his pint. ' 'Ere's to us, all on us, an' me an' all. May we nivver want nowt, none of us, nor me neither. Good 'ealth, Mester Phinn.'

' 'As tha sooarted out them squirrels yet, then?' Harry asked me.

'Yes, all sorted out,' I said.

'Tha got rid on 'em, then?'

'Yes, I got rid of them.'

'What's this about squirrels?' asked George.

' 'E's 'ad an hinfestation,' Harry told him.

'Two actually,' I said, 'but they've gone.'

'That's what thy thinks,' chuckled Harry. 'They'll be back. Mark my words.' Ever the prophet of doom, I thought.

'We used to eat squirrels, tha knaas,' said George.

'Eat them?' I exclaimed.

'I'm telling thee, my owld mam used to cook 'em,' said George. 'An' they were very tasty, an' all. My owld mam used to mek one o' them stews wi' taties an' carrots and onions. Tasted a bit like rabbit.'

'I like rabbit,' said Christine, 'but I don't think I could bring myself to eat squirrel and certainly not cook it.'

'Sometimes it were t'only thing what there were to eat,' said George. 'When I were a lad, times was 'ard. Many's t'time we 'ad to mek do wi' bread an' jam an' what we could scavenge from fields an' hedgerows. It were quite a treat to 'ave squirrel 'ot-pot.' He took a gulp of beer. 'Aye, times were 'ard, all reight, but we was 'appy.'

'More than can be said for us now,' grumbled Harry.

'Tha reight theer,' agreed George.

'Aye,' sighed Harry sadly.

211

'Come on, you two misery-guts, stop yer moanin' and a-groanin',' said Thomas. 'Tha two are abaat as 'appy as a pair o' funeral bells.'

'What about a poem, Mr Umpleby,' I said.

'Nay, I'm not reight in t'mood for poetry today, if truth be towld,' he replied.

'Oh, please,' pleaded Christine.

'Gu on then,' he said, taking very little persuading. 'Just for thee, Missis Phinn, but only one mind, I'm not doin' no epics today. I'll give thee "The Laugh of a Child". Mi sainted mother, God rest her soul, used to recite this. It were one of 'er favourites. She did a sampler of it when she were a little 'un. Beautiful it is. I 'ave it on mi wall.'

The old man stood and, with one arm outstretched, he declaimed his poem in a voice as bracing as a Yorkshire moor, and as clear and sparkling as the singing becks.

> Luv it! Luv it! 'Tis the laugh of a child,
> Now ripplin', now gentle, now merry and wild.
> It rings in t'air with t'innocent cush
> Like t'trill of yon bird at t'twilight's soft 'ush.
> It floats on yon breeze like t'toll of a bell,
> Or t'music which dwells in t'heart of a shell.
> 'Tis best music of all, so wild and so free
> 'Tis merriest sound in t'whole world to me!

We all applauded vigorously, and would have stamped our feet on the ground had we been able to reach the floor but the stools were too high; instead, we banged our glasses on the table.

The young landlord appeared at the bar. 'Could you keep the noise down in here, please?' he asked. 'You're disturbing the other customers in the lounge. And,' he added, 'all breakages will have to be paid for.'

*   *   *

'You know, I do feel sorry for Harry and his pals,' said Christine later when we were back at the cottage. She took a steaming casserole out of the oven and placed it on the table.

'That smells good,' I said, creeping up behind her and kissing her on the neck.

'They were so out of place sitting on those horrible modern stools. They looked like parrots on a perch. And there was certainly no need for the landlord to say what he did.'

'You're the best cook in Yorkshire, Mrs Phinn, do you know that?' I said, lifting the lid of the large metal dish and sniffing the contents. 'Mmmmm.'

'They looked quite pathetic. Like fish out of water. And you should have seen poor Mr Umpleby's face when he was told to be quiet.'

'I thought they were parrots on a perch?'

'You know what I mean. It's such a pity,' she said. 'That traditional eighteenth-century inn with its timber frames, oak beams and horse brasses.'

'You've changed your tune,' I said. 'You were all for change before we went out.'

'That was before I saw the changes,' she said. 'The place now looks so pseudo. It's lost all its character.'

'There's always the Golden Ball,' I said. 'They could go back there.'

'That's worse.'

'They'll get used to the changes,' I said dismissively. 'Now, can we eat? I'm starving.'

213

'I don't think they will ever get used to the changes,' Christine replied. 'And, yes, we are ready to eat. Will you call to Mum? She'll be upstairs putting Richard down for his sleep.'

I shouted up the stairs, then turned back to Christine. 'Now the landlord at the Royal Oak—'

'The Oak, you mean.'

'The Oak, then. You have to admit that he's a vast improvement on the last miserable specimen.'

'Now who's changed his tune?'

'And he is making a bit of an effort to brighten up the place.'

'Well, I didn't like him—or his decor,' said Christine.

'At least he smiled,' I said, 'and we didn't have to wait an age for the drinks.'

'Well, I didn't like him,' she repeated. 'He had clammy hands.'

'Look, Christine, I'm starving,' I said. 'Can we eat?'

Christine's mother appeared in the kitchen. 'Hello, Mum, all well?' she said.

As she ladled out the steaming casserole, I said grace in the style of Thomas Umpleby, a true Yorkshire grace: 'God bless us all and mek us able, to eayt all t'stuff 'at's on this table.' Then I asked, 'What are we eating by the way? It smells delicious.'

'I'm trying out an old Yorkshire recipe,' she told me, her eyes full of mischief. 'Very traditional. It's called *écureuil bourguignonne*.'

'And what's that when it's at home?' I asked.

'Squirrel hot-pot!' she replied.

214

CHAPTER THIRTEEN

The Reverend Percival Featherstone, Chairman of the Governing Body at St Margaret's Church of England Primary School, was a stern-looking cleric with a sizeable hawkish nose, grey strands of hair combed across an otherwise bald head, and heavy-lidded eyes. His large eyebrows met above his nose giving one the impression that he was permanently scowling. Because he wore thin, gold-framed spectacles and sported great bushy grey sideburns, he looked every inch the Victorian parson. I could visualise this grimly-serious figure walking the streets of Barchester for he looked as if he had stepped out of the pages of Trollope's most celebrated novel.

I had inspected St Margaret's at the end of the previous term and had promised to make a return visit to the school—an austere Victorian grey stone building adjacent to the church in the village of Hutton-with-Branston—at the beginning of the new academic year to go through my conclusions and recommendations. Prompted by the situation that had arisen at Ugglemattersby Junior School, I had quickly arranged a visit.

Fortunately for me, and in a quite unexpected way, things seemed to have sorted themselves out with regard to Ugglemattersby. The first meeting with the headteacher, Mrs Braddock-Smith, and the governors of the Infant School, where I had outlined the suggestions for the amalgamation, had gone amazingly smoothly and everyone present had been strongly in favour of the recommendation.

The meeting with the headteacher, Mr Harrison, and governors of the Juniors, had been less good humoured but, again, it appeared that my lucky star was shining brightly for the predicted 'fly in the ointment', Councillor Sidebottom, was 'down with the flu' and couldn't attend the meeting. All in all, things seemed to be working out fairly well.

St Margaret's had an excellent reputation for creative arts and Mrs Kipling, the headteacher, a small wiry-haired woman with smiling eyes, was a regular delegate on Sidney's art courses. In fact, it was rumoured that she had quite a crush on him.

During the summer inspection, I had been given pride of place in the front row to watch the end-of-term musical concert. The choir had sung confidently and with genuine enthusiasm, the small brass band had played with gusto, and the twin girls playing the piano duet had been most impressive. But the star of the show had been a boy of eleven who had delighted the audience with a selection of violin solos. When he had finished, the applause had been loud and enthusiastic and the boy, with a massive grin on his face, had taken a very low and prolonged bow.

After the concert, I had gone backstage to congratulate the young performers.

'You were excellent,' I had told the budding Paganini.

'Oh, thanks, sir,' the boy had replied. 'I was really, really nervous with all those people out there and my violin teacher as well. When miss said we'd got a school inspector in the front row, I thought I'd be sure to fluff it.'

'Well, your nerves didn't show,' I had told him.

216

'And I was impressed with that very professional bow at the end. You looked like a seasoned performer.'

'Oh, the bow,' the boy had said. 'The reason I bent so low was to check the front of my trousers to see if I'd wet myself.'

After my inspection the previous term, I had written a very positive report but I guessed that the chairman of governors, the fearsome-looking Mr Featherstone, would have something to say on this Tuesday afternoon. I had spent a couple of hours in the classrooms, and was now sitting in the headteacher's study, together with the clergyman in question. His thin white hands were clasped before him and dark eyes stared pointedly at me, nodding slowly and solemnly as I talked through my report and my findings. He looked dramatically tight-lipped and thoughtful. The headteacher, sitting next to him, awaited his response.

The cleric took a deep and audible breath and rubbed his long nose. 'So,' he said finally, 'things seem to be very much in order then, Mr Phinn.' He didn't look all that pleased, I thought.

'Yes, indeed,' I replied chirpily. 'In fact, Mrs Kipling and her staff should be commended for all their hard work and dedication. This is a very good school with many outstanding features. The children work hard, achieve good results and their behaviour appears to be good. As you have heard, there are only a few minor issues to be addressed.'

'Very gratifying, I'm sure,' said the chairman of governors sonorously, again stroking his nose. He thought for a moment before continuing. 'I have to say that I had little doubt that the school would receive a praiseworthy report but it is good to have

217

one's observations reinforced. I was particularly pleased to hear that the children's religious education was satisfactory.' There was another long pause. 'I think I mentioned to you at our last meeting, Mr Phinn,' he continued, 'that I am deeply saddened by the children's lack of biblical knowledge generally.'

'Yes,' I replied, 'and I think I said that this is certainly the case in many schools I visit, although I have to say that the pupils here do seem to have a better knowledge than most. Children do not, as a rule, know as much about the Bible as they used to do.'

The vicar took a deep breath and stared heavenwards. 'Very regrettable,' he sighed. 'I think this school endeavours to create the Christian ethos while considering other people's beliefs, as indeed it should do. But you know, it is all very well children learning about other religions, cultures and ways of life, but we are living in a Christian country and I think first and foremost they should have a good grounding in Holy Scripture and a sound knowledge of Jesus. It is so important that children know about Him and His works. Archdeacon Richards was only telling me last week that he was addressing an assembly at a school in Fettlesham last Easter and was telling the children that Jesus had risen from the dead and had returned to see His disciples. He asked the children if they knew what words Jesus had spoken when He walked through the door to face His apostles. One child apparently stood up, threw out his arms like a magician and shouted, "Ta-da!"'

'Oh dear,' I said, biting my lip to hide a smile.

'Archdeacon Richards also told me about the

time,' continued the cleric, 'he was telling the children the parable of the Feeding of the Five Thousand. He asked the children what important lesson Jesus had taught to the multitude. He was saddened, as I frequently am, by the one answer he received: "Remember to take your litter home with you."'

I could have added to the cleric's stories. I was once addressing an assembly at a school in Bartondale and asked the children who the Good Shepherd was. One bright spark had waved his hand in the air. 'I know! I know!' he'd cried. 'It's Jack Farrell. Mi dad reckons 'e's not lost a sheep in fotty years.' In another school, the student teacher had asked if the children could remember the name of the famous King of Babylon mentioned in the Bible whom they'd been reading about the previous week. She persevered for a time, trying to elicit the answer, until one boy told her wearily, 'Miss, nae bugger can tell ya.' 'Very good,' she replied, 'well tried, but try to remember that the name is pronounced Nebuchadnezzar.'

'It's all very regrettable,' continued Mr Featherstone now, 'and so very depressing.' It was obvious he was getting well and truly into his stride. 'I am afraid we live in a secular and affluent society, Mr Phinn, in a world of what I consider quite unsuitable television programmes, loud music, convenience foods and expensive holidays. I may sound a little old-fashioned, but I do sometimes despair at the way things are going.'

'Times do change,' I murmured.

'*Omnia mutantur nos et mutamur in illis,*' he intoned.

'I'm sorry?' said Mrs Kipling.

219

'All things change and we change with them,' I said.

'I am glad you know a little Latin, Mr Phinn,' said the vicar. 'That is another of my regrets—the decline in the teaching of the classics in schools.'

'I recall that we had a conversation about christenings the last time we met, Mr Featherstone,' I reminded the cleric. 'About all the unusual names that parents give their children.'

'Indeed,' he said stroking his long nose again. 'So many children these days are named after pop stars, footballers and television personalities. It's the cult of the celebrity. The old biblical names seem to be fast disappearing—Samuel and Simon, Mary and Michael, Joseph and James are now replaced by Dean and Darren, Carlie and Crystal, Shane and Sharlene. And some parents give little thought to the fact that their children, when they arrive at school, have to cope with some quite bizarre names. I've even had a request to christen a child Kipper! Kipper, I ask you? I really think it very unkind to saddle a child with such an unusual name.'

'I have come across some very unusual names, too,' I said. 'I've met children called Walter Wall, Duncan Biscuit, Teresa Green, Brent Willey, Rose Bush, and one child with the surname Pipe who was burdened with a first name of Duane.'

'Dear me,' sighed the clergyman. 'Do you recall, Mrs Kipling, when we had the Smout children here?'

'I do,' replied the headteacher. 'There was Paris Smout, Vienna Smout, Seville Smout. It is just as well the parents didn't go on a City Break to Brussels.' She chortled gently.

'Indeed,' sighed Mr Featherstone, without the trace of a smile.

'I have a pet theory about first names,' said Mrs Kipling. 'Over the many years I have been in education, I have come to the conclusion that Shakespeare got it wrong when he said that "a rose by any other name would smell as sweet". I learned very early on that boys called Richard tend to be well behaved, quiet children who work hard, Matthews are very polite and thoughtful, Dominics are little charmers, Damiens have far too much to say for themselves and Kevins are accident-prone. Penelopes tend to be lively and interested, Traceys too big for their boots and Elizabeths little darlings.'

'And what about me?' I asked. 'What are little boys like with a name such as mine?'

Mr Featherstone looked in my direction. 'I don't think I know your Christian name, Mr Phinn,' he said.

'Gervase,' I told him, smiling.

'Really?' he murmured. 'How very droll.'

When the vicar had departed, I went through the school report in greater detail with the headteacher.

'Your chairman of governors does have a bit of a bee in his bonnet about the lack of religion in people's lives and the decline in the teaching of scripture in schools,' I observed. 'I guess he can be rather difficult at times.'

'He's actually a very caring and committed priest,' said Mrs Kipling, springing to the cleric's defence. 'He spends a deal of time in the school, and he encourages the children to visit the church. He might look a little severe, Mr Phinn, but appearances can be deceptive. Remember the parable of the Good Samaritan? Underneath that rather hard shell, Mr Featherstone is a very kindly man and has been most supportive of me personally. You might be surprised to hear that his church is full on Sundays and people come a fair distance to hear him preach.'

'Really?' I said with some amazement.

'We had a wonderful Harvest Festival at St Margaret's church the Sunday before last, and every elderly person in the village received a hamper of food delivered by the children and then a visit from Mr Featherstone. He also raises a great deal of money for the Children's Society. When I started as headteacher here, I took the children over to the church. The little ones, much to the teachers' embarrassment, were rather boisterous and noisy and we were about to take them out when Mr Featherstone stopped us. I was quite taken with what he said. "Please don't worry about a bit of noise," he told me. "To me, there is nothing like the sound of little children's voices." Yes,' she concluded, 'I consider myself very fortunate to have someone so actively interested in the life and work of the school.'

'Well, I'm very pleased to hear it, Mrs Kipling,' I said. 'To be honest, I would never have guessed, from listening to him, that your chairman of governors was so supportive and positive. He seems somewhat dour to me.'

'He's a most thoughtful and gentle-natured man, is Mr Featherstone,' she said, 'a man of high principles and uncompromising views. He's also chairman of governors at St Cuthbert's High School, you know, and last summer was asked by the headmaster to act as Solomon in the case of the cricket nets.'

'That sounds intriguing,' I said.

'Three girls in the sixth form,' continued Mrs Kipling, 'were up before the headmaster for vandalism. They had taken a pair of scissors and had cut holes in the new and expensive cricket nets. The headmaster, a passionate cricketer himself, was not well pleased, as you might imagine, discovering his precious nets wilfully damaged. Mr Featherstone was asked to arbitrate, and he took the side of the students.'

'If you were to ask me, it seems a pretty open and shut case,' I told Mrs Kipling. 'There seems to be no excuse for hacking holes in brand new cricket nets.'

'Well, it's not as simple as that,' the headteacher told me, a small smile playing on her lips. 'You see, the girls who were on their way across the school fields and were passing the cricket square came on a squirrel entangled in the nets.'

'A squirrel?' I mouthed. When, I thought to myself, will I be free from mention of the pesky little tree rats?

'It was trying desperately to extricate itself, poor, exhausted creature, but with no success and the more it tried to untangle itself, the more it became enmeshed. So the girls cut away the netting and freed it.'

'They freed it?' I repeated.

'Mr Featherstone was very impressed with their actions and reminded us of the hymn "All things bright and beautiful, all creatures great and small" etc. He considered it to be a very noble act.' Mrs Kipling paused. 'I mean, Mr Phinn, who would want to see a little squirrel harmed?'

'Who indeed,' I murmured.

*   *   *

The Staff Development Centre looked particularly clean and bright when I arrived there later that afternoon to prepare for a course I was to direct the following day. Since I had last been in the Centre, everything—the walls, ceiling, window frames, shelving and cupboards—had been painted a startling white, which gave the building the appearance of a hospital. It had a most unfriendly atmosphere. As I headed for the kitchen area to make my presence known to Connie, I passed a veritable gallery of new and very conspicuous signs, written in large red lettering: STRICTLY NO SMOKING! THIS DOOR MUST NOT BE USED AS AN ENTRANCE OR AN EXIT. DO NOT BLOCK THE FIRE DOORS. RETURN ALL CROCKERY TO THE KITCHEN AFTER USE. NO FOOD TO BE CONSUMED IN THE MEETING ROOMS.

Calling in at the Gents, I found another selection of strident instructions: NOW WASH YOUR HANDS! DO NOT DEPOSIT FOREIGN BODIES DOWN THE TOILET! TURN OFF TAPS AFTER USE! And on each of the toilet doors the somewhat ambiguous injunction: IN CASE OF FIRE EVACUATE IMMEDIATELY!

I found Connie, in her regulation pink overall, up her stepladder scraping paint off a window with a vicious-looking kitchen knife. Her face, beneath an ocean of copper-coloured curls, was red with exertion. 'If you want a cup of anything, you'll have to get it yourself,' she told me bluntly. 'I'm busy.'

'So I see,' I said.

'I spent all day Monday on my hands and knees and I'm still not finished. The mess those decorators have left behind!' she complained, attacking a particularly stubborn bit of paint. 'More like defecators than decorators. They were worse than Mr Clamp on a bad day, and that's saying something. Only lads by the look of them, and I reckon the last time they had a paintbrush in their hands they were in the infant school. I had to tell them to do my pelmets again and touch up the skirting boards. There's paint everywhere. More on the floor than on the walls.'

'Well, the Centre looks a lot better,' I said.

Connie stopped scraping, swivelled round and peered down at me. 'Does it?' she snapped.

'Well, it's cleaner and brighter for one thing.'

'Mr Phinn,' she said looking down from the stepladder and wielding the knife like Lady Macbeth on the battlements of Glamis Castle, 'what are you incinerating? I'll have you know, this Centre is *always* clean and bright. I makes sure of that. You'll have all on to find so much as a speck of dust, a marked wall or a scuffed floor in the building.'

'Of course,' I said quickly. 'I didn't mean it was dirty or anything like that. You always keep the Centre pristine.'

'Prissy-what?'

'Spotless, in an excellent state of cleanliness and care.'

'Well, what did you mean then when you said it looked a lot better?' she asked sharply, in no way mollified.

'I meant it looks . . .' I struggled for the right

word. 'It looks . . . whiter.'

'Whiter?' she repeated.

'The paint. It makes it look whiter.'

'Well, of course it does,' she said. 'It's white paint they've used. I must say for the inspector in charge of English you do say some funny things.'

I left her at her labours, made myself a cup of coffee and headed for the meeting room to prepare my course. It wasn't long before Connie joined me.

'How many are coming on your course?' she asked. 'It's just that I have to know the numbers for the refreshments.'

'About twenty,' I told her.

'Is that all?'

'Yes, that's all.'

'I don't know how that Mr Clamp does it,' she told me. 'They queue up to get on *his* courses. I wouldn't give them the time of day myself but they're always full to bursting. Same with Dr Mullarkey. She never has less than thirty coming on hers and they always go away saying how wonderful they are.'

'Thank you, Connie,' I said. 'That makes me feel a whole lot better.'

'Anyway, I can't tell you how glad I was to see the back of the decorators.'

'Yes, I bet you were pleased,' I said.

'Pleased?' she cried. 'Pleased? I was ecstatical. You would never believe the carry-on we had here last week. It was enough to drive a person to drink. Fire alarm going off, fire brigade, ambulance, paramedics, hospitalisation—you name it, we've had it.'

'Why? What happened?' I should never have

asked.

Connie perched on the side of a desk. 'One of the decorators, a young lad, not started shaving yet by the look of him and with more silver rings through his ears than they have in a jeweller's shop and a head as bald as a coot, ended up in Casualty.'

'His name wasn't Kevin, by any chance?' I asked, thinking of Mrs Kipling's assertions about names that I had heard earlier that day.

'I think it was, as a matter of fact,' said Connie. 'Why, do you know him?'

'No, it was just a wild guess.'

'Well, this Kevin ended up in hospital with a broken leg,' Connie told me.

'Ladders can be dangerous,' I said. 'I nearly fell off a ladder last week trying to mend the guttering on our cottage. I brought the whole lot down and nearly ended up flat on my back. And *you* want to be careful, Connie, up that stepladder of yours.'

'Oh, he didn't fall off a ladder,' said Connie. 'He was sitting on the toilet.'

'How on earth do you break a leg sitting on the toilet?' I asked, intrigued.

'I'll tell you, if you let me finish,' she said. 'His mate, Shane I think they called him, legarthic individual with more hair than a sheepdog, had just finished painting the toilet doors in the Gents and before he sets off home he goes and puts his brushes in a jar of turpentine substitute to stop them getting hard. Anyway, next morning the silly lad pours the contents of the jar down the toilet bowl but doesn't think to flush the toilet. Fancy putting inflammatory material down the toilet. Then this Shane goes off to paint the doors in the Ladies. In goes this Kevin into the Gents—he was

227

another gormless piece of work—and he sits on the toilet and lights up a cigarette.'

'Oh, no,' I said. I could predict what was to follow.

'I told them when they started it was a no-smoking environment but they just don't listen, youngsters, these days, do they? Just do as they want. He thought he'd have a surreptitious smoke, didn't he? Well, he's learnt his lesson good and proper this time, I can tell you. It's not the best way of giving up smoking but I bet it will be a while before he has another cigarette after that fandango.'

'So what happened?' I asked, as if I didn't know.

'When he'd finished his cigarette, what does he do?'

'Puts it down the toilet bowl?' I suggested, with a strangled expression.

'Yes,' said Connie, 'he puts the lighted tab-end down the toilet and he does it while he's still sitting there.'

'Oh no!'

'Oh yes. There was this great big flash and the next thing you know he's emerging from the Gents, screaming and shouting, his overalls around his ankles and jumping down the corridor like a kangaroo with rabies. Fortunately for him, I've been on a first-aid course and did what I could. I can tell you it was very embarrassing for yours truly, not to mention the lad himself, with me having to put all my clean dishcloths and tea-towels on that particular part of his anatomy.'

'But how did he break his leg?' I asked.

'I'm coming to that,' said Connie. 'I called the ambulance and it was here in quick time and the

228

lad was carted off, moaning and groaning, wriggling and writhing, to the Royal Infirmary. "So how did it happen?" asks one of the ambulance men as they were carrying the injured party down the steps at the front of the Centre. Well, when I told him he began to laugh and this started the other ambulance man off laughing and they laughed so much that they dropped the stretcher and this Kevin broke a leg.'

'You are joking,' I said.

'As God is my judge. They just creased up and the lad was tipped off of the stretcher, rolled down the steps and he broke a leg.'

'It's like a Whitehall farce,' I said. 'And how is the lad?'

'Oh, he's getting on all right,' Connie told me. 'I phoned the hospital this morning and he's on the mend.' Connie stood and brushed the creases out of her overall. 'Mind you,' she said, 'there was one good thing about it all.'

'What's that?' I asked.

'He'd finished painting the Centre before he had the accident.'

CHAPTER FOURTEEN

The first school visits of the following week were to the primary school at Foxton in the morning and then to Hawthwaite Infant School in the afternoon. In the first school, I was due to observe the lessons of a young probationary teacher, and in the second a teacher who was only in his second year of teaching. It was one of the inspectors' responsibilities to assess the competency of those new to the profession by observing their lessons three or four times over the course of their first year, evaluating their teaching, assessing their planning materials and examining the children's exercise books and test scores. If the inspector felt that a new entrant possessed the necessary ability and knowledge and maintained good classroom control, the teacher would pass the probationary year and be deemed fully qualified to enter the profession.

It was understandably a nerve-racking time for many a young teacher to have to perform with a school inspector sitting at the back of the classroom with his clipboard on his lap and his pen poised, watching everything going on, and there had been occasions when the lesson had not gone as well as it should have because of the teacher's nerves or some unexpected occurrence. That morning at Foxton there was indeed a surprise in store for me.

Foxton School was a sprawling, flat-roofed structure erected in the 1950s to cater for the children who lived on the large council estate surrounding it. As a building, it had little of character; it was a purely utilitarian construction with large classrooms, huge square, metal-framed widows, long narrow corridors and a multi-purpose hall. In summer the school was a hothouse, in winter it was icily cold. The floors consisted of brown reconstituted tiles and the shelving was of the cheap-looking plastic-coated variety. The field to the rear of the building, despite the notices, was used after school and at weekends by dog-walkers to exercise their pets, would-be golfers practising their strokes and adolescents on motorbikes. Break-ins and vandalism were regular occurrences.

Knowing the area that Foxton School served, with its deserved reputation as being one of the most problematic and socially-deprived parts of the county, I guessed that Miss Bailey would need all the support and encouragement she could get. On my last visit, Mrs Smart, the headteacher, had listed for me a whole catalogue of difficulties faced by those who lived on the estate: petty crime, drug-related problems, absentee fathers, poverty, unemployment and low levels of literacy, all of which had a real impact on the children's achievement. But she was by nature a steadfastly optimistic and enthusiastic woman, not given to complaint and she was fortunate to lead a team of like-minded colleagues: keen, committed, experienced teachers who had a genuine concern for the children and their parents. Bearing in mind the children's background, the school was achieving pretty good results.

'Most of the parents are the salt of the earth,' the headteacher had told me on my last visit. 'They cause me no trouble and, on the whole, they want the best for their children. They have so little and are so very grateful for anything we do for them. We have a breakfast club so children can start off the day with a meal inside them. There are regular jumble sales, bingo nights and school discos. With the money we raise, we're able to help the least fortunate families to buy the school uniform. Many of the parents themselves fell through the net in the school system and a surprising number are barely literate so on one evening a week we have what we euphemistically call a 'Brush Up Your

231

English Group'. Basically, it's to teach them to read and write better so they can help their own children with their schoolwork. Sometimes I have to smile,' she had continued. 'One young mother with four children—she can't have been much older than twenty—had real problems filling in the forms when she registered the children to start school, having just moved into the area. She knew the children's dates of birth and who the fathers were but when I asked if all the children were natural born British citizens she told me that the youngest child was born by Caesarean. When it got to "length of residence" she said it was about fifty feet although she couldn't be sure. I once asked a young single-parent mother, whose son had a wonderful head of curly ginger hair, if the boy's father was redheaded, too. "I don't know," she had told me in all seriousness, "he kept his cap on."'

As I drove to Foxton that morning I thought about Mrs Smart, of her dedication and all the extra effort she and her staff made to better the lives of the children, and I thought too of the cynical, lazy, nine-to-four teachers at Ugglemattersby Junior School. Closing that particular school, I said to myself, would be the best thing to do.

I arrived at Foxton just as the bell, shrill and peremptory, sounded for the start of school and, after signing in at the office, I joined the throng of chattering children as they made their way down the long corridor to their various classrooms. Mrs Smart was at her classroom door and greeted me with a broad smile. Unlike many of her headteacher colleagues, she insisted on doing some teaching, rather than spending all her time in

232

her office on administration.

'Good morning, Mr Phinn,' she said in a hearty, welcoming voice, 'and how are you this bright Monday morning?'

'All the better for seeing you, Mrs Smart,' I said.

'Here to see our new member of staff, are you?'

'Yes, but I thought I'd pop in to see you first.'

'Always a pleasure,' she replied. 'I think you will find that I have discovered a real gem in Miss Bailey. She's settled in really well and the children love her.'

Mrs Smart, a small, tubby woman with a jolly pinkish face and large blue eyes, reminded me of a brightly-painted Toby jug one sees displayed in old country inns; indeed, one could visualise her pulling the pints with gusto.

'Come into the classroom for a minute,' she said, 'while I mark the register. I'm sure the children would like to meet you.'

The class of eight- to nine-year-olds stared at me inquisitively as they filed into the room and took their seats.

'Sit up smartly, children,' the headteacher said. 'Straight backs, arms folded, all eyes this way.' The children did as they were told. 'We have a very important visitor. This is Mr Phinn, children.'

'Good morning, Mr Phinn,' the children chanted.

'Good morning,' I replied.

'Some of you might remember Mr Phinn when he came into our school last time,' said Mrs Smart.

'I remember him, miss!' called out a boy with a thin-boned face, very short hair and large low-set ears.'

'Yes, I thought you might remember him,

233

Justin,' said the headteacher, glancing in my direction and giving me a knowing look. 'As I recall, you and Mr Phinn had a very interesting conversation at the school office when you were sent there to cool off.'

'I couldn't stop winking,' said the boy, a cheeky grin spreading across his face.

'I do remember,' I said, trying to suppress a smile.

'I am glad to say, Mr Phinn,' said the headteacher, 'that Justin has now got out of the habit of winking at everybody.'

'I am very pleased to hear it,' I said in a mock-serious tone of voice.

'Now,' said Mrs Smart, addressing the class, 'before I collect in the dinner money, are there any absence notes?'

Three children came forward, two of who passed the headteacher scraps of crumpled paper. The third child, a pale-faced girl with large glasses and untidy hair, leaned over the teacher's desk.

'Miss,' she said, 'mi mam says can mi name be changed in t'register?'

'Whatever for, Darlene?' asked the headteacher.

'Because she said she dunt want me called Darlene Nixon any more. She wants me to be called Darlene Smith.'

'But why?' asked the headteacher, clearly as puzzled as I was.

'Because mi dad keeps goin' off wi' women an' my mam says she's not 'avin' 'im back this time. Mi mam's sick of 'im goin' off wi' women an' then comin' back an' causin' trouble so she dunt want 'im round t'house any more and she says if 'e comes to collect me from school, I've not got to go wi' 'im.' The child continued hardly seeming to draw breath. 'Anyway, mi mam's got a new boyfriend now an' 'e's moved in wi' us, an' 'e's called Ron Smith an' she wants me to 'ave 'is name.'

'I think I had better have a word with your mother, Darlene,' Mrs Smart told her. 'I can't just change your name like that. Tell your mother that I'll write to her.'

The child continued regardless. 'But mi mam says you've *got* to change mi name to Darlene Smith from now on cos she's got this new boyfriend called Ron Smith.'

Justin, who had been eavesdropping on the conversation, nodded wisely and remarked, 'We 'ad 'im—'e were rubbish!'

*   *   *

Miss Bailey was a handsome young woman with a friendly smile and a lively, cheerful nature. When I observe young teachers, I find I can usually tell within just a few minutes how good he or she really is; it is the way they react to the children. The teacher must, of course, be first and foremost a performer, able to interest and entertain as well as having a sound knowledge of their subject; they must be always in command of the classroom, their stage, and employ the techniques of seasoned actors. I was impressed immediately by Miss Bailey, who had that certain presence. She had a winning smile and a patient and even-tempered manner; it was clear that the six-year-olds in her care liked her enormously. They clustered around her desk, chattering excitedly about what they had been doing over the weekend and several had brought her little presents of flowers and sweets.

'It's my birthday,' she explained. 'I think Mrs Smart must have let the cat out the bag.'

'I suppose the last thing you were expecting on your birthday,' I told her, 'was a visit from the school inspector.'

'I could think of a pleasanter present,' she replied good-humouredly.

The classroom was tidy and colourful, and it was obvious Miss Bailey had made a real effort to provide a stimulating environment for the children. If she was nervous about my visit, Miss Bailey certainly didn't show it. I had an idea that the headteacher's assessment of her was spot on.

'We usually have a story on Monday mornings,' Miss Bailey told me, showing me a large picture book with a collection of colourful animals and birds on the front cover. 'So if you would like to join us in the reading corner, Mr Phinn, we'll make a start.'

Without being instructed, the children gathered around the teacher on the small square of carpet, with me sitting at the back. Some of the infants yawned widely and rubbed the sleep out of their eyes, two stuck thumbs in their mouths, while another began energetically poking his nose with his index finger. One little shuffler, right at the front, not really on the carpet, looked as if he were polishing the floor with his bottom. I was grateful that I had not been prevailed upon to read a story on this occasion. I had only just got over my experience telling the tale of *The Three Billy Goats*

Gruff.

'We have a visitor this morning, children,' said the teacher, 'and his name is Mr Phinn.' The children all swivelled round and stared at me. 'I wonder what letter Mr Phinn's name begins with? What do you think, Daisy?'

The child removed her thumb from her mouth. ' "F",' she said.

'It's a good guess, but it doesn't. The fin on the back of a shark begins with the letter "f" but Mr Phinn's name begins with another letter.' She smiled at the little shuffler who was still restlessly shifting his position. 'I bet Philip knows.'

' "D",' he said.

'Think of your name, Philip,' said the teacher. 'What does your name begin with?'

The child's hand shot up in the air. ' "P" and "h"!' he shouted out.

'Good boy,' said the teacher. 'Well, Mr Phinn's name is just like the beginning of your name. I bet Mr Phinn likes stories, don't you, Mr Phinn?'

'Yes, indeed,' I replied.

'This morning's story, children,' she began, showing her little audience the cover of the book and pointing to the title, 'is *The Tale of Chicken Licken*. It's a story that my mother used to read to me when I was a little girl and it's about a rather silly chicken that spreads a foolish rumour.'

'Miss,' volunteered Philip, 'we had chicken for dinner this Sunday. I had the parson's nose.'

'Yuk,' said another. 'We had sausages and chips.'

'We went out on Sunday,' volunteered a third, 'to our Gran's.'

'I know you've all got lots to tell me,' said the

237

teacher, 'but if you keep interrupting, I'll never get on with the story. Now, let's all sit up smartly, eyes front and pin back those little ears, and listen.'

As soon as the teacher began reading, in a loud, expressive voice, the children turned their attention to her and listened intently. They were a picture: open-mouthed, wide-eyed, completely still, hanging on every word. She can tell a story rather better than I can, I thought to myself.

' "Once upon a time there was a little chicken called Chicken Licken. One day an acorn fell from a tree and hit Chicken Licken on the head." '

'I bet that hurt,' observed Philip.

'I'm sure it did,' said the teacher.

'A conker fell on my head once, miss,' said the child, 'and it really hurt.'

'Philip,' said the teacher is a patient voice, 'I would like you to listen. We can talk about you and your accident with the conker later. "Now, when the acorn fell on Chicken Licken's head, the silly bird thought that the sky was falling down so he ran off to tell the king." '

'Miss,' interrupted Philip, 'Chicken Licken wouldn't be a *he*.'

'And why's that, Philip?' asked the teacher.

'Because a chicken would be a *she*. If it was a *he*, it would be a cockerel.'

The teacher smiled and shook her head. 'Do you know, you're right, Philip. I never thought of that. I shall change it to a *she*.' The teacher continued with the age-old story of the foolish chicken that, on the way to tell the king that the sky was falling down, meets a series of gullible and equally silly fowl that agree to join her on her trek. She is joined by Henny Penny, Cocky Locky,

238

Ducky Lucky, Drakey Lakey, Goosey Loosey, Turkey Lurkey and finally by the wily predator, Foxy Loxy.

Miss Bailey beckoned with a long finger. ' "I know where the king lives," growled Foxy Loxy, "follow me and I'll lead you there." '

'Miss,' interrupted Philip again, 'Foxy Loxy wouldn't do that with a finger. Foxes don't have fingers, they have paws.'

The teacher smiled and shook her head again 'Yes, you're quite right, Philip.' At last she finished the tale where the cunning fox persuades the credulous birds to follow him to his den where they end up as his dinner.

Miss Bailey closed the book, paused and looked up at the children. 'What a silly chicken she was, children, wasn't she, and what foolish birds to follow her. I wonder,' she pondered, 'what the wise old king would have said to Chicken Licken when the silly bird told him that the sky was falling down. What do you think he would have said, Philip?'

The little boy had started to shuffle again and I guess the teacher had asked him the question to gain his attention.

'Pardon, miss?' asked the boy.

'I said, what do *you* think the wise old king would have said if Chicken Licken had told him that the sky was falling down?' repeated the teacher.

The child thought for a moment and scratched his chin before replying, 'Bloody hell, a talking chicken!' he said.

At the sound of a spluttering from the back, all the children whirled round and witnessed the school inspector biting his fist in an attempt to

239

stem his laughter.

At morning break, I discussed the lesson with Miss Bailey.

'I'm glad you saw the funny side,' the young woman said. 'I always imagined that school inspectors were rather serious-minded people and certainly not given to laughing out loud in class. I was expecting Philip to tell me that the king told the animals not to listen to such a foolish rumour. You just don't know what they will say, do you?'

'I think you will find, Miss Bailey,' I said, 'that children are a constant surprise. They frequently say funny things, make amusing mistakes, conscious or otherwise, and very often come out with the most unexpected comments. One of the best pieces of advice given to me when I started as a teacher in Rotherham was from the first headteacher I worked for, a splendid man called Dennis Morgan. "With young people," he once told me, "always expect the unexpected." I suppose that is why teaching has got to be the most interesting job in the world—nothing is predictable, every day is different, and you are in the company of children, which tends to keep you young at heart. Expect the unexpected,' I told her, 'and you'll not go far wrong.'

I had smiled when I saw the children giving Miss Bailey her little birthday gifts. It reminded me of an occasion a couple of years before when I was observing a probationary teacher in the same way as I was now. It was just before Easter and an angelic-looking little girl had presented the teacher with a small bag of sugar-coated chocolate eggs.

'These are for you, miss,' the child had whispered sweetly, 'because you are my very

240

favourite teacher.'

The teacher had blushed with embarrassment and obvious pleasure. 'Oh, what a kind thought,' she had said. 'A present for the teacher. Thank you so much, Amy.' She had given the child a peck on the cheek. 'Do you think I might have one now?'

The little girl had nodded and watched as her teacher had popped one of the chocolate eggs in her mouth.

A small boy had then approached the teacher's desk, with a little egg in the palm of his hand. 'This is for you, miss,' he had told her.

'My goodness,' the teacher had said, 'another present. Thank you so much.' She had popped that egg in her mouth—just as the small boy announced proudly, 'Our budgie laid it this morning.'

That had been a time when the school inspector had had to take charge as the horrified teacher had bolted from the classroom with a hand slapped over her mouth.

It had taken all my powers of persuasion later in the staff room to convince the poor young woman that these things did sometimes happen in the classroom and that she should be prepared for many more in the years ahead. She had brightened up when I had reassured her that I had judged her teaching to be very good and that I would be recommending that she passed her probationary year with flying colours. I was pleased to give Miss Bailey the very same reassurance, telling her I fully endorsed the headteacher's opinion of her; she was an excellent teacher.

Driving back to the office, little Philip's blunt observation about Chicken Licken brought to mind an occasion when something similar had happened to me.

I had been telling a group of infant children at Crompton Primary School the story of *The Three Little Pigs*. I had reached that part of the story where the wolf knocked on the cottage door of the second little pig, the one who had built his house of sticks.

'All the second little pig wanted to do was sleep and play,' I had told them. 'He built his stick house quickly and went inside to have a sleep but he was woken up by the deep, growling voice outside.

' "Who's there?" called the second little pig.

' "It's the Big Bad Wolf," said the Big Bad Wolf, "and if you don't let me in, then by the hair on my chinny, chin chin, I'll huff and I'll puff, and I'll puff and I'll huff and I'll blow your house in!"

' "No," squealed the little pig, "I will not let you in."

' "Then by the hair of my chinny, chin, chin, I will blow your house in." And so the Big Bad Wolf huffed and he puffed and he puffed and he huffed and he blew the house in and he gobbled up the little pig.'

'The bastard!' had come a voice from the back.

*   *   *

It took me a good hour and a half to get to Hawthwaite. For several miles along a twisting narrow snake of a road, I was stuck behind a large caravan as it meandered and swayed at a leisurely pace. I became increasingly frustrated as the vehicle teetered along, the driver no doubt taking in the magnificent views across the panorama of rolling green dales and entirely oblivious of the driver behind him. When I finally managed to overtake, the driver and his passenger, both extremely elderly people, gave me a nonchalant wave and smiled happily. I sped past only to be slowed down again when a tractor pulled out of a field in front of me. He might have waited, I growled to myself: the English disease, pulling out in front of cars. I managed to get past eventually, only to come round a bend and find a herd of young bullocks blocking my path. The creatures filled the entire road, pushing and bumping each other, and lowing in complaint as the farmer and his collie dog chivvied them along. When the creatures turned into a field half a mile further on, the herdsman also gave me a casual wave and a cheery smile as I drove past. It was no wonder that I arrived in Hawthwaite in a ferment.

Hawthwaite Infant School was in the centre of one of these picturesque Dales villages so common in the heart of the National Park. It was sandwiched between a row of carefully-maintained grey stone cottages with mullioned windows and blue slate roofs and the imposing Victorian vicarage. The village had everything for those who desired a country life in idyllic surroundings and was therefore extremely popular with commuters wealthy enough to afford the inflated house prices, or weekenders who had the funds for a second home. Hawthwaite had an elegant Norman church, a traditional country inn, a village store, and an immaculately kept village green in the centre of which stood an impressive stone monument built in honour of a past lord of the manor. On a mound a little out of the village were the ruins of a medieval castle.

I was looking forward to sitting in on the class of Mr Pannet, who was in his second year of teaching at Hawthwaite School, because Geraldine's little boy, Jamie, was in his class and my colleague had spoken very highly of this particular young man. When Jamie had started school, the usually unflappable Dr Mullarkey had apparently been in a highly-agitated state. She had described tearfully to Julie how Jamie had clung on to her pathetically when she had tried to leave him, and then he had begun screaming and shouting, tugging and writhing, begging to be taken home. She had worried all day about him but, not wishing to be the over-anxious parent, resisted the temptation to call the school to see how he was. We heard later that when Geraldine had gone to collect Jamie at the end of the school day, she had found a happy smiling little boy who didn't want to go home.

'We do football, Mummy,' Jamie had told his mother, pointing at his new teacher. 'And he can pull funny faces and play the guitar, and he tells smashing stories.'

Mr Pannet was a fit-looking young man with close-cropped sandy hair. He had obviously prepared for my visit since he wore carefully-pressed grey flannel trousers and a smart blazer with silver buttons. He looked more like a young off-duty army officer or city accountant than an infants' teacher. Despite his formal appearance, Mr Pannet was far from conventional. He was loud and jolly and, like Miss Bailey, he had the same solicitous and kindly manner with the children. Far from being intimidated by the presence of a school inspector, he appeared very much at ease and was keen to show me the work the children were

244

undertaking and all the topics he had planned for the term.

I knew that Mr Pannet had a wry sense of humour because Geraldine had regaled us in the office about the term's first parents' meeting that had taken place the week before. She told us that she had been very circumspect with the school about what she did for a living. She had thought that should Mr Pannet learn that he taught the child of a school inspector, and one who possessed more degrees than a thermometer, he might be somewhat daunted. There was, of course, little chance of that for, as she was soon to discover, this confident young man fully appreciated his own abilities and was not reticent in telling others. When she had registered Jamie at the school, Geraldine had merely told the headteacher that she worked in an office in Fettlesham. Since she had never visited Hawthwaite in her capacity as a school inspector, the headteacher and the staff were in ignorance about her profession.

Geraldine had told us in the office the next morning that she had been very pleasantly surprised by this new entrant to the profession who had displayed such remarkable self-assurance at that first parents' evening. Mr Pannet had rested a solicitous hand on her arm, she had said, and, in the most sympathetic of voices, had told her that he understood how difficult it must have been bringing up a child alone, and if ever she needed any help or advice, Geraldine only had to ask. He confided that he was from a 'broken home' himself and went on to say that many children from one-parent families do very well in school, as he had done, despite what the newspapers might say. He had leaned back in his chair and told an amused Geraldine that it was fortunate her little boy had a male teacher since Jamie, lacking a father, now had a male influence in his life. He had told her that it was extremely important that her son was read to every night. 'Half an hour of reading before bedtime,' he had told her, 'will bear the fruits of a lifetime.' Mr Pannet had then gone on to advise my colleague how she might help with Jamie's number work, history and science. 'Young children find science particularly difficult,' the teacher had explained to the inspector for Science and Technology.

When Geraldine had finally found the opportunity to get a word in, she had told Mr Pannet that her son liked school, was happy in his class and seemed to be coping with the work very well. For her, that was all that mattered at this stage in his education. 'That's such a sensible attitude,' Mr Pannet had told her, smiling sympathetically and again patting her arm. 'I just wish all parents were like you, Ms Mullarkey.'

When Jamie had arrived at school the next morning, Mr Pannet had told him that he had had a most interesting little talk with his mother, and asked what she did in her office in Fettlesham.

'She goes out in the morning with a black bag,' the little boy had told his teacher, 'and comes in late with a black bag.'

'Is she a doctor?' Mr Pannet had asked.

'She is,' the child had replied, 'but not a real one. She's a school inspector.'

When Geraldine had opened Jamie's reading book that evening, she discovered an envelope addressed to Dr Mullarkey. It was from Mr Pannet and all it contained was a scrap of paper on which was written in large letters: 'Ha! Ha! Bloody ha!'

CHAPTER FIFTEEN

The Chief Education Officer's headquarters, a large oak-panelled room in the main building at County Hall, smelt of lavender furniture polish and seasoned wood. It was a sumptuous room with a thick-pile maroon carpet, heavy mahogany chairs upholstered in dark green simulated leather with the county crest emblazoned in gold on their backs. Glass-fronted bookcases stocked with red leather-bound tomes lined one wall, and framed paintings by some of the county's most talented children were displayed on the other. A large picture window looked out over Fettlesham and up to the moors beyond.

The Chief Education Officer for the county of Yorkshire sat at a huge partners' desk set in the middle of the room, resting his elbows on the highly-polished surface and steepling his fingers before him. Dr Gore was a tall man with deep-set, earnest eyes and the unabashed gaze of one who knows his position in the world. Next to him, straight-backed and severe, sat his Personal Assistant, the redoubtable Mrs Brenda Savage, dressed in an expensive dark tailored suit with small gold buttons, a lilac silk scarf at her throat and wearing an assortment of expensive-looking jewellery. As always she looked immaculate.

'Do sit down, will you, Gervase,' said Dr Gore, indicating a chair facing his desk. 'Thank you for coming to see me. I know how very busy you are, especially at this time of the year.'

'As indeed we all are, Dr Gore,' observed Mrs Savage, cocking her head in a somewhat arrogant fashion.

'Quite,' said the CEO, nodding and giving her a cursory glance. 'Now, Gervase, I have a little job for you.'

I might have guessed as much, I thought to myself. Over the four years I had been a school inspector in the county, I had been summoned to 'the holy of holies', as Julie termed the CEO's office, about nine or ten times and on every occasion I had left the room with one of Dr Gore's 'little jobs'. I had been asked to conduct a countywide reading survey, undertake an audit of the secondary school libraries, investigate standards of spelling, chair working parties, accompany members of the Education Committee, foreign inspectors and important visitors around schools, compile discussion papers and organise a poetry festival. And they were never ever 'little jobs'.

'I have had a word with Miss de la Mare,' continued the CEO, unsteepling his fingers and tilting back in his large swivel chair, 'and she agrees with me that you are the person best placed to take on this particular little job.' He smiled like a basking shark and fixed me with the dark, heavy-lidded eyes. 'Strictly speaking, it doesn't fall into your bailiwick, but you have had the experience of organising conferences and events and such—very successfully, too, I may add. I am sure that this little job will not take up too much of your time. Mrs Savage will, of course, be working closely with

248

you to deal with all the administration and to keep me fully informed of developments.'

'So, it's a conference you wish me organise, is it, Dr Gore?' I asked.

'Not as such,' said the CEO. 'Much of the work was done early last term when I selected the speakers and discussed the topics for their lectures. I just want you to deal with one or two aspects. You'll be pleased to hear it's not a massive undertaking. Now,' he said, leaning forward again, 'you may or may not be aware that I have been elected the President of NACADS for this academic year.'

'NACADS,' I repeated.

'The National Association of Chief Administrators and Directors of Schools,' explained Mrs Savage.

'Thank you, Mrs Savage,' said the CEO, holding up a hand to stop her speaking, 'I am sure Mr Phinn has heard of NACADS.'

Mr Phinn had not heard of NACADS but, if he had, he might very well have suggested a more suitable acronym.

'It is the only occasion in the history of the association,' said Mrs Savage, 'when a member of council has been elected a second time. Dr Gore was the president some twelve years ago and has been prevailed upon to serve again. It is quite a feather in the cap for Dr Gore and, indeed, for the county.'

'Be that as it may,' said Dr Gore, giving a thin-lipped smile which conveyed little more than a slight interest in what his PA was saying, 'in my capacity as the President of NACADS, it falls upon me to host the annual weekend conference. It will begin on the Friday evening and conclude at Sunday lunchtime, so it's nothing prolonged.'

'It is an opportunity for delegates to hear the very best national speakers and for chief administrators and directors of schools and colleges to network,' said Mrs Savage, adding that 'Sir Bryan Holyoake, the Minister of Education and Science, has already intimated that he might be present.'

Dr Gore sighed and drummed his fingers on the desktop. 'Mrs Savage,' he said, turning to face her and removing his spectacles, 'I should be very much obliged if you would refrain from intervening. Time is of the essence. As you have pointed out, we are all very busy people.' He replaced his spectacles.

Mrs Savage, having been put firmly in her place, pursed her lips and examined one of her long painted nails.

'Where is the conference to be held?' I asked.

'Ah,' said Dr Gore, 'thereby hangs a story. It was to be held in the Broddington Hall Conference Centre but, as you may have read, it recently suffered a great deal of damage following a fire. I believe it won't be open again for several months. We have had to find another venue.'

'That sounds serious. Have you managed to find an alternative?' I asked, knowing how difficult it was to get conference facilities at short notice.

Dr Gore beamed at me, with obvious satisfaction. 'We have been fortunate, most fortunate indeed with the venue. Lord Marrick, in his capacity as Chairman of the Education Committee, has very kindly offered his own country residence, Manston Hall, as the venue for the conference. It is a quite superb Regency house and ideally suited to our purposes.'

'Actually, Dr Gore,' interposed Mrs Savage, unable to keep quiet for very long, 'I believe Manston Hall was built some time earlier.'

The CEO made a small dismissive gesture. 'The age of the building is of no consequence, Mrs Savage,' he said testily. 'It is an ideal venue for my conference.' His PA leaned forward and was about to respond but thought better of it. 'What I would like you to do, Gervase, is organise things from the school side, while Mrs Savage deals with all the administration. I was thinking that it would be appropriate to have a display of children's work, a performance from a school choir or ensemble, perhaps a small piece of drama, an art exhibition, that sort of thing. I want the delegates to leave the county with a very good impression.'

'If I might be allowed to say something, Dr Gore,' said Mrs Savage.

'Yes, of course,' sighed the CEO.

'I just wish to impress on Mr Phinn that he needs to liaise closely with me and keep me fully up to speed on everything that he intends to do.' Her voice dripped with condescension. 'It is essential that he touches base with me before organising anything and keeps me in the loop so I can see the big picture.'

'I am sure Mr Phinn is aware of that,' said the CEO.

Mrs Savage, as was her wont, persisted. 'It is just that on previous occasions, as Mr Phinn well knows, there have been—how shall I put it—certain crossed wires and misunderstandings when we have been liaising and—'

'Be assured, Mrs Savage,' I told her smiling, 'I will fill you in.'

'That's settled, then,' said Dr Gore. 'I look forward to hearing about how things are progressing.'

'There is just one other thing, Dr Gore,' I said. 'What are the dates for this conference? Some time next term, I assume?'

'No, no,' replied the CEO, 'the end of next month.'

*   *   *

'So what was your little *tête-à-tête* with the good Dr Gore about?' asked Sidney when I arrived back at the inspectors' office at lunchtime. He was leaning back precariously in his chair, with his feet on the desk and a mug of steaming coffee in his hand.

'He's given me another of his little jobs,' I grumbled, flopping down in my chair.

'You shouldn't be so industrious and malleable,' said my colleague, taking a huge and noisy gulp from his mug. 'You should have told him you were far too busy and stressed.'

'Well, I am busy,' I said, 'but I don't know about being stressed.'

'I have to say, my dear friend,' said Sidney, 'that I have perceived that you have recently been without your usual *joie de vivre*. There is a certain *froideur* about you, a lassitude and earnestness which is quite *outré*. You are positively neurasthenic.'

'Hark at Dr Freud,' said David, looking up from his papers. 'Sidney, you are the last person in the

252

world to counsel anybody. You would drive the most carefree, well-adjusted soul to suicide. You may recall that when you went on one of those stress-management courses, the tutor told you that you didn't suffer from stress, you were more of a carrier. And, anyway, what's with all this French? You spent your summer holidays in Italy but now you are spattering all your conversation with silly French phrases.'

'I am a man of the world,' said Sidney, spreading his arms expansively.

'Give me strength,' said David. 'The man gets worse.'

'It's just that things are a bit heavy-going at the moment,' I told them.

'Tell me about it,' said David. 'These school closures are highly contentious and I have had to brave two acrimonious meetings with governors when insults and recriminations were thrown about like confetti. I am dreading speaking to the parents' association next week.'

'Actually, my meetings on that subject have gone pretty smoothly,' said Sidney. 'I merely told the audience of aggrieved governors and parents not to shoot the messenger. I was merely an unwilling conduit, a harbinger sent from County Hall to present the unwelcome news and had no power to prevent the closures. I said I fully sympathised with their concerns, agreed with their comments and would take back their views to the powers that be. They seemed quite satisfied with that. Anyway, Gervase, with regard to Dr Gore and his wretched little jobs, you must tell him No. You are far too easily persuaded, dear boy. You should have told him that you were suffering from mental, physical and emotional strain and couldn't possibly take on anything else at the moment.'

'What?' I exclaimed. 'Tell Dr Gore that? I'd have got the sack.'

'Nonsense!' cried Sidney. 'You could have wrung your hands, sighed and shuffled in your chair, wiped your fevered brow and told him it was all becoming too too much for you. It would have been a *coup de maître*,' said Sidney.

'If you continue talking like a French phrase-book, Sidney,' said David, 'I'm off.'

'Of course,' continued his colleague unabashed, 'I put it down to post-natal depression.'

'Post-natal depression?' I repeated.

'Oh yes,' said Sidney. 'It doesn't just affect mothers, you know. Fathers are susceptible too and you seem to me like a classic case. You look tired, overworked and ill-at-ease.'

'Well, that should cheer the man up and no mistake,' said David.

'It happened to me when my daughter, Tanya, was born,' said Sidney. 'After all the euphoria of the birth and holding the little bundle in my arms, the despondency and dejection set in. I couldn't put paintbrush to canvas for a whole year. I had sleepless night after sleepless night. I would doze off and then be woken up in the early hours to feed this wrinkled, little piggy-faced whelp, squawking and squealing and wriggling about. It was like listening to a bat being nailed to a door. And then having to change her and get her off to sleep again. It was a waking nightmare. The next morning I would struggle downstairs, and I can promise you that there's nothing more guaranteed to bring on nausea than having to face a bucket full of dirty nappies first thing.'

'My dear departed Welsh grandmother had thirteen children and brought them up in a terraced house with only one tin bath,' said David. 'You never heard her complain. You want to count yourself lucky.'

'Sweet angels of mercy!' cried Sidney, 'Please, oh please, spare us from the dear departed Welsh grandmother.'

'Actually I don't mind changing the baby,' I told Sidney, 'and since Christine is breast-feeding, I don't have to get up in the middle of the night, so it's certainly nothing to do with that.'

However, it worried me that Sidney had noticed I was under something of a strain. There was no doubt that the problems at Ugglemattersby were still preying on my mind. I would shortly be attending a meeting of the parents of the children at both schools, something I was not looking forward to at all.

'Lucky you,' said Sidney. 'My wife had cracked nipples and, as I recall, I came out in sympathy. Lila couldn't wear anything tight-fitting for a month. She had to express the breast milk using this peculiar-looking rubber-nozzled gadget given to her by the health visitor. Now, she was a Gorgon if ever there was. I gave her the *nom de guerre* of Sister Enema since she constantly asked about the baby's stools. "My dear woman," I told her, "the baby cannot sit up yet, never mind coping with a stool." She was not amused.'

'I'm not at all surprised,' said David. 'Very feeble. Anyway, do we have to hear all this?' he asked. 'If we have to talk about something, couldn't it at least be a pleasanter topic than

255

cracked nipples and stools?'

Sidney, however, was not in the mood to be stopped. 'You'll have far more important things to worry about raising a child, Gervase, than cracked nipples and stools. When that cuddly little bundle of joy gets to adolescence, shaves all his hair off, comes home sporting tattoos on his chest, answers you in grunts and lives in squalor in his room, when he wants to roam the streets at night because all his mates' parents allow them to, and when he hogs both the telephone and the bathroom, then you will have something to worry about.'

'What an optimistic view of adolescence,' observed David.

'And, later,' Sidney went on, 'when he embarks on a twenty-six-year-long art course at university in London, you will have to pay through the nose for his lodgings and upkeep. Then you will question whether it is worth being a father.'

'Can you imagine having Sidney for a father?' sighed David.

'I'm a splendid father, I'll have you know,' exclaimed Sidney, 'and always have been. I was both a model husband and father. Before work, I would take Lila her morning tea, then breakfast in bed, newspaper and the baby, all changed, washed and scrubbed. Our first Christmas with Tanya, just for a bit of a wheeze, I wrapped the turkey in the baby's shawl and took that up instead of the baby. Lila opened the shawl to find this turkey looking up at her. Well, of course, it didn't actually look up at her. It was plucked. "Where's the baby?" screamed Lila. "Oh gosh!" I said. "I must have put her in the oven."'

'Sidney!' I exclaimed. 'That's dreadful.'

256

'That's what Sister Enema said,' Sidney continued, 'when Lila told her about it. She said I could have dried her milk up.' He tipped his chair forward from its perilous position, and put his elbows on his desk. 'You know, I came in early this morning, hoping to finish some reports. It is always the same when you two are in the office together. I can never get a thing done.'

David and I looked at each other but didn't say anything.

After a minute's blissful silence, David asked, 'So what's this little job that Dr Gore has given you, Gervase?'

'He's asked me to help organise a conference,' I said. 'Our esteemed leader is this year's president of some high-powered association called NACADS.'

'NACADS!' exclaimed Sidney.

'No! No!' exclaimed David. 'He can't be. You have to work in the mines to be a member of that. Dr Gore wouldn't recognise a pit if he had one at the bottom of his garden.'

'Mining?' I asked puzzled. 'What's mining got to do with it?'

'Ours is a strong mining family,' David told me. 'Generations have worked down the pit.'

'I can see her now,' said Sidney, 'that old Welsh grandmother of yours, in pit boots and helmet and carrying her lamp, emerging black as the ace of spades from the mine, having shovelled nutty slack all day and wending her weary way home to prepare tea for her thirteen hungry children. It brings a tear to the eye.'

'If you must know—' began David.

'Actually, we really don't need to know,'

interrupted his colleague, leaning lazily back in his chair and looking at David with humorous idleness.

'If you must know,' continued David, ignoring Sidney, 'my father was an official in that association. He rose up the ranks from miner to deputy. Forty-five years my father worked down the pit. Forty-five years and never missed a day.'

'I bet he missed a few baths, though,' said Sidney, 'what with the thirteen children and the one tin tub.'

'My father was the local convener for NACODS,' said David. 'The National Association of Colliery Overmen, Deputies and Shotfirers.'

'No, this is NACADS,' I told him, accentuating the second "A". 'The National Association of Chief Administrators and Directors of Schools.'

'NACADS,' mused Sidney, leaning back precariously on his chair. 'It sounds like a self-help group for world-weary geriatrics. Mind you, I guess if it were, Dr Gore would feel very much at home being president of that. I've noticed of late how tired and irritable he's getting. Two peas in the old colloquial pod, you two, Gervase.'

'Perhaps he's suffering from post-natal depression as well,' said David.

'I've been given the job of organising various exhibitions and events,' I told them. 'Displays of children's work, the usual sort of thing.'

'And does this little job of Dr Gore's mean having to liaise with Mrs Savage?' asked David.

'Yes, it does,' I replied glumly. 'I wouldn't mind doing his little job for him but the thought of having to liaise with the Ice Queen herself fills me with dismay.'

'Poor you,' said Sidney.

'Oh dear,' groaned David. 'I can hear the rumble of enemy fire. I suppose this is the conference she was going on about during the summer holidays.'

'When? I never heard any mention of it,' said Sidney, twiddling a pencil round and round in his fingers.

'No, it was when you were swanning around Italy, and we were packing up the office, including all your things,' I replied.

'Ah, yes, that was most kind of you—if only I could find where you've put everything. I still haven't found my earthenware vase. However, that is nothing compared to having to work with our Brenda.'

'That woman is insufferable!' said David. 'Last week she had the brass neck to send back two of my reports with corrections. Corrections! The impertinence of it, correcting my English.'

'Well, I would have thought you would have welcomed that,' said Sidney, being deliberately provocative. 'I well recall a conversation we had last year when you were bemoaning the sloppy use of English.'

'As usual, Sidney, you are missing the point,' said David irritably. 'You are quite happy giving everyone the benefit of your views whether they want to hear them or not but you are incapable of listening to others. I am perfectly capable of using correct English, thank you very much. My point is that Mrs Savage returned a report to me with corrections on.'

'On which there were corrections,' interrupted his colleague.

'On which there were corrections,' repeated David, 'but these corrections did not need to be corrected.'

'Well, that sounds perfectly clear to me,' said Sidney. 'Did you understand him, Gervase?'

'Behave yourself, Sidney,' I told him. 'What did you write, David?'

'I wrote,' said David, 'that the Head of the Mathematics Department at Lady Cavendish High School for Girls, and I quote, "sets the standard by which the remainder of the department is judged". Mrs Savage took it upon her self to change it to "are judged", which is, of course, incorrect. I told her in no uncertain terms when I saw her swanning down the top corridor at County Hall with a face as hard as a diamond, like some mature model out of a woman's magazine, pretending to be all important, that I was not going to put up with it.'

'You mean up with it you were not going to put,' said Sidney.

'I'll come over there in a minute, my friend,' exclaimed David, 'and knock you off that chair and put you flat on your back!'

'Mrs Savage is the last person to start advising people how to use English,' I said. 'She continually uses a whole new vocabulary of dead terms and office catchphrases: "coming aboard", "running things up flagpoles", "getting up to speed", "blue sky thinking", "squaring the circle", "touching base". It's a whole new language.'

'She goes on a one-day course in office management,' said Sidney, 'and comes back with all this gobbledegook.'

'Like a certain art inspector who goes to Italy for a fortnight and comes back peppering all his

260

conversation with French phrases,' said David.

'*Touché*!' said Sidney.

'I mean, I don't mind being picked up by someone who uses English well, but certainly not by Mrs Savage. As my dear departed Welsh grandmother used to say'—Sidney sighed dramatically and rolled his eyes—'"before you look at the mote in someone else's eye, take a look at the tree in your own."'

'I don't see how you could see anything with a tree in your eye,' said Sidney.

'And what surprises me,' continued David, deciding to ignore Sidney's flippant remark, 'is why Dr Gore allows her to get away with it. Take that crass document she sent about the school closures. It was incomprehensible.'

'Maybe because our dear Dr Gore is just too exhausted and worn out. She is enough to make the most even-tempered person exhausted and irritable. I should think the old man feels thoroughly NACADS.'

'Well,' said David, 'I wish you luck working with that woman, I really do.'

'In the long tradition of *esprit de corps*, which exists in our little team, Gervase,' said Sidney, 'you know that if we can be of any help we would be only too happy to oblige— *tous ensemble*.'

'Of course,' agreed David, 'that goes without question. I am more than happy to help you. I will, of course, produce an exhibition of mathematics teaching and children's work and, if you wish, I could arrange a gymnastics display and perhaps a performance of traditional dancing.'

'That sounds excellent,' I said.

'I don't mind a bit of gymnastics,' said Sidney,

261

'but could we leave out the Morris dancing? And I shall be only too pleased to mount *une exposition magnifique* of children's painting and sculpture. I like nothing better than celebrating young people's efforts and I have just the person in mind to help me. The newly appointed Head of Art at Crompton Secondary Modern, *la charmante* Colette, an inspirational teacher and also an inspiration to look at.'

'Ah! I thought there would be a woman somewhere in your scheme of things,' sighed David. 'And I suppose she's French, is she?'

'However did you guess?' asked Sidney with mock surprise in his voice.

'I wondered why we have been bombarded with all these Gallic phrases,' said David. 'Been brushing up on your French, have you?'

'She is the perfect Pre-Raphaelite beauty,' said Sidney, raising his hand like a priest about to give a blessing. 'Tall, pale-complexioned with piercing violet eyes and delicate slender hands, and with an explosion of auburn hair cascading straight down her back. A long-legged goddess. *Une belle femme.* She could have walked out of the canvas of a Burne-Jones masterpiece. I shall get onto it *pronto.*'

'Give me strength!' cried David. 'He's gone into Italian now.'

'I'm feeling better already,' I said.

'And no doubt Geraldine will come up with something spectacular,' said David. 'Now there's an example to any parent. You don't hear her complaining about sleepless nights, changing nappies and post-natal depression. I take my hat off to her, bringing up a child single-handed.'

'I wonder if she suffered from cracked nipples,' mused Sidney.

At that moment my telephone rang.

'Brenda Savage here,' came a sharp voice down the line.

'Oh, hello, Mrs Savage,' I said, emphasising her name to let my colleagues know to whom I was speaking. Sidney pulled a gruesome face, David grimaced.

'Following our discussions with Dr Gore this morning,' she said formally, 'I feel it is important that we need to expedite matters ASAP. As time is very short and there is much to do, particularly in incentivising your colleagues to get aboard this project, I suggest we put our heads together. I have produced a possible paradigm and need to flag up a few things with you. Have you a window in your diary next week?'

'No,' I replied simply. 'I've a full programme of school visits, an English course to run and three governors' meetings.'

'I cannot impress upon you too strongly, Mr Phinn, that we must push ahead with this,' she said testily. 'Are you available now?'

'Now?' I asked. 'This very minute?' Better get the inevitable meeting with her over and done with, I thought. 'I am free until two o'clock, and then I have to join an appointments panel.'

'Then I shall come over and see you,' she said. 'I shall be over straight away.' The phone clicked.

'Mrs Savage is on her way over,' I told my colleagues insouciantly.

David snatched up his briefcase and made a hurried exit, followed by Sidney. '*Adieu, mon brave!*' he cried as he left the office.

* * *

'Do you think I'm malleable?'

I was helping Christine wash the dishes that evening when I put the question to her.

'What a strange thing to ask,' she said.

'Well, do you?'

'Think you're malleable?' she repeated. 'You mean like a lump of clay that's moulded into shape?'

'Well, not really like a lump of clay,' I said. 'What I mean is "easily persuaded".'

'Why do you ask?'

'Sidney says I'm malleable, that I take too much on because I can't say No to people.'

'Well, for once I think Sidney's got it right,' said Christine, 'You do take on too much and do tend to say Yes to people far too often.'

When Winco Cleaver-Canning had shown his whiskered face at the door that morning, clutching the playscript of *The Dame of Sark*, Christine had discovered that I had virtually agreed to join the cast. When I arrived home, she had shaken her head and asked me crossly why I hadn't said I was too busy. She had asked the very same question when I had agreed to speak at a charity dinner, join a sponsored walk, help a dyslexic boy in the village with his reading and write an article for National Poetry Day for the *Fettlesham Gazette*. 'It's a simple enough word,' she had told me. 'Just say No.'

Later that evening, when I was reading the paper and Christine was doing some sewing, she said, 'I meant to tell you that Andy is coming up on

Saturday to fix the guttering. I don't know why you didn't wait until he could help you instead of trying to fix it yourself and bringing the whole lot down. Andy said it's a two-man job, so I'm assuming you will be able to give him a hand?'

'I think, my dear,' I said jokingly, 'that I shall follow your very good advice.'

'And what advice is that?' asked Christine.

'I shall just say No.'

CHAPTER SIXTEEN

By the end of that week, I was feeling more settled, under less strain. There had been no further sign of our visitors with the bushy tails and I hoped that they were settling down on the Manston estate. On Saturday, Andy, with limited help from myself (I held the ladders) fixed the guttering and finished tidying up the garden, and Christine cooked the most delicious pheasant and venison casserole for dinner on the Saturday night—on the proceeds of a little present Harry Cotton had brought round during the week. 'What the eye doesn't see, the heart doesn't know,' said Christine bravely, as she prepared the meat for the oven. She had prevailed upon Andy to pluck and gut the pheasant.

On Sunday, a gloriously sunny day, we decided to give ourselves a day off, and went to Whitby. The tide was out, and Christine and I strolled along the vast sandy beach to Sandsend with little Richard strapped on my back. How I looked forward to the time when he was old enough to help me build castles, collect crabs from the rock pools in a plastic bucket, search for fossils, paddle in the cold grey waters of the North Sea and join me on a trip around the harbour in the old lifeboat.

That evening I read *The Dame of Sark*, which I enjoyed hugely, and became quite excited about 'treading the boards' once again with the Fettlesham Literary Players. Sitting in front of the fading fire before going to bed, I also felt happier about taking on Dr Gore's latest little job. The discussions with Mrs Savage had gone surprisingly well, and we had arranged to meet again this coming week, when we would visit Manston Hall. We were both a little concerned that Lord Marrick's home would not have the same facilities as a conference centre, and we needed a 'site visit', as Mrs Savage called it, to acquaint ourselves with the layout, the lie of the land.

Both David and Sidney had been busy planning their contributions for the exhibition, and Geraldine, as I knew she would, had immediately agreed to put on a science display. As well as telephoning the schools that I wanted to provide material for an exhibition of children's writing, I had contacted the County Music Adviser, Pierce Gordon, and enlisted the services of the Young People's Brass Band to entertain the delegates on the Sunday morning. The brass band had at first been reluctant to change their normal rehearsal morning—'Christmas is a very busy time for us,' I was told—but when their band-leader understood that they would be playing at Marrick Hall, he agreed to switch rehearsal times.

Mrs Savage, for her part, busied herself confirming details with the hotels where

266

accommodation had been booked earlier in the summer. She drew up the invitation list for the reception on the first evening, and finalised arrangements with the caterers for both that and the dinner on the Saturday night. She was planning to provide a short history of Manston Hall that would go into each delegate's pack along with the official programme, digests of the speakers' lectures, directions to the venue etc., and this was one of the reasons she wanted to go down to the Hall as soon as possible. All in all, things were progressing well.

*   *   *

I was in excellent spirits, therefore, when I walked into the entrance of Daleside Primary School on the Monday lunchtime. I had a veritable spring in my step. I was there to observe Miss Graham, a probationary teacher.

In the headteacher's room, with a cup of coffee in my hand, I explained to Mrs Blackett, a small, dark-haired, softly-spoken woman, what I intended to do while I was in the school that morning and asked if she had any questions or observations before I went into the first class.

'You don't remember me, do you?' she enquired.

I looked at her a little more closely. 'I'm afraid not,' I replied. 'As you are no doubt aware, I meet many people on my travels.' I sounded terribly pompous, so added quickly 'And I'm afraid I'm not very good at names and faces.'

'I thought you might have remembered me, and the occasion when we met.' A small smile played on the woman's lips.

I was pretty certain she wasn't an ex-girlfriend; was she a former colleague from my teaching days or, even further back, someone I was at school with? I looked again at the smiling face but no recognition dawned. 'There are so many schools in the county,' I told her defensively, 'and I meet many other people during the year at the conferences and courses I run.' She still held the amused expression. 'One of my colleagues,' I continued, 'worked out that it would take over twenty years for one of the inspectors in the team to visit every school in the county.' She continued to smile at me, and when she didn't offer to tell me where we had met, I said, 'I'm sorry but you will have to remind me.'

'We were on interview together,' she replied, 'at County Hall for the post of inspector.'

'Of course!' I said, and then did recall her. 'It's ...er...'

'Dorothy.'

'I remember now,' I said. 'Dorothy Blackett. We had a very interesting conversation. You were a headteacher in the Midlands, as I recall, but you were born in Yorkshire.'

'That's right,' she said, 'and neither of us thought we were in with much of a chance.'

'It was a pretty daunting experience,' I said, 'with all the other hugely-qualified and experienced candidates, bursting with confidence, and that battery of questions from the interview panel. There was no one more surprised than I when I was called back into the room and offered the job.'

'Oh, I had a sneaking feeling you would get it. I

could see how keen you were. I recall thinking you were a bit of a dark horse at the interviews and that you didn't give very much away about yourself.'

'That was nerves,' I told her.

'I've followed your progress,' she continued, 'and from what I have heard, you are doing very well and are making quite an impression.'

'And I remember your saying, when you congratulated me, that you were rather relieved that you didn't get the job because you weren't sure whether you wanted the post or not.'

'I did,' she replied, 'and I guess that uncertainty came over at the interview. You see, my dream was to work in the Yorkshire Dales. That is what I really wanted. I was brought up here and wanted to return to my roots.'

'And your dream came true,' I said.

'It did,' she replied. 'After the debriefing interview afterwards, Dr Yeats told me that the panel was impressed with my answers and any further applications I should make for posts in the county would be looked upon favourably. Last year, this headship came up. I applied, got the job and here I am.'

'I'm so pleased,' I said, 'and if I can—'

A sharp rap on the door interrupted me.

'I'm sorry to disturb you, Mrs Blackett.' It was the school secretary. 'I thought you ought to know that Gavin is in a bit of a state. His, er . . .' she paused, struggling for the right word—'er . . . little problem seems to have flared up again. Shall I send for his mother to come and collect him?'

'Yes please, Vera,' said the headteacher, 'that would be a good idea and I would like a word with her when she arrives. I really don't think he should have been sent to school in this state.' The secretary nodded and after she had closed the door behind her the headteacher shook her head and smiled. 'Not a day goes by when there isn't some incident or crisis,' she told me.

'It's the same in my job,' I said.

'I suppose that's what makes what we do so different and challenging,' she said. 'One day is never the same as another.'

'So, what's the little problem with Gavin?' I asked, reaching for my coffee.

'Little Gavin, all of seven,' said the headteacher, 'arrived at school this morning obviously in some discomfort. He was shuffling away during assembly and I had to tell him to sit still on a couple of occasions. At the end of assembly, I saw him heading out of the hall like a miniature cowboy who had just got off his horse after a hard day in the saddle. He was walking down the corridor bow-legged. I asked his teacher, Miss Graham, to find out why he was behaving in such a strange manner. In the classroom, Gavin produced an absence note from his mother—he'd been away from school for much of last week—explaining, as she put it, that he was "a bit sore in the downstairs department" because he'd been into hospital for an operation. She had written that it was nothing very serious, just that he'd been castrated.'

'Castrated!' I exclaimed.

'Yes, castrated,' said the headteacher. 'Well, a very red-faced Miss Graham—she's in her first, probationary year of teaching and is of a rather delicate disposition—brought little Gavin and the note straight along to me. I discovered that he had not, in fact, been castrated—he'd been circumcised. I thought it more appropriate that the deputy headteacher, Mr Johnson, rather than myself, should have a look at it. Les was not at all keen, telling me that he could get thirty years for "looking at it". Eventually, he was prevailed upon to examine the little boy's problem but only in the presence of the caretaker as a witness that nothing untoward happened. Les reported back to me that Gavin's little problem "in the downstairs department" didn't look that bad and that the child had been sent back to his class. Gavin returned to his classroom and seemed a lot better. Then just before morning break, Miss Graham noticed to her horror that little Gavin, sitting at his desk, had his trousers and pants around his ankles and, to put it euphemistically, had everything on display for the entire world to see. "Whatever are you doing?" she asked him and he replied, "Mr Johnson told me to stick it out for the rest of the day."'

I spluttered and spilt coffee all down the front of my suit.

One of the delights of working in schools is to hear of, and on occasions witness, such humorous episodes. Children and young people have a wonderful capacity to make us laugh—sometimes consciously but more often than not, unconsciously. Many children, particularly the little ones, are disarmingly naïve and possess the ability for such inventive thought and often use language in a surprisingly and keenly intelligent way.

*　　　*　　　*

271

A short while later, I joined Miss Graham in her classroom. I little thought that I would be taking over her lesson that Monday afternoon but that is what happened.

Miss Graham was indeed, as the headteacher had intimated, of a rather delicate disposition. She was a tall, mousy-haired, pale-faced woman whose dark brown eyes, like those of some small nocturnal tree-climbing creature, were alarmingly magnified behind large round glasses. Despite my reassurances she looked agitated when I joined her in the classroom after lunch.

'I must tell you, Mr Phinn,' she said at once, 'that I've never had a school inspector watching me before so I am rather apprehensive.' There was a slight quiver in her voice. She touched the nervous red rash that had appeared at her throat. 'When I was at college, I used to get very worked up when the tutor visited the school where I was on teaching practice.'

'I'm quite harmless, Miss Graham,' I said, 'and I'm sure my visit won't be too much of an ordeal for you.' I could not help but compare this apparently frail, frightened-looking young woman to Miss Bailey, the probationary teacher at Foxton, with her quiet assurance and disarming personality. I just wondered to myself how Miss Graham would cope in a career where she was very likely to come across some very demanding and difficult children. Perhaps she had been unusually alarmed by the incident with Gavin and 'his little problem in the downstairs department', so I did not allude to it and complimented her instead on the splendid classroom displays.

272

'Art was my specialist study at college,' she told me, allowing herself a small self-conscious smile.

'And where was that?' I asked.

'The College of Ripon and York St John,' she replied.

'Ah, a very fine college,' I said. 'One of the very best teacher-training institutions in the country. You can't go far wrong if you have studied there.' I was attempting to boost her confidence and put her at ease since her voice was still trembling noticeably. 'And how are you getting on in your first year?' I asked cheerfully.

'Oh, it's not too bad,' she said, 'but I have to admit I do find the children very blunt and to the point.'

'That's Yorkshire children for you,' I told her.

'Yes, and they do tend to speak their minds. It's a very mixed catchment area. A growing number of children come from the estate, some from the village and a large number live on the surrounding farms. The world of the estate children usually centres on what is on the television, and for the farming children it revolves around sheep, cows and pigs.' She looked wistfully out of the classroom window at the great sweep of the dale outside. 'Sometimes they come out with things which are quite unexpected.' I immediately thought of little Gavin and smiled. 'The farming children will insist on bringing things to school,' she told me. 'Sheep's skulls, dead birds, hedgehogs in boxes, wasps' nests, newts in jam jars, frog spawn, owl pellets. One day, there was a dreadful smell in the classroom. I discovered that one child had brought his ferret to school and was keeping it in his bag, which he'd rested on the radiator. He insisted on

273

telling me all about catching rabbits with his ferret, putting a net over the entrance to their burrows and flushing out the poor creatures, which he promptly killed.' Poor nervous Miss Graham looked like a frightened rabbit herself. 'It's all very interesting, I'm sure, but I have an aversion to anything like that. I don't mind cats and small dogs but snakes and spiders and creepy-crawlies just freak me out. Last April Fools' Day, when I was on teaching practice, one of the children in the class put a plastic spider on my desk.' She shuddered at the thought. 'Uuhhhh! I know it was only a silly toy but just the sight of it made me go into a cold sweat. I was not best pleased, I can tell you, and had to sit in the staff room for half an hour to compose myself. I am sure that if my college tutor had been in the classroom at the time I would have gone to pieces.'

'Well, I promise you, Miss Graham,' I reassured her, 'that I haven't a ferret in my bag and no creepy-crawlies up my sleeve.'

Having listened to this timid and rather anxious young woman, I had to admit that I was not expecting the most riveting of lessons that afternoon but I was pleasantly surprised. As soon as I had been introduced and the children were sitting up smartly at their desks, Miss Graham seemed to come to life. The nervousness she had shown earlier disappeared, and she became animated and encouraging. She had a friendly and supportive manner with the children and they listened attentively and readily responded to her questions. After she had set the children the task of writing a story entitled 'A Day to Remember', Miss Graham moved from table to table, smiling and helping the children with their work. She clearly had forgotten about the man in the dark suit with the notebook who sat inconspicuously in the corner of the classroom watching her.

After a while, I joined a small group of children to talk to them about their work and to look at their books.

'So what are you writing about?' I asked one child.

'My holidays last summer,' she replied.

'And where did you go?'

'Spain.'

'Do you know the capital of Spain?' I asked.

'Course I do,' she replied. 'Letter "S".'

One boy, a large lad with pale eyes and a rather mournful expression, sat staring at the blank piece of paper before him.

'You haven't started,' I said.

'No.'

'Aren't you going to have a go?' I asked.

'I don't know what to write about,' he told me, screwing up his nose and scratching his thatch of thick fair hair.

'"A Day to Remember",' I said. 'There must been a special day in your life which stays in your mind.'

'No.'

'Something memorable,' I said. 'There *must* have been something that you can recall—a happy memory, an accident, a visit, something like that?'

'No.'

'What about your birthday?'

'I had mumps.'

'Christmas?'

'My granddad died.'

'Where did you go for your summer holidays?'

'Nowhere.'

'Well,' I said giving up, 'you put on your thinking cap. I'm sure something will occur to you.'

He looked up at me with a lugubrious expression. 'I wish I knew what to write about,' he told me again and stared down at the piece of paper, and then turned to gaze out of the window onto the dale, where no doubt he would have preferred to be.

It was towards the end of the lesson that things went wrong for Miss Graham. She went into the storeroom for some exercise books and emerged a moment later carrying a little toy bat, black with rubbery wings and a furry body—the sort children buy in joke shops at Halloween.

She held the toy between her finger and thumb. 'Now, this is very silly, children,' she said. 'Firstly, you know I don't allow anyone in my storeroom. Secondly, you all know I don't like creepy-crawlies and, thirdly, you know I warned you about playing tricks. I don't find it at all funny, and I'm sure that Mr Phinn, the school inspector'—all eyes turned in my direction—'is not very impressed with this kind of behaviour, are you, Mr Phinn?'

What could I say but, 'No, I'm not'?

'Now,' continued Miss Graham, 'who does this toy bat belong to?'

The question was greeted with complete silence and blank stares. 'Come along, whose is it?' Still there was no response. 'Well, if the person who brought it to school doesn't own up, then I shall put it in the waste-paper basket and it will stay there.' Just as she was about to deposit the toy in the basket, the thing she held moved. It was a real

276

bat. It had probably found its way into the storeroom through a skylight. The little creature turned its head and squeaked. Miss Graham went rigid. The children stared dumbstruck. I could see by the teacher's expression that she was having some difficulty in maintaining a measure of perpendicularity so, dropping my notebook and grabbing the blackboard duster, I rushed to her assistance. Taking the small trembling creature from her, I cradled it in the soft material. Miss Graham remained frozen to the spot.

'You go to the staff room,' I whispered in the teacher's ear, 'and make yourself a cup of hot strong sweet tea. I'll deal with the little visitor.' Miss Graham, ashen-faced, headed for the door without a word, as if in a trance.

Having deposited the bat in a small box and quietened down the now very excited and voluble class, I told the children to get on with their stories.

The taciturn boy with the pale eyes who had spent his time until then contemplating the blank piece of paper on his desk, suddenly came to life. He waved his hand madly in the air like a poplar in a high wind. 'Sir, please, sir!' he cried. 'I want to tell you something.'

'Whatever is it?' I asked.

'I've got something to write about now, sir,' he said with a great beaming smile. ' "The Day our Teacher went Batty!" '

*　　　*　　　*

I had to go back to the office before going home that evening, and I found David and Geraldine already there. David was lounging at his desk and Geraldine was pushing files into her briefcase. They were laughing at something as I walked in.

'You two seem in good moods,' I commented, dumping my own bulging briefcase on my desk. 'Had a good day?'

'I was just telling Gerry about something that happened at Highcopse Primary that I visited today,' said David. 'The children were doing fractions and I thought I'd test them. I said, "If there are four children in a family sitting down for a meal and there are only three potatoes between them, how would you divide the potatoes equally between them?" The answer, of course, is give each of them three-quarters of a potato. One bright spark called out, "That's easy," he said. "I'd mash the potatoes."'

I laughed out loud. That was exactly the sort of unpredictable comment that I had been trying to explain to frightened little Miss Graham that afternoon.

'I think that's a very sensible answer,' remarked Geraldine. 'Mash would go much further with lots of lovely butter mixed in.'

'That's not the point, and well you know it,' responded David crossly.

Geraldine laughed and closed her briefcase with a sharp click. 'Bye, you two, I'm off. See you tomorrow.'

'What a waste of a pretty woman,' sighed David after Geraldine had left the office. 'It would be so nice if she would join in a bit more. Perhaps have an evening drink, or something—just occasionally.' He looked morosely at his rather full in-tray. 'I think I've had enough myself today. Are you in a rush, too, Gervase, or do you fancy a quick drink?'

I glanced at my watch. There wasn't enough time to start on the notes of the English course I was due to give soon, and I thought a drink would be nice, so the pair of us walked down into Fettlesham High Street to a small pub that we sometimes used. Once we were ensconced comfortably, with pints in our hands, David returned to the theme of the things children come out with.

'On one occasion—I think it might have been at St Helen's—' he said, 'the chairman of governors was addressing the children in a primary school assembly. He was a rather pompous man, an accountant by profession, and told the children that he had been particularly good at mathematics when he was a child. "We had mental arithmetic every morning," he informed the children, "and I was taught to calculate very quickly in my head. I can add up the bill in my head at the supermarket check-out faster than the person on the till can do it using the cash register. I wonder how many young people today, for example," he continued, "could multiply eight hundred and eighty-eight by eighty-eight?" As quick as a flash, a voice from the back of the hall called out: "Seventy-eight thousand, one hundred and forty-four." The pompous fool was most surprised. "That's correct!" he spluttered. "Well, well!" On leaving the school, he complimented Mrs Smith, the headteacher, on the outstanding mathematical ability of the child. Mrs Smith—who told me the story—had apparently observed the incident from the side of the hall, and decided not to mention that she had seen the mathematical genius using the calculator on his wristwatch.'

'Clever clogs!' I remarked. 'I had a nice one the other day. A child informed his teacher that the boy sitting next to him kept "pissing" in his ear.'

'Nasty habit, that,' chortled David.

'The bemused teacher,' I continued, 'asked him what he meant. "He keeps on going 'Pssst! Pssst!' in my ear when I am trying to get on with my work," the child explained.'

It was turning into one of those occasions when one silly story led to another.

David then told me about one student PE teacher, jogging with a class of fourteen-year-old students on the school fields, who had told his young charges to start running. ' "Where to?" one boy asked. "Anywhere," the teacher replied. The class promptly ran home, leaving behind one very cross PE teacher—I bet he didn't make that mistake again.' He laughed. 'Children are so unpredictable.'

'And yet so innocent,' I added. 'I heard the other day about a child who told her teacher that she knew a naughty word beginning with the letter "F". "Well, I hope I don't hear you using it," the teacher said. And the child replied primly, "Oh, I don't, miss. I always say 'trump'." '

'Hearing that story about swearing,' David said, 'reminds me about a conversation that followed a lesson in which the teacher had tried to impress on the young children how naughty it was to swear. A small girl hurried into the classroom after playtime and informed the teacher that a boy in the playground had used a very rude word. "And what was this word?" the teacher asked. After a thoughtful pause, the precocious informant had said, "Miss, I mustn't say it but if you say all the rude words you know, I'll stop you when you come to it." '

I chuckled with laughter. 'Time I made a move. I've got a feeling I'm on cooking duty this evening,' I said, draining my beer mug.

CHAPTER SEVENTEEN

I made my way towards the main entrance of Castlesnelling High School for the rehearsal of *The Dame of Sark*. It was the last thing I wanted on a Friday evening but Raymond, the producer, had phoned the office earlier that day and had very nearly burst into tears when I had told him that it was going to be very difficult for me to attend.

'No, no!' he had moaned, when I explained that I had a meeting that evening, which might go on until quite late. 'But, Gervase, you have only made one or two of the rehearsals so far, and tonight is when I go through the play's *dénouement*. Granted yours may only be a smidgen of a part but it is a cameo.'

My character appeared at the end of the very last act and it was true that I had only attended a couple of rehearsals. I was thankful for that and determined that never again would I be persuaded to get involved in amateur dramatics. So far it had been something of a stressful experience and was likely to continue to be so.

'Very well,' I had told him resignedly. 'I'll be there.'

Raymond was a frenetic little man with cropped

dyed blond hair and a round, pixie-like face; he invariably wore a pair of extremely tight jeans and a close-fitting T-shirt, usually with some suggestive motif emblazoned on the front. He seemed to live constantly on his nerves and certainly got on everybody else's. Rehearsals were lively affairs with him rushing around the stage, pointing, shouting, prancing, pulling faces, jumping up and down and waving his hands in the air. It was a bravura performance in itself. If someone fluffed a line or missed a cue, he would utter a sort of strangled cry before calling out in an irritatingly high-pitched, piercing voice, 'No, no, no, no, no!' Then he would add, brushing his brow dramatically with the back of his hand, 'Why, oh why, do I have to work with amateurs?'

'That's because we are amateurs,' one brave member of the cast had once informed him.

I was met at the entrance to the school by the caretaker, a sallow-faced, skeletal figure of rather menacing aspect. He wore a grubby grey overall, huge black boots, a greasy flat cap and jangled an enormous set of keys on a long chain. Standing foursquare and ferocious next to him was Daisy, his barrel-bodied bull terrier. The creature, catching sight of me, displayed a set of vicious-looking teeth and growled threateningly.

I had first come across the beast when I had attended a school production of *Oliver!* some years before, when it had played Bill Sikes' dog, Bullseye. The creature had stolen the show. The maxim that one should never share the stage with an animal or child rang very true that evening. The actor playing Bill Sikes (the head of the PE Department at the school) had, in the last act, rather foolishly jerked on the rope attached to the dog. 'Come on, Bullseye!' he had commanded in a voice as rough as gravel. The dog had lifted its fat, round head, fixed him with its cold button eyes and then had shot like a cannonball straight for him, snarling and slavering. As I entered Castlesnelling High School now, I gave the dog a very wide berth, knowing full well how unpredictable it could be.

There was no friendly word of greeting from the caretaker but an angry, 'I'll be glad when this bloody play of yours is over,' he told me. The dog rumbled as if in agreement. I'll be glad when it's over as well, I thought to myself, but I kept my own counsel.

'Good evening,' I said, rather overdoing the smile. 'Bit nippy, isn't it?'

'That's because the heating's off,' he informed me bluntly. 'Friday afternoon after school I always turn it off. There's never any heating on of a weekend and I'm buggered if I'm keeping all the school heated for you lot. Any road, I should think there's enough hot air from you amateur fanatics to heat the whole of the bloody Arctic Ice Cap.'

'In the hall?' I asked, not wishing to pursue this line of conversation.

'Aye,' replied the caretaker, jangling his keys like a warder, 'and making a hell of a racket as well and, no doubt, scuffing up my floor, dropping litter and leaving marks on my walls.' He sounded unnervingly like Connie. 'Times I have to tell that producer of yours to tidy up after you're done. You're worse than the bloody kids in the school and that's saying something. But I might as well talk to myself.' Perhaps he didn't realise that he was. The dog growled. 'I don't know why you lot

283

have to rehearse here, what with all the other schools there are around. I've had to stay on to keep the place open for you lot and it'll be after nine before I gets home. Why can't you use another school for a change?'

'I really wouldn't know,' I told him, heading down the corridor. 'I am just a mere member of the cast and a minor one at that.'

The caretaker wasn't going to let me escape so easily and he and the dog pursued me as I made for the school hall. 'You were the SS hofficer in *The Sound of Music*, weren't you?'

'I was.'

'Aye, I thought it was you—the one who had to rush off after the last performance because your wife was in hospital having a baby.'

'The very same,' I told him and added, 'She had a boy, by the way.'

Any normal person might have enquired after the baby, but no congratulations were forthcoming.

'It was a right carry-on was that,' he complained. 'Talk about bloody drama. You rushing about like a chicken with no head and that big woman with the red lipstick and a face like a battleship shouting her head off, and that little producer fellow nearly having a nervous breakdown on stage.' I speeded up but he kept apace. 'I didn't know you were in *this* play.'

'Just a small part,' I said, quickening my step.

'I said to that producer of yours,' he told me, 'I said, why do you always have to do plays about the Nazis. Anybody'd think it was them what won the war. My father was a Dunkirk veteran and a member of the Royal British Legion. He'd turn in his grave to see you lot marching about in German

284

uniforms.'

'I'm a British soldier,' I told him.

He wasn't going to be put off. 'We've had *Cabaret* with blackshirts goose-stepping all over my floor, *Sound of Music* with the Gestapo chasing nuns all over the place and now we've got the SS taking over the Channel Islands. It'll be a musical about Hitler next. Why do they always do plays about the Nazis?'

'I wouldn't know,' I said again, finally leaving him behind. 'I don't pick the plays, I merely act in them.'

The caretaker shouted after me, 'Well, tell that producer of yours to leave the place as he found it and you have to vacate the premises before eight.'

In the hall, a knot of people, wrapped up in thick coats with gloves and scarves, was standing on stage with Raymond. The producer was encased in a bright red duffel coat, a woolly hat was pulled down over his ears and he was wearing multi-coloured woollen gloves. He was barking out instructions and the group didn't look particularly happy. I stood at the back to watch.

'I know it's cold, my lovelies,' Raymond was telling them, 'but the sooner we get moving about, the sooner we will get warm. Now, from the beginning of the act, please, and Cecile, darling, your line is: "That young soldier's at the door, madam, with a message for you" and not "with a massage for you". There is a subtle difference.'

'But I'm tryin' to do mi French accent,' said the girl peevishly, moving from one foot to another to keep warm. She was a large young woman swathed in a vast khaki anorak with fur-lined hood and wearing substantial brown boots. She looked as if she could be auditioning for the musical version of 'Eskimo Nell'. 'It sounds more sexy to 'ave a French accent,' she said. 'Anyway, my mam says that if I was called Cecile I would be French and I'd 'ave a French accent.'

'And tell me, Sharon,' asked Raymond, controlling his obvious irritation, 'does your mother have qualifications in performing arts, dramatic production and theatre direction?'

'No.'

'Did she perhaps study at RADA?'

'Rather what?'

'And is your mother producing this play?'

'No,' replied the girl, defensively folding her arms across her chest.

'Well, I am,' he told her, raising his voice, 'and what I say, goes. *Comprenez?*'

'Eh?'

'This is not a Whitehall farce,' groaned Raymond. 'It is a deeply poignant drama about the triumph of courage and perseverance over tyranny and oppression and there is no place in it for a sexy French maid. This is one of the last rehearsals before the dress rehearsal, so it's not the time to suddenly try something new. So—stick to the English accent, please, but try not to make it so Yorkshire.'

'It'd liven things up a bit,' observed one of the actors, 'a sexy French maid and a German soldier offering the Dame of Sark a massage.'

'I could do with a massage,' announced a tall man in a black overcoat, black leather gloves and a black trilby, sitting in one of the seats at the side of the hall. 'I can't feel my feet, it's so ruddy freezing. It's colder than a morgue in here—and I should

286

know.'

The figure in black was George Furnival, proprietor of Furnival's Funeral Parlour in Collington. He was a tall, cadaverous and sinister-looking individual with short black brilliantined hair parted down the middle. He had played the part of Herr Zeller, the Gauleiter, who came to arrest Captain von Trapp in the previous production of *The Sound of Music*. I had thought at the time how perfect he was for the part of an official in the Nazi secret police with his long pallid humourless face and cold grey eyes. Here he was again in the role of the sinister Dr Braun, covert Gestapo officer. He suddenly caught sight of me standing at the back and loudly announced the fact.

' 'Ey up, Colonel Blimp's arrived,' he called up to the stage. 'All we need now is the pantomime dame and her husband and we've very nearly got a full pack of cards.'

Ray swivelled round and gazed out into the hall. 'At last,' he sighed, his breath pluming out into the cold air, 'the Colonel's arrived. We were going to send out a search party. I can't tell you how stressful it's been, Gervase. It really has. This is one of the last rehearsals and half the cast is missing. There's no sign of Margot and Winco, and Mrs Bishop's come out in a rash. Then you didn't turn up for your scene. It's all too too much. I feel like abandoning it—but that wouldn't be professional.'

'I'm sorry,' I said, 'the meeting went on rather longer than I thought.'

'This is important you know, Gervase,' Ray said sharply. 'This is one of the last opportunities we have before the dress rehearsal to get it right and it still is far from perfect.'

'Well, shall we get on with it, then?' called George from where he was sitting in the hall. 'The sooner we do, the sooner we'll be on our way. I've got an extra-ordinary meeting at the Rotary tonight, so I can't stay much longer.'

'Give me strength,' said Raymond. 'Why do I put myself through this? Why do I bother? On stage, please, Gervase. I'll read in the lines of the Dame. Cecile, you enter stage right with Colonel Graham behind you. And can you not stomp on to the stage like a constipated elephant? Lightly, lightly does it. You stride into the room, Gervase, the conquering hero, having just taken the German surrender. You look pretty pleased with yourself. You smile, look around, nod knowingly. Then you salute and extend a hand to the Dame and bow your head. I'd like to see a little more gravitas in your manner, Gervase, than I have seen to date. At the last rehearsal, you tended to be a bit louche.'

'Louche?' I repeated.

'Remember you command a crack Scottish regiment,' Raymond told me.

'Will he be wearing a kilt?' asked George.

'No, he won't,' I said quickly.

'Or tartan trews?'

'Definitely not!' I told him.

'Now that's not a bad thought,' pondered Raymond, tilting his head to one side and looking at me as a professional photographer might examine a model before taking the picture. 'It might be quite colourful for you to appear on stage, Gervase, in a bright tartan. It would have to be a kilt, of course, you don't really have the buttocks for trews.'

'Raymond,' I said firmly, 'there is no way I am wearing a kilt or tartan trews.'

'Will I have a uniform this time, Raymond?' asked George. 'I had to wear a dirty old raincoat in *The Sound of Music* and everybody else was in uniform. Even the nuns got to dress up a bit.'

'We will discuss your wardrobe, George, all in good time,' said the producer, still staring at me with the thoughtful expression on his face.

The rehearsal continued until, ten minutes later, the redoubtable Mrs Cleaver-Canning made her grand entrance followed by her husband, Winco. He was an elderly, slightly stooping man with thin wisps of sandy-grey hair and a great handlebar moustache and he was struggling with a large hamper. The Dame of Sark was attired in a substantial fur coat with matching hat, puce leather gloves and knee-length black boots.

'Come along, Winco,' she said.

'Righto,' he growled.

'Margot!' exclaimed Raymond, throwing up his hands. 'You've arrived.'

'With some hot soup and little nibbles to keep us going,' she said.

Despite Raymond's protestations, the whole cast descended on Winco chattering like a bunch of excited school children.

'I give up,' he moaned, flopping onto a chair. 'I give up.'

*   *   *

When the rehearsal was finally over, I declined the invitation to join the rest of the cast to go for a drink. I was keen to get home—not that I was going to spend it quietly reading or watching television. I knew I still had quite a bit of preparation to do for the forthcoming English course, and a couple of school reports to proof-read that evening.

I was heading down the corridor towards the front entrance, when a stentorian voice echoed behind me.

'Hold up!' It was George Furnival. 'I want a word.'

Now what, I thought. 'Yes, George?' I waited for him to catch me up.

'You, my friend, might very well be the answer to my prayers,' he told me, hurrying down the corridor to join me.

This sounded ominous. 'I am not carrying a coffin,' I said.

'No, no, it's nothing like that,' he said. 'I have all the pallbearers I need. Anyway you haven't got the right features for a funeral assistant. You have to have a mournful expression, a sorrowful countenance, and a sombre outward bearing to carry a coffin. You look far too fit and happy.' I didn't feel it at that moment. 'I'm in search of a speaker.'

'No, no,' I began, 'I know nothing whatsoever about funerals.'

'Listen a minute,' he said, extending a thin white hand, which he placed around my shoulder. His cold grey eyes looked into mine and I could smell the rather sickly odour of embalming fluid. 'I was just telling Margot Cleaver-Canning about the dreadful fix we're in over the Rotary District Governor's Conference in the Memorial Hall tomorrow. That's why I'm rushing to this extra-ordinary meeting now. It's crisis time. We're short of a speaker. We have tried a number of people already but they're all booked up—inevitable, really—and I was asking Mrs Cleaver-Canning if Winco might fill the slot with memories of his wartime experiences as a fighter pilot, but they're going to be in London for some big Air Force do, so that's no good. Anyway, to cut a long story short—'

I knew full well what I was about to be asked and made to move off. 'Goodnight, George. I really do need to get home.'

'Hold on, hold on!' said George, gripping my arm. 'Mrs Cleaver-Canning said you'd be just the ticket.'

'I'm busy tomorrow,' I said quickly.

'Let me finish,' he said. 'This isn't any old meeting, you know. It's the highlight of our Rotary calendar. There'll be upwards of five hundred people there. One of the speakers—Chuck Wiseman from Seattle, he's the International President's representative, by the way, and we were so over the moon to have secured him—well, he was to speak but he's had to cancel. Well, he hasn't had to cancel as such, but his widow has. I was looking forward to meeting Chuck and comparing notes because he is, or was, I should say, in the same profession, running a very successful funeral business in the States, very successful. You might have heard of it—the Primrose Path Bereavement Parlour. They're way ahead of us in embalming over there, you know. Anyway, as I was saying—'

'This is all very interesting, George,' I told him, looking at my watch, 'but I really can't help.'

291

'It's only a paltry ten minutes,' he said.

'Well, I can't.'

'He was carrying a casket out of the Heavenly Meadows Chapel of Rest to the strains of Elvis Presley singing "Return to Sender" and he just keeled over.'

'Who?' I asked.

'Chuck. Heart attack. Best way to go, in my opinion. Fortunately, the bearers managed to hang on to the coffin—they call them caskets over there—otherwise it would have been even more tragic if they had dropped the corpse as well. There's nothing worse at a funeral than dropping the body. Anyway, he was going to speak.'

'Well, I'm not!' I said firmly. 'I have things planned for tomorrow.'

'Come on, it's only ten minutes of your time,' he persisted. 'We've got a really good speaker before you, a brigadier with experiences of commanding front-line troops. Since you're playing a colonel in the play you could pick up a few tips.'

'No.'

'It's not that it's a dinner where you would have to sit through the meal, and then listen to all the other speakers. It is just ten minutes of light-hearted banter before the District Governor rounds things off.'

'Light-hearted banter!' I repeated. 'I'm not a comedian.'

'I know that and, as I said to Mrs Cleaver-Canning, a school inspector isn't likely to have us rolling about in the aisles, but we are desperate and she said you'd spoken at her Golf Club Dinner and you were all right. She also said you didn't charge a fee and so they were able to afford a

292

really good speaker for the following year.'

'That's good to know,' I said, accepting the backhanded compliment with a wry smile. 'I'm glad I was "all right".'

'I mean, we don't want anything smutty, mind. Rotarians are professional business people. They don't like *risqué* material. We had a blue comedian once who used the DG's wife as the butt of his jokes. We don't want a repeat of that.'

'There won't be anything smutty, *risqué* or otherwise, George,' I told him, 'because I am *not* doing it. Much as I would like to help, I can't. I am really busy tomorrow.'

'I see,' he said, looking deflated. 'Well, you can't say I didn't do my best. As I said, it would only be ten minutes of your time which doesn't seem much to ask and we would, of course, be prepared, if you insisted, to give a donation to a charity of your choice and we are desperate. I understand the Committee has tried everyone else, but if you won't do it . . .' He looked at me expectantly.

Malleable, Julie had called me and malleable I was. 'Oh, for goodness' sake,' I sighed. 'Go on, then, but ten minutes only and not a second more.'

'You're a gentleman and a scholar, that's what you are,' he said, clapping me on the back, 'and if you are ever in need of my funeral services, I shall be happy to give you a good discount. The conference starts at nine thirty but you needn't be there until eleven.'

I heard the jangling of the keys that signalled the arrival of the caretaker and a moment later he appeared like the Ghost of Christmas Past around the corner.

George observed him for a moment. 'Now, he'd

be ideal as a pallbearer,' he said. 'Mind you, he would make a bloody good corpse as well.'

* * *

I duly arrived at the Memorial Hall just before eleven the following morning. To be honest, I wasn't sorry to get out of the house because Christine was not best pleased at my having agreed to give a talk on a Saturday morning. She had said some rather unflattering things about my resolve to say No.

I was met in the foyer by a large man sporting a straw boater and wearing a bright yellow sash with a wheel displayed prominently on the front.

'I'm the Sergeant-at-Arms,' he announced, smiling widely. 'Welcome to the District Governor's Conference.'

'Good morning,' I said. 'I'm one of the speakers.'

'Chuck?'

'No, no,' I said, 'I'm standing in for Chuck.'

'Is he not well?'

'He's dead.'

'Oh dear,' he said, shaking his head. 'How did that happen, then?'

'He was carrying a coffin—they call them caskets in the States—and I think he had a heart attack.'

'I see.'

'Fortunately they didn't drop the coffin.'

'That's a blessing, anyway. Does the District Governor know that Chuck won't be speaking?'

'I believe so, yes.'

'Everybody was expecting Chuck.'

'Well, he's not here.'

'You had better come this way. Where are you from?'

'Hawksrill.'

'We've a Hawksrill in Yorkshire, you know.'

'Yes, I know. I live there.'

'I thought you were from America.'

'No, that was Chuck,' I said.

'Poor old Chuck. Did you know him?'

'No, I never met him.'

'No, neither did I, but we were all looking forward to hearing him,' said the man disconsolately. 'People will be very disappointed.'

'Well, I'm afraid it can't be helped,' I said.

'That's life, isn't it,' said the man. 'It comes to all of us eventually—death, I mean.'

'I think perhaps I should be making a move,' I said. 'I'm supposed to be speaking in ten minutes' time.'

'Things have been moved back,' said the man. 'The brigadier's delayed. They're all having coffee at the moment so you've plenty of time. I mean, we can't start proceedings without the brigadier.'

'No,' I sighed, 'I guess not.' So much for the ten minutes, I thought.

'First-class speaker, the brigadier, I'm told.'

'Yes, so I hear. Incidentally, has George Furnival arrived yet?' I asked.

'George? No. He had a ten o'clock funeral this morning, and will be here a little late.'

'I see,' I said. I was somewhat irritated by the fact that the person who had inveigled me into doing this wretched talk would not be here himself.

'Are you a friend of George's, then?' asked the Sergeant-at-Arms.

'Not really,' I said. 'I'm doing him a favour and standing in for Chuck.'

'So you're an undertaker like George, then?'

'No, a school inspector.'

The man looked at me for a moment. 'A school inspector?'

'That's right.'

He sucked in his breath, 'And what are you talking to us about then?'

'My experiences in education.'

'Doesn't sound a barrel of laughs,' he said.

'Still, you've got the brigadier,' I told him.

'That's true enough. Well, if you'd like to follow me," said the man, 'I'll take you to the District Governor and his guests.'

I was shown into an ante-room by the Sergeant-at-Arms. There were several knots of middle-aged and elderly men, all heavily chained and bemedalled, in earnest conversation. I joined a man standing by the window, furtively smoking a cigarette.

'Good morning,' I said.

'Morning,' he replied, breathing out a cloud of smoke. 'Nasty habit. I'm trying to give them up.' It certainly didn't look like it to me. 'Are you a delegate?'

'I'm one of the speakers,' I told him.

'Oh, you must be Chuck.'

'No, I'm not Chuck. I'm standing in for him.'

'Is he ill?' asked the man.

'Dead,' I said.

'Dear, oh dear, how did that happen?'

'He was carrying a coffin and had a heart attack.'

'Well,' said the man, inhaling the smoke from his

cigarette, 'if you have to go, I suppose that's the best way.' He coughed loudly.

'Thankfully they didn't drop the coffin that Chuck was helping to carry,' I told him.

'There's a blessing,' said the man. 'Could have been nasty.'

'So, you see, Chuck couldn't make it,' I said, 'and I've been asked to speak instead.'

'I was really looking forward to hearing old Chuck,' said the man sadly. 'He was supposed to be a brilliant speaker, by all accounts. Spoke from the heart. Still, we've got the brigadier and are in for a real treat. Have you heard the brigadier speak before?'

'No, I haven't.'

'Supposed to be one of the best speakers in the British Army.'

'Really?' I was heartily sick and tired of hearing about the wonderful speaking skills of the brigadier so decided to move on. 'If you'll excuse me,' I said, 'I must get some coffee.'

Reaching for a coffee cup, I accidentally knocked the arm of the man next to me in the queue. 'I'm sorry—' I started.

The man turned slowly and smiled a wide rather unnerving smile.

'Hello, Gervase,' he said pleasantly.

'Dr Gore!' I spluttered.

'And what are you doing here?' he asked.

'I've been asked to speak,' I told him.

'Really?'

'I'm standing in for Chuck.'

'Can't he make it?'

I was tempted to relate the whole sorry saga again, but resisted and settled for, 'He's indisposed.'

'Pity,' said Dr Gore, 'we were all looking forward to hearing him. Quite a speaker, I am told. Still, we've got the brigadier to look forward to. The brigadier comes highly recommended. So you've been asked to speak to conference, have you?'

'George Furnival asked me to stand in for Chuck,' I said.

'And how do you know George?' he asked.

'We act together in the Fettlesham Literary Players,' I told him.

'Well, well, well. I didn't know you were an actor *and* a raconteur as well as a school inspector.'

'I dabble,' I said.

'Good, good! I hear from Mrs Savage that arrangements are progressing very well for my NACADS Conference.'

'Yes, everything's in hand,' I told him. Butterflies were beginning to flutter uncontrollably in my stomach.

'I said it would be a little job, not too onerous,' said the CEO, smiling his thin-lipped smile. 'Anyhow, I very much look forward to hearing what you have to say about education.' My heart now sank down into my shoes. 'Nothing too controversial, I hope.'

'No, no,' I said quickly, 'nothing controversial.'

'You had better come and say hello to the District Governor,' Dr Gore instructed me, taking my arm. I accompanied the CEO dutifully and was introduced to a craggy-faced man with thick wavy silver hair.

'I'm Harry Cockburn,' he said, 'District Governor, for my sins. And you must be the young man George was telling me about who has so kindly stepped into the breach.'

Before I could answer a loud, harsh voice I knew only too well came from behind me.

' 'E gets everyweer, this chap.'

I turned to find a large man with a fat red face, purple pitted nose and mop of unnaturally shiny, jet black hair. It was Councillor George Peterson, the most self-opinionated and wearisome member of the Education Committee, and husband of the headteacher of Highcopse Primary School.

'You know our speaker then, Mr Deputy Mayor?' asked the District Governor.

'I do indeed,' said Councillor Peterson, sticking out his chin. 'Gev my wife a right goin' over when 'e hinspected 'er school. Looked at everythin' from t'books in t'library to t'locks on t'lavatory doors.'

'Good morning, Councillor Peterson,' I said.

'Mr Deputy Mayor,' he corrected me. 'I've been elevated since we last met. Oh yes,' he continued in that strident tone of voice, 'I know Mester Phinn very well. We've crossed swords—paradoxically, of course—in t'past, 'ave we not, Mester Phinn?'

I gave a weak smile. *Why* had I let myself get into this, I asked myself? Could things get worse? First, to have to deputise for Chuck, the outstanding orator everyone was so looking forward to hearing, then to have to speak after the brilliant brigadier, and then to discover that my boss *and* Councillor Peterson would be in the audience. At that moment, I completely identified with Raymond's plaintive cry that it was 'all too too much'.

'I was just saying to Dr Gore, Mr Deputy Mayor,' commented the District Governor, 'that it is very kind of Mr Phinn to stand in for one of our speakers who unfortunately is unable to be with us.'

' 'Appen it is,' said Councillor Peterson, 'but I wasn't aware that hofficers of the Hauthority were allowed to moonlight.'

'I'm hardly moonlighting, councillor,' I told him, irritated by his comment. 'I'm giving up a Saturday morning to help a colleague.'

'Aye, well, I would 'ave thought you 'ad enough on yer plate what wi' all these school closures wi'out speakin' at conferences. I've said it once, and I'll say it again—'

'Please, Mr Deputy Mayor,' interrupted Dr Gore, 'let us not discuss Education Authority business. That is best left for the Council Chamber.'

' 'Appen so,' said Councillor Peterson, 'but it's huppermost in my mind at t'moment. I'm gerrin' a lot of flak, as you well know, Dr Gore. Bullets comin' at me from every direction, same as what I got when I tried, wi'out success, I may add, to close t'school in the village where Mester Phinn lives.'

'I think it is so very important to preserve these little village schools,' observed the District Governor. 'To my mind, they are so much a part of the fabric of rural existence and so important in the life of the small community.'

'Aye, well, I can see you've never 'ad to manage a budget with a bloody gret deficit, Dr Cockburn,' said Councillor Peterson, clearly stung by the remark. 'I could say a few things about 'ospitals and doctors and t'waste in t'National 'Ealth Service, if I'd a mind.'

'If indeed,' murmured the District Governor.

'Beg pardon?' asked Councillor Peterson.

'I said, "Shall I lead?" I think we are about to start.'

The Sergeant-at-Arms shouted from the door. 'Mr Deputy Mayor, District Governor, fellow Rotarians, honoured guests, gentlemen, if you please. Could you take your seats? The brigadier's car has been sighted and is pulling into the car park.'

I was conducted to the wings of the stage by the Sergeant-at-Arms and told to wait while the brigadier, who would be speaking before me, was freshening up.

'They like to look smart and well presented, these military types,' he said.

I was getting more and more irritated as the time ticked on. Eventually a woman in a dark blue suit joined me.

'Good morning,' she said.

'Good morning,' I replied.

'Are you one of the speakers?' she asked.

'I am,' I said, 'I was supposed to be on half an hour ago but we've all been waiting for this bloody brigadier. He's arrived at last, but now we're waiting for him to powder his nose, or something.'

The woman gave a lop-sided smile. 'I'm the bloody brigadier,' she said, holding out a hand. 'Nice to meet you.'

CHAPTER EIGHTEEN

'It's the Black Widow on the phone for you,' said Julie, grimacing, and passing over the receiver as if it harboured some dire infection. It was a quarter to three on Wednesday afternoon and I was about to leave the office.

'Who?' I asked.

'Brenda the Impaler. Who do you think?'

'Mrs Savage?'

'Right! And, as usual, she sounds as sharp as a bottle full of sulphuric acid. Shall I say you've already left?'

'No, no,' I said hurriedly. 'I had better speak to her because it's probably about the meeting later this afternoon.'

I took the receiver from Julie who waited, a hand on her hip, smiling and listening.

'Mr Phinn?' came the brusque and imperious voice.

'It is,' I said.

'Brenda Savage here. There is a slight problem with regard to our intended visit to Manston Hall this afternoon to discuss the arrangements for the NACADS Conference. If you recall, we agreed to meet there for four o'clock. I'm afraid my car is . . . it's . . . well, it won't start . . . so I shall have to travel with you.'

'Travel with me?' I repeated.

Julie pulled a face.

'Yes, indeed,' said Mrs Savage. 'There is really no alternative.'

'The problem about travelling with me, Mrs

302

Savage,' I told her, 'is that I have a couple of calls to make on my way to Manston Hall.'

'A couple of calls?' she repeated.

'I agreed to collect some things for Sister Brendan at St Bartholomew's.'

'Collect some things?' She sounded like an echo.

'Yes, Sister Brendan is organising a charity auction next week in aid of disadvantaged children and is collecting contributions. Fettlesham Social Club has donated a television, Fine Wines of Fettlesham a couple of cases of wine, and there's a hamper from Roper's Salesroom. I have agreed to collect them on my way to Manston Hall, so I can drop them off when I visit St Bartholomew's on Friday. So you see, I have to set off quite a bit earlier—in fact, I am just leaving now—and my car will be pretty full.' Julie raised a thumb and grinned at me. 'Unfortunately, therefore, I cannot take you with me.'

'I wasn't aware that collecting and delivering goods was part of the inspector's duties,' she observed.

'It's no trouble,' I told her. What I should have said was it is really none of your business, but I bit my lip. 'All the pick-up points are *en route* to Manston Hall so I am not going out of my way and it is for a very good cause.' I often wondered why people felt it necessary to explain themselves to her. She seemed to have this bizarre effect.

'Nevertheless, it does seem to me—' Mrs Savage began.

'So you see,' I said, cutting her off mid-sentence, 'I have things to do and the car will be full. I suggest you get a taxi.'

'That is out of the question!' she retorted

sharply. 'The County Treasurer would not be best pleased to receive a claim for a taxi fare right out to Manston Hall, particularly when another member of the Education Department will be going there. No, no, I shall have to travel with you. When will you be ready?'

I looked heavenwards and sighed. 'As I said, I'm just about to set off.'

'Well, if you could collect me from outside the main entrance to County Hall in ten minutes, I—'

'Mrs Savage,' I said, interrupting her again, 'you may recall the conversation we had the other week on the top corridor of County Hall, when you were at great pains to point out to me that the inspectors' office is but a short distance and it is not that onerous for us to walk over. I am sure, therefore, that it would not be too much of a hardship for you to "walk over" and meet me here. It's such a lovely sunny day, too. Apart from anything else, I would not want to venture near County Hall in case I am clamped.'

There was a silence at the end of the line. I could visualise her, drumming her long, red-nailed fingers testily on the desktop, her face tightening with displeasure. Julie continued to make faces at me. 'Very well, Mr Phinn,' she said at last. 'I shall be with you directly.'

'I'll meet you in the car park outside this office.' I put down the phone. 'She's coming over,' I told Julie.

'Well done!' she said sarcastically. 'You had every reason *not* to take that woman with you to Manston Hall, yet here you are about set off with venomous Brenda. I just hope you live to tell the tale.'

'I'll try.'

'Why can't she make her own way there?' Julie asked.

'Her car won't start.'

'What, that swanky red sports convertible?'

'It appears so,' I said.

'She could get a bus.'

'Now, can you imagine Mrs Savage on a bus?'

'Tell her to get on her bike, then,' said Julie.

'I can just see it,' I laughed. 'Mrs Savage on a bicycle!'

'Well, I hope for your sake she gets her car fixed soon, otherwise you'll be chauffeuring her all round the place, and people will start talking.'

'That I shall *not* be doing!' I spluttered.

'Well, you are today,' said Julie, teetering towards the door on her ridiculously high heels. 'The trouble with you is that you're too easily persuaded. Dr Gore gives you all those "little jobs", Sister Brendan has you collecting things for her raffle, and now the Bride of Dracula has you chauffeuring her around. You ought to put your foot down.' Before I could respond, Julie was through the door. 'See you tomorrow,' she called over her shoulder, 'if you survive this afternoon, that is.'

*   *   *

Mrs Savage kept me waiting a good ten minutes, and I was about to go when she eventually appeared, strolling down the white gravel path leading from County Hall to where I was parked. For all the world, she looked like a model from a fashion magazine dressed to kill. She was wearing

305

a grey herringbone tweed jacket with black velvet collar and cuffs, a blue pencil skirt and navy suede shoes. Around her shoulders was draped a pale brown woollen overcoat, while tucked under one arm was an expensive-looking ruched velvet handbag and she was carrying a slim leather document case. She had obviously made a considerable effort, and would appear very much at home amongst the aristocrats at Manston Hall. In fact, she looked every inch a duchess.

As she climbed into the car, her ostentatious jewellery jangling, she sniffed the air.

'Babies,' I said.

'I beg your pardon?'

'The smell of babies,' I said. 'It's my little boy. He tends to splash a bit when he has his milk.'

'I see.'

'The smell lingers.'

'Yes, it does,' she agreed, winding down the window a fraction. She then produced a bottle of scent from her handbag and sprayed herself liberally.

I set off. There was an embarrassed silence as we made our way down Fettlesham High Street. It appeared that Mrs Savage was not, for once, in a very talkative mood.

'So what's wrong with your car?' I asked, deciding to break the ice.

'Oh, it's . . . er . . . something mechanical,' she replied evasively, examining a long red nail.

'Did it just cut out,' I asked, 'or wouldn't it start?'

'I don't know anything about cars,' she said dismissively, turning to stare out of the window.

Good gracious, I thought, so there *is* something

that Mrs Savage doesn't know about.

There was another protracted silence.

'And how are the school closures progressing?' I asked.

'Slowly,' she replied.

'Things certainly seemed to have moved with regard to the schools I have been involved with,' I told her.

'The schools at Ugglemattersby are somewhat different,' she said. 'They are not in actual fact closing, they are merely amalgamating. Everyone there, with the exception of a few mavericks, as Dr Gore is wont to call them, is in favour. Would that were the case with the others.'

'So they're not going too well?' I asked.

'I am not at liberty, Mr Phinn,' she said, 'to discuss the other schools.'

And that was the extent of our conversation until we arrived at our first port of call.

After I had collected the two cases of wine from Fine Wines of Fettlesham, and a hamper from Roper's Salesroom, we left the centre of Fettlesham, and headed for the rather insalubrious northern side of the town. The area was run down, and the road sweepers that kept the High Street as neat as a pin obviously never came out here. I pulled up outside an ugly grey building. High walls topped with broken glass enclosed the litter-strewn car park. A sign above the entrance announced in large red letters, 'FETTLESHAM WORKING MEN'S CLUB'. Below it, a notice warned would-be trespassers that they would be prosecuted, that the building was protected by security cameras and alarms, that guard dogs patrolled and that no money was kept on the premises.

'I shan't be a moment,' I told Mrs Savage.

'I don't intend to remain in the car,' she told me curtly, hurriedly unfastening the safety belt. 'This area does not look at all safe and I would be foolhardy indeed to be sitting here with two cases of wine and a hamper full of food on the back seat. I'd be a sitting target for muggers.' She touched the gold necklace at her neck. 'I shall come in with you.'

Pasted on the wall outside the club, between the graffiti, was a series of bright and showy posters, advertising the 'star turns' that were due to appear. The first one brought a grin to my lips. 'Hello to Striptease!' it stated in large red letters. 'Featuring the ravishing and adorable Big Brenda of the Body Beautiful. She's pert, pleasing and tasty.' Mrs Savage averted her eyes. Another poster announced, 'Olga, one of Sweden's loveliest models and her muff in classical nude studies. She's saucy, spicy and sexy.'

'Are we going to be long in this establishment?' asked Mrs Savage, looking decidedly uncomfortable.

'Not long,' I replied jovially.

After repeated ringing and banging, I managed to gain the attention of someone who poked his tousled head out of an upstairs window. He looked like a tortoise emerging from its shell.

'What?' he shouted.

'It's Mr Phinn,' I shouted back.

'Who?'

'Mr Phinn. I think you were expecting me.'

'You're early!' he snapped.

'I can't recall giving a time,' I replied.

'Well, you're early,' he repeated. 'I was told

308

you'd be arriving at six. I haven't had time to finish the cleaning. I've the dressing rooms to finish and then the bar to sort out.'

'There's no need to worry about that,' I called up to him.

A group of youths appeared from around the corner of the street and paused to observe us. One wolf-whistled.

'Do you think we might get inside?' asked Mrs Savage, stepping closer to me.

'Shall I call back later?' I asked the head at the window.

'No, hang on, I'll come down.'

After a great deal of noise from chains and bolts from the other side, the substantial door finally opened. An overweight and under-shaved man, dressed in a threadbare cardigan and shapeless grey flannel trousers, peered myopically at me. A cigarette dangled from the corner of his mouth.

'You'd better come in,' he said. 'I'm Reg, by the way. Watch them barrels. I'll have to shift them before tonight's show. You'll be pleased to hear that it's a full house. Very popular is Friday night. We've got Dougie Draper, the comedian. Have you heard of him?'

'No, I'm afraid not,' I said, following the man, with Mrs Savage close behind.

'He's brilliant!' exclaimed Reg. 'Back by popular demand. Has them rolling in the aisles and he's got a lovely voice. And then we've got Patsi Ronaldo with 'Songs from the Shows'. She's appeared here a few times. Bit past it now, but she can still belt out a good number.'

'Sounds a good evening,' I said.

'Oh yes, we have class acts here,' the man said.

'The sound system is on the blink again, but we've got someone coming to see about it.'

I had no idea why the man thought I would be interested in all this technical information but I nodded politely and said, 'Really?'

Reg took us into the vast hall, which had a big stage at the far end, a long curved bar area, an assortment of tables and chairs, while the unmistakable smell of stale beer, old smoke and toilets permeated the air. The walls, painted in garish greens and blues, were lined with photographs, no doubt of performers who had appeared at the club.

The grubby caretaker stared at Mrs Savage as she walked into the room with her usual long and decisive step. He observed her as one might study a strange decorative item on show in someone's house. Mrs Savage sniffed the air, placed a finger delicately under her nose then sat down at a small round plastic-topped table near the door, having first dusted down the plastic chair with her hand. From her ruched handbag, she produced her perfume, and sprayed her wrists liberally. She looked most ill at ease, perched on the edge of the chair. Her face was as set as a death mask.

'Would you like a drink?' Reg asked, still with his eyes fixed on Mrs Savage.

'No, thank you,' I replied.

'What about . . . er . . .' he gestured in Mrs Savage's direction.

'I don't think so,' I said.

The man turned slightly so we were facing away from the door and from where Mrs Savage was sitting. He leaned towards me and whispered, 'You'd never tell, would you?'

'Tell what?' I asked, recoiling from the man's foul breath.

'You know.'

'No, I'm afraid I don't.'

He came closer. 'That it was a man.'

'What?' I said. 'I honestly don't know what you're on about.'

'We've had one or two performing here before but I could always tell. It's the hands that are the give-away, that and the prominent Adam's apple. Yes, I've seen one or two in my time,' he continued in a hushed voice, 'but I have to say, he's the best. He's incredible. Spit and image of Danny la Rue. I suppose he's had cosmetic surgery and had his hormones seen to and, of course, make-up covers up a multitude but he certainly could have fooled me.'

Was I in some parallel universe? 'What on earth are you talking about?' I asked.

'Veronica.'

'Who?'

He tilted his head in the direction of Mrs Savage. 'Him, the female impersonator.'

'Female impersonator!' I exclaimed. 'I think we have some crossed wires here. Who in heaven's name do you think I am?'

'You're the agent for Veronica, the female impersonator who's appearing here tonight.' Then a shadow of doubt crossed his face. 'Aren't you?' He nodded towards Mrs Savage. 'That's Veronica, the drag act, isn't it?'

I nearly choked. 'No, no, I've come to collect the television for Sister Brendan's charity auction. That's . . . that's not a man—it's Mrs Savage!'

'Bloody Nora!' he exclaimed. 'I'm sorry, mate, I

thought you were this evening's drag act. I've been expecting them for a sound and lighting check before the show. And when I saw you both standing out there, well, I put two and two together.'

'How long is this going to take?' asked Mrs Savage impatiently, getting to her feet and smoothing her hands down the front of her skirt.

The man started to stifle a laugh and so did I. Our amusement became so much greater when we caught sight of the stiff-backed figure with the stony countenance, looking at us as if we had both gone completely mad. Thankfully, it appeared that Mrs Savage hadn't heard any of the previous exchange.

'You won't tell her, will you?' Reg spluttered.

'No, no, of course not,' I replied as I headed for the door, indicating to Mrs Savage that we were on our way.

A few minutes later, the television set was safely stowed on the back seat, and we set off for Manston Hall.

'Something seems to have amused you and that awful man,' Mrs Savage said as we drove out of the car park.

'Yes,' I said, smiling.

She was clearly curious. 'Are you going to share it with me?' she asked.

I thought for a moment. 'It was nothing, really,' I said. 'Not worth bothering about. I'm sure you'd find it a bit of a drag if I told you.'

*   *   *

Yorkshire is blessed with many gracious stately

homes, from magnificent piles to handsome manor houses. Manston Hall, although not a large house by the standards of Castle Howard or Harewood, is undoubtedly one of the most elegant. The visitor drives though great black ornate gates, past the gatehouse, and along a seemingly endless avenue of beech trees, until he arrives at this perfectly proportioned early eighteenth-century mansion. Built in warm, red brick and standing square and solid amongst lawns, rose gardens, scenic lakes and woodland, it had been the home of the Courtnay-Cunninghame family since the eighteenth century.

I pulled up in front of the flight of steps that climbed up to the great black front door, which was flanked by two stone pillars. Above, carved into the stone lintel, was the family motto writ proud and large: *Lancastrienses manu dei occidantur*. I smiled to myself. My Latin wasn't that good, but I got the gist.

As Mrs Savage and I got out of the car, the door opened and a tall man appeared and stood at the top of the steps, his feet slightly apart and his hands in the pockets of his dark green corduroy trousers.

'Mr Phinn, is it?' he called down.

'That's right.'

'You were expected,' he said. 'Do come along up.'

The speaker was a striking-looking man with broad, brown face creased on the forehead and around the eyes, and with a crop of curly brown hair—attractively flecked with grey at the temples. His gaze settled on Mrs Savage as she came up the steps towards him.

'This is Mrs Savage,' I told him, 'Dr Gore's

Personal Assistant.'

'I say,' he murmured, clearly taken with the vision who, having got to the top of the steps, stroked the creases out of her skirt, draped her coat around her shoulders and looked around imperiously. She nodded at the man.

'I'm Tadge, by the way,' he said, giving her a broad and winning smile.

'Good afternoon,' she said formally.

'Good journey?' asked the man.

'Interesting,' replied Mrs Savage. Her tone was undisguisedly sarcastic.

'The last time I came to Manston Hall,' I said, 'it was shrouded in thick snow. It looks very different at this time of year. Very beautiful.'

'Autumn is my most favourite season,' said the man. 'The colours are magnificent, the beeches in particular . . .' he waved his hand towards the beech avenue we had driven through. 'All the golden and red, the bracken slopes rusty brown and, of course—'

'Do you think we might go inside?' enquired Mrs Savage. 'It is getting quite chilly.'

'Of course, of course,' he said. 'How very remiss of me. Do come along in.'

The spacious entrance hall, which was decorated in the palest of yellows and blues, was dominated by a magnificent ornately-carved chimneypiece in white Italian marble. Hanging above was a large oil painting depicting a heavily bemedalled, moustachioed and severe-looking soldier in crimson uniform.

'One of the ancestors,' Tadge explained, seeing me look up at it. 'Not a happy chappie, is he?'

Tadge led us from the hall and down a long

corridor, past numerous shut doors, to the room I knew was the library. On my first visit to Manston Hall—on another of Dr Gore's 'little jobs', of course—we had met in this elegant room. The walls were lined with bookcases, from floor to ceiling, and there was a not unpleasant smell of leather from the handsome bindings. Over the fireplace was a large portrait of a young woman with pale blue eyes and a dreamy look. Dressed for the hunt, she was astride a dashing chestnut horse. I didn't remember seeing that before.

'What a handsome room,' observed Mrs Savage, taking in everything with a sweep of her head. She then glanced in my direction. 'Somewhat a contrast to the last one we were in.' She allowed herself a small, self-satisfied smile.

Our host indicated a large green leather armchair. 'Do have a seat, Mr Phinn,' he said to me, smiling. He waited until Mrs Savage was seated on the matching chesterfield sofa and then sat down beside her.

The man stared at her like a hungry cat might watch a bowlful of goldfish. 'I've arranged for a cup of tea later, when we've dealt with all the business,' he said. 'I thought we'd discuss your requirements first and then have a look around the house.'

Mrs Savage opened the leather document case, removed a wad of papers and put on a pair of stylish small gold-rimmed spectacles.

'We have two halls,' said Tadge, 'North and South. Either would be suitable as the main conference hall. I suggest you have the lectures in one and the exhibitions in the other. Delegates are very welcome to use the billiard room, this room and the dining room but the drawing room and the morning room—the private apartments—will not be available. Of course, the grounds are—'

'Excuse me,' interrupted Mrs Savage, her carefully-plucked eyebrows arching, 'do I take it that *you* will be liaising with us?'

'That's right,' Tadge replied good-humouredly.

'Oh,' she said, clearly sounding disappointed. 'My understanding was that Lord Marrick would be meeting with us to discuss arrangements for the conference.'

'He's with the gamekeeper at the moment,' she was told, 'but he will be along later.'

'So he is leaving the organisation to *you*?' asked Mrs Savage, stressing the last word. Her tone was as sharp as ever.

'Yes, indeed.'

For goodness' sake, I thought, will the woman shut up! 'Mrs Savage—' I started.

'One moment, Mr Phinn,' she said. 'I do like to know with whom I am dealing. I take it then, Mr Tadge, that you are Lord Marrick's secretary or an administrator of some kind?'

'I suppose I am, in a way,' said Tadge, smiling widely.

'Well, you are or you are not,' said Mrs Savage, somewhat coldly and pulling one of her faces. Her tone bordered on the brusque. 'I do like to know with whom I am liaising. As Mr Phinn is well aware, on previous occasions when I have been asked to take on various initiatives, there have been certain crossed wires and misunderstandings.'

'May we get on with the meeting, Mrs Savage,' I said irritably.

'No, no, Mr Phinn,' said our host amiably. 'I

foolishly imagined you knew who I was. I clearly didn't introduce myself properly. I deal with most of the business now at Manston Hall, running the estate, managing the business interests.'

'Oh, I see,' she said. 'So you are the Estate Manager?'

'I'm Lord Marrick's son,' replied the man. 'Tadge Manston.'

Mrs Savage jumped as if touched by a cattle prod. 'Oh!' she exclaimed. 'Lord Marrick's son?'

'Most people call me Tadge—it comes from my names, Thomas, Arthur, D'Aubney, George, Edmund Courtnay-Cunninghame—Viscount Manston, if you want the full thing. Bit of a mouthful, isn't it?'

Mrs Savage's demeanour changed completely. 'Oh,' she cooed, smiling so widely that it was a wonder she didn't leave traces of her red lipstick on the lobes of her ears. 'I'm so very sorry, Lord Manston. You must have thought me extremely rude. I had no idea you were Lord Marrick's son.'

'Please, please, Mrs Savage,' he said, patting her hand. 'Think nothing of it. I don't stand on my dignity. Dignity to me is like a top hat, it looks rather silly when you stand on it.'

She ought to take a leaf out of his book, I thought to myself.

'I'm so sorry. I just didn't realise who you were,' said Mrs Savage in a syrupy tone of voice. She looked quite flustered.

'That's the second case of mistaken identity in one day,' I said.

'Did you say something, Mr Phinn?' asked Mrs Savage tartly.

'No, nothing,' I said, smirking before asking,

317

'Shall we get back to the business in hand?'

Tadge took us on a tour of the house, at least of the rooms which the conference delegates would be permitted to use. When we returned to the library, a tray with the promised pot of tea was waiting for us. As we finalised the arrangements for the NACADS Conference, Mrs Savage never took her fluttering eyes off Tadge Manston, and smiled winsomely every time he opened his mouth. He, too, seemed equally struck with Mrs Savage. I might have been invisible for all the notice they took of me.

'Well, Lord Manston,' said Mrs Savage finally, 'I think we have dealt with everything most satisfactorily, and may I say it has been a very great pleasure and indeed a privilege to have met you and to have been made so very welcome.'

'The pleasure was entirely mine, Mrs Savage,' he replied, patting her hand that was lying on the chesterfield next to him, 'and do please call me Tadge. Everyone does.'

'Tadge,' she said with a small smile. 'And I do hope you will call me Brenda.'

I was beginning to feel like a gooseberry so to put an end to their little *conversazione*—as Sidney would have said—I coughed. 'Was it your son, Tadge, that I met when I visited Manston School?' I enquired. That observation should pour cold water on their intimate little chinwag, I thought.

'Sorry, what did you say?' his lordship asked, just about managing to take his eyes off Mrs Savage.

'Your son,' I said. 'I believe I met him when I visited the school on your estate.'

'Young Tommy?' he said.

'He was a bright boy as I remember,' I told him.

'Yes, he's got quite a bit about him,' Tadge said. 'At prep school now, at Cransworth, and doing very well by all accounts. He's had a rough time of it over the last couple of years.'

'Oh dear,' said Mrs Savage, with a rare show of sympathy. It was clear she was determined not to be excluded from the conversation.

Tadge turned to Mrs Savage. 'His mother died when he was six,' he said, nodding sadly and looking up at the portrait above the fireplace.

'I am so sorry,' said Mrs Savage, following his gaze to the portrait. 'Was that your wife?'

'It was. She had a riding accident, fell from her horse at a jump, broke her neck.'

'How tragic,' said Mrs Savage.

' "Who never ate his bread in sorrow,' said Lord Manston, ' "who never spent the midnight hours, weeping and wailing for the morrow, he knows ye not, ye heavenly powers." '

'I beg your pardon?' said Mrs Savage.

'Goethe,' he replied.

'Of yes, of course,' she said. There was a sigh. She looked wistfully through the window. 'I too lost a spouse and know full well how it feels to be left alone in the world.'

'Really?' Tadge said, leaning forward.

Before Mrs Savage could regale us with the tragic details of her dear departed husband, and much to my relief, the door burst open and Lord Marrick made his ebullient entrance. Valentine Courtnay-Cunninghame, the 9th Earl Marrick, MC, DL was a rotund, ruddy-cheeked individual with a great walrus moustache and hair shooting up from a square head. I had met Lord Marrick on

319

a number of previous occasions—at interviews for teaching posts, Education Committee meetings, governors' conferences and various school events, and always found him an extremely warm, good-humoured and plain-spoken man with a deep sense of reverence for the land his family had owned for many generations.

'My apologies for not being here to greet you,' he growled, slamming the door shut behind him. 'Bit of business with the gamekeeper. Good to see you, Mrs Savage, Mr Phinn. I hope my son has been taking care of you both?'

'Yes, indeed,' replied Mrs Savage.

'Good show,' replied Lord Marrick, at which point there was a crashing noise from the other side of the library door, and the earl moved to open it. Two bulldogs catapulted into the room and rushed across to jump up at Tadge's chair.

'Get down, you brutes,' he said good-naturedly. 'You're wet! Go and lie down.'

The two barrel-bodied animals, drooling from their pink jowls, ambled across the floor and collapsed in front of the fireplace. I had met them on previous visits to Manston Hall, but I noticed Mrs Savage was eyeing them with grave suspicion.

'Sorry about that,' said Lord Marrick. 'Anyway, everything's sorted out for this conference, is it?'

'It is,' I replied.

Lord Marrick turned to his son. 'Still trying to catch the blighters,' he said. 'Jameson's set a couple more traps near the forty-acre. Just a matter of time before we get 'em.'

'Is it poachers?' enquired Mrs Savage.

'Squirrels, Mrs Savage,' replied the peer. 'Squirrels!' Then he turned to me. 'Do you know anything about squirrels, Mr Phinn?' he asked.

'Squirrels?' I murmured, with a sinking feeling but attempting to look as insouciant as possible.

'Squirrels,' he repeated.

I could feel myself colouring up. The gamekeeper had told him about my releasing the squirrels on his land, I was sure of it. Now he was setting mantraps. 'I can't say I know a great deal about squirrels,' I said.

'We have rather an odd problem with squirrels on the estate at the moment. The first we knew about it was when the local rag printed a report of a new breed of squirrels having been seen up in the woods near the forty-acre. Seen by a party of wretched ramblers who were walking there, and one of them sent a report in to the newspaper. They claimed to have seen a cross between a red and a grey squirrel—had grey coats, white bellies and bright red tails. Would you believe it, tails as red as a pillar box!' Lord Marrick brushed a hand across his large moustache. 'Stuff and nonsense, of course, reds and greys don't interbreed. Any damn fool knows that.'

I gulped. 'Really? Squirrels with red tails. How unusual.'

'I've no idea what they are. Had the fellows from CAPOW sniffing around—that's the Countryside Association for the Protection of Wildlife,' he expanded. 'If I have my way, it won't be a case of "protection", I can tell you, when we catch up with the varmints. Wreck my trees, they do. Anyhow, Jameson and I have been putting out traps this afternoon.'

'Amazing,' simpered Mrs Savage. 'Grey squirrels with red tails.'

'Once we catch them,' said Lord Marrick, 'the wildlife people can do what they like with them—so long as it is a long way away from my woods.'

'You think you'll catch them, then?' I asked in the most innocent of voices.

'Oh, we'll catch them all right,' growled the peer, 'and then we'll get to the bottom of this daft bloody business. Pardon my French, Mrs Savage. Grey squirrels with red tails, I ask you!'

'Might some children have painted their tails red for a prank?' suggested Mrs Savage. 'It is just the sort of thing some repellent boy would do.' I could have strangled her.

'Now there's a thought,' mused Lord Marrick. 'You might just have something there, Mrs Savage, and if it is mischievous young hooligans, I won't tell you what Jameson will do to them if he get his hands on them. The trouble they've caused him.'

'Perhaps we should be making tracks, Mrs Savage,' I said, keen to put an end to the conversation and see the back of Manston Hall.

CHAPTER NINETEEN

'You're a saint,' trilled Sister Brendan, the headteacher at St Bartholomew's Roman Catholic Infant School, as I lugged the last of the donations into her office. The nun, a diminutive woman with small, sparkling black eyes and a little beak of a nose, was like a twittering blackbird. 'It is so very good of you to collect all these items for my auction. I am sure we will raise a veritable fortune for those poor unfortunate children. People have

322

been so generous.'

'I've been called a number of things in my life, Sister,' I told her, panting under the weight of the huge hamper, 'but never a saint.'

'We all have the makings of a saint within us, Mr Phinn,' she told me. 'Just put the hamper down there near my desk, will you? My goodness, you look quite out of breath. Would you like to sit down for a moment?'

'No, no, Sister,' I said, breathing heavily and wiping my brow. 'I'm fine. It was just rather heavier than I imagined, and it's quite a walk from the car park.'

The school caretaker, an emaciated individual in a spotless brown overall and with a face the colour of putty, had observed me without a word as I had struggled with my burden but never suggested giving a helping hand. 'I would have asked the caretaker to help,' said the nun, peering into the hamper, 'but since his heart murmur, he can't exert himself or get excited. And, of course, he gets vertigo so can't climb ladders, and then there's his asthma . . . Poor man, he can't carry or climb or dust. He's a martyr, is Mr Sharrock, a true martyr.'

He sounded like a walking pathological museum and not a great deal of use as a caretaker, I thought, but I didn't comment. 'Well, Sister,' I said, 'that's the lot. Good luck with your auction. I must be making tracks.'

'You can't leave without having a little tour of the school!' cried the nun.

'Actually, I'm in rather a hurry, Sister,' I told her. 'I have an appointment with the headteacher of Crompton Primary School, and Mrs Gardiner is

323

a bit of a stickler when it comes to punctuality.' I glanced at my watch. 'In fact, she will be expecting me about now.'

'Come on! It's not half past eight yet,' said Sister Brendan, 'and Crompton Primary is just round the corner. You can't leave before having a little look round the school and Mrs Webb, my wonderful assistant, will be devastated if you leave before saying hello.'

She was somewhat fond of the hyperbole was Sister Brendan.

'No, I really must go, Sister,' I said. 'Perhaps another time.'

'Just a few minutes,' pleaded the nun. 'Please.'

I surrendered. 'Very well, just a few minutes.'

The headteacher took me on a tour of the school, gliding down the corridor before me as if she were on castors, stopping occasionally to admire a child's painting or to tell me how well the pupils were progressing. St Bartholomew's was indeed a rich and colourful place and she was justifiably proud.

I finally escaped—or thought I had. Sister Brendan came out into the playground with me, to see me off to the car park.

'Ah, here's Mrs Webb,' said Sister, 'manning the yard as usual. Look who I've brought to see you,' she told the teacher.

'Oh, Sister,' simpered Mrs Webb.

'You remember Mrs Webb, don't you, Mr Phinn?' said the nun.

'I do, yes,' I replied. 'Good morning, Mrs Webb.'

How could I forget Mrs Webb! Today, she looked as if she were about to embark on an Arctic expedition. The small, red-faced teacher with dyed black hair and bright red lips was wearing a shapeless grey duffel coat, thick scarf, fat woolly gloves and substantial leather boots.

'You gave her such a lovely report when you observed her lessons,' said the nun before the teacher could respond. 'You were very impressed with her drama work, as I recall. You've not quite got over it, have you, Mrs Webb?'

'No, Sister,' replied the teacher, nodding her head like a puppet. 'Good morning, Mr Phinn.'

'And when I was away ill,' continued Sister Brendan, 'she held the fort magnificently.'

'I didn't know you'd been ill, Sister,' I said.

'Heart attack,' said Mrs Webb, nodding. 'You would not believe the suffering and discomfort she endured, Mr Phinn. Never thinks of herself, always of others.'

'I had no idea,' I said.

'Collapsed in assembly, didn't you, Sister?'

'You make it sound very dramatic, Mrs Webb,' said the nun. 'It was just a small turn.'

'You see what I mean,' said her colleague. 'Never complains.'

'I'm so sorry to hear you've not been well, Sister,' I said. 'Well, it's good to see you looking your old self. And now, if you will excuse me—'

As I turned to leave, the nun touched my arm. 'That's why we teach, Mr Phinn,' she said.

'I beg your pardon, Sister?' I asked.

'Look at that little child by the wall.' She gestured across the playground. Standing there alone was a small boy, hugging himself against the sharp wind. 'We have such an awesome job, those of us who teach, watering these little seeds, watching them grow and flourish and bloom.' She sighed. 'In all the seeds of today are all the flowers of tomorrow.'

'Indeed,' I said, desperate to get away, 'and time waits for no man so, if you will excuse me, I really must—'

'Some are planted in very fertile soil,' continued Sister Brendan, 'but, sadly, others fall on hard and stony ground.'

'He's such a sorrowful child is Jasper, isn't he, Sister?' observed Mrs Webb.

'Indeed he is, Mrs Webb,' agreed the headteacher, nodding. 'A sorrowful child. He looks as if he has the troubles of the entire world on his little shoulders.'

'He only just started with us this last week,' Mrs Webb explained to me, 'and we do so worry about him. I think he's finding it a bit difficult at home at the moment.' She lowered her voice. 'His parents have recently divorced and I expect he's trying to adjust to a new life with just his mother, and in rented accommodation. I'm sure he must miss his daddy, poor little mite. He never smiles, never plays with the other children, and rarely says anything. He just keeps himself to himself.'

'I'm sure he'll soon settle in, Mrs Webb,' I reassured her. 'Children are very resilient and he couldn't be in a better school environment.'

'Bless his heart,' sighed Sister Brendan. 'You know, Mr Phinn, if an angel were to descend to earth he would have the countenance of Jasper. He reminds me of one of those little cherubs with golden wings that you see on Christmas cards.'

'Raphael,' said Mrs Webb.

'I'm sorry?' I said.

'When Sister and I went to Rome on the parish

pilgrimage with Monsignor Leonard, we saw these paintings by Raphael,' Mrs Webb told me.

'Really?' I said, looking at my watch.

'He painted these cherubims,' explained Mrs Webb, 'little chubby pink children with wings. Jasper's just like them.'

The child did indeed look angelic, with his mass of golden curls, great wide eyes and round red cheeks. 'You're so right, Mrs Webb. Come along, Mr Phinn, let's go and have a little word with him.'

'No, no. I really must go,' I said for the umpteenth time.

'It'll only take a minute,' she said, heading for the child. 'Come along.'

So I traipsed after her. The child stared up at us with a serious expression on his small face as we approached.

'Hello, Jasper,' said the nun. 'This is Mr Phinn who is visiting our school today. He's a school inspector.'

The child observed me with no change to his mournful expression. He was shivering with cold and had a glistening frozen teardrop on his cheek.

'Aaaaah,' sighed Mrs Webb.

'Have you been crying, Jasper?' warbled Sister Brendan, bending down and taking his little hand in hers.

The child shook his head, making his golden curls swing.

'You have, haven't you?' said the nun with the most sympathetic of smiles. 'You've been crying, poor mite. Here, let me wipe that little teardrop away.' Sister Brendan gently brushed the child's cheek with a finger.

The child stared her straight in the eyes. 'It's

snot,' he told her.

*   *   *

Crompton was a gloomy place. On the outskirts of the town was evidence of its industrial past; tall blackened chimneys, now redundant, rose from a wasteland of derelict buildings, half-demolished houses, boarded-up warehouses and abandoned factories. There was not a tree or a bush or even a square of grass in sight. What a contrast it was to the rolling hills and picturesque landscape of the Dales.

Crompton Primary School was built in the latter part of the nineteenth century to cater for the needs of the children of the factory workers employed in the newly-constructed mills, factories and steel works. It looked more like a Victorian workhouse than a school, with its shiny red-brick exterior, cold grey slate roof, mean little windows and enveloping black iron fencing. Despite the efforts of the headteacher and staff to brighten up the interior with pictures and plants, the place still felt strangely musty and inhospitable.

Mrs Gardiner, the headteacher, a big-boned woman with bobbed silver hair and thin lips, had the no-nonsense look of someone who is very confident of her own abilities. Despite the dismal environment, some very difficult and demanding parents and a relatively large proportion of children one might euphemistically describe as having 'challenging behaviour', she ran a well-ordered and successful school and was highly respected in the Education Department at County Hall. Mrs Gardiner was, by her own admission, not

328

one to beat about the bush. She had a startling bluntness and such formidable self-assurance that even the most hard-bitten and awkward parent would never be so foolhardy as to take her on.

'I say what I have to say, Mr Phinn,' she once told me. 'I say it how it is. People might not like it, but they know where they stand with me. What you see is what you get.'

Mrs Gardiner was waiting at the entrance to the school to greet me, and looked theatrically at the small gold pendant watch suspended around her neck on a thin gold chain as I walked towards her. She looked as intimidating as the exterior of her school.

'Overslept?' she asked bluntly, as I hastened into the building.

'I'm really sorry, Mrs Gardiner,' I explained. 'I called in at St Bartholomew's and just couldn't get away.'

She gave a small smile. 'Sister Brendan.'

'Sister Brendan,' I repeated.

'You have to be firm with our dear Sister Brendan, Mr Phinn,' said Mrs Gardiner, 'particularly when she waxes lyrical. She can talk for a good hour without seeming to draw breath. I believe she went on one of these weekend silent retreats and was back in the convent by coffee time of the first day. Just couldn't keep quiet by all accounts. Anyway, now you are here, you are in time for assembly and you can do me a great service this morning.'

'Oh?' This sounded slightly ominous.

'I want you to sit at the front with me, and I want you to glower at the boys I have asked to remain behind after the infants and the girls have gone to their lessons.'

'Glower?'

'I want you to scowl and look angry,' she said.

'Why?'

'All will be explained at the end of the assembly,' said Mrs Gardiner.

The children marched into the hall, heads up, arms swinging, accompanied by stirring martial music played on an old upright piano with great gusto by a small man who bobbed up and down on the piano stool in time with the beat. Mrs Gardiner took centre stage, legs slightly apart, her large hands clasped before her, eyes ever watchful. I, the visual aid, was placed behind her on a large wooden chair with arms, trying to look solemn. The children lined up in rows like little soldiers, they sang the hymn lustily and said the prayer with downcast eyes and then, at the signal from the headteacher, they sat cross-legged on the floor, looking at Mrs Gardiner expectantly.

'Good morning, children,' said the headteacher, loudly and clearly.

'Good morning, Mrs Gardiner,' chanted the children. 'Good morning, everyone.'

'I think I must be going deaf,' said Mrs Gardiner. 'Shall we try that again and this time with a bit more enthusiasm.'

'Good morning, Mrs Gardiner,' shouted the children. 'Good morning, everyone.'

'That's much better,' announced the headteacher. 'Now, sit up smartly, children. I would like to introduce our special visitor, someone very important from the Education Office. This is Mr Phinn, a school inspector.'

'Good morning, Mr Phinn, a school inspector,'

chorused the children loudly.

'Good morning, children,' I said seriously. I felt like a king, enthroned in my heavy wooden chair, set high on the stage.

There followed a small homily from Mrs Gardiner about good manners and consideration for others and then the children, with the exception of the upper junior boys, were dismissed.

Mrs Gardiner turned to face me and, in a hushed voice, said, 'Now, Mr Phinn, I want you to look really angry and scowling.' She turned to the pupils and placed her hands firmly on her hips. 'Down to the front, you boys!' ordered the headteacher. A nervous group of pupils lined up before her. The children could see by her body language that Mrs Gardiner was angry about something. 'You are a group of dirty, dirty, dirty little boys, do you know that?' Mrs Gardiner enunciated each word clearly and slowly. A sea of faces stared back at her. Some of the younger pupils shuffled uneasily, others bit their lips and one boy looked like a terrified rabbit caught in a trap. 'You might well look shamefaced and sheepish. You are dirty, disgusting little boys and you know what you have done and why you have been asked to remain behind.'

'Miss, is it because—' began a boy.

'Be quiet!' snapped the headteacher. She paused for effect and scanned the faces. 'Last night, when Mrs Garbutt—who keeps this school so clean and tidy—went into the boys' toilets, she was disgusted. *Disgusted!* She came straight away to find me and when I saw the floor and the walls in the boys' toilets and the mess you had made, I too was disgusted. The floor was awash—and I do not mean with water!' She stabbed the air with a finger. 'I know full well what you have been up to. You've been seeing who can get highest up the wall.' I suppressed a smirk quickly, and continued to glower. 'Oh, yes,' continued Mrs Gardiner, 'I know what you've been doing. You have been having a competition to see who can reach highest up the wall, you dirty little boys.'

At this point, all the boys stared at a small lad with spiky black hair and a very embarrassed expression on his face. He was clearly the winner of the contest. Mrs Gardiner's furious gaze settled on him. The boy rubbed his eyes and began to sniffle.

'The waterworks won't wash with me, Jimmy Sedgewick, so don't bother with the crocodile tears. It is not Mrs Garbutt's job to clean puddles up after you. And let me tell you this,' Mrs Gardiner shook a finger at the boys, 'if there is so much as a drop or a drip, a splash or a smidgen on the floor today, you will all get down on your hands and knees and clean it up. Is that clear?'

'Yes, Mrs Gardiner,' replied the children in subdued voices.

'Mr Phinn,' continued the headteacher, pointing in my direction, 'is a very important school inspector sent especially from the Education Office about the toilets, and he was appalled, appalled, when I told him what you have been up to. Just look at his face. See how disgusted he is.'

All eyes focused on me as I sat on my throne. I pulled a particularly gruesome face. There was a laboured pause before the headteacher continued and, when she did, I could not, in all my wildest dreams, have imagined what she would say next. I was, to use the old Yorkshire expression, 'gobsmacked'.

'When Mr Phinn goes to the toilet,' said Mrs Gardiner—I looked at her in horror, dreading what was to follow—'he doesn't flip it about like a fireman's hose. Do you, Mr Phinn?'

'N . . . no,' I replied feebly with an even more woebegone expression on my face.

'He directs it where it should go. And that is what you boys will do in the future. Is that clear?'

'Yes, Mrs Gardiner,' replied the boys.

'Have you anything to add, Mr Phinn?' asked the headteacher.

'No, nothing,' I murmured, attempting to take in what I had just heard. 'Nothing at all.'

Later in her room, Mrs Gardiner sat behind her desk and remarked, 'I think we made our point, don't you think, Mr Phinn?'

I still had nothing to add.

* * *

I was not looking forward to my afternoon in Ugglemattersby. The meeting, held a short time earlier with the parents of the children who attended the two schools, could not have gone better. The gathering, held in the village hall, had been very well attended, and the general feeling was that the amalgamation was an excellent idea. The parents of the Juniors, especially, no doubt liked the idea of the modern, attractive premises. The two teachers from the Junior School, Mrs Battersby and Mrs Sidebottom, had sat at the back like stone statues, hands knotted tightly in their laps; it was clear that they were not in favour of the proposal and had simmered in angry silence.

Councillor Sidebottom, who had got up from his sickbed, determined to make this meeting, had soon discovered that the parents were vociferously in favour of the proposal. With an eye to the next county elections, he had obviously felt it prudent not to exacerbate his voters and had been remarkably restrained. He had explained that he was in an invidious position and could not speak freely, but had added that he did want to register his opposition. It would have been interesting to have been a fly on the wall in the Sidebottom home after the meeting. The evening had ended with the parents voting in favour of the change. I had even received some applause at the end of my presentation.

After this meeting, I had written to the two headteachers explaining my purpose for wanting to see them, and had enclosed copies of the proposals from the Education Committee. These two meetings were likely to be difficult since I anticipated that both Mr Harrison and Mrs Braddock-Smith would expect to take on the role of the new headteacher. I decided to see them separately to explain the situation and to sound out their views. Now, driving out of gloomy Crompton and into open countryside, I rehearsed what I would say.

The closure of a school, as I knew from personal as well as professional experience, often proved to be a highly contentious affair. Two of my colleagues had already found the process extremely stressful, as Miss de la Mare had predicted it would be. In the schools destined for closure that David and Geraldine had visited, parents, governors, local residents, former pupils and members of staff had objected strongly and that was only the beginning. Pressure groups were being formed, petitions raised, local councillors and even Members of Parliament were becoming involved, columns of newspaper articles were appearing, and there were interminable and acrimonious meetings. If a school closure went ahead, there would be redeployments and redundancies accompanied by another set of disagreeable meetings and interviews.

Sidney, of course, could run through a minefield and emerge unscathed; his discussions, as he was at great pains to tell us, had gone 'swimmingly'.

To my surprise and relief, Mrs Braddock-Smith had seemed veritably elated when, a few weeks before at the governors' meeting, I had explained that the proposal was to close the Junior School and relocate the children on her premises. Now I was meeting with her to discuss the amalgamation in more detail.

'Well, I think,' she said with obvious self-satisfaction, 'it's the only course of action. There's plenty of room on this site and, let's face it, the Junior School is in decline.' She sounded somewhat smug. 'As you are aware, Mr Phinn, many of the children in the village, after an excellent start here in the Infants, are being sent by their parents to other primary schools and even to preparatory schools. It is a sad fact but true that the Junior School does not provide the sort of education these upwardly mobile, professional parents are looking for. Now, I don't want to appear unprincipled, but Mr Harrison has not been an unmitigated success at the Juniors, has he? Sadly, for whatever reason, he has had his share of problems, and parents in the community just don't have any confidence in the school. After all, at the recent meeting, the parents of the Juniors were in complete support for the merger, as were my parents. In my considered opinion, it's a very appropriate move on the part of the county to close the Juniors and for the children to be educated at my school. I feel fully confident I can take on the headship of the amalgamated school and—'

'It's not quite as simple as that, Mrs Braddock-Smith,' I told her, irritated by her smugness.

'Oh?'

'The schools will amalgamate, as you rightly say. It is proposed that the current Junior School will close and two temporary classrooms will be erected on this site to house the Junior children, until an extension is built.'

'Isn't that what I was saying?' enquired the headteacher, looking puzzled.

'The Infant School will also cease to exist,' I said, 'and become part of a county primary school with a new headteacher.'

'A new headteacher!' exclaimed Mrs Braddock-Smith. 'How can there be a new headteacher when I am already in post?' The colour drained from her face as what I had said sunk in.

'Well, both you and Mr Harrison will be considered for the position in the first instance, and then if neither of you is appointed, it will go to national advert.'

'You mean I will be in *competition* with Mr Harrison for the post?' asked Mrs Braddock-Smith. 'And it may go to national advert?'

'Yes,' I replied. She had obviously assumed that the position would be hers.

She gave a wry smile. 'Well, I may sound as if I am blowing my own trumpet, Mr Phinn, but when you compare my track record with that of my colleague down the road, I should think there will be little doubt which one of us is the better suited for the position of headteacher at the new school. You yourself have seen the quality of the education I provide here and the excellent standard of work the children achieve. And, though I say so myself, I feel I run a school second to none in the county.'

'That may very well be the case, Mrs Braddock-Smith,' I told her, 'but the appointment will be in the hands of the governors. I can only advise.'

'My governors,' she said, 'have always greatly valued the work I have done here and know that I will be able to rise to the challenge.'

'There will be a new governing body,' I said, 'comprising of governors from both schools.'

'I see,' said the headteacher. Mrs Braddock-Smith's elation had evaporated like a burst balloon. She rose from her desk in queenly fashion. 'Well,' she said, 'I naturally assumed that I would be asked to become headteacher of the amalgamated schools. I thought that is why you wished to see me. As you might imagine, this has come as some surprise. I shall have to see what Archdeacon Richards has to say about all this—and my union. And now, if you will excuse me, Mr Phinn, I have a great deal to do. As you are no doubt aware, half-term starts this afternoon and there is much to be done before the children break up for their holiday.'

Oh dear, I thought, a minute or so later as I stood at the gate looking back at the school building; this situation was likely to be more contentious than I had imagined. I sensed a presence behind me and, turning, discovered the same hawk-faced crossing patrol woman I had encountered when I had visited the Infant School earlier in the term. She was now wielding her lollipop sign emblazoned with 'STOP!' most aggressively.

'I hear that you're closing the Juniors,' she said sharply.

'Not me personally,' I said.

'Well, I don't like the idea.'

'Really? Why not?'

'It will mean a whole lot of new kiddies coming to this school and crossing the road up here.' She pushed her lollipop in my face.

'That's very likely,' I told her, moving back a pace.

'Older children, who can be real nuisances and not do what they're told. And there'll be many more cars hooting and puthering out exhaust fumes. It'll be like a war zone up here. Well, will I be getting some help?'

'I've really no idea.'

'I hope I will because I won't be able to cope on my own.'

'It may well be,' I said mischievously, 'that the crossing patrol warden down at the Junior School, who I believe is extremely well thought of and very good humoured, is asked to take on the job up here.' With that and a hearty 'Good afternoon', I headed for my next appointment, leaving the vision in luminous yellow open-mouthed and lost for words.

*   *   *

At the Junior School, Mr Harrison was waiting in the entrance to greet me. He looked a whole lot better than when I had last seen him at the parents' meeting and was actually smiling.

'Good afternoon, Mr Phinn,' he said cheerfully.

'Good afternoon.'

'It's been a beautiful day, hasn't it? Getting a bit nippy now, but it's been bright and fresh.'

'Yes, indeed,' I said, surprised by his obvious good humour.

I followed him to his room where he sat at his desk, rubbed his hands together vigorously and asked, 'Cup of tea?'

'No, thank you,' I replied, bemused by his manner. Mr Harrison was grinning like a cat that had got the cream.

I had written to him after my last visit, explaining that I had seen the Chief Inspector with the intention of recommending that a thorough inspection of the school would take place, but events—namely, the proposed amalgamation of the two schools—had changed things.

'As you know,' I said now, 'the plan is to close down this school and move the Juniors in with the Infants at the school up the road.'

The headteacher leaned back in his chair, placed his hands behind his head and looked up at the ceiling. 'I think it's an excellent idea,' he said.

'You do?' I said, taken aback.

'I do,' he said. 'Numbers are declining here, there's plenty of space up at the Infants and I think a fresh start with new teachers and a new headteacher will make all the difference.' I considered for a moment how to approach the thorny question of the new headteacher. He must have been reading my mind. 'And then, of course,' he said, 'there'll be the appointment of the headteacher of the amalgamated schools.'

As at the meeting with the headteacher of Ugglemattersby Infant School, I explained that, in the first instance, he would be in competition with Mrs Braddock-Smith for the headship of the new school, and if neither was deemed satisfactory to the board of the newly-elected governors, then the position would be advertised nationally.

'I think she deserves the job,' he said. I detected a slight sardonic inflection in his voice.

'Who?'

'Mrs Braddock-Smith,' he replied.

'You do?'

'I do,' he said. 'She's a very successful headteacher and runs a popular and high-achieving school, as she is always at great pains to point out, and I am certain she will rise admirably to the challenge.' There was undisguised sarcasm in his voice.

'So you won't be applying for the post?' I asked.

'No, I won't,' he told me, a smile still playing across his face. 'You see, I am resigning.' He looked as pleased as Punch.

'Resigning?'

'Yes,' he said. 'My wife is a great one for telling me that things have the habit of working out for the best. Well, I'm pleased to say that they have now for me. The chairman of governors of my last school down in London phoned me a few weeks ago, when I was at my lowest ebb, to tell me that the present headteacher is retiring at the end of this term. He asked if I would consider putting in an application for the post. I was, of course, very flattered. I then received such encouraging letters from my former colleagues on the staff urging me to apply. Why, even the caretaker wrote asking me to return. I cannot tell you how I felt receiving such letters. I applied, went for the interview last week and was offered the position. So, you see, Mr Phinn, the amalgamation of the schools is all academic as far as I am concerned. I shall be returning to London.'

'Well, congratulations,' I said, and meant it.

'And I do hope that Mrs Braddock-Smith is appointed as the headteacher of the new primary school, I sincerely do.' He looked well pleased with the situation. 'She always told me that she welcomed a challenge and I have no doubt in my mind that should Mrs Battersby and Mrs Sidebottom be redeployed to the new school, they will provide her with all the challenge she needs.'

CHAPTER TWENTY

It was the opening night of *The Dame of Sark* and I was ready to head off home from the Staff Development Centre, shower, change, have some tea and get to the Fettlesham Little Theatre in good time. Much to the cast's amazement and despite Raymond's frequent panic attacks and periodic theatrical outbursts, the production had fallen into place and it seemed that we might not make total fools of ourselves on the night.

I was tidying up after an English course I had just directed; it had been a tiresome afternoon with a number of would-be Philip Larkins testing my patience. I was about finished when Mrs Kipling from St Margaret's Church of England Primary School popped her head around the door of the room.

'Hello, Mr Phinn,' she said brightly.

'Good afternoon,' I said.

'I've been here on one of the art courses,' she told me. 'We've been doing collage work this afternoon and it's been truly inspirational. Yesterday, we did batik and screen-printing. He's such a character isn't he, Mr Clamp, and so artistic?'

'He is,' I agreed.

'And so very talented.'

'Yes, he is.'

'I try to come on all the courses he holds,' she said, beaming pinkly.

I curtailed the eulogy to my 'artistic', 'very talented' and 'truly inspirational' colleague by asking, 'And how are things at St Margaret's?'

'Fine,' she told me, coming into the room.

'I meant to get in touch with you,' I said. 'I'm sorry if I was a bit hard on your chairman of governors. When I thought about it later, you were quite right—one shouldn't judge by appearances.'

'Don't worry your head about that, Mr Phinn,' she said. 'Mr Featherstone does have that effect on people until you get to know him. He looks rather Dickensian with his whiskers and gold-rimmed spectacles but he's not the dour and daunting person he appears to be. What he needs is a good wife, a jolly, homely, good-humoured woman and a large family of lively children to get him to take things less seriously, but I guess he is too set in his bachelor ways and will remain so. He likes children but just can't seem to get on their wavelengths. But I do have to say, Mr Phinn, his heart is in the right place and I would much rather have a really interested and concerned chairman of governors like Mr Featherstone, than one who is constantly interfering or someone who is apathetic and can't be bothered.'

'I suppose so,' I said.

'Actually, poor Mr Featherstone is a little nervous at the moment,' she confided in me.

'Why so?' I asked.

'Well, it's getting near to Remembrance Sunday and last year he was a bit shell-shocked after an incident at the war memorial in the village.' Mrs Kipling pulled a face. 'Oh dear, perhaps that's not quite the right phrase to use in the circumstances.'

'What happened?' I asked, intrigued.

'If you have a minute, I'll tell you,' she said, bringing up a chair. 'Mr Featherstone came into school last November in the week leading up to Remembrance Sunday. He explained to the children in assembly about the significance of the poppies and the importance of the special service at the war memorial when people gathered in the village to remember those who had given their lives in the two world wars. It was a very emotional assembly, particularly when he told the children that his own father had been killed in the last war and his grandfather had died in the trenches at Ypres in the first. He told the children,' Mrs Kipling continued, 'that they might like to attend the service with their parents on the Sunday but that, if they did, they had to remain perfectly still and silent during the two-minute silence. "If you feel you want to say something," he told them, "put your finger over your lips to stop yourself." He demonstrated by placing his index finger over his own lips and the children did likewise. "And if you really want anything, then raise your hand like this." He held up his right arm to show them how.'

Mrs Kipling stood up to demonstrate what Mr Featherstone had shown the children to do, then sat down again.

'Well, on the Sunday, quite a few of the children did attend the service. We crowded around the memorial on the village green and Mr Featherstone gave a very moving address. The children behaved themselves but I could see a few of them were getting a bit fidgety. When it came to the two-minute silence several did as they had been told. They put their fingers over their lips, and three young lads raised their arms. No doubt, you can imagine the surprise on the faces of all the old soldiers when they saw a group of little children facing the war memorial and giving what to them looked like the Nazi salute.'

I smiled as I pictured the scene. 'Well, I'm sure it will all go swimmingly this year,' I said.

'Would you like to see my masterpiece?' she asked, standing up.

'Your masterpiece?'

'My collage. I'm really proud of it.'

'Yes,' I told her, having a surreptitious look at my watch, 'I'd be most interested to see it.'

'It's in the corridor.'

I followed Mrs Kipling and there, propped up

on a chair, was a garish jigsaw of material mounted on a large piece of card.

She looked at her handiwork with obvious pride. 'We were asked to express a mood such as happiness, anger, frustration, affection, depression, that sort of thing. I call mine 'In the Pink' and I know exactly which wall I will display it on back at school. I shall put it in the entrance hall in order to cheer people up.'

'It's very striking,' I commented, thinking to myself that I wouldn't even hang such a hideous creation, with all those clashing pinks and corals, on my toilet wall, let alone in my hall.

'I thought of the school entrance,' Mrs Kipling told me, 'to give it maximum impact and exposure.'

'It will certainly turn heads,' I said. As I looked closer at the collage, I seemed to recognise some of the material—a bright pink nylon fabric, and had a sudden dreadful thought.

'So where did the material come from for your collage?' I asked casually.

'Mr Clamp brought along black bags containing all sorts of woven, knitted or felted fabric, wool, cotton, scraps of silk, bits with different textures and in various colours. He told us that he often got old clothes and pieces of material from charity shops. As soon as I saw this really unusual pink overall—you must admit it is so wonderfully bright that it sort of shimmers—I commandeered it.'

'Pink overall,' I repeated.

'Yes, I thought it would be ideal.'

'And it was one of the things that Mr Clamp brought to the class in his black bags?'

'Yes—at least I think so,' replied Mrs Kipling, fingering a piece of the garishly coloured material.

'Or was it already out of the black bag when I saw it? Yes! That's it. It was over the back of a chair.'

'In the art room?' I asked.

'Yes, over the back of a chair in the art room.'

'And you cut it up?'

'Yes, I cut it up and transformed it into my collage,' said the headteacher. 'I can quite understand how it came to be thrown out. I mean, I can't imagine anyone wanting to wear such a hideous garment, can you?'

Oh dear, oh dear, I thought. It was Connie's pink overall, I was sure of it. I could imagine the mayhem when she discovered that her coveted pink nylon overall, her trademark uniform, had been vandalised and mounted.

When I saw the woman in question heading down the corridor, I quickly picked up the creation and retreated back into the room. 'I'd like to see it in a better light,' I told a rather surprised Mrs Kipling.

I waited until Connie was out of sight and then helped Mrs Kipling carry her creation out to her car.

'I did wonder, you know,' she said as I negotiated 'In the Pink' onto the back seat, 'if I should offer to let Mr Clamp display it in the Staff Development Centre but then decided I wanted it back in school.'

'A wise decision,' I murmured.

It was with a great sense of relief that I saw Mrs Kipling drive out of the car park.

Back in the Centre, Connie, hands on hips and minus overall, was surveying the art room. 'Just look at this mess,' she complained. 'Everywhere he goes he leaves a trail of debris and destruction, that Mr Clamp. There are bits of cloth and old clothes all over the place. It's like an explosion at a jumble sale in here.' I wondered what the state of the room would be like the following day when Sidney and the teachers had finished silkscreen printing. Connie shook her head. 'I was hoping to get off a bit earlier this afternoon. It's my bingo night.'

'Have you ever won at bingo, Connie?' I asked, changing the subject.

'Not a lot,' she said. 'A few pounds here and there, that's all. I'm always optimistic, mind. I've got my eye on the Christmas accumulator. It's the jackpot prize, and is over fifteen thousand pounds now. What I could do with that sort of money!'

'How long have you being playing bingo for?' I asked.

'Oooh, over twenty years,' she said.

'And you've only won a few pounds? You would have been better putting it into a deposit account,' I told her.

She looked at me and pursed her lips. 'If I want a financial adviser, Mr Phinn,' she told me, clearly nettled, 'I'll find one in Fettlesham, thank you very much. Bingo might not be the cup of tea for you academical sorts, but it gets me out, I meet my friends and I enjoy it. Enough said.'

I changed the subject again. 'Have you had any news of that young man who had the unfortunate accident in the Gents?' I asked.

'Young Kevin? Oh, he's been out of hospital a while now, and has just gone back to work. I saw him in Fettlesham the other day. He's given up painting and decorating because he says he'll never be able to give up smoking. He's cleaning shop windows, now. And speaking of the incident in the gentleman's cloakroom,' she added, 'you know who showed her face up here at the Centre the other week, testiculating all over the place? It was that Mrs Savage woman, Lady High and Mighty.'

'What did she want?' I asked.

'She comes in here like something off of a catwalk and starts telling me she's in charge of "Health and Safety" at County Hall, and she's here to look into the accident. Then she waves about these guidelines what she's written and warns me about the dangers in the workplace.'

'Mrs Savage went on a one-day course last year and now thinks she's the expert,' I told Connie.

'Well, there's nothing she can tell *me* about health and safety. It's like telling your grandmother how to poach eggs. She drives into the Centre car park like a cat out of hell in that red car of hers, blocks my entrance, clatters up the steps in her stilettos, clutching this clipboard to that expensive bosom of hers, and then she has the brass neck to quiz me like one of those interyregulators. My goodness, she's got an attitude, that woman, and does she know how to use it! "I've got to hascertain what happened," she says, all snooty-like. I said to her, I said, "You can hascertain all you want to, I've got work to do." I told her it was all in the report what I sent in to County Hall. "Did you undertake a risk assessment?" she asks me. I told her straight, I said, "Risk assessment—of a toilet?" I mean there's not a lot of risk sitting on a toilet, is there, apart from picking up something nasty from the toilet seat and that wouldn't happen here because I bleach them down regular. I told her, "You're not likely to fall down the toilet and it's not every day that half a pint of turpentine substitute is put down the bowl and then somebody is daft enough to light up afterwards and post the cigarette between their legs and set themselves alight." Flaming cheek of the woman. Pardon my pun. Anyway, off she goes to examine the cubicle. She comes back with paint all over her fancy black outfit. You should have seen her face!'

'But surely the paint would have been dry by the time she went to carry out her inspection,' I said.

'Course it was, but I had been doing a bit of touching up of the paintwork that morning. There were scorch marks on the wall after the incident, and you know what I'm like with marks on my walls.'

'And you didn't think to tell her?'

'No, I didn't,' Connie said with a smug expression on her florid face. 'Since she's so good at hascertaining, I thought, she could hascertain where the wet paint is.'

'Connie,' I said, shaking my head, 'you're incorrigible.'

'I don't know what that means, Mr Phinn, but I'm sure I'm not,' she told me.

'I hear from Mr Pritchard that Willingforth School is taking part in the mathematics display at Dr Gore's conference at Manston Hall next month,' I said, changing the subject. 'Are your grandchildren involved, Connie?'

She smiled. 'Our Lucy is,' she told me. 'She's a real whiz when it comes to sums. Can add up like nobody's business. Miss Pilkington's been having them doing mental arithmetic every morning for the past few weeks.'

'It's an excellent school, Willingforth,' I said. 'Mr Pritchard told me that overall it achieves the best mathematics results in the county.'

'Oh,' said Connie suddenly, and casting her eyes around, 'speaking of overalls, you haven't seen mine, have you?'

*   *   *

I arrived at Fettlesham Little Theatre during the interval. It appeared, judging by the number thronging the noisy bar area, that the play was going well so far. The doorman told me that it was almost a full house, and the audience had been responding enthusiastically. The worst scenario, and one which Raymond had predicted in one of his blackest moods, was that the audience would vote with its feet if the play didn't come up to scratch before the interval and we would play the second half to an almost empty auditorium.

'And that frightful Marcia McCrudden, theatre critic of the *Fettlesham Gazette*, will be there,' he had moaned, 'sitting like an evil presence in the front row, scribbling invective in her little black notebook. I shudder at the very sight of the woman and can just imagine what her review will be like when it appears in the paper the following Friday. She said my production of *Cabaret* was "unimaginative" and after all the time and effort I put into *The Sound of Music*, she wrote that it "lacked vitality and verve". I dread to think what she will say about this play. It could well be the end of my career in the amateur theatre.'

'Raymond!' Mrs Cleaver-Canning had told him. 'Pull yourself together, for goodness' sake. It will

350

be fine. Everything will fall into place as it always does. Marcia McCrudden is but one person and her opinion counts for very little in my book.'

It seemed, however, that since no one was making for the door when I arrived that Raymond's prognosis was unfounded, that Mrs Cleaver-Canning's reassurance was being proved right and that the first half of the play had gone without a hitch. I was soon to learn differently.

I went backstage where I came upon Percy, the Stage Manager, a rotund little man with a flushed complexion. His substantial stomach bulged beneath an old brown sweater and above a pair of grubby trousers. I noticed he was without socks but was wearing a pair of carpet slippers with 'Mr Grumpy' embroidered on the tops. He was squatting on a small stool by the fire exit, beneath a large sign that stated in bold red letters: 'STRICTLY NO SMOKING'. He held a smouldering cigarette in one hand and a bottle of brown ale in the other; a second bottle lay on the floor near the stool.

'I see the cavalry's arrived,' he said, as he caught sight of me trying to negotiate the narrow door, squeezing through with my holdall containing cap, Sam Browne belt and boots, my uniform over my arm. He made no effort to give me a hand but took a swig from the bottle of beer and then puffed away on his cigarette, blowing out clouds of smoke and wheezing loudly in the process.

'Good evening, Percy,' I said, putting down my heavy load on a table.

'Is it?' he replied.

'So, how's the play going?' I asked brightly.

'How's it going?' he repeated. He gave a hollow

little laugh. 'How's it going? You don't want to know, squire.'

'Oh dear,' I sighed, 'as bad as that. The people in the bar seem happy enough.'

'It's worse than bad,' Percy said. He finished the bottle of brown ale noisily, burped, dropped the stub of his cigarette and ground it into the floor with his slipper. 'Raymond, our creative director and revered producer, has buggered off.'

'He's what?' I exclaimed.

'He's done a runner, scarpered, deserted, gone to ground. He had one of his paddies at the end of the first half, stormed off and nobody's seen him since. Mind you, he's not missed. It's always the same on the opening night. He gets into this state, flapping about like a constipated bat, getting himself all wound up and winding everyone else up in the process.'

'He doesn't seem to have wound you up, Percy,' I observed.

'No, that's because I won't let him. I just let it all flow over me. I turn off like a wireless when he has one of his tantrums.'

'It's his artistic temperament,' I said. 'You have to make allowances.'

'He's like a big daft girl, the way he goes on. Actually, it was a big daft girl that got him wound up in the first place.'

'So what's upset him?' I asked, shaking out the uniform, and hanging it up on a hook.

'Well,' said Percy, lighting another cigarette, 'Sharon, you know, the lass playing Cecile, the Dame's maid, she arrives all dolled up to the nines, wearing enough make-up to sink a bloody battleship and wrapped up in a great cloak-thing

352

like what a pantomime magician would wear. Shortly before the performance started, she takes off the cloak, and all she's got on underneath . . .' Percy paused, and chortled at the memory of what the girl had been wearing but he unwisely took another drag on his cigarette at the same time and his laugh turned into a coughing spasm. When he had got himself under control, he continued: 'She were wearing just a strip of a skirt, black fishnet stockings and a blouse that revealed more than a liberty bodice. Ray had a fit, as you can imagine. "You're not going on stage in that get-up," he says. "You're supposed to be the Dame's maid during wartime, not a common back-street tart." Well, Sharon storms off and when she does walk on stage in the proper costume, what does she do?'

'What *does* she do?' I asked.

'She puts on that daft French accent Ray told her not to do when she came out with it at the rehearsal. Did it just to be awkward. She can be a right madam, can that Sharon. I remember her when she was playing a nun in *The Sound of Music*. The words "modesty", "chastity" and "obedience" don't readily some to mind when it comes to that young woman. What went on backstage with that spotty beanpole of a youth playing Rolf is nobody's business. They were at it like nine-pins behind that curtain. I've never seen such carryings on. Talk about "Climb Every Mountain", he was all over her.'

Perhaps he shouldn't have been so interested in what was going on behind the curtain, I thought to myself, but said nothing.

'Anyway,' Percy continued, 'Ray went ballistic when she comes off stage, just as George Furnival brings in the coffin.'

'What coffin?'

'The coffin for the last act.'

'There isn't a coffin in the last act,' I told him.

'I know that,' said Percy, 'but George thought it would be a good idea if he used one of his spare coffins in the last act. He told Raymond it would be more dramatic if the young German soldier, Wilhelm Muller, him who gets blown up by the mine at the end, were brought on stage in a coffin. He'd got this lovely black affair with brass handles. Course, George never misses a trick when it comes to advertising his business and he'd put down the side of the casket: "Furnivals for the Finest in Funerals. Coffins to die for." Well, I won't repeat where Raymond told him to stick his coffin. George didn't take it too kindly and stormed on stage with a face like thunder. Then Lady Hatchet—'

'Who?'

'That Mrs Cleaver,' said Percy. 'I wouldn't like to take her on in a wrestling ring if her hands were tied behind her back and she was blindfolded. By heck, she's got a gob on her. She could have won the war single-handed, that one. Well, she starts adding to her lines, upstaging everyone, and Ray just cracked. "I can't stand any more," he says and buggers off.'

'Well, just make sure that you are there when I go on stage, Percy,' I told him. 'The sound effects are pretty complicated in that last scene.'

'No worries,' he said, blowing out a great cloud of cigarette smoke. 'It's all in hand.'

I had to admit that I did worry. The final scene of the play involves me, playing Colonel Graham, bringing news to Mrs Hathaway, aka the Dame of Sark, that the island has been liberated and that her husband is safe and well. As the curtain rises on the final scene, Handel's *Water Music* is playing on the wireless and this is followed by the announcement from Alvar Liddell: 'This is London. We are interrupting programmes with the great news that Berlin has fallen and that the German Armed Forces in Italy have surrendered unconditionally to Field Marshal Alexander.' Then the *Trumpet Voluntary* plays. I enter with the good news of the German surrender of the island but, during my conversation with the Dame, there is an explosion offstage. Mrs Hathaway switches on the wireless to listen to Winston Churchill announce: 'The cease-fire began yesterday to be sounded all along the fronts, and our dear Channel Islands are also to be freed today.' Then the telephone rings with news that the young German soldier, who has been kind to Mrs Hathaway during the Occupation, has been blown up while dismantling a mine in the harbour. So, in terms of sound effects, it was the most demanding part of the play and had only been rehearsed once properly at the dress rehearsal. I had a feeling that things might not go to plan.

In the dressing room, I found the male members of the cast, most of them in their German uniforms, in argumentative mood and far too involved to notice me. I stood in the doorway to listen.

'The lights are too bloody bright,' complained Winco. 'It's like flying a Hurricane into the sun out there. Couldn't see a blasted thing. Put me off my stride. Kept on forgetting my lines. Damned hot as well.' He dabbed at his make-up, which was indeed glistening.

'And why don't they ask that man with the infernal cold to leave,' said Malcolm, the man playing the part of Major Lanz. 'It's very disconcerting when you're trying to say your lines, with him sneezing and spluttering and coughing.'

'You should complain,' moaned George Furnival. 'If this Luger pistol was real, I'd shoot that ruddy woman on the front row. Every time I walk on stage she says, "Oh, it's him again."'

'And who gave permission for them to take photographs and blind people with the flashing?' asked Malcolm of no one in particular.

'It's the last time I'm doing this,' said George Furnival. 'I nearly did my back in getting the coffin up those stairs, and then that little lunatic who is supposed to be directing this farce and has now gone AWOL, says I couldn't put it on the stage. It would have been a really good way to close the play.'

'Quite apart from giving yourself free advertising,' said Malcolm.

'That's not the point!' snapped George. He caught sight of me standing by the door, smiling. 'And you can take that silly grin off your face as well,' he said. 'You've missed most of the rehearsals and now only arrive when it's nearly all over.'

'Good evening, my happy band of fellow thespians,' I said cheerfully, heading for the corner where I relieved myself of my burden.

'Don't get settled in there,' said George. 'You're in the other dressing room.'

'I'm all right here, thank you,' I replied. 'I can

356

squeeze in.'

'No, no, you're not!' exclaimed George. 'You're in dressing room two. It's the Germans in here. The British are next door.'

'What?'

'We can't be fraternising with the enemy,' he said. 'We're on opposing sides. Getting pally with you lot will interfere with us getting into our roles as Nazis so you can clear off to the other dressing room. *Schnell!* It's Germans only in here.'

'George,' I said, 'may I remind you that this is a play. It is not for real.'

'A play,' he snorted. 'Is that what it is? I thought it was more of a fiasco.'

*   *   *

The production was saved, as ever, by the remarkable improvised efforts of Mrs Cleaver-Canning. In Scene Five, Winco, no doubt still dazzled and disconcerted by the stage lights, missed out half his lines with the result that we were into the final scene a good five minutes earlier than we should have been. Percy, no doubt still squatting on his stool like a gnome with his bottle of brown ale, missed the cue for both Handel's *Water Music* and the *Trumpet Voluntary*. When Mrs Cleaver-Canning switched on the wireless, no voice of Alvar Liddell came across the airwaves. Undaunted and with the aplomb of a seasoned actor, she blamed the batteries and did a very fair summary of what the announcer would have said had the wireless worked. Luckily, I was alert to what was happening and I entered on cue with the news that Mrs Hathaway's husband was safe and well, and that the Germans had handed in their guns and were now clearing the mines in the harbour. This was the point when there was to have been the loud explosion but, of course, nothing was heard. There was still no sign of Percy who should have been positioned in the wings, controlling the sound effects. I looked desperately at Mrs Cleaver-Canning.

'What was that?' she exclaimed, ad-libbing and staring into the wings with an excessively dramatic gesture.

'What?' I replied nervously, following her gaze.

'I thought I saw a flash.'

'A flash?' I repeated.

'From the harbour.'

'The harbour?'

'Yes, the harbour,' she said, slowly and deliberately. 'Could it have been a mine exploding?'

'A mine?'

'Please don't keep repeating me, Colonel,' said Mrs Cleaver-Canning. 'Did you not inform me that you had instructed the Germans to dismantle the mines in the harbour?'

'I did?'

'Yes, you did,' she said. 'Perchance one has exploded.'

'Ah yes,' I said, 'I believe it could have been a mine.' Some of the audience, aware that things were not going exactly to plan, began to titter. Please let this end, please let this end, I kept repeating to myself. I was frozen to the spot and quite unable to keep up with Mrs C-C. Then I caught sight of a small woman in black, sitting in the very centre of the front row. She had a crab-

358

apple-sour mouth and was holding a small notebook. I knew at once it was the feared theatre critic, Marcia McCrudden.

'What's the time?' asked Mrs Cleaver-Canning.

'W-what?' I stuttered. Someone in the audience, quite close to the front, chuckled, which added further to my discomfiture and, out of the corner of my eye, I caught sight of the theatre critic scribbling something in her notebook.

'I asked if you could tell me the time, Colonel,' she said.

'The time?' I repeated. I knew I was beginning to sound like a parrot.

'We're forgetting Mr Churchill,' announced Mrs Cleaver-Canning.' She fiddled with the knobs on the wireless. 'You don't mind, do you?'

'No, I'd like to hear it,' I replied, knowing full well that there was no chance of that. I looked despairingly into the wings but there was still no sign of Percy. Where the devil was he? He should be getting ready to play the broadcast.

'Flat batteries, I'm afraid,' said Mrs Cleaver-Canning, banging the top of the cabinet with the flat of her hand. 'Everything seems to stop working in wartime. Perhaps you know what Mr Churchill would have said, Colonel Graham, had we been able to listen to it on the wireless?'

'Erm, erm,' I stuttered. 'I'm . . . I'm . . .'

'No?' she said. 'Well, I imagine he would have announced the cease-fire, informed us that the dear Channel Islands have been liberated, that the war is over and that the cause of freedom has triumphed over the scourge of tyranny.'

'I guess he would,' I mumbled.

Following the Prime Minister's broadcast, the

telephone should have rung. The stage was deathly silent. Mrs Cleaver-Canning and I looked at each other for a moment.

She then picked up the receiver. 'Oh, it seems to be working again,' she said. 'I think I'll ring Major Lanz and see what that explosion was.' She dialled a number. 'Hello, hello, is that Major Lanz? A soldier? What? One of ours? One of yours? What happened? Was there a fight? A mine? The English colonel's here. I'll tell him.' She replaced the receiver. 'A young German soldier's been killed by a mine down at the harbour.'

'Oh,' was all I could manage to say.

At this point Percy finally arrived, offstage right. The next moment, the wireless came to life with a loud rendering of Handel's *Water Music*, the telephone rang and a loud explosion could be heard offstage. Through all the cacophony, Mrs Cleaver-Canning bravely and very loudly declaimed the final words of the play.

'It goes on, Colonel Graham,' she said. 'It goes on. When will it ever stop?'

*　　　*　　　*

As soon as I was offstage, I hurried to the dressing room and changed quickly, keen to be on my way. Percy was the one who had now 'done a runner' and couldn't be found. Raymond, who had surfaced just in time to observe my dismal performance, was being comforted by Mrs Cleaver-Canning with the aid of a wet flannel and Winco's brandy flask. I decided to slope off before the post-mortem but as I reached the stage door George Furnival appeared like the pantomime villain.

'Well, that was a bloody masterful performance of yours tonight,' he said.

'Thank you for those few kind words of encouragement, George,' I replied. 'If Winco had not cut short half his words, and if Percy had provided the sound effects as he should have done, I would—'

'It's all very well you blaming others,' he interrupted. 'You know what my old dad used to say?'

'No, I don't and I'm really not that interested,' I told him.

'A good workman never blames his tools.'

'And what exactly is that supposed to mean?' I asked.

'Well, I thought you were supposed to be good with words. You could have made a bit up instead of leaving it all to Margot. You could have done a bit of improvisation.'

'Improvisation?' I repeated. 'Ah yes, improvisation. You mean like introducing a coffin into the play? Goodnight George.'

I left him open-mouthed, and headed for the stage door.

CHAPTER TWENTY-ONE

It was a bright but chilly November afternoon as I drove along a narrow ribbon of empty road beneath a pale cloudless sky on my way back to the office from Willingforth, a small rural village set in the depths of the Dales. The countryside was

361

looking as though it were ready to settle down for the winter. In the corners of fields, where the sun had not reached, I could still see traces of the morning's hoar frost. The heather on the moors beyond was now dead, and appeared like a dark troubled ocean. Here and there, the colour was broken by clumps of ochre-coloured bracken that were still standing.

Suddenly, as I turned a sharp bend, a small boy, perhaps ten or eleven, ran across the road straight in front of me, his elbows moving like pistons. I slammed my foot on the brake and screeched to a halt, missing him by a whisker. The boy scrabbled over the drystone wall encrusted with lichen, and shot across the fields like a hare pursued by hounds.

A moment later three other boys, much bigger in build, emerged from a small copse at the side of the road, red in the face with exertion and panting like greyhounds. They stopped at the roadside when they caught sight of me, said something to each other and then moved off down the road away from me, looking back occasionally to see if I were still there.

I sat for a moment with my hands resting on the steering wheel, thinking what might have happened had I been travelling down that road a few seconds earlier.

Then I started forwards again, driving extra slowly and keeping my eyes peeled just in case there should be a recurrence of the incident. Half a mile along the road I spotted the boy who had run out in front of me; he was sitting on the grass verge. I pulled over and wound down the car window.

'Whatever were you playing at, running out in front of me like that?' I asked him angrily and, as I did so, immediately recognised who it was. His wavy red hair was the giveaway.

'I was in an 'urry,' the boy replied, refusing to look at me but staring down mulishly at his feet.

'I could see that,' I said, 'but you might have got yourself killed—Terry Mossup!'

At the sound of his name, the boy looked up, surprise showing on his little sharp face. I had met this young lad a couple of years before when I had gone out to Willingforth Primary School at the request of the headteacher, Miss Pilkington, who wanted my advice on how to deal with a particularly disruptive pupil—one Terry Mossup.

He had come from a deprived background, where there had been some abuse and certainly a great deal of neglect, but was now being fostered by a local doctor and her husband who were trying their best, under difficult circumstances, to give the boy some affection and stability. When he had started at the school, Terry had been rude, very naughty and destructive, shouting out in class and refusing to do his work but Miss Pilkington had persevered. After showing incredible patience and tolerance and investing a great deal of her own time, she had made real progress with Terry, and the boy's behaviour had improved by leaps and bounds.

The headteacher had discovered that the boy had a natural way with animals. He was the only pupil that the school cat would allow to stroke her, and he liked nothing better than feeding the birds at playtime; they would fly down to him in the small playground as if knowing that they had nothing to fear. On a visit to a farm, he had been fascinated by the cows and the sheep, and was determined that when he left school he would work on the land and one day have a smallholding of his own.

'Do you remember me, Terry?' I asked him now.

The boy stared up at me, with a suspicious expression on his small face. 'No, should I?'

'Mr Phinn.'

'Are you a social worker?'

'The school inspector.'

He smiled and nodded. 'Oh, aye, I remember thee,' he said. 'You're the one who asks all them questions.'

'And I judged the public speaking competition at the Fettlesham Show when you won first prize for your performance of a piece of verse about cricket.'

'Aye, I did an' all,' he said nodding, and then recited the first verse:

> Whativer task you tackle, lads,
> Whativer job you do,
> I' all your ways,
> I' all your days,
> Be honest through and through:
> Play cricket.

As he said the lines, I recalled the boy's face beaming with pleasure and pride as he had been given the award—a face like a footballer who had just scored the winning goal.

'And do you still play cricket?' I asked.

'Naw, not any more.'

'So what school are you at now?' I asked.

'West Challerton 'Igh,' he told me.

'They have a good cricket team there, don't they?'

'Yea, well, I'm not in it,' he told me, getting to his feet.

'And how are you getting on at West Challerton?'

'I'm not,' he said. 'It's crap.'

'Terry, why were those boys chasing you?' I asked.

He bent down and picked up a stone, which he examined as if he had found something precious. 'They gang up on me,' he said.

'Why do they do that?'

'Cos I'm little and don't give 'em what they want—money and sweets—but I don't take any crap from 'em.'

'Have you told anyone that these boys are bullying you?'

'I can handle missen,' he said, as if I had said something offensive. 'They think they're tough when they're in a gang but on their own they're like all bullies—bloody cowards.' He threw the stone at some rooks in the field behind him. 'Bloody rooks. Eat owt they do. Farmers 'ate 'em.'

'Did they hurt you, those boys?' I asked.

The boy rubbed a red mark on his neck. 'I've 'ad worse,' he said looking me in the eyes.

I guess you have, I thought. 'I think perhaps you should tell somebody at school,' I said.

'Naw,' he said dismissively. 'What's the use? They never do owt. You just 'ave to put up wi' it.'

'No, you don't,' I said. 'You don't have to put up with it. If you are being bullied, you should tell someone you trust—your foster parents, a teacher,

365

a friend. You must never ignore bullying. It won't just go away. Something should be done about it.'

'Aye, well,' he said, stuffing his hands in his pockets, 'they'll 'ave got tired of waitin' by now, so I'd best be off 'ome.'

'Just a minute, Terry,' I said.

'What?'

'Have you told your foster parents you're being bullied?'

'Naw, it'd only mek things worse.'

'No, it wouldn't,' I said.

He looked at me, and his face tightened. ' 'Ow would you know? 'Ave you been fostered, lived in a children's home, taken away from your mam, not allowed to see your little brother, always movin' around from one place to another, switchin' schools, 'avin' to go to all these meetin's when they talk about you? Then you get to this new school an' all the teachers know you're in care and then everybody knows an' you stand out an' kids start to pick on you cos you're different. Then they say things about your mam an' where you come from, an' you get into a scrap and sent to the deputy 'ead an' you can see it in the teacher's eyes—"These kids are all the same—trouble."'

I listened to his outburst but couldn't reply. I really had no conception of the life this child led. What a sad, angry and troubled boy he was, standing on the grassy verge, his blazer ripped and his eyes filling with tears.

'Terry—' I began.

'See ya,' he said and, with that, the boy set off running down the road.

'Terry!' I shouted after him. 'Will you promise me you will tell someone?'

366

He turned and called back to me, 'I've told *you*, haven't I?'

As I drove to the office on that cold afternoon, I recalled the time when I was about Terry's age and I too had a problem with a bully—but that's a story I'll tell another time.

*   *   *

In the office I sat at my desk, staring out of the window wondering just what I could do about Terry Mossup.

'Penny for them,' said Julie, who had come in to put some papers on Geraldine's desk.

'Sorry, what—' I asked.

'You were miles away.'

'I was thinking,' I said.

'What about?'

'About a little boy who leads a life no child should lead,' I said.

'Sounds serious,' said Julie. 'I think I'd better make you a strong cup of tea.'

'Thanks, Julie, that would be great. But first, could you get me the school secretary at West Challerton High on the phone, please? I need to arrange a visit.'

At that moment, David and Sidney arrived noisily in the office—arguing as usual.

'We shall have to agree to disagree,' said David crossly.

'Fine,' said Sidney. Then, after a pause, added, 'But I know I'm right.'

A few minutes later, after I had spoken to West Challerton School, arranging to go and see the headmaster the next morning, Julie tottered in with a tray of cups of tea for all of us. It was some feat to carry them without spilling a drop, considering the height of her heels.

'Do you remember, Mr Phinn,' she asked, 'when Mrs Savage told you that her car wouldn't start the other afternoon and she had to cadge a lift from you to get to the planning meeting at Manston Hall?'

'Yes.'

'Well, it wasn't that it wouldn't start,' said Julie gleefully. 'She'd been clamped!'

'Mrs Savage clamped!' repeated Sidney. 'Oh goody!'

'Makes a change from Mr Clamp being savaged,' chuckled David.

'According to Marlene on the switchboard,' said Julie, 'she had parked her car in one of the councillors' bays and she got clamped. She goes round telling everyone not to park in those bays and then she goes and does it herself. Typical! Well, what's sauce for the goose is sauce for the gander. She had to show herself at the Admin. office, and pay a fine to get the clamp taken off.'

'Hoist by her own petard,' I observed.

'Her what?' asked Julie.

'Nothing,' I said. 'Just an expression.'

'Well, whatever it means, it serves her right,' said Julie. 'It's poetic justice.'

'What's all this about you giving Mrs Savage a lift anyway, Gervase?' asked Sidney. 'You seem to be getting mighty pally with her, if you ask me. You'll be making old Todger jealous.'

'First of all, Sidney,' said David, 'his name is Tadge and not Todger, as you well know. Secondly, Gervase is a happily married man with a young

368

baby, so has no interest in other women and, finally and most importantly, Mrs Savage is the last person in the world he is likely to get pally with.'

'Thank you, David,' I said. 'I couldn't have put it better myself.'

'Oh, by the way,' said Julie, holding up a copy of the *Fettlesham Gazette*, 'you're in the paper.'

'I am?' I asked.

'And there's a photograph of you with a group of soldiers and a seedy-looking man in a raincoat,' she told me.

'I knew that your nocturnal exploits in the gentleman's lav on Fettlesham High Street would eventually catch you out and get to the press,' said Sidney. 'You've been exposed, dear boy, if you will excuse the pun.'

'It's a real rag that paper,' I said. 'They rarely check their facts. It was pure luck that we were able to scotch that article about Tarncliffe School and Mr Hornchurch's English lesson. And when I wrote an article for National Poetry Day, it was full of errors.' I reached for the paper and began looking through it. 'It'll be a review of the play I was in the weekend before last. I'm dreading to see what it says. The night the critic was there was a humiliating failure.'

'I recall once there was a wonderful headline in the *Gazette* about the Lady Cavendish High School,' said Sidney. ' "HEADMISTRESS UNVEILS BUST AT DEDICATION CEREMONY". I can just imagine the redoubtable Miss Bronson unveiling her bust.'

'I can't find this review,' I said.

'Page eight,' Julie said. 'Marcia McCrudden's column.'

'Give it here,' said Sidney, coming across the room and snatching the paper from me. 'I'll tell you what it says and spare your blushes.' He turned to the page. 'Here it is,' he said, taking a theatrical stance before reading: ' "The staging of a wartime classic drama, based on the autobiography of the Dame of Sark, was performed last week by the Fettlesham Literary Players at the Little Theatre. It was a bold undertaking by any standards and was warmly received by a most appreciative audience." '

'Does it really say that, Sidney?' I asked. 'That's not bad.'

'Scout's honour.' He read on. ' "The undisputed star of the show was Margot Cleaver-Canning who gave an inspired performance as the formidable Dame of Sark, Mrs Sibyl Hathaway. She captured the larger-than-life character superbly, dominating the stage with her imperious presence. In her voluminous black dress, she was every inch the powerful matriarchal figure whose courage and determination remained steadfast during the occupation of her island home. She was ably supported by Norman Cleaver-Canning as the mild-mannered, aristocratic, rather bumbling German commander, who was no match for the Dame. It was a delight to see them on stage together. Sharon Mawson, playing the part of Celine, Mrs Hathaway's French maid, brought sparkling humour and vitality to a very demanding role. She maintained the Breton accent throughout the drama with great authenticity. I look forward to seeing much more of this talented young woman." '

'It gets better,' I said.

Sidney read on. ' "Another sterling performance was given by George Furnival, the sinister Dr Braun, whose angry delivery of his lines showed his displeasure and hostility when in the presence of the Dame. His pale deadpan features and slimy manner were perfectly suited to the role of a member of the feared Gestapo." '

'Sounds a *tour de force* to me,' said David. 'I should have got tickets to take Gwynneth. Why didn't you tell us about it?'

'Do I get a mention?' I asked, ignoring him.

'Yes, here you are at the end,' said Sidney. He read in silence.

'Well, go on,' I said. 'What does it say?'

'Perhaps you ought to read it yourself, old boy,' said Sidney, with a rather hangdog expression.

'No, no,' I said, 'go on Sidney. I'd like to hear. I don't mind what it says.'

I should have thought back a moment to my performance.

'Very well,' said my colleague. He coughed. ' "Gervase Phinn, playing the part of the British Colonel Graham, was . . ." ' Sidney paused.

'Was what?' I asked.

' "Lacklustre",' said Sidney.

' "Lacklustre"!' I cried.

'That's what it says.' Sidney continued, ' "He mumbled though his few lines with little conviction and it was hard to suspend one's disbelief and accept that one so youthful looking—" '

'Well, there's a compliment, at least,' interrupted David.

'Go on, Sidney,' I said quietly.

' ". . . that one so youthful looking and so lacking in assertiveness could have been the senior British officer who liberated the island."' Not an overwhelmingly good review, is it, old boy?'

'It's awful,' I said. 'I was fine at rehearsal. It was the blasted sound effects or, rather, the lack of them that did for me. It put me completely off my stroke.'

'Well, it rules you out for a role at Stratford,' said David.

' "Lacklustre"!' I said again. It was then that I recalled this was the very same word I had used to describe the two teachers at Ugglemattersby Junior School.

'I'd best get on,' said Julie, giving me a sympathetic glance as she left the office.

'Never mind, Gervase,' said Sidney, returning to his desk and leaning back in his chair. 'You have to look on the positive side of this. One good thing is that you won't be called upon again to tread the boards, having to give up all those evenings rehearsing with a group of broken-down amateur actors. You can now, as the politicians frequently say, spend more time with your family.'

'Cheer up,' said David. 'You'll have forgotten all about it by tomorrow.'

'Yes,' I said, feeling rotten inside. 'It's just that I'm a bit taken aback by the review. I didn't think I was that bad. Anyway,' I said, picking up my briefcase, 'I must be away to a governors' meeting.' To be honest, I was relieved to have an appointment to go to.

*   *   *

The following morning, I went straight from home to West Challerton High School. I was glad that I had been able to get an early appointment to see the headmaster because I really wanted to get this bullying problem sorted out.

Mr Pennington-Smith was thin and stiff as a broom handle. He had short-cropped iron-grey hair and eyes like blue china marbles behind thick black-framed glasses. He was wearing, as always, a black academic gown.

'And what have we done to deserve a visitation from yet another school inspector?' he asked, with undisguised sarcasm in his voice. He had kept me waiting in the entrance hall for a good ten minutes before emerging from his room to meet me. 'You inspectors must enjoy coming to West Challerton,' he continued in his deep and grating voice. 'You seem to spend so much time here.'

It was true that Sidney, David and Geraldine had visited the school frequently in recent months, largely because several areas of weakness had been identified in their reports. Despite his grandiose claims when he had taken over the headship, little had been translated into good practice. Mr Pennington-Smith was, as David's old Welsh grandmother might have described him, 'all wind and no substance'.

At our first meeting, when I had visited the school to introduce myself and offer what help and advice I could, I very soon discovered that this overweening and arrogant man felt he was in little need of any assistance or guidance from anyone, least of all a school inspector who, I guess, he thought was still wet behind the ears. I had been subjected to a lengthy monologue in which he had described his impeccable credentials in the education world and his vast experience. I had bristled when he had launched into a diatribe of the previous headmaster. His predecessor, Mr Blunt, ('Blunt by name and blunt by nature') was a large, bluff and outspoken Yorkshireman yet, despite his brusque manner, I had rather liked the man.

'I am afraid, Mr Phinn,' Mr Pennington-Smith had confided in me at that first visit and fixing me with his cold, fishy eyes, 'that the former incumbent tended to—how can I put it diplomatically?—to let things drift. I don't wish to be too unkind and I have no doubt that, at one time, Mr Blunt ran a tight ship, but sadly things got slack.' I quickly discovered that he was very big on nautical metaphors, and thoroughly deserved the nickname we inspectors soon bestowed on him—Captain Bligh. I had thought at the time that such observations about his predecessor were unfounded and I had told Mr Pennington-Smith as much. Under Mr Blunt's leadership, the school had achieved commendable examination results, was relatively successful in sports, had a thriving brass band, staged good-quality drama productions and there was a positive atmosphere. It wasn't the county's flagship school but it certainly was not in the doldrums.

At the school's prize-giving ceremony and speech day that I'd attended, it had been clear to me and everyone else hearing Captain Bligh's 'performance' behind the lectern that only the most successful students in the various academic subjects and those who did well in sport would be presented with any awards, and that the emphasis in the school, under Mr Pennington-Smith's leadership, would be on the more able and the high achievers. So, when young Andy, standing in the garden at Peewit Cottage, had assessed his headmaster as being 'only bothered abaat bright kids and them what are good at sports,' he reinforced an opinion I had already formed.

After a little over a year in the job, things had not altered at all for the better at West Challerton High School. In fact, if anything, they seemed to have worsened and my colleague inspectors had submitted a series of critical reports, all of which had been challenged by the headmaster, supported by his chairman of governors, none other than Councillor, Mr Deputy Mayor, George 'pain in the neck' Peterson.

'I've come about bullying,' I told Mr Pennington-Smith now.

'Bullying,' he repeated.

'Yes. I have reason to believe that one of your pupils is being bullied.'

'You sound like a policeman, Mr Phinn,' he said raising an eyebrow. ' "Reason to believe"?'

'Yes,' I said. 'I am not certain of the facts but—'

'And you have made a special visit to inform me about one pupil,' he interrupted.

'Yes, I thought I should draw it to your attention.'

'I would have thought that you have many more pressing matters than making a special visit to the school over a single pupil. I am sure a telephone call would have sufficed.'

'Perhaps,' I said, 'but I thought I should acquaint you personally with the situation.' I realised with horror that I had unwittingly aped Savage-speak. 'I am sure that you take bullying as seriously as I do, and if it is one or one hundred pupils being bullied it is important to tackle it. In fact, the boy concerned could very well have been killed.'

'Well, you had better come to my room,' he said. I followed him down the corridor. He glanced at a shiny watch on his wrist. 'I have a Senior Management Meeting to chair at ten o'clock and several pressing matters to deal with—but I can spare you ten minutes.'

He sat at his desk and, to my surprise, listened impassively and without interruption as I related the incident with Terry Mossup and how I had very nearly knocked him down.

'But from what you have told me,' he said when I had finished, 'this incident took place off school premises and out of school hours. Am I right?'

'It did, yes,' I replied.

'I can hardly be expected to police society as a whole, Mr Phinn,' said Mr Pennington-Smith pompously. 'What am I expected to do—escort the student home, patrol the highway, stand on street corners on the look-out for bullies? I deal with things which happen in my school, and have no control over what happens out of it.'

'But would you not agree,' I asked him, 'that the bullying of one of your pupils outside school should concern you since the bullying is more than likely to continue on school premises.'

'Of course I'm concerned with the pupils in my school,' he said, 'and I shall take any action I deem fit.'

'May I ask what action you might take?' I asked.

'I shall ask my deputy headteacher, Mr Stipple, to investigate the matter. If, indeed, this is a case of victimisation, I shall deal with these three boys

376

you can be certain of that. I will not tolerate any form of bullying in West Challerton High School. As you may be aware, I have a very thorough and well-tried anti-bullying policy.'

'May I ask—' I started.

'One moment, please. I will get you a copy of our policy.' He pressed a buzzer on his desk. A disembodied voice asked, 'Yes, Mr Pennington-Smith?'

'Mrs Rogers, would you bring me a copy of our anti-bullying policy, please?'

The headmaster smiled. 'You might wish to take it with you when you leave,' he said.

*   *   *

On my way to the car, I came upon a knot of large boys having a crafty smoke well out of sight of the main building. The cigarettes miraculously disappeared as I approached. I smiled, recalling the time when I was their age and had snuck off with several pals behind the bicycle sheds to do the same. I was not a very successful smoker and after several bouts of vomiting gave up the dreaded weed for good.

'Morning, boys,' I said cheerfully as I passed.

One of the group, a large pink-faced lad with coarse bristly brown hair and enormous ears, emerged from the group of lads, flicking his cigarette stub into a bush.

'Hey up, Mester Phinn.'

'Hello, Andy,' I said.

' 'Ere on hofficial business, are tha?' he asked.

'Something like that,' I told him.

'Are tha closin' t'school down, then?' he asked.

'No,' I replied.

'Pity.'

'By the way, the garden is looking really good.'

'An' t'gutterin'?'

'Fine.'

'An' no more squirrels?'

'Not one.'

''As thy 'eard abaat mi Uncle 'Arry?' the boy asked.

'No, what?' I replied.

''E's been barred.'

'Barred?' I repeated.

'From t'Royal Oak. New landlord got sick on 'im complainin' all t'time, moanin' abaat all t'changes so 'e barred 'im. Telled 'im not to come back an' to tek his pals wi' im.'

'All four have been banned?' I asked. 'That's a bit much.'

'Well, to be 'onest, Mester Phinn, it were a bit cheeky-like fer mi Uncle 'Arry to get up this pertition an' ask people comin' into t'pub to sign it.'

'I suppose it was,' I said, although it was just the thing Harry Cotton would do, I thought to myself.

'Any road, 'e's in a reight temper these days, angry as an 'ungry ferret in a sack.'

'I'll remember to keep out of his way,' I said.

'Well, let us know if there's owt else I can 'elp thee wi'.'

'There is something,' I said, having a sudden and inspired thought. 'Could you walk with me to the car? I'd like a quiet word with you.' When we were out of earshot of the other boys, I stopped. 'Andy,' I said, 'there's a boy in the first year here at West Challerton called Terry Mossup. He's a bit of a loner, small for his age with ginger hair.'

'Aye, I reckon I've seen 'im abaat. Funny kid. Allus on 'is own.'

'Well, he's had a fair bit of trouble in his life and I think you can be of help.'

'What's tha want me to do then, Mester Phinn?' he asked.

'He's being bullied by three older and much bigger boys and it occurred to me that—'

He finished my sentence. 'Tha wants me to put a stop to it.'

'Well, what I was thinking was, that you might—'

'No problem, Mester Phinn,' he said. 'I'll fettle it for thee. Nob'dy'll pick on 'im from now on. I 'ates bullies, there's summat up wi' 'em. Anyone who likes to mek others upset must be a bit tapped in t'ead.'

'I don't want you to do anything in particular, Andy,' I said. 'Just keep a watchful eye on Terry.'

The boy winked. 'I follow yer drift, Mester Phinn,' he said knowingly, tapping the side of his nose. 'I'll not do nowt in particular.'

'Thank you,' I said.

'But there's summat tha can do fer me,' he told me.

'Yes, of course,' I replied. 'What that?'

'Keep thee gob shut abaat t'smokin'.'

CHAPTER TWENTY-TWO

On a morning towards the end of November, I visited King Henry's College in Brindcliffe to observe some English lessons. On my previous visit, I had been mostly impressed with the quality of teaching. The exception was the head of department, Mr Frobisher, a pale-complexioned individual, with large hooded eyes magnified behind rimless spectacles. He seemed to be totally devoid of humour and had the arrogance of a Spanish conquistador.

Following my very critical report, he had decided to take early retirement.

I was surprised this morning, however, to find Mrs Todd back at King Henry's. When I had first met her, here at this school, she had recently retired as the head of the English Department in a large comprehensive. She had been persuaded to do some supply teaching at King Henry's and had been there during the Frobisher affair. She had told me some time later that she was moving on to The Lady Cavendish High School for Girls, to cover for a maternity leave. She was a petite woman with neatly-permed, tinted hair and clear rather piercing blue eyes behind small round spectacles. Having sat in on one of her lessons, I knew she was someone who clearly enjoyed the challenge presented her by lively, intelligent but sometimes rather difficult and demanding students, and that, I suppose, was why she had been prevailed upon to return to the classroom once her own family had grown up.

She met me now outside the staff room, and she explained as we walked together to her classroom.

'My contract at The Lady Cavendish ended when the teacher I was covering for returned to work. She had a little boy called Harry, by the way.'

'And you were persuaded to come back here as the acting head of department?' I said.

'Dragooned more like.' She laughed. 'After Mr Frobisher left, they appointed a teacher who I believe they were pleased with. Most unfortunately, however, she had to stand down when her teenage son was involved in a serious motorcycle accident during the summer holidays, and now requires round-the-clock care at home. The school got in touch with me, and here I am.'

'It's nice to see you again,' I said warmly. 'And you don't mind being back in the old routine?'

'No, I am very happy to be back in the classroom. It didn't take much to persuade me. When I'm away from school, I miss teaching terribly.'

The sixth form group stood up when we entered the classroom.

'Do please sit down, boys,' said the teacher. She faced the class and smiled. 'It will not have escaped your notice that we have a visitor with us today. This is Mr Phinn.'

'Excuse me, sir.' The speaker, sitting at one of the front desks, was a gangly boy with lanky brown hair and angry acne across his forehead and cheeks. 'I know you, don't I?'

I recognised the boy immediately. Who could forget such a character? I had met Hugo Maxwell-Smith on my last visit to King Henry's. He had been extremely obstreperous, constantly challenging Mr Frobisher, trying to catch him out, or making some clever comment and demonstrating his undoubted ability. He was an extremely bright but belligerent student. I wondered how Mrs Todd was coping with such a tricky and troublesome individual.

'Do you?' I asked the boy innocently.

381

'You're the school inspector,' said the boy. 'The man in black who sits in the corner of our classroom with his little notebook and a set of questions. I'm sure you remember.'

'Ah, yes,' I said, recalling well the occasion when the boy had grilled me. 'Who exactly are you?' he had asked 'And what is it that you do?' When I had informed him that it was usually the inspector and not the pupils who asked the questions, he had replied, 'But surely in a good school, the pupils are encouraged to ask questions, are they not?'

'You will have to be careful, Mrs Todd,' Hugo told her with a smirk on his face. 'It was after Mr Phinn's last visit to King Henry's that Mr Frobisher suddenly and mysteriously left. I think the term is "The Kiss of Death".'

'I shall have to watch my step then, Hugo, won't I?' replied Mrs Todd pleasantly. 'Now, why don't you get out your books and we can begin.'

The lesson was extremely well taught but, as expected, Hugo was at pains to be clever and an insufferable show-off. When asked by the teacher what was Romeo's last wish he replied, 'To get laid by Juliet.'

The innuendo was not lost on the teacher who remained unflustered and affable. 'By that, do you mean Romeo wished to be buried in the crypt next to Juliet, Hugo, or to have sex with her? You really have to be more explicit in what you mean.'

The boy didn't give up and continued to try and embarrass the teacher. 'There's a lot of erotic imagery in the play,' he observed, 'isn't there, Mrs Todd?'

'Indeed there is, Hugo,' said the teacher, 'but then there is a great deal of sexual language in many of Shakespeare's plays. It appealed to the groundlings, just as smutty humour and suggestive allusions appeal to some people today.' She gave him a long and knowing look. 'So what was the point you wished to make?'

'It was just an observation,' replied the boy.

'Well, thank you for that,' said Mrs Todd. 'I am most grateful to you for pointing it out, and I am sure that I don't need to spell out all the sexual allusions to you, Hugo, do I, your being a man of the world?' There were a few sniggers from the rest of the class. 'But if you are unsure about anything, I shall be most happy to explain things.'

'Of course I know what they mean,' he replied, clearly put out, 'but—'

'Was there something else?' asked the teacher.

'No,' said the boy.

'Then we can get on,' said Mrs Todd. 'Perhaps, Hugo, you might like to read on from where we were at the last lesson. Act 1, Scene 5, line 47.'

The boy sighed and read the verse in a sing-song manner:

O! she doth teach the torches to burn bright.
It seems she hangs upon the cheek of night
Like a rich jewel in an Ethiop's ear;
Beauty too rich for use, for earth too dear!
So shows a snowy dove trooping with crows,
As yonder lady o'er her fellows shows.

'Hugo,' said the teacher, in mock-horror, 'you have the greatest words of love at your disposal and you are reading them like an inventory. I want to hear passion in your voice. Romeo's smitten, he can hardly breathe for love of this beautiful young

383

woman.'

'Can someone else read it, Mrs Todd,' said the boy, blushing and clearly irritated. 'I think it's rather soppy.'

'Self-indulgently sentimental, I think might be a better description if you were making this observation on your examination paper. Examiners do not take kindly to colloquialisms. But, of course, I don't agree with you that this is mawkish. I think the lines are rather beautiful. Perhaps, Hugo,' she said smiling, 'when you are in love, the words of Romeo might ring true.'

There were more titters from the class.

The boy brooded for much of the lesson but as it neared morning break he thought he would have another salvo. 'Mrs Todd,' he said, 'you know you said there is a lot of sexual language in many of Shakespeare's plays.'

'Yes,' replied the teacher.

'I've never been quite sure,' he said, nudging the boy next to him, 'what the difference is between the word "erotic" and the word "kinky".'

'Well, perhaps I can explain,' said the teacher, without the least sign of any embarrassment. 'Let me see. "Erotic", I think, comes from the French *érotique* meaning "sexual love", but "kinky" will have a much more recent provenance. Let me give you an example. To have a long soft ostrich feather brushed enticingly across your cheek by a beautiful woman might be considered erotic. To use the whole ostrich would be, I guess, regarded as kinky. Does that explain?'

'Yes, miss,' replied the boy sullenly, as the rest of the class burst out laughing.

After the lesson, when I was chatting with

Mrs Todd, she said, 'I think I mentioned on the last occasion we met, Mr Phinn, that I have brought up four boys of my own and know all too well how the adolescent's mind works. I taught for many years in a tough inner-city school, and I have always found that the rebellious and unmanageable boys tend to seek attention by misbehaving or trying to provoke the teacher. There is nothing I haven't seen or heard when it comes to teenagers. Hugo tries it on but he will soon learn that I am not the one to rise to his clever comments.'

'I thought you handled him very well,' I said. 'I remember what a thorn in the flesh he was for Mr Frobisher.'

'I know I might sound uncharitable,' she said, 'but Mr Frobisher did rather ask for it. I remember the time the school staged the Scottish play. Mr Frobisher, rather puritan in his views, if you recall, tinkered about with the text in case anything should give offence to anyone in the audience. Our colleague, the inestimable Mr Poppleton, was incensed that anyone should have the impertinence to alter Shakespeare but Mr Frobisher carried on regardless, chopping and changing. He told young Hugo, who was playing the part of King Duncan, to adjust the language of his very first line. You may remember, Mr Phinn, that in *Macbeth*, the King, seeing a survivor of the battle staggering on to the stage, asks his attendants, "What bloody man is that?" Hugo, as directed, changed the line to his own version, "And who's that silly bugger, then?" You can imagine Mr Frobisher's reaction!' She smiled and shook her head. 'Hugo will either end up in prison or become a very successful barrister like his father.'

*   *   *

Later that morning, I arrived at Westgarth Primary School. I had visited this school, an ugly, sprawling building enclosed by black iron railings, when I had first started as a school inspector. I had accompanied Harold Yeats, the then Senior Inspector, and we had been mistaken for the men from the Premises and Maintenance Section of the Education Department who were due to come to fix the leak in the boys' toilets.

I had made a return visit to Westgarth School the following year to speak at a parents' meeting and had found the chairman of governors, Mr Parsons, to be an insufferable individual. He was loud, extremely portly, and had a profound sense of his own importance. He had berated me, as I prepared to give my talk, about the decline in educational standards, the lack of discipline and manners in the young and the increase in juvenile crime. I had listened to him wearily.

As I made my way up the path to the school entrance now, to attend the interview panel for a new deputy headteacher, I hoped that Mr Parsons wouldn't be there, but I knew full well he would be, no doubt spouting his outrageous views. I noticed a red sports car parked in the road outside the school, which told me that Dr Gore's representative on the panel, the redoubtable Mrs Savage, had already arrived. This was likely, I thought, to prove a very interesting morning.

I could hear the chairman of governors' loud and abrasive voice at the end of the corridor as I approached the headteacher's room. Taking a deep breath I knocked and entered. There were five people present, four of whom were being lectured by Mr Parsons. The speaker stopped mid-sentence when he saw me. 'So, if you want my opinion—'

'Good morning,' I said brightly.

'Oh,' said Mr Parsons. 'It's Mr Flynn. We can make a start now you've arrived.' There was the hint of criticism in his voice.

'Phinn,' I said.

'What?'

'It's Mr Phinn,' said Mrs Thornton, the headteacher, moving forward to shake my hand. 'Thank you for coming.'

Mrs Thornton was dressed in a thick green tweed suit in contrast to the CEO's Personal Assistant who was standing by the window. Mrs Savage was attired in an elegant salmon-coloured dress with a black velvet jacket. She looked as stylish as ever. 'You know Mrs Savage, of course,' continued the headteacher, 'but may I introduce two of my governors, Mrs Smethurst and Mrs Curry.' The headteacher gave me a knowing look as she said, 'And, of course, you've met Mr Parsons.'

'Well, now we're all here,' said the chairman of governors, 'shall we make a start? I've a business to run and don't want these interviews dragging on.'

'I don't think it will take us long,' the headteacher told him. She turned to me. 'Unfortunately, two of the candidates have pulled out at the last minute so we only have three applicants to consider. I did suggest to Mr Parsons that perhaps we ought to re-advertise—'

'But I said we should go ahead,' he interrupted. 'I'm the sort of person who likes to get things done.'

The interviews took place in the school hall. The six of us, with Mr Parsons positioned in the centre, sat in a row at a long trestle table in front of which was a hard-backed chair for the interviewee.

First of all, the candidates' application forms were considered by the governors and the headteacher and, much to my horror when I heard the name, it became clear that the chairman had a preferred choice. Neither Mrs Savage, who was present to record the deliberations and report back to Dr Gore, nor I, who always preferred to wait until I had seen and heard what each applicant had to say, gave an opinion. However, from what I had read on the application form, one of the candidates seemed eminently suitable, another was a strong possibility and the third, Mr Parson's obvious favourite, was quite unsuitable.

I had met Miss Pinkney, the first candidate, when I had inspected St Catherine's, a school for those with 'special needs', some two years earlier and had been very impressed by her teaching. I had arrived in the hall to watch a drama lesson, where I had met this larger-than-life, bubbly, middle-aged woman with long hair gathered up in a tortoiseshell comb. She had been dressed in a bright pink and yellow Lycra tracksuit, and I remember thinking at the time that she looked like a huge chunk of Battenberg cake.

'Come along in, Mr Phinn,' she had boomed. 'Shoes by the door, jacket on a peg. There's a spare leotard if you want to slip into it.' When she had seen the appalled look on my face, she had added, 'Only joking!' She had then informed me that her students, all of whom were disabled but 'very talented', were her 'stars'. It was transparent that this teacher had a very positive relationship with the children; she was sensitive, encouraging, and good-humoured.

I had met a cheerful and obviously clever young man at St Catherine's whose ambition was to study English at university. Michael, aged sixteen, had been blind since birth but announced when I spoke to him that his blindness was not a 'handicap' nor a 'disability'; it was 'more of an inconvenience' and that if sighted people like myself were a little more considerate and put things back in their proper place, then he wouldn't bang into them. I had learnt to read Braille when I had studied for a teaching diploma but had become very rusty and Michael had been most amused at my miserable efforts to decipher the dots on the page.

'Not the world's best reader,' he had told me, good-naturedly. 'I think you need to brush up on your Braille, Mr Phinn.'

He'd had no problems, of course, reading the text and his fingers had moved across the page at a remarkable speed.

'You're a pretty important person, aren't you?' Michael had told me.

'Not really.'

'Yes, you are,' he had said. 'The atmosphere in the school since the teachers knew you were coming has been manic. You write a report about the school and how things can be improved and the teachers have to do it.' He waited for a response but when I didn't reply, he added, 'Well, don't they?'

'I suppose that's how it's supposed to work,' I had told him. 'So what improvements would you recommend?'

'Not many,' he'd said. 'It's a good school. There's not much wrong with it.' The boy had thought for a moment and then added, 'The library could do with more good-quality books in Braille and Moon.'

'Moon?'

'Moon is an easier alternative to Braille,' he had explained. 'It was invented by Dr William Moon back in 1854. I'm surprised you've not heard of it, you being a school inspector. Braille is a better system in lots of ways but Moon is pretty good for kids who can't manage Braille. You ought to look at it. You see, someone with a visual impairment is likely to be behind in his or her reading and they need really good material to get them turned on to books. It's awfully expensive to convert a book into Braille so lots of books aren't available.'

'I will certainly take that on board when I write my report,' I had told him. 'So tell me, Michael, what is the best thing about St Catherine's?'

'That's easy,' he had replied without a moment's hesitation. 'Miss Pinkney.'

That same Miss Pinkney now entered the hall for her interview like a seasoned actress coming on stage. The door was thrown open and she made a grand entrance, dressed in a multicoloured smock of a dress, red leather sandals and a rope of enormous amber-coloured beads.

'Good morning to you all,' she said in a deep, resonant voice. She approached the chair, her sandals making a slapping sound on the wooden floor. 'May I sit?' Without waiting for an answer,

390

she plonked herself down and smiled widely at the panel.

The interview went very well for Miss Pinkney. She answered the questions fully and confidently, and it was clear that she was a highly-committed and enthusiastic teacher with the experience, expertise and the force of character to be a first-rate deputy headteacher. When Mr Parsons climbed on his hobbyhorse about decline in standards, poor behaviour in the young and lack of discipline, she challenged him.

'My goodness,' she chortled, 'you do sound so dreadfully pessimistic. The picture is not quite as bad as you paint it, you know, and I speak from working with children for many years. On the whole, I have to say that I am very impressed by the youth of today. I love working with them and I have a great deal of faith in them. I know there are the awkward and the demanding and, on occasions, the repellent youngsters who are hard to cope with, and it is always these who seem to get into the newspapers, but there are many many children who come from caring, supportive homes and are in the hands of dedicated and talented teachers.'

Out of the corner of my eye, I could see Mrs Thornton beside me nodding. She was obviously impressed with what she was hearing.

The chairman of governors grunted. 'Mr Phinn,' he said, 'would you like to say something?'

'What do you think are the keys to educational success?' I asked her.

Miss Pinkney answered without a moment's thought. 'Great expectation and high self-esteem.' She clasped her hands in front of her, displaying a set of large coloured rings. 'Shall I go on?'

'Please,' I replied.

'If you feel good about yourself, you feel good about others, don't you? And, you are more likely to feel confident of your own worth and abilities. I think it's so important to build up a child's feeling of self-worth. I work with dyslexic and autistic youngsters and many have such low self-esteem. They think they're useless. I try and build up their self-confidence and convince them that they aren't on the scrap heap and can achieve great things. I firmly believe that if a teacher expects the moon, perhaps her pupils will go through the roof and dwell amongst the stars. Sounds a bit fancy that, doesn't it, but I certainly have great expectations of the children I teach at St Catherine's.'

'Ah yes,' interrupted Mr Parsons, 'St Catherine's. That's a special school, isn't it?'

'Yes, it is,' she replied.

'And you work with handicapped children?' he asked.

'Disabled,' she said. 'Handicapped is a word we no longer use.'

'Yes, well, I'm not big on so-called political correctness,' mumbled the Chairman.

The smile disappeared from Miss Pinkney's face. 'It is really not a question of political correctness,' she retorted. 'It is more to do with sensitivity and respect. It wasn't that long ago people were calling children with cerebral palsy, "spastics", and those with Down's Syndrome, "mongols". The appropriate term is "disabled" and, yes, I have worked with these children for a number of years.'

'And don't you think you might find it a bit

392

different working with *normal* children?' asked Mr Parsons.

'And what do you mean by *"normal"* children?' she asked.

'Well, children that have all their facilities, that aren't handi—disabled.'

'Children with a disability are like any other children,' she told him. 'They have the same feelings and fears, likes and dislikes. They enjoy the same things. They can be as delightful, difficult, happy, moody, sad, loving, naughty as any other children. It is just that they have rather more difficulties in life to face than many others. And I have to say that many disabled children show remarkable courage and forbearance. Shall I go on?'

'No,' grunted Mr Parsons, 'that's quite sufficient.'

When Miss Pinkney had left, the Chairman turned to the headteacher. 'Not very appropriate outfit for an interview, was it?' he observed. 'I'm of the opinion that teachers should be dressed like teachers. She looked like a gypsy fortune-teller in that coloured tent. And fancy wearing sandals for an interview.' He shook his head. 'And I can't say I liked her manner. Over the top with her answers, I thought, and I didn't like the way she was always asking me questions. It's for us to ask her, not her to ask us.'

I noticed Mrs Savage producing a thin silver pen and small leather-bound notebook from her handbag and proceed to make a note.

'So what did you make of her then, Mrs Thornton?' he asked.

'I should prefer to see all the candidates before I

express my opinion, Mr Parsons,' she told him.

'Which is normal interview procedure,' added Mrs Savage.

'Oh, is it?' said the Chairman.

The second applicant was a tall, pale-faced man in his twenties, with an explosion of wild, woolly hair and a permanently surprised expression. It was Mr Hornchurch.

'Take a seat,' said Mr Parsons. I could see from his expression that he was less than impressed with the outfit that this candidate too was wearing. Mr Hornchurch was attired in a loud checked jacket, pale grey trousers, pink shirt and a multicoloured tie. 'It occurs to me,' continued the Chairman, flicking through the application form, 'that you're a bit on the young side for this position.'

'It is true,' Mr Hornchurch answered, crossing his long legs, 'that I have only been in the profession for a relatively short time, but I feel quite confident about taking on the role of the deputy headteacher.' He went on to give a series of splendid answers, outlining what he had developed at Tarncliffe Primary School, the results the children in his class had achieved, the prizes they had won and the fact that the headteacher had actively encouraged his application.

Mr Parsons gave a cynical smile. 'Some might say she was keen to get rid of you.'

'Some might say that,' replied Mr Hornchurch pleasantly, 'but I am led to believe that I am a valued member of her teaching staff, which I hope is reflected in her reference.'

When it came to my turn, I asked the candidate what, in his opinion, characterised a good school.

He uncrossed his legs, leaned forward and rested his hands on his knees.

'A good school,' he said, 'is cheerful and optimistic, a place where children can learn in a safe and secure environment, where they feel valued and respected, where the teachers are enthusiastic and committed, and the leadership is purposeful and dynamic. There should be no bullying or racism, and there should be decent toilets. For me, the good school—'

'Toilets?' exclaimed Mr Parsons.

'Yes, of course,' replied Mr Hornchurch. 'If you were to ask children what they think characterises a good school, the state of the toilets is always high on their list. You see, if the toilets are clean and attractive, everything else in the school is likely to be the same.'

'That's, of course,' said the headteacher, glancing in my direction, 'if they are working properly.'

I determined that my first port of call back at the Education Office would be the Premises and Maintenance Section.

The third candidate, a lean woman with a pale pinched face and dressed in a black suit and prim white blouse buttoned up to the neck, looked startled when she saw me. She drew her lips together into a tight little line and stared at me with Medusa ferocity. It was Mrs Sidebottom from Ugglemattersby Junior School.

Mr Parsons was clearly taken with her tidy appearance for his manner changed. I suppose she looked to him like the good old-fashioned, I-stand-no-nonsense sort of teacher that he wanted at Westgarth.

'Do take a seat, Mrs Sidebottom,' he said amiably. 'I'm sorry you have had to be the last in, but somebody has to be.'

'That's quite all right,' she replied, giving a thin-lipped smile. 'And my name is pronounced Siddybothome.'

'So,' said Mr Parsons, 'can you tell us why you want to leave your present position?'

She smiled wanly. 'I feel I need a greater challenge,' she said. 'As you may know, the Junior School in which I teach at present is due to amalgamate with the Infant School.' She glanced briefly in my direction. 'I really feel that it is time for me to take on greater responsibility. I have to say that I believe in very high standards, some might say my expectation is rather too high, but in my opinion there needs to be discipline, routine, good order in the classroom, and well-behaved children, attributes which I feel are sadly lacking in society as a whole.'

'Indeed,' agreed Mr Parsons. 'I'm constantly saying so myself.'

'I am, and I make no apology for this, a traditionalist, some might say rather old-fashioned.'

'Not a bad thing,' said Mr Parsons, nodding.

'And were I to be appointed to the position of deputy headteacher,' she continued, cheered by the supportive comments and friendly nods of the chairman of governors, and preparing to give us the benefit of what no doubt was a prepared statement, 'I should endeavour to develop in the children self-discipline, acceptable behaviour and good manners as well as teaching them the essential basic skills of reading, writing and arithmetic. I do have managerial skills and a great deal of classroom experience with difficult children. I am efficient, punctual and have had few absences, qualities which are essential for the deputy headteacher.'

'Very good,' said the Chairman, nodding again.

After the interview panel had each put a question to Mrs Sidebottom, I asked her, 'And how important in a school, do you think, are extra-curricular activities?'

'Extra-curricular activities?' she repeated.

I elaborated. 'School concerts, Saturday sports activities, trips out of school, that sort of thing?'

'They have their place, I am sure,' she said, 'but the main function of the teacher is to teach children—as I have just said—good behaviour and manners as well as the usual lessons. In my opinion, such things as those you describe decorate the margin of the more serious business of a school and, in any case, should be left largely to the parents.'

'I see,' I said. 'No more questions thank you, Mr Chairman.'

When the time came for the panel to consider the three applicants, Mr Parsons said straight away, 'I have to say that the first two candidates didn't *look* like teachers to me. Neither of them was, in my opinion, dressed properly for an interview. Nor was I impressed by their answers— far too airy-fairy, for my liking. The last candidate seems to me to have her feet firmly on the ground. She looks the part, sounds like a teacher after my own heart and, as far as I'm concerned, she's the one we should appoint, and I don't think we need waste any more time—'

'Might we hear what the inspector has to say?' asked Mrs Curry who, apart from asking one question of each candidate, had sat quietly, listening intently.

'Yes, I suppose so,' said Mr Parsons.

I was careful, when giving my assessment of the candidates, to outline what I considered to be their strengths and weaknesses without indicating which one I favoured. I explained that I had observed all three applicants actually teach so was in a position to comment on their classroom practice.

'Thank you for that,' said Mr Parsons. 'Now, in my opinion—'

'And might we now hear what the headteacher has to say?' asked Mrs Smethurst. 'After all, it is Mrs Thornton who will be working closely with the successful candidate.'

'Yes, yes,' said Mr Parsons, somewhat flustered. 'I was just about to ask her.'

It was clear to all that Mrs Thornton preferred the first candidate and considered the last totally unsuitable.

'I just don't think,' persisted Mr Parsons, when Mrs Thornton had finished speaking, 'that this Miss Pinkney *looks* like a teacher who will fit in here.'

'May I ask, Mr Chairman,' said Mrs Savage, asking a question for the first time, 'if you are judging the candidates *only* on their appearances?'

Bravo, Mrs Savage! I thought to myself.

'Well, that and what I've heard,' he replied, testily.

'It seems to me, Mr Chairman,' she continued, 'that Mr Phinn, having seen all the candidates teach and observed them in a school environment, has a clearer picture than any of us here as to what they are really like. In addition, the headteacher has clearly intimated her preference for the first candidate. I should also like to draw your attention to the references, which do indicate that there are strong reservations about the last candidate. Appearances can be deceptive, as I am sure we are all aware.'

'Mrs, er . . . ?' began Mr Parsons.

'Savage,' she replied. 'Personal Assistant to Dr Gore, the Chief Education Officer, and his representative on the Appointments Panel, here to ensure that the rubric of the "Procedures for the Appointment of Staff" is adhered to.'

'Mrs Savage,' said the chairman of governors, speaking her name with deliberate emphasis, 'I don't need to remind you that it is the governors of this school who make the decisions in appointing staff, not inspectors nor education officials.'

'No, Mr Chairman, you do not need to remind me,' replied Mrs Savage, with an edge to her voice. 'It is I who send the "Instruments of Governance" to schools and am more conversant with them than anyone.'

'That's as may be—' he began.

'If I may finish,' she interrupted, like a politician during an awkward television interview. 'I shall say this, Mr Chairman, that if the governors decide to ignore the advice of Mr Phinn and of the headteacher, who has expressed her preference, and they disregard the references, which of course they are at liberty to do, and Mrs Sidebottom, were she appointed, turns out to be unsuccessful in this important managerial role, then it will be the governors' entire responsibility.'

'There's not much chance of that,' said Mrs Curry. 'My vote goes to Miss Pinkney.'

'And so does mine,' agreed Mrs Smethurst.

'Thank you, colleagues,' said Mrs Savage in her most obsequious voice, her small silver pencil poised over her notebook. 'I take it, then, that I may record that Miss Pinkney is to be offered the position?'

CHAPTER TWENTY-THREE

'Well, that's another of Dr Gore's little jobs about ready for the off,' I said, snapping the red folder shut. It was Thursday morning, during the last week of November, and I was trying to catch up on the paperwork that was piled high in my in-tray. When two of my colleagues arrived, however, I pushed the work away, deciding to finish the rest at home that evening. There was little chance of getting anything done when both Sidney and David were in the office.

'And what little job is that?' asked David, peering over the top of his spectacles.

'The NACADS Conference,' I told him.

'Well, all I can say, dear boy,' said Sidney, leaning back on his chair and puffing out his cheeks dramatically, 'is that you deserve a medal for working with that domineering, disagreeable, umbrageous, bad-tempered woman.'

'You have to know how to handle Mrs Savage, Sidney,' I told him. 'You just rub her up the wrong way. I've become quite adept at dealing with her now. And, actually, she's not been too bad.'

'I just ignore her,' said David. 'That's the best way.'

'The only way I would handle that virago,' said Sidney, 'is to place my hands around that long swan-like white neck of hers and throttle the life out of her. She's unbearable. She's more strident than a tree full of screeching crows. Do you know that when I arrived at Manston Hall first thing this morning, to drop off my exhibits for your FRACAS conference, she was standing at the entrance, hands on hips, dripping with gewgaws—'

'Dripping with *what*?' asked David at the same time as I muttered 'NACADS' rather crossly.

'All that ghastly showy jewellery she is wont to wear,' explained Sidney. 'She was dressed in a ridiculous peasant-style blouse with great balloon sleeves and a flouncy red skirt, looking just like an ageing Heidi. Anyway, she asks me, "I take it you are here to put up the art display?" I was tempted to reply, "No, Mrs Savage, I'm here to rip off my clothes and dance naked up and down the drive singing selections from *Oklahoma!*" What did she think I was there for?'

'So, what did you say?' asked David.

'I merely told her that I was there, as instructed, to mount my exhibition for this wretched "knackers" conference.'

'NACADS,' I repeated, loudly and very crossly.

'Well, whatever,' said Sidney. 'Do you know what she said when I got the paintings and sculptures out of the car?'

'No, but I guess you are going to enlighten us,' said David wearily.

'She said, "I hope you are aware that this is a listed building of great historical interest, and that

401

there must not be the slightest damage to the fabric." I told her that I knew more about architecture and listed buildings than she did, and to go and irritate someone else. It was as if she owned the place, waltzing around with a clipboard like some manic television producer, ordering people about. "Put that here, don't leave that there, do this, do that, go here, go there." She even had the nerve to tell me not to stick drawing pins in the wainscoting or staples in the doors. "Don't stick sellotape on the wallpaper," she told me, "and nothing sharp on the polished wooden floor." I told her straight. I said, "Mrs Savage, I have been mounting displays for over thirty years. I do not need to be told how to do it. Please depart and let me get on with it." Insufferable woman!' snorted Sidney.

'I'd have liked to have been a fly on the wall,' chuckled David.

'And when I arrived in the South Hall, can you imagine what the stupid, foolish woman had done?'

'No,' I said, 'but I have an idea you are going to tell us about that, too.'

'She had shrouded those wonderful Italian white marble figures, the glorious sculptures that one of Lord Marrick's forebears no doubt filched when he was on his Grand Tour of Europe, those beautiful classical figures of Venus and Leda with her swan, she had obscured them with fronds.'

'With what?' exclaimed David.

'She had draped these wispy ferns all over the statues' most beautiful and intimate features, and then placed potted palms in front of them. All you could see were the heads peeping out through the undergrowth as if they were in a jungle. It looked quite ridiculous. "We can't have delegates coming into a room full of naked women," she told me. "Mrs Savage," I said, "it might have escaped your notice but they are statues, inert objects, representations, works of art. They are not delegates at a strippers' convention. The British Museum doesn't cover up the statues of the human form, the Pope in Rome doesn't cover up the statues of the human form and I am not in the business of covering up statues of the human form. There is nothing offensive about them. They are works of art. The human form at its most beautiful. The shrubbery must be removed forthwith."'

'It's the woman's profoundly irritating sense of self-importance which makes my blood boil,' said David, 'and her patronising manner. As Julie would say, "She's all fur coat and no knickers."'

'Oh, I think there was a very expensive pair of knickers under the Gypsy Rose Lee outfit she was wearing,' said Sidney.

'How did you get on with your mathematics display?' I asked David.

'Oh fine,' said David. 'Fortunately the woman in question was busy elsewhere, giving the audio-visual technician a hard time, so she wasn't about when I took in my materials. I shall put up my display tomorrow afternoon, which won't take me long. My contribution is only on a small scale compared to Sidney's. I'm going for the more practical. I think I mentioned that I've asked Miss Pilkington to bring some of her pupils along on the Sunday to do a demonstration. Wonderfully talented children she's got, all keen and confident.'

'Yes, and I understand Connie's grandchildren

are involved,' I said.

'There's another woman I could throttle,' mumbled Sidney.

'You want to be careful Connie doesn't throttle you first after what you've done,' I told him.

'Oh, she's forever moaning and groaning about the mess I leave,' said Sidney casually. 'It's par for the course with Connie.'

'It's not the mess I'm talking about,' I told him, 'it's her prized pink overall.'

'Pink overall!' exclaimed Sidney. 'Whatever do you mean? Explain yourself, dear boy!'

So I related the incident at the SDC and how Mrs Kipling had used Connie's pink overall as part of her collage.

'Oh dear,' said Sidney, laughing. 'You won't tell her, will you? If she found out, she'd put bleach in my coffee.'

'Depends what it's worth,' I said.

'You will just have to get her another one, Sidney,' said David.

'And where in heaven's name would I get such a horrendously bilious garment?'

'That's your problem,' said David. 'Anyway, as I was saying, Miss Pilkington has some very talented youngsters and they will be demonstrating their mathematical skills.'

'And then,' exclaimed Sidney, sitting up on his chair and thrusting his chin forward, 'she had the brass neck to tell me that she hoped the paintings and sculptures I would be exhibiting would not include anything *risqué*.'

'Yet again, we're back to Mrs Savage,' I sighed.

'*Risqué*? "Look here, Mrs Savage," I said,' continued Sidney, ' "it is not your function to tell me what I should or what I should not be displaying. You are the administrator, not the art critic."'

'Was Lord Manston around?' I asked.

'Who?' Sidney asked.

'Lord Marrick's son and heir. He's rather more in charge of the conference than Lord Marrick is.'

'Tadge?' said David.

'You know him?' I asked.

'Of course, I know him,' said David. 'He's Captain at the Golf Club this year. Decent fellow is Tadge but a bit of a ladies' man.'

'Yes,' I said, 'I detected something of that when Mrs Savage and I were over there for a planning meeting. He couldn't take his eyes off her, nor she off him. They flirted shamelessly!'

'What! Lord what's-his-name and Mrs Savage!' exclaimed Sidney. 'This Todger, or whatever he's called, wants his head examining, getting involved with her. She's like a praying mantis. She'll eat him up and spit him out.'

'She's a very attractive woman,' said David. 'I'd be the first to admit that. It's just a pity she's got a personality bypass. Anyway, she'll never get her hooks into Tadge. He's too big a fish. Many have tried, but none have succeeded in landing him. He's had more lady friends than I've had rounds of golf. The merry widower is Tadge and likely to stay like that.'

'Can you imagine if something did come of it,' groaned Sidney. 'Mrs Savage with a title. She'd be even more insufferable. Aaaaahhh!'

At this point Julie arrived in the office. 'I could hear you right along the corridor, Mr Clamp,' she told him.

'He's been regaling us with the saga of Mrs Savage and the naked statues at Manston Hall,' I told her.

'You'll all be naked and whipped if you don't get over to the Centre for your meeting. Dr Mullarkey went ages ago,' said Julie.

'Great Scot!' exclaimed Sidney. 'I had forgotten the inspectors' meeting has been brought forward.'

I think we had all forgotten, and the three of us set off post-haste for the Staff Development Centre for the monthly meeting of the inspectors, which had been brought forward to the Thursday. This would give us the following morning to finalise our various exhibitions at the NACADS Conference, which was due to start that evening.

* * *

'I have asked Mrs Savage to join us this morning,' said Miss de la Mare.

The CEO's Personal Assistant sat, legs elegantly crossed and looking as chic as ever in a navy-blue suit, pink blouse and sporting a string of delicate pearls and matching earrings. If she looked at all disconcerted by the row of stony-faced inspectors facing her, she certainly did not show it.

'Thank you for coming to the meeting, Mrs Savage,' continued the Chief Inspector. Mrs Savage gave a small nod. 'I know what a very busy time it is for you. I thought it would save a great deal of time—and paperwork—if we heard the latest developments from the horse's mouth, so to speak.'

The pointed mention of the 'very busy time', the paperwork and the reference to the horse's mouth

406

was lost on Mrs Savage, who rested her long pink-nailed fingers on two huge red files that sat on the table before her. 'Thank you, Miss de la Mare,' she said.

'Before I ask Mrs Savage to give us the latest information about the CEO's conference at the weekend and the situation concerning the school closures,' said the Chief Inspector, 'I should just like to take this opportunity of thanking you for the hard work you have undertaken during the past six weeks. It has been a particularly frenetic and demanding time, and you have all risen to the challenge superbly. You have been more than generous with your time, attending the frequent evening meetings of governors and parents, interviewing headteachers, as well as your regular weekend courses, Saturday morning workshops, organising book days and art festivals, mathematics seminars and science sessions, quite apart from your main function of inspecting schools. You really have worked so very hard, so thank you.'

She was a clever woman was Miss de la Mare. This eulogy was clearly intended for the ears of the CEO's Personal Assistant, who, for a rare moment in her life, was a captive audience. Miss de la Mare knew that Mrs Savage, a stickler for protocol and procedure, had a somewhat jaundiced view of the school inspectors, who appeared to her to have far too much power, influence and freedom for her liking. This was the Chief Inspector's way of letting the CEO's PA know just how hard the team had worked and the amount of time we had devoted to extraneous activities.

'It's nice to be appreciated,' said David, with just

a hint of a smirk.

'And, as a mark of my appreciation,' said Miss de la Mare, 'I should like to invite you all to a small Christmas get-together at the end of the school term on the 18th, here at the Centre. Just a glass of sherry and a few nibbles at the end of the day, about six o'clock, I suggest. Nothing special. I'm only telling you now so you can put it in your diaries.'

'Excellent,' said Sidney.

'Very decent,' added David.

'Now to business,' said the Chief Inspector. She turned to Mrs Savage. 'First of all, Dr Gore's conference. I am exceedingly sorry that I shall not be able to be there myself. However, as you know, I have to represent Dr Gore on the European Intermediary Education Initiative being held in Belgium this weekend. The EIEI—'

'Oh,' said Sidney.

'I'm sorry, Sidney, did you say something?' asked Miss de la Mare.

'No, no, merely clearing my throat,' he replied, smiling.

'The EIEI,' continued the Chief Inspector, 'is very close to the CEO's heart—but then so is this conference. Now, perhaps you might like to update us, Mrs Savage, on how things are progressing at Manston Hall.'

'Yes, indeed,' said Mrs Savage, opening the first capacious folder. 'The NACADS Conference, which will take place this weekend at—'

At this point the door burst open and Connie appeared, pulling behind her a large metal trolley on squeaky wheels. She was attired in an electric-blue overall which clashed alarmingly with her florid complexion and copper-coloured hair. There was no 'Excuse me' or 'I'm sorry to disturb the meeting' or 'Is it convenient to bring in the coffee?' She just barged in noisily without a by-your-leave.

'I'm bringing your elevenses in now, Miss de la Mare,' Connie announced, cutting Mrs Savage off mid-sentence. 'It's in flasks so you can have it at your own convenience. I've got Miss Kinvara and the psychologists in this morning, and you know what a noisy lot they are. You can hear them psychologising from the kitchen. And eat! You can say goodbye to at least two packets of Garibaldis when they get cracking, and the amount of tea they drink would sink a battleship.'

Miss de la Mare gave a small, indulgent smile. 'Thank you, Connie.'

Connie manoeuvred the trolley into position at the side of the room and was about to leave the room, when Sidney stretched out a hand to her as she was passing. 'Your new overall is the *most* wonderful colour, Connie, truly—er, electrifying.'

Oh Lord, I thought, here we go.

Connie halted, and looked down at herself. She was obviously quite taken aback by Sidney's praise. 'Well, I don't know, I'm sure,' she said, smoothing her hands down her front. 'I don't think blue is my colour. But what with my pink overall gone missing, I've had to use this substitution.' She looked up at us, where we were sitting round the table. 'I know I've asked you all before—except perhaps you, Miss de la Mare—but has *anyone* seen my pink one?'

'I'm afraid I haven't seen it,' said the Chief Inspector, obviously quite amused by the interruption, for I could tell she was attempting to stop herself smiling.

I shook my head and tried to appear the picture of innocence. Geraldine looked genuinely innocent, of course. Mrs Savage pursed her lips and said nothing. David looked pointedly at Sidney who stared heavenwards as though examining something of unusual interest on the ceiling.

'Well, it's a mystery and no mistake,' said Connie, placing her hands on her hips. 'I mean you can't miss it. It's bright pink.' She pointed at Mrs Savage's expensive silk blouse. 'Not dissimilar to that colour.'

Mrs Savage pulled an extremely cross face.

'I am sure it will turn up, Connie,' said Miss de la Mare. 'Thank you for the—er, elevenses.'

'I've put a few custard creams and ginger nuts on the plate with the Garibaldis, Miss de la Mare,' said Connie. 'I know you have a particular pendant for them.' With that, she headed for the door but once more stopped and turned. 'Oh, and if Health and Safety, particularly toilets, is on your agenda this morning,' she said, staring accusingly at Mrs Savage, 'you might like to fill me in.'

'How I would like to,' muttered Sidney, looking at his hands.

When Connie had departed, Mrs Savage continued. 'As I was saying, before I was so rudely interrupted, the NACADS Conference at Manston Hall at the weekend appears to be up to speed. Dr Gore was particularly keen that it should have a Yorkshire flavour to it. With that in mind he has secured the concert pianist, Vincent Barrington, himself a Yorkshireman, to entertain the delegates after the Friday evening reception.'

Geraldine, who was so often very quiet at our meetings, suddenly became animated. 'Vincent Barrington!' she exclaimed. 'Oh, that's wonderful! How clever of Dr Gore.'

'Might we be permitted to know more about this Mr Barrington?' said Sidney, obviously rather piqued that he had not heard of him, since he considered himself quite a connoisseur of classical music.

'Yes, indeed,' purred Mrs Savage. 'This talented young man took third prize in last year's Leeds International Pianoforte Competition. He was, I believe born in that city, and attended the university there.'

'I heard him earlier this year in the Bridgewater Hall, and I would dearly love to come and hear him tomorrow,' said Geraldine.

'I'm afraid that will not be possible, Dr Mullarkey,' said Mrs Savage, with a patronising smile on the pale pink lips. 'Seats are at a premium.'

I winked at Gerry to let her know that somehow I would find her a seat.

'On the Saturday morning,' continued Mrs Savage, pointing a long finger at an item in the file, 'the Minister of Education and Science, the Right Honourable Sir Bryan Holyoake, QC, MP, will give the keynote lecture, and this will be followed after the coffee-break by a presentation on "Inspirational Leadership and Effective Management" by the eminent educational consultant Mr Alan Vaughan who, as it so happens, is another Yorkshireman.'

'Let's hope our CEO is listening,' muttered Sidney to David. 'He might pick up a few tips.'

'I beg your pardon?' asked Mrs Savage.

'I said, I look forward to listening,' Sidney replied. 'I might pick up a few tips.'

'Indeed,' said Mrs Savage.

'He's very good, is Alan Vaughan,' said David. 'I've heard him several times. Good-natured chap, feet on the ground, good speaker.'

'So I believe,' said Mrs Savage. 'After the buffet lunch, there will be seminars during the afternoon, the speakers for which Dr Gore has organised and will preside over. For the formal dinner on Saturday evening, Dr Gore is delighted to have secured the lawyer, author and raconteur, Mr Stephen D. Smith, as the after-dinner speaker. He is, of course, another Yorkshireman.'

'If we might continue,' said Miss de la Mare quietly.

'Then, on the Sunday morning,' said Mrs Savage, 'and this is where the inspectors come in, the delegates will have the opportunity during the morning of viewing the displays, observing the children's demonstrations, joining in the students' workshops and listening, before lunch, to the Young People's Brass Band directed by Mr Gordon of the Music Service.'

Mrs Savage looked up from her file, which she then closed quietly.

'That all sounds excellent,' observed the Chief Inspector. 'Thank you for bringing us up to date, Mrs Savage.'

'I cannot stress,' said Mrs Savage, 'how very important it is that things go smoothly. Dr Gore is particularly keen that we, as he told me this morning, put all our hands to the wheel and pull together.'

412

'Always the master of the mixed metaphor, our CEO,' muttered Sidney.

'I'm sorry, Mr Clamp,' said Mrs Savage sharply. 'Did you say something?'

'I merely observed, Mrs Savage,' Sidney replied, 'that I shall endeavour to do so.'

'The Viscount Manston,' she continued, 'who is spearheading arrangements from his end and who has been liaising closely with me over the last few weeks, has assured me that everything at the Hall is up and running.'

'Good,' said Miss de la Mare.

'The delegates will be bussed in each day for the conference from their hotels, which are all in the proximity. Mr Phinn and I, who need to be on call at all times, will be staying at Manston Hall for the duration of the conference.'

'How very cosy,' mumbled Sidney.

Mrs Savage gave him one of her famous withering looks.

'I was merely commenting that everything in the garden appears rosy, Mrs Savage,' he said.

'I am sure,' she continued, 'that I do not need to impress upon everyone that this is a very prestigious conference and the CEO wants it to be the very best. I was only saying to Dr Gore this morning—'

'Yes, thank you, Mrs Savage,' said the Chief Inspector quickly. 'That was a splendid presentation. Does anyone have any questions for Mrs Savage?' She paused.

'No? Well, then, I think this is a good time to break and have our elevenses, and then we can discuss the school closures.'

When I arrived home that evening, I found Christine standing by the kitchen table nursing a sleepy baby, and sitting opposite her was Andy, clutching a large mug of tea.

'Hey up, Mester Phinn,' he said, smiling widely.

'Hello, Andy,' I said as I entered. I kissed Christine and tickled Richard under the chin. 'And how's my little Tricky Dicky been today?' I asked. The baby continued to suck his thumb earnestly.

'Teething and nappy rash,' replied Christine, 'and he's certainly let me know all about it. He's been tetchy all day. The moment you walk through the door, he starts to settle down, the little tinker.'

'I were tellin' Missis Phinn that goats' milk's t'answer,' said Andy. 'Milk from my nanny goats works wonders on t'skin. Missis Poskitt swears by it an' she's got a skin as soft as a babby's bottom an' she's gerrin on for eighty. I read it were reight good for clearing up eczema, rashes, impetigo an' other skin complaints. Worked wonders on Bianca's spots. I put this advert in t'doctors' surgery sayin' there were goats' milk for sale an' delivered to t'door an' I'm doin' quite a bit of business now.'

'Quite the entrepreneur,' I said, recalling that Bianca was the girl who rather fancied him.

'You must put me on your list of customers, Andy,' said Christine.

'Nowt up wi' your skin, Missis Phinn,' he replied, reddening a little.

I had an idea that this young man had a bit of a crush on my wife, and his frequent visits were less to do with the garden and guttering than with

414

seeing Christine.

'Anyway,' said Christine, 'since Richard looks as though he might at last go to sleep, I'll take him up.'

I slipped off my jacket, poured myself some tea and then joined Andy at the table. The boy's large pink face looked scrubbed and the coarse bristly brown hair had been slicked back, accentuating the enormous ears. He was dressed in a clean white shirt, leather jacket and denim jeans. The green tie that he was wearing, on which a variety of game birds were disporting themselves, looked incongruous on such an outfit.

'You look very smart, Andy,' I told him.

'Young Farmers meetin' toneet, Mester Phinn,' he told me. 'I'm doin' a bit of a talk like, so thowt I'd gerra bit dressed up.'

'Doing a talk,' I said. 'What about?'

'Well, not poetry,' he said, laughing. ' "Preparation for Sheep Breedin" ', an' I tell thee this, I'm reight frit.'

'Go on,' I said, 'there's nothing to be frightened about. From what your Uncle Harry tells me, there's few who know more about sheep than you do. And, as you well know, your Uncle Harry is not one to throw out compliments lightly.'

'Aye, 'appen I do know summat abaat sheep,' said the boy, 'but it's different tellin' folk abaat it, standin' theer wi' all these eyes like chapel 'at pegs starin' at thee.'

'You'll be fine,' I reassured him. 'So is preparing sheep for breeding a long business then?' I should never have asked.

The boy jerked upright in the chair, like a marionette that has had its strings pulled. 'Oh aye,

Mester Phinn, it's a reight carry-on. You see, choosing yer ram is reight important. 'E's got to come from good breeding stock for a start an' be in tip-top physical condition afoor yer let 'im loose on t'yows. It's no use at all 'avin' a ram what's well 'ung an' wi' an active sex drive if 'e can't walk to 'is food an' watter an' can't eat or drink when 'e gets theer. You 'ave to start well in advance wi' t'routine 'ealth treatment like foot inspection an' cleanin', dippin', drenchin' an' clippin'. Yer ram's got to be in prime condition to serve a yow so you 'ave to examine 'im good an' proper at 'is feet and joints, look for swellin's, check teeth an' gums for damage, back o' mouth an' cheeks for any lumps. Then you 'ave to check 'is penis.'

'Would you like another mug of tea?' I asked the boy, keen to change the conversation.

'No, ta, Mester Phinn. As I was sayin', you 'ave to check 'is penis.' Andy was now well into his stride and was enhancing his description with various arm and hand movements. 'This is best done by gerrin yer ram in a sittin' position so 'e's upright an' then yer can give t'area a good goin' ovver, mekkin' sure it's free o' sores an' scars. What you do is carefully force out t'ram's penis manually. This is done by graspin' 'old of—'

At this point, Christine returned to find me open-mouthed and lost for words. 'And what are you two talking about?' she asked.

'Just saying what lovely weather we're 'avin' for this time o' year, Missis Phinn,' said Andy, winking at me.

'And how's your Uncle Harry?' asked Christine. 'He wasn't too happy last time we saw him.'

'Oh, abaat t'Royal Oak, tha means.' Andy shook

416

his head. ' 'E were abaat as miserable as a love-struck rigg, but 'e's been as 'appy as a pig in shit lately. Sorry, missis, I dint mean—'

'It's all right, Andy,' said Christine, smiling, 'I've heard worse.'

'And what's put your Uncle Harry in such a good frame of mind?' I asked.

' 'Ant thy 'eard? That new landlord at t'Royal Oak is up an' leavin'.'

'I didn't know that,' said Christine. 'My, my!'

'Aye,' said Andy. 'Tha knaas Mester 'Ezekiah Longton, who used to be 'ead gard'ner up at Manston 'All? Nice enough owld fella but dunt say much. 'E were a reg'lar in t'Royal Oak an 'e were not 'appy abaat all t'change, like rest o' reg'lars. 'E were given 'is marchin' orders wi' mi Uncle 'Arry when 'e was banned. Well, 'e's up an' bought it.'

'Bought the Royal Oak?' I exclaimed.

'Aye, lock, stock an' barrel. There were a big piece abaat it in t' *Fettlesham Gazette*—"Regular buys t'village pub that barred him". Mester Longton's become quite a celebrity.'

'What made him think of buying it?' asked Christine.

'Place were goin' dahn t'nick. Trade waint as good as t'new landlord were expectin' an' 'is missis never settled. Southerners, tha sees. Any rooad, landlord thowt it'd be filled to burstin' wi' folks out from town, "off-comed-uns", ramblers an' cyclists and such, but it never 'appened. Fact is, 'is trade dropped reight off. Then t'plannin' people told 'im that 'e needed permission to mek all t'changes 'cos pub were a listed building and of gret 'istorical hinterest, so 'e 'ad to put t'roof back as it were an' change t'winders an' all. 'E must 'ave been pig sick.

417

Any road, 'e 'ad this offer to gu in wi' a couple o' pals who was openin' a bar in Majorca. That an' t'fact that Mester Longton med him a fair good offer, one 'e couldn't refuse.'

'Sounds like the Mafia,' I said, laughing.

'Mester Longton 'ad a bit put by, like,' continued the boy, 'an' 'is wife weren't short on a bob or two, an' left 'im a tidy sum when she died.'

'So Hezekiah Longton's bought the Royal Oak,' I said. 'Well, well, well.'

'An' from what 'e says, 'e's gunna put things back as they were inside. All owld tables an' chairs, the lot, an' it'll be a traditional country inn ageean, wi' nowt fancy. 'E reckons, from what mi Uncle 'Arry says, that 'e's gunna get owld Missis Poskitt to cook some good owld Yorkshire food.'

'Tripe and onions, black pudding, pigs' trotters?' I suggested.

'Nay, good owld Yorkshire hot-pot, that sort of thing.'

'I think you'll find it's Lancashire hot-pot, Andy,' said Christine.

'I waint trust a Lancastrian as far as I could spit. Steal pennies from t'eyelids of dead men, they would. I reckon they pinched t'idea of t'hotpot from a good Yorkshirewoman.'

'And how's young Terry getting on at school?' I asked Andy. 'You remember I wanted you to keep an eye on him.'

' 'E's doin' champion,' said the boy. 'Few days after yer were in school, I saw them three bullies follow 'im into t'boys' toilets. I knew what they were up to, so I followed 'em in, and I 'ad a quiet word wi' 'em.'

'Had a quiet word?' I repeated. I was worried

418

that Andy might have had rather more than a quiet word.

'I told 'em face-to-face—well, more hand-to-throat, really—that it wasn't very nice to bully little kids. I explained to 'em that if they laid a finger on 'im ageean, I wunt be best pleased. They soon came round to my point o' view an' they 'aven't touched 'im since. Young Terry's been 'elpin' me on t'farm, an' I'll tell thee what, Mester Phinn, 'e's reight good wi' beeasts. 'E's gor a way wi' 'em. I don't know wor it is but, even Conrad, that Limousin bull in Mester Price's top field, reight big, bad-tempered bugger 'e is an' all, well, 'e's putty in t'hands of that Terry. Aye, 'e's been a real good 'elp to me.' Andy paused, running a careful hand over his slicked-back hair. 'I was tellin' thee abaat how I prepare jocks for breedin', weren't I, an' 'ow yer get yer ram in a sittin' position so 'e's upright. Well Terry were a gret 'elp an'—'

I cut the boy short. 'And what about you, Andy? How are you getting on at school?' I asked.

'Oh, all reight, I suppose.'

'You know, if you really do want to go to Askham Bryan College,' I told him, 'you do need a few qualifications.'

'Aye, I suppose I do but I just can't get mi 'ead round all this learnin'. I'm not a one fer books an' that. I'd sooner be out on t'land, in t'fresh air, wi' t'wind in mi face an' a view over Wensley like there's no other in t'world. I told mi form teacher, Mester Fairclough—'e's not a bad chap, Mester Fairclough—I told him that I was 'avin' t'day off come Friday to gu to t'sheep auction at Bentham. "Yer can't just 'ave a day off like that, Handrew," he told me, "it's truantin'. You 'ave to be at school workin' an' not gallivantin' off to Bentham." I said, "Look, Mester Fairclough, I'm bein' 'onest wi' thee. I could 'ave telled thee I were dowly."'

'You were what?' I asked.

'Ill, took badly, under t'weather, tha knaas. Any road, he said, "Well, Handrew, that would be deceitful, wouldn't it?" I said, 'That's reason I'm tellin' yer t'truth, Mester Fairclough, I shan't be in t'school because I'm off to t'sheep auction. Tha sees, I've got two prime yows an' a gradely jock up for sale an' I wants to see 'ow they do." "Well," says 'e, "I commend your 'onesty but I can't give yer permission to take the day off. Ye'd be missing your school work an' it would be against the law." I said, "Look 'ere, Mester Fairclough, if you don't let me 'ave t'day off, up till Friday I'd be whittlin' an' werritin' abaat not bein' able to gu to Bentham Market so I wunt be concentratin' on mi work, now would I? Mi mind would be on other things. Then come Friday when t'auction were on, I'd come to school in a reight mardy mood, an' mi mind wunt be on owt but 'ow mi sheep were doing at t'auction. I wouldn't be concentratin' on school work an' that's fer certain. Then t'whole week afterwards, I'd be feeling really 'ard done by abaat not bein' able to go to t'auction so I wunt be concentratin' on mi work then neither." I explained to 'im that if 'e were to let me gu to t'auction, I'd work really 'ard up to Friday an' catch up on t'work I'd missed. "So tha sees, Mester Fairclough, if tha was to let me gu to t'auction, tha'll be gerrin' a lot more work out on me in t'long run."'

'And what did Mr Fairclough say?' I asked.

420

'He thought a bit, an' then 'e said 'e'd put it down to work experience, an' 'e 'oped mi sheep gu fer a good price at t'auction on Friday, an' to be sure to let' im know.'

'Well, you had better be making tracks to the Young Farmers,' I said. 'I hope your talk goes well.'

'There's a little matter of wages, Mester Phinn. That's reason for comin' to see ya. I've spent all mi brass an' cum to get paid. Got to have enough to impress that Bianca toneet.'

'Of course,' I said, reaching for my jacket and taking out my wallet. 'You've done a super job for us, Andy, and we are both very grateful.'

'I mean,' said the lad, 'I liked doin' that work for thee, Mester Phinn, but as mi Uncle 'Arry is allus remindin' me, nob'dy does owt for nowt in Yorkshire, tha knaas.'

CHAPTER TWENTY-FOUR

On the Friday morning, having collected some material for the English exhibition at the NACADS Conference, I reached Manston Hall about eleven o'clock. On my way from the car to the steps that led up to the front door, I passed a gardener who was forking a large pile of greenery into a wheelbarrow.

When I arrived in the South Hall, I discovered the inspector for Visual and Creative Arts in the middle of complete disorder and confusion. My heart sank when I saw the chaos. There stood Sidney, this great bear of a man, surrounded by cardboard boxes and crates, wooden sculptures, strange three-dimensional structures in shiny metal, stone carvings, twisted wire structures, bolts of brightly-patterned fabrics, collages, squares of batik, empty picture frames, not to mention dozens of paintings and photographs. He was shouting at and gesticulating to the three teachers who had agreed to help him, while Geraldine and David stood at the side, watching with folded arms and bemused expressions. I walked through the clutter to join them.

'When Picasso has quite finished,' David informed me in his sonorous Welsh accent, 'Geraldine and I will try and squeeze in our modest efforts.'

'Is there any sign of Mrs Savage?' I asked. I could just imagine her reaction to this complete mayhem.

'She made her bellicose appearance earlier,' David said, chuckling, 'and did attempt to engage Sidney in conversation but to no avail.'

'And a battery of well-chosen words from our bearded colleague,' Geraldine added, 'were enough to send her on her way.'

'What did he say?' I asked.

'When she mentioned the mess—and it was much worse fifteen minutes ago, I can tell you—' David said, 'he retorted that he had a profound belief that chaos and confusion had the effects of engendering seriously remarkable thinking, and that creative geniuses, such as himself, flourished in disorder and that the sooner she left him to get on with the exhibition, the sooner the hall would be tidy. As she was leaving, he yelled after her, "And take that blithering greenery with you!"'

'When she had gone,' Geraldine said, 'Sidney

told us that great creative minds very often encounter mindless opposition from those with mediocre ones.' I flinched and Geraldine, seeing the anxious look on my face, rested a hand on my arm. 'Don't worry, Gervase,' she reassured me, 'everything will be fine. For a start, Mrs Savage did remove—or, rather, sent some flunkey to remove—the potted plants and the greenery she had draped over the Italian nudes.'

Geraldine was right. By the end of the afternoon, the exhibition looked stunning. The visitors would enter the South Hall to be confronted by a mass of brilliant colours and shapes, and a most impressive range of work from the county's talented youngsters. Even Mrs Savage, when she finally dared to make an appearance, was impressed and nodded approvingly as she cast a critical eye over everything.

*   *   *

I had just an hour's turn-round at home; enough time to sit and chat with Christine, and dangle little Richard on my knee.

'Most of the time, I don't miss the world of education at all,' she said, 'but on occasions like this, I wish I could be there with you, especially staying at Manston Hall. Make sure you behave yourself, mind!'

I laughed, gave both her and the baby a kiss and went upstairs to pack.

The Manston estate looked magnificent that evening as I drove through the ornate iron gates, past the small lodge and up the long avenue to the great red-brick house, which stood square and solid before me, floodlit from the far side of the gravel sweep in front of the Hall. There was a clear sky above me and frost was already forming on the grass.

It was now six o'clock and the delegates were due to arrive in an hour's time for the reception. I wanted to make a final check that everything was in place and ready.

A gigantic Christmas tree dominated the impressive entrance hall. It was rather early for a tree—Christmas still being several weeks away—but when Tadge had offered one from the estate, we had accepted graciously. However, this was no ordinary Christmas tree—it was white! Earlier in the afternoon, I had come through the hall and seen Mrs Savage organise the tree's decoration, directing operations from both the grand staircase and the gallery above. No flickering fairy lights or coloured baubles for her: the tree was simply but most beautifully decorated with small fuchsia-coloured silk bows. Against the shimmering white of the painted branches, the effect was most dramatic. Even Sidney had approved.

My eyes now, however, were not drawn to the tree, but to Mrs Savage herself. Wearing a long burgundy-coloured and daringly low-cut dress, which clung to her as if she had been poured into it, and with a pale silk shawl draped around her shoulders, she stood beneath the portrait of the crusty old general, looking for all the world as if she were the chatelaine of Manston Hall.

'Good evening, Mrs Savage,' I said as I approached her. 'You are looking quite splendid, if I may say so.'

'Good evening, Mr Phinn,' she replied. 'And,

since this is a special occasion, yes, you may.'

At that moment, Tadge arrived in the hall. He stood a little way off, gave a low whistle and said, 'My goodness me! How very flippercanorious you are this evening, my dear Brenda.'

I sensed Mrs Savage stiffen beside me. 'Flipperwhaty, Lord Manston?' she enquired in her most starchy voice.

'Flippercanorious, Mrs Savage. Isn't it a simply splendid word? I discovered it the other day.'

'Well, it might be splendid if I knew what it meant,' she replied.

'Elegant, my dear, wonderfully elegant, is what it means. And I think it calls for a toast to the evening.' With that, he turned on his heel and walked back across the hall.

I watched him go and realised that I was clearly underdressed for the occasion in my simple grey suit, white shirt and college tie. The heir to Manston Hall was no longer in his usual garb of old tweed jacket and corduroy trousers, but was now sporting a burgundy-coloured smoking jacket—had he and Mrs Savage consulted each other about their colours for the evening, since they matched perfectly—and a pair of close-fitting, red-and-green tartan trews. I immediately thought of Raymond, the producer, and his comment that I didn't have the buttocks for trews. Tadge certainly had.

Tadge returned with a bottle of champagne and three glasses, but I politely refused the offer. 'A bit early for me,' I said.

'We are merely making certain that the Moët is at the right temperature,' Tadge said, pouring generous glasses for Mrs Savage and himself.

'In my opinion,' said Mrs Savage, holding the long-stemmed champagne flute delicately between finger and thumb, 'there is nothing worse than warm champagne.' She saw me smiling. 'I do want everything to be just right,' she added testily.

'Of course,' I said. 'That is what I came to check with you. Have there been any problems?'

'Only that the caterers arrived with the savoury nibbles but forgot the salmon vol-au-vents for the buffet,' she told me. 'I told them to go and get them back here ASAP. Then I was less than happy with the floral centrepieces for the serving tables so they had to be done again. You just can't rely on people these days. Apart from that, everything else seems to be in place.'

'You're a perfectionist, Brenda,' Tadge commented. 'A true perfectionist.' Mrs Savage accepted the compliment with a slight nod of the head.

'What an amazing Christmas tree!' I said. 'I've never seen one painted white before.'

'Ah, then you've not seen our escutcheon,' Tadge said. 'The white tree has been on our coat of arms since the fifteenth century when Sir Launceston Whiteleaf-Cunninghame was ennobled. Back in the last century, when fir trees became all the fashion, the old Dowager Countess Elvira decided to have the Christmas tree painted white and we've kept up the tradition.'

'In years hence,' remarked Mrs Savage, 'they might become all the fashion.'

'I very much doubt it,' I murmured.

'One year, we couldn't be bothered to paint the tree,' said Tadge, 'which obviously displeased the long-since dead Lady Elvira because she was seen by one of our guests in the dead of night wandering along the top corridor. Well, I must press on, so if you both will excuse me. I need to make sure Lucretia and Caesare are penned before the guests arrive. They get a bit frisky with a lot of people around. Wouldn't want any accidents.'

'Lucretia and Caesare?' said Mrs Savage.

'The dogs,' he told her. 'I'll see you both later.' He topped up Mrs Savage's glass, and then strode off, whistling loudly.

'I can't say that I am at all keen staying here with a ghost wandering the house,' said Mrs Savage.

I could have said she need not worry since she could put the wind up a banshee, but I said nothing.

'Are you content with the decision over the headship of the new combined Ugglemattersby School?' she asked, taking a sip from her glass.

'Yes,' I replied. 'Mrs Braddock-Smith needs taking down a peg or two, I think, but the governors will see to that. However, to have a familiar person in place is so much better than having to go through all those interviews.'

At that moment, a young man with curly hair and wearing a long black overcoat walked through the door, and hovered indecisively.

'Good evening,' he called across the hall.

'Round the back, please,' Mrs Savage instructed, pointing over the man's shoulder to the front door.

'I beg your pardon?' he asked, looking thoroughly mystified.

'Would you take the vol-au-vents round the back,' she told him. 'This is not the caterers' entrance.'

'Oh, I'm not here with the vol-au-vents,' he replied, taking off his coat and revealing a shirt that sported an outrageously multicoloured parrot on the front. 'Actually I could do with one or two vol-au-vents. I'm famished. No,' he said, running a hand through his hair, 'I'm here to work. I'm Vincent Barrington.'

'Vincent Barrington, the pianist?' exclaimed Mrs Savage.

'The same,' replied the young man.

'Oh, maestro,' she cooed, immediately changing her tone of voice, smiling widely to display a set of rather too white teeth and gliding towards him, extending a long red-nailed hand. 'I'm so terribly sorry. I foolishly assumed you would be wearing rather different attire.'

'Oh, I don't travel in evening dress,' Vincent Barrington told her amiably, 'since it tends to get creased. It's in the car.'

'Well, it is such a great pleasure to make your acquaintance,' said Mrs Savage. 'I have heard so many wonderful things about you.'

'I'm sorry,' said the young man, 'but I don't know who you are.'

'How remiss of me.' Mrs Savage tinkled a little laugh. 'I'm Brenda Savage, who, for my sins, is the organiser of the conference. I'm Dr Gore's Personal Assistant.'

'Ah, yes. It was Dr Gore who invited me to play. I was at university with his niece.'

'Hello, I'm Gervase Phinn,' I said, offering my hand. 'I am helping Mrs Savage with the conference.'

'I knew a cellist once called Gervase,' said the young man. 'A very nice man.'

428

'I expect you would like to freshen up,' simpered Mrs Savage. 'But first, let me show you where you will be giving your recital, and then I will show you where you can change.'

I stayed in the hall while Mrs Savage took Vincent Barrington to the North Hall and a few minutes later Dr Gore arrived, accompanied by Councillor Peterson.

'Well, Gervase,' said the CEO, rubbing his long hands together and taking in the surroundings. 'This looks splendid, quite splendid!'

'And no doubt costing a pretty penny, as well,' grumbled the councillor, sniffing.

'Not at all, councillor,' replied Dr Gore good-humouredly. 'Lord Marrick has very kindly allowed us to use Manston Hall without charge, and all other expenses are paid for by NACADS. It would be insensitive, to say the least, for the county to spend money on a conference when we are closing schools to cut costs.'

'Just as well,' mumbled the overweight councillor.

Dr Gore turned back to me. 'Is Lord Marrick about? I'd like to have a word with him before the guests arrive?'

'I'm afraid he's been delayed in Italy, Dr Gore. He rang Lord Manston earlier this evening to say that a baggage-handlers' strike has meant his plane from Rome has been delayed. He is expecting to arrive some time after midnight, and will be with us in the morning.'

'Oh dear, what a shame. He will miss young Vincent Barrington who—'

'And while we are on the subject of closing schools,' interrupted Councillor Peterson, 'in my

429

opinion, I—'

I quickly made my escape. The very last thing I wanted to hear was George Peterson's undoubtedly biased opinion about school closures.

I found Mrs Savage with Vincent Barrington and Tadge by the grand piano in the North Hall. I thought she was looking rather flushed. No doubt a surfeit of the champagne she had been testing was having its effect.

'I do so love pianoforte music,' she gushed at the pianist, 'particularly the works of Brahms and Liszt.' Rather appropriate composers, I thought to myself, considering the state she was getting into.

'And do you have a favourite piece, Mrs Savage?' Vincent Barrington enquired.

'*Liebestraum*,' she sighed. 'I do so love that melody. It was my dear late husband's favourite.' I couldn't believe what happened next. I saw Mrs Savage's eyes mist over and she began to sniff inelegantly. A tear dribbled down her cheek. Perhaps, I thought, there was a sensitive soul after all beneath that icy exterior, that hard carapace. But, of course, it could have been the drink.

'Ah, the "Dream of Love",' said the young man. 'I shall play it tonight, especially for you.'

'Really?' simpered Mrs Savage. 'Would you?'

'And what about you, Lord Manston?' he asked. 'Have you a piece you would like me to play?'

'I like the works of Schumann,' he said. 'He was my dear late wife's favourite. I would love to hear one of the "Woodland Scenes".'

'Ah yes,' said the concert pianist, 'the great Schumann, who dedicated so much of his work to his beloved Clara. I see I have two romantics here. "You are my heart and my soul," he wrote. "You are the world in which I live. You are the heaven to which I soar. You are my grave into which I will forever pour my grief." '

'How very beautiful,' sighed Mrs Savage, dabbing her nose with a lace handkerchief. With glistening eyes, she looked in Tadge's direction and smiled.

This was getting maudlin to say the least, so I left them to it.

* * *

The evening, thank heavens, seemed to be a great success. After the reception and buffet, the guests settled down to listen to young Vincent Barrington. Even I, who didn't know much about classical music, recognised real quality. His playing of Beethoven's *Hammerklavier* was superb, and Geraldine, whom I had smuggled in at the back and was next to me, sat eyes closed and totally enraptured, drinking in the wonderful music. At the end of the recital, the whole audience rose to its feet and gave the pianist a standing ovation. Everyone, that is except Councillor Peterson, who had slept through most of the evening.

'And for an encore,' announced Vincent Barrington, 'I should like to play a beautiful piece especially requested by my elegant hostess. *Liebestraum*—the "Dream of Love" by Franz Liszt.' He smiled at Mrs Savage who, true to form, was not going to be relegated to the rear of the hall, out of the limelight, and had added a chair to the end of the front row. 'And for Lord Manston, a piece by Schumann: *Freundliche Landschaft*—"Friendly Landscape".'

'If you're doing requests,' came a booming voice, 'what about "On Ilkla Mooar baht 'at"?' It was Councillor Peterson who had been roused from his slumbers by the applause.

I winced, imagining the expressions on the faces of Dr Gore and the pianist.

'Of course,' said Vincent Barrington, without a trace of annoyance. 'It will be my pleasure.'

The guests clapped enthusiastically after the Liszt and Schumann pieces, but they sprang to their feet following a bravura rendering of the good old Yorkshire melody, played in the style of Beethoven, Chopin, Mozart and Rachmaninov. The pianist was indeed a maestro.

*   *   *

Once the delegates had departed for their hotels, the concert pianist had left in his taxi and I had seen Dr Gore's car disappear down the drive, I trudged up the great staircase, more than ready for my bed. I had no idea where Mrs Savage was—I had expected her to be there, saying goodbye to the delegates with me. I had been a mass of nervous energy all evening and all I wanted now was to climb into bed and get a good night's sleep. I had just changed into my pyjamas when there was a light tap on my door.

'Yes?'

'May I have a word?' It was Mrs Savage's voice.

'I'm just about to go to bed,' I called, standing rigid in the middle of the floor.

'This is important,' she insisted.

'Wait a moment, please.' I was taking no chances with an inebriated and concupiscent Mrs Savage at eleven o'clock at night. She had a reputation as a man-eater but she was certainly not going to get her teeth into me. She had tried it once, just after I had started as a school inspector, fluttering her eyelids and telling me how we 'clicked'; she had terrified the life out of me.

I grabbed at my dressing gown, thankful that Christine had made me put one in. 'You never know when you might need it,' she had said. 'Emergencies—like a fire in the middle of the night.'

I opened my bedroom door cautiously. Mrs Savage stood in the corridor in an expensive-looking smoky-grey dressing gown, probably silk. 'Yes?' I asked, keeping a foot firmly placed behind the door. 'What is it?'

'This may sound a rather bizarre question to ask,' she said in a hushed voice, 'but do you have a facility in your bedroom?'

'A facility?' I asked, utterly mystified.

'A toilet?'

'Toilet?'

'Yes, a toilet, a lavatory.'

'Yes, I do,' I replied. 'I have a connecting bathroom.'

'I've got a bathroom, too, but it appears I have no—er, facility.'

'You must have.'

'Well, I haven't.'

'Have you looked?'

'Of course I've looked,' she said in an exasperated voice. 'I've been looking for the last ten minutes.'

'Is there no one around that you can ask? A member of the household,' I suggested.

'There's no one about,' she said in a weary tone. 'Everyone must be in bed, and I can hardly go knocking on strange doors.' Just mine, I thought.

'So what now? Do you wish to use mine, is that it?'

'Certainly not!' she exclaimed. 'I would like you to come with me and see if you can locate it. I mean, there must be a toilet somewhere. I've got a bath and a basin, but no toilet.'

'Couldn't you use the one downstairs?' I asked. 'There's a cloakroom near the North Hall.'

'No, I couldn't,' she replied. 'I do not intend to wander around in the dark. Those dogs might be loose.'

'And, of course, there's the mysterious Lady Elvira,' I said, wickedly.

That wasn't a sensible thing to say since Mrs Savage gave a little shriek, and clutched at my arm. 'Please, please, will you come and see if you can find it?' she asked.

I followed her charily down the dimly-lit corridor, watched by the stern-featured figures in the gold frames that covered the walls. They seemed to have warning expressions on their faces. I just hoped this wasn't some sort of ruse for Mrs Savage to get me into her room and have her wicked way with me.

Mrs Savage led me through her bedroom—and I quickly averted my eyes from the chair where her underwear was neatly laid out—into a spacious marble-floored bathroom. As she had said, there was a bath—a vast old-fashioned affair on claw feet—and a wash basin. The room was so big—bigger than our guest room at Peewit Cottage—that there was space for a circular alabaster table

434

in the centre on which were copies of various journals, *Horse & Hound*, *Country Life* and *The Dalesman*. There was also a *chaise longue*, an elegant highly decorative eighteenth-century chiffonier and two heavy, ornate Chippendale-style chairs—but there was no sign of a lavatory.

'Perhaps aristocrats don't go to the toilet,' I suggested flippantly.

'Mr Phinn!' said Mrs Savage sternly. 'This is neither the time nor the place to be frivolous. I am in desperate need of a toilet.'

I examined one of the chairs. 'Perhaps this is a commode,' I said, poking and prodding at it.

'A commode?' Mrs Savage curled a lip in distaste.

'A chair which conceals a chamber pot,' I informed her.

'I do know what a commode is,' she told me, 'and I have already looked there. In any case, I do not intend to avail myself of a chamber pot. I want a proper toilet. Oh dear, I suppose I shall have to use your facility after all.'

'Perhaps it's in here,' I said, examining the chiffonier.

'In a cupboard?' she said.

I pulled at the door and the whole front of the cabinet opened to reveal the lavatory—a polished wooden seat beneath which was a large glazed blue and white earthenware bowl.

'Well, will you just look at that!' I said. 'How fascinating.' I examined the bowl, which depicted three large, crudely painted Chinese figures beside a rickety bridge. 'Good heavens! We have a plate just like that at home. It's Delft. This is probably very old and valuable.'

'Mr Phinn,' said Mrs Savage, crossly, 'it could be Royal Doulton, Clarice Cliff or part of the Ming Dynasty for all I care, but I have a pressing need to go to the toilet and I do not intend to use that. I require one of the flushing variety.'

'Hold on, what's this?' I said, and pulled a small gilt fleur-de-lis on the back of the chiffonier. The bowl descended, hot scented water gushed out from the side and swirled around the bowl. Then, having been thoroughly scoured, it returned to its original position, spotless.

'Good gracious!' exclaimed Mrs Savage. 'How remarkable.'

'How the other half live,' I commented. 'I will leave you to your ablutions, Mrs Savage.'

As I reached the door leading into the corridor, she called after me. 'I do hope I can rely on your absolute discretion in this little matter, Mr Phinn? I am sure that neither of us wishes this evening's adventure to become tittle-tattle around the corridors of County Hall.'

'Of course, Mrs Savage,' I said, smiling. 'I shall be the very soul of discretion. May I bid you a good night?'

*　　*　　*

The Rt Hon Sir Bryan Holyoake arrived the following morning in a shiny black limousine at precisely nine o'clock. Dr Gore, Lord Marrick and Tadge Manston were in the grand entrance hall to greet him. Mrs Savage and I stood a little distance away. The delegates were all assembled in the North Hall, ready to listen to the CEO's lecture.

The Minister of State for Education and Science

was a lean, angular individual with a prominent Roman nose and well-cut silver hair. Sir Bryan was a man of few words and forceful opinions. He did not like any fuss, drank only mineral water, insisted on seeing the itinerary in the minutest detail before any visit, and was punctilious about keeping to schedule. I had only been in my job for a few months when he had visited the Staff Development Centre and, as we had toured the building, he had been embarrassingly uncommunicative. Despite my best efforts to engage him in conversation, the man had remained resolutely unsmiling and tight-lipped. It was clear he was taking in everything he saw and heard, but he expressed no view nor made any comment. He merely nodded and grunted when spoken to.

'Sir Bryan,' chortled Dr Gore now, as the minister walked through the door with his two colleagues. 'Such a pleasure to see you again. I trust you have had a pleasant journey?'

'Passable,' he replied.

'And how are things at the seat of government?' asked the CEO. The minister stared at him, raised a silver eyebrow but made no reply. 'So much legislation,' Dr Gore rattled on. 'So much to do and education always seems to be at the top of the agenda, doesn't it? Education, education, education.'

The minister nodded. 'Indeed.'

'Well, let me introduce you to the Earl of Marrick in whose magnificent home the conference is taking place.'

'Morning, Sir Bryan,' growled the peer, who was looking somewhat worn out after the trials of his journey back from Italy.

437

'Good morning, Lord Marrick,' replied the minister.

'Do you know Yorkshire at all?' he was asked.

'A little,' he replied.

'You must spend more time here,' said Lord Marrick. 'God's own county.'

'An interesting family motto you have above your door, Lord Marrick,' said the Minister of State.

'*Lancastrienses manu dei occidantur,*' said the peer. 'Been the family motto for generations: "Let the hand of God smite the Lancastrians". Typically Yorkshire, of course—blunt and to the point.'

'I should perhaps tell you, Lord Marrick, that I was born in the Red Rose County,' said the Minister of State.

'Well, you can't help that,' said Lord Marrick. 'Best thing that ever came out of Lancashire is the road to Yorkshire.'

'I fear, my lord,' said Sir Bryan with a thin smile, 'that we will be fighting the Wars of the Roses all over again if we continue this conversation.'

'Perhaps we should move on,' suggested Dr Gore, clearly worried that hostilities might break out at any minute. 'I appreciate that you are on a very tight schedule. May I introduce Lord Marrick's son, Sir Bryan—Lord Manston.'

'Good morning,' said the minister. He then caught sight of Mrs Savage standing a little behind Tadge, and extended a long white hand. 'And you must be Lady Manston. Good morning.'

'Oh no, Sir Bryan,' simpered Mrs Savage. 'I'm not Lady Manston. I'm a mere minion.' I could think of many words to describe Mrs Savage but 'minion' was not one of them. She was the least obsequious person I knew.

'This is my Personal Assistant,' explained Dr Gore, 'Mrs Brenda Savage, who has organised the conference and next to her is—'

'Ah, yes, Mr Phinn,' said Sir Bryan. He turned to the CEO. 'We met when I last visited the county.'

'Yes, yes, of course you did,' said the CEO.

'You may recall, Mr Phinn,' said Sir Bryan, 'that you took me around the Teachers' Centre where that remarkable janitor—Connie, wasn't it?—kept everything so spick and span.'

'That's right. What a memory you have!' I said. 'She will be very pleased to hear that you remembered her, Sir Bryan.'

The minister thought for a moment and then became uncharacteristically eager to impart his pet philosophy. 'I make a point of never forgetting a name nor a face, Mr Phinn,' he told me. 'In life, one meets many people, particularly if, as I, one is in the political arena. All people are significant in their own way, and all deserve our attention. Whether one is a peer of the realm or a gardener, a chief education officer or a cleaner, a minister of the Crown or a chauffeur, all play their part and have important jobs to do.'

'Indeed,' said Dr Gore. 'Now, if I may lead the way . . .'

*   *   *

Later that afternoon, when the delegates broke into discussion groups, I rushed home to get my dinner jacket. I certainly did not wish to be underdressed at the formal dinner that evening. As I drove through Hawksrill, I smiled as I passed the

439

pub. The brightly painted board with the outline of an oak tree and the lettering THE OAK had been replaced with the original sign featuring the oak tree in full leaf, with the smiling figure of the restored Merry Monarch standing beneath it. I could imagine the contents of the interior: the round tubular steel stools, matching tables and minimalist prints would have been consigned to the skip or given to a charity shop, and the trestle tables, hard wooden chairs, old photographs, hunting horns and horse brasses would have been reinstated.

'I see the pub is back as it was,' I said to Christine, as I rootled in a drawer for the studs of my dress shirt. 'That'll please the "gang of four".'

'Yes,' she said. 'I saw Harry earlier today when I took Richard out in the buggy for a walk. He was looking almost ecstatically pleased.'

'That makes a change from his grumblings. Oh come on, where are these wretched studs?'

'Are these what you're looking for?' Christine asked, holding up a cupped hand.

'What would I do without you?' I said, pecking her cheek. 'And now I must get back to Manston Hall. The evening awaits me.'

The after-dinner speaker, a round, jolly man, was a great success and he entertained the delegates for a good forty minutes with anecdotes about the world of law courts, police cells and solicitors' offices. Even Mrs Savage managed a smile or two.

On Sunday morning, everything went to plan. My fellow inspectors joined me in the South Hall, and the delegates seemed genuinely interested in the various exhibitions that we had mounted. After

440

coffee, the delegates returned for a final time to the North Hall. Here they listened to a short but very impressive performance by the brass band. Finally, wearing his chain of office, Dr Gore gave a rather tedious presidential address, which generated polite applause, and by noon the delegates had all departed for their hotels.

Mrs Savage and I wandered through the now strangely silent building.

'It went well,' I said.

'Yes, it did,' she replied. 'And now we are left to organise all the clearing up.'

'Where's Dr Gore?' I asked.

'A good question,' she replied. 'I believe he's gone off with Lord Manston for lunch at his golf club.' I could tell by the tone of her voice that she was distinctly peeved. 'It certainly wouldn't have hurt him to invite us. After all, we did all the work.'

'Ah well, Mrs Savage,' I said with a smile, 'that is the fate of the mere underlings of the powerful. We are the foot soldiers and not the generals, the workers and not the master builders, the minions and not the powers-that-be, but we too play our small part in the scheme of things.'

She looked at me for a moment. 'Nonsense!' she said. Then with long decisive steps, her high heels clicking on the polished marble floor, she walked towards the South Hall. And as she passed the portrait of the crusty old ancestor hanging on the wall, she tossed her head at him.

CHAPTER TWENTY-FIVE

I was the last inspector to arrive at the SDC for Miss de la Mare's Christmas get-together. Everyone had gathered in the lounge area, which had been decorated with silver streamers and coloured balloons, sprigs of mistletoe and holly. A large, slightly straggly Christmas tree, over-decorated with bright baubles and fairy lights, stood in one corner where I saw David and Miss de la Mare deep in conversation.

I approached Sidney, who was dressed in a black velvet jacket and ostentatious pink bow tie. He was explaining to Geraldine the finer points of modern art, waving a newspaper in front of her as if swatting flies. Julie was standing next them, with a weary expression on her face. She grimaced, rolled her eyes and tilted her head in Sidney's direction as I approached, which told me he was in the middle of one of his loud, passionate and not-to-be-interrupted monologues. Julie was dressed in an incredibly tight-fitting, crimson polo neck, a thin black strip of a skirt and her red stilettos. She wore silver earrings the size of onion rings.

'It is all a matter of symmetry and balance, my dear Geraldine,' Sidney was telling her, 'and the dexterous juxtaposition of primary colours and shapes which give that stunning, symbolic effect. I would not expect that a scientist would, for one minute—' He caught sight of me, stopped mid-sentence and made a deep flourish. 'Hail the conquering hero cometh, sound the trumpets, beat the drums.'

'And what is that supposed to mean?' I asked.

'Our esteemed leader, Dr Gore, was singing your praises to high heavens when he spoke to Della recently—so I have been reliably informed by Julie here.'

'Really?'

'Yes,' said Julie. 'He phoned her up saying how well things had gone and what a good job you did at his conference. Marlene on the switchboard just happened to hear the conversation when she put Dr Gore through to Miss de la Mare the other day.'

'Evidently that "knackers" conference of his was a huge success,' added Sidney.

'From what I heard, Sir Bryan singled out the art display for special mention,' said Geraldine, 'so you too can feel a little bit smug, Sidney.'

'It is a miracle I was even able to start to set up the wretched exhibition,' said Sidney, 'with Mrs "I'm in charge and do as you are told" Savage doing her utmost to jeopardise it with her shrubbery and fronds—the patronising, tyrannical besom.'

'Sidney!' said Geraldine. 'It's the season of goodwill. Show a little more Christmas spirit.'

'But to give her her due,' I told him, 'she did have all the shrubbery removed.'

Sidney waved around the newspaper theatrically, dismissing Geraldine's gentle reprimand. 'Be that as it may, I have to agree that it was an unusually impressive display but the teachers are the ones who did all the work. I merely *designed* it. I believe the part our young Lochinvar here played is more deserving of the plaudits. I am sure after this last startling success,

443

our malleable colleague will have quite a few more of the CEO's "little jobs" to take on.'

'No fear,' I spluttered.

'Sidney's in a particularly good mood,' Geraldine told me, 'because his exhibition in York has caused something of a stir. Listen to what it says in the review in the *Post*.' She took the newspaper from Sidney and read. ' "Sidney Clamp's sumptuous, decadent oil on canvas paintings are a welcome breath of fresh air. His vibrant landscapes both shock and delight the eye. They are fast and furious, bold and strongly wrought energetic contortions in bright crimsons, saffron, vivid greens and blues. His images of the frenetic nudes dancing through a rural landscape are stunning and his neurotic expressionist portraiture is both grotesque and glorious." '

'Wow!' I said. 'I'm planning to go to the exhibition as soon as term ends. Well done, Sidney.'

'A trifle wordy, perhaps,' observed Sidney, looking immensely pleased with himself, 'but very gratifying nevertheless. I must let David read this.'

I left Geraldine and Sidney to continue their discussions of modern art and turned to Julie. 'So are you looking forward to Christmas?' I asked.

'No,' she told me bluntly.

'Why?'

'Because I'm not,' she said. 'I'm one of those people who finds it a real drag.'

'Come on, Julie,' I said, 'it's the best time of year. Where's the Christmas spirit gone?'

'Down the neck of my father if he gets his hands on it.'

'I love Christmas,' I said. 'There's something so

444

special about it.'

'It might be for you, but you don't live at our house. Christmas always ends in arguments, recriminations, simmering silences and some sort of disaster. Last year was worse than usual. My granddad dropped his false teeth down the toilet bowl, Gran nearly choked on a silver sixpence put in the pudding, Uncle Albert had one of his turns and had to lie in a darkened room until the Queen's Speech. My little nephew Kenny spilt gravy all down my mum's new skirt, and Paul, my boyfriend, sat in front of the television all afternoon watching *The Towering Inferno*, which he must have seen ten times. Why they have to put on a disaster movie at Christmas time, I don't know. Then my Great Auntie Doreen, who must be a hundred if she's a day, went on and on about my cousin Bethany who's just got married. "It'll be your turn next, our Julie," she says. The number of times I've heard her tell me that.' Julie adopted a squeaky quavering: '"Oh yes, it'll be your turn next, our Julie." I was tempted, when we went to my Great Uncle Horace's funeral to say the same thing to her. "It'll be your turn next, Great Auntie Doreen." You have no idea the stresses and strains Christmas puts on me, Mr Phinn. I'm always glad to get back to work.'

I left Julie and joined Connie. She looked very Christmassy, dressed in a scarlet blouse buttoned high at the neck and with balloon sleeves, and a green and red apron. Her hair was newly permed and tinted, and she was sporting a pair of dancing reindeer earrings. She was standing by the buffet, watching proceedings with eagle eye.

'Good evening, Connie,' I said. 'You're looking

445

very festive.'

'I don't feel very festive,' she said. 'I'm thinking about all the clearing up which will have to be done when you lot have finished. Them pine needles get everywhere.'

'No overall today?'

'I don't sleep in my overall, you know, Mr Phinn,' she said sharply. 'When the occasion merits it, I do dispensate with it. In any case, as you well know, my pink one went walkabouts and I'm not at all happy with the colour of that blue one. Incidentally, I have a good idea who walked off with my pink one.'

'Really?' I said with feigned innocence.

'I reckon it was Mr Clamp. He was always making disparaging comments about it, and that I looked like a stick of Blackpool rock. It's just the sort of thing he would do. He's forever moving my stepladders, rearranging things, putting his horrible pictures up all over the place and playing tricks. He wants to grow up. It was him what told me that that flowering plant in the tub at the front of the Centre was a flaming alopecia and that creeper up the wall was a clitory, or something. Oh yes, he thinks he's very funny. Anyways, I won't be requiring any overall after this week.'

'Why's that?' I asked.

'Because I'm leaving, that's why.'

'You're not!' I exclaimed.

'I am. Finishing at the end of the week.'

'For goodness' sake, why didn't you say something?'

'You know I'm not a one for any fuss,' she told me. 'I can't be doing with it. As I put in my letter to Dr Gore, I've done my job to the best of my facility and now I want to enjoy my retirement while I can, with only my own house and the caravan to clean. Also, I want to be able to spend a bit more time with the grandchildren.'

'But you must have a send-off, Connie,' I said. 'You can't walk out of the door after all these years, not finish without a bit of a do.'

'It's been a bit of a do all these forty years, Mr Phinn, having to deal with all the destruction and debris you inspectors leave behind. I don't want no "bit of a do". They had a "bit of a do", as you call it, when my Ted retired from driving buses for forty years, rain or shine, wind and snow, ice and fog. They gave him a clock, ugly shiny gold thing it were, far too fancy for us. It stopped a week later. Anyway, I've got more clocks than I know what to do with. I don't know why they always give you a clock at the end. Is it so you can spend the rest of your time looking at it and seeing your life ticking away? Anyway, Ted's clock had a label on the bottom saying where they bought it from—Just Clocks in Station Parade in Brindcliffe—so I took it back and got a refund. Do you know that when my Ted retired, the General Manager—some youngster, wet behind the ears—said what a valued colleague he had been and how much he'd be missed. Didn't even know my Ted's name. Kept on calling him Ed. Didn't know him from Adam.'

'I think everyone knows *your* name, Connie,' I said, 'and I know for certain that you'll be greatly missed.'

'Well, that's as may be,' she replied, dismissing the compliment with a shrug. 'Any road, when I won on the bingo, I said to Ted—'

'You won on the bingo!' I exclaimed.

'I did,' she hissed, 'but keep your voice down. I don't want all and Sunday knowing. I scooped the Christmas jackpot, so you see going to bingo wasn't such a waste of time, like what you said.'

'Congratulations! How much did you win?'

Connie shrugged again. 'That's for me to know,' she told me. 'It's given me and Ted a bit of a nest egg, and it will supplicate my pension. So, you see, I won't be needing no overall after this week. Mr Clamp is welcome to it.'

For a moment, I considered telling her the truth, that her prized pink overall would be enshrined forever on the wall at St Margaret's School, preserved for all time in a fancy frame for the entire world to see, but I thought better of it. I somehow didn't feel she would find it amusing. 'I'm sure Sidney didn't take it, you know,' I said.

'Oh, yes he did,' said Connie. 'He went all quiet and guilty-looking when I brought it up at your meeting. He looked like a naughty child who had just been found out. I've known him long enough to be wise to his little japes and shenanigans. And if he thinks I'll take that letter he sent me seriously—'

'Letter?'

'He's sent me a joke letter.' She reached underneath the table for her handbag and, after rummaging through the contents, found a rather crumpled envelope, which she handed to me. 'He must think my brains are made of porridge to fall for this one.'

I read the letter. I was stunned.

'The Prime Minster has asked me to inform you, in strict confidence, that he has in mind, on the

448

occasion of the forthcoming New Year Honours, to submit your name to The Queen with a recommendation that Her Majesty may be graciously pleased to approve that you be appointed a Member of the Order of the British Empire.'

'Connie, this is no joke,' I told her, running my finger over the embossed crest and address at the top of the letter. 'It's the real thing!'

'Don't be so daft!'

'It is.'

'And who would want to give a medal to a cleaner?' she asked.

'The Queen,' I said, 'that's who.'

'It's Mr Clamp's idea of being funny,' she said, but there was a hint of doubt now in her voice. 'Isn't it?'

'No, Connie. This is an authentic letter from 10 Downing Street. You're getting a medal.'

'Are you kidding?'

'Not at all.'

'You mean they want to give me this—what was it?' she asked. 'An MBE?' Connie stood there, shaking her head.

'This is wonderful,' I said. 'Many many congratulations,' and I planted a little kiss on her cheek.

'Mr Phinn!' Connie squeaked, turning bright pink.

'But it's got to be kept secret until the Honours List is announced in the New Year,' I cautioned her. 'You shouldn't have told me or anyone— except perhaps Ted—until it's official. It says in the letter that you have to keep it to yourself, it's in the strictest confidence, until the announcement.'

'Well, I didn't know it was for real,' she said. She looked flustered and now her face began to drain of colour. 'You wouldn't have me on, would you?' asked Connie, gripping my arm.

'No, Connie, I'm not having you on.'

'You mean I'm getting a medal?' she murmured. 'You mean, I'm actually getting to meet Her Majesty at Buckingham Palace, that I'll get to talk to the Queen? I mean, how would the Queen know about *me*?'

'I believe she—or more likely the Government—reviews recommendations that are sent in. It's not only retiring politicians, pop stars or footballers that get medals. You'll now have the letters MBE after your name,' I told her.

'I think I'm going to faint,' she said, resting her hand on the table and bending over like a broken puppet.

'Don't forget—you mustn't say anything to anybody,' I warned her as I caught sight of Geraldine and Sidney heading in our direction.

'Connie, are we going to get a glass of sherry or not?' asked Sidney. 'We've been here a good half hour and not a sign of any libation. And when can we make a start on that delicious-looking repast which you have so beautifully prepared?' Connie stared into the middle distance and said nothing. She had a puzzled faraway look on her face. 'Connie! Are you all right? Did you hear me?'

'You look ill, Connie,' said Geraldine taking her arm. 'Would you like to sit down?'

'No, I'll be fine, Dr Mullarkey, thank you very much,' she replied vacantly. 'I just feel a bit funny, that's all. I'd better see to the drinks.'

After she'd left the room Sidney said to me, 'I

don't know what you were saying to Connie but you appear to have frightened the life out of her. She went out of this room looking like an extra from *The Village of the Damned.*'

'I'll go after her,' said Geraldine.

'No, I'll go,' I said.

I found Connie in the kitchen. She was sitting behind the hatch crying. 'Now, now, Connie,' I said, putting my arm around her shoulder. 'Why the tears? You should be over the moon.'

'I don't know what's the matter with me,' she said, sniffing noisily. 'I've come over all unnecessary, as my mother used to say. It's the shock, I suppose. Meeting the Queen. I thought it was a joke, that it was Mr Clamp playing his usual fun and games.' She shook her head. 'To think that anybody would want to give me a medal for cleaning toilets and doing a bit of dusting.'

'You do more that that Connie,' I told her, 'much, much more.'

'Brave people like my father, they get medals,' she said. 'People what make a difference in life. I have Dad's medals on the sideboard at home. I polish them every week. I don't know what he'd make of this, I really don't.'

'He'd be so proud of you,' I said. 'You make a real difference to people's lives, Connie, and if anybody deserves a medal, it's you.'

'I just do my job, that's all,' she said, choking back a sob.

'You do more than that. Now, come on, dry those eyes and I'll help you with the sherry. And, remember, you must reply to the letter at once telling them you will accept the award or they'll think you don't want it. Also, remember, not a word about the letter to anyone.'

When we arrived back in the lounge area, we discovered Dr Gore had made an appearance with Mrs Savage. His PA was dressed in a striking cerise silk dress with a feather boa draped around her shoulders and, as ever, jangled with expensive jewellery. She was never knowingly underdressed was Mrs Savage, and rarely missed an opportunity to show off yet another new outfit. She was in conversation with Miss de la Mare and David as I approached them with the tray of sherry.

'So is it a quiet Christmas for you this year, Mrs Savage?' the Chief Inspector was enquiring.

'Good gracious, no, Miss de la Mare,' Mrs Savage replied, giving one of her all-too-familiar patronising smiles. 'Quite the opposite, actually. I'm spending the holiday with a friend in the South of France. The Riviera is quite something at this time of year.'

'Whereabouts?' asked David.

'I beg your pardon?' asked Mrs Savage.

'Whereabouts on the Riviera are you going?'

'San Tropez,' Mrs Savage told him. 'And are you familiar with the French Riviera, Mr Pritchard?'

'Not at all, never been,' he replied.

'Then why do you ask?' she asked, giving him a withering look.

'Just interested, that's all,' he said, helping himself to a glass of sherry. There was mischief in his eyes. 'As a matter of fact, our Captain at the Golf Club has a place in the South of France. Now that's a coincidence isn't it? And I believe *his* place is in San Tropez. He always spends Christmas out there.'

'Really,' said Mrs Savage, taking a glass from the

tray and assuming total disinterest.

'Of course, you know Tadge—Lord Manston—don't you, Mrs Savage?' said David. 'You did a bit of the old liaising with him over the CEO's conference.'

'Our paths have crossed,' she replied, looking extremely uncomfortable.

'Perhaps you'll bump into him in San Trop,' said David casually.

'If you will excuse me, Miss de la Mare,' said Mrs Savage, turning to the Chief Inspector. 'I think Dr Gore wants a word.'

'That was very naughty of you, David,' I said after Mrs Savage had moved away with a jangle of jewellery. 'You don't really think she's spending Christmas with old Tadge, do you?'

'Very likely,' replied David. 'Plenty of other women have stayed with him over the years, from what I've heard. I told you he was a bit of a *roué*.'

'You never know,' said Miss de la Mare, chuckling, 'Mrs Savage might return after Christmas as Lady Manston. Now, that *would* be interesting.'

'Perish the thought!' exclaimed David. 'Mrs Savage with a title! Lady Brenda! I can't bear to think about it.'

Sidney gatecrashed the conversation. 'So what was all that about with Connie?' he asked me. 'She was uncharacteristically taciturn.'

'She's leaving,' I told him.

'Leaving!' exclaimed Sidney and David together.

'I didn't know about this,' said Miss de la Mare.

'Nobody did,' I said, 'well, apart from Dr Gore. Connie says she wants to go quietly.'

'Go quietly?' repeated Sidney. 'Connie?'

'That's what she said.'

'Whatever will we do without her?' said David.

'The place just won't be the same,' added Sidney.

Our discussion was interrupted by Dr Gore who, tapping a spoon on his glass, called for attention.

'Colleagues, friends, before we enjoy the Christmas fare that Connie has prepared for us, I guess it is incumbent upon me to say a few words at this convivial occasion.' He coughed and then slipped with ease into one of his famous monologues. 'This term has been a particularly successful one. Standards in schools have continued to rise, the Education Department's budget looks as though it should see us through to the end of the financial year, the school closures—which could very well have been most contentious and time-consuming—were effected with the minimum of complaint and only one or two hiccoughs, and my NACADS Conference was a resounding success. Indeed, Sir Bryan told me as he departed back to the metropolis that he was most impressed with the sterling work we undertake in the county.

'But, colleagues, friends, I cannot let this occasion pass without mentioning one particular individual, someone who has been a stalwart in the Education Department—loyal, reliable, hard-working and never stinting in the work she has undertaken for the many years I have known her. She has been a great asset to the Education Department and I would like to acknowledge that this evening.'

Mrs Savage, standing to the right of Dr Gore, gave a slight smile of appreciation. She reminded me of a film star waiting to receive an Academy Award.

The CEO continued. 'I have discovered that in life there are four kinds of people. There are the wishbones and they are the dreamers. There are the jawbones and they are the talkers. There are the knucklebones and they are the critics. And then there are the backbones and they are the ones who carry the load and do the work. The person to whom I am referring has been the very backbone of the Education Department. I speak, of course, of Connie.'

I was watching Mrs Savage, and her face was a picture. She looked like a startled ostrich. In contrast, the colour drained again from Connie's face and she looked ashen and deeply uncomfortable. Fortunately, I was holding the tray of sherry or, had she been dispensing it, it would undoubtedly have clattered to the floor.

'Connie wrote to me at the beginning of this month,' continued Dr Gore, 'tendering her resignation and saying she wished to leave at the end of this term. She wanted no fuss, no leaving celebration, nothing special. She wished to retire quietly. Well, for once, Connie, you are not getting your own way.' Dr Gore reached behind him for a large box wrapped in silver paper. 'I should like to present you, on behalf of all in the Education Department who have so valued your good offices, with this gift, in appreciation of your loyal and devoted service over the last forty years.' There was a round of enthusiastic applause. 'And, you know, Connie,' said the CEO, raising a hand, 'if it were up to me, I'd give you a medal.' I knew then who had recommended her for the award. 'Perhaps

Miss de la Mare, you might like to say a few words.'

'Thank you, Dr Gore' said the Chief Inspector, moving forward. 'I should just like to echo your comments. None of us, with the exception of yourself, had any idea Connie was leaving us. She will be greatly missed. To repeat one of my colleagues, the place won't be the same without her. I speak for everyone here, Connie, when I say thank you for all you have done and may I wish you a very happy, restful and well-deserved retirement.'

'Hear, hear!' said Sidney, not very *sotto voce*.

'And I should also like to put on record my own appreciation for all the hard work everyone has put in this year, and for the welcome you have given me as Head of Department. I came to this great county of rolling fells and trickling becks, austere moorland and soft green dales, twisting roads and endless limestone walls, and felt immediately at home. It is a vast and beautiful landscape, God's own country, but it is the people in Yorkshire who make it so special—their warmth, hospitality, blunt honesty and cheerful good humour. So thank you, thank you so much for making me feel so very welcome. Now,' she said, turning to Connie who was standing in front of her, clutching the large silver box, 'perhaps you would like to open your present.'

Connie took the box to the table and loosened the paper from around it. She lifted the lid off the box, and peered inside. 'Oh, goodness me, how I . . . lovely!' she said, and drew out a large ugly shiny gold clock.

CHAPTER TWENTY-SIX

During the final few weeks of term, teachers and pupils everywhere had been preparing for Christmas. Highly-decorated fir trees in large tubs stood in entrance halls, wreaths of holly and laurel hung on doors, cribs with brightly-coloured figures had been taken from storeroom shelves, dusted down and arranged in classrooms, walls had been decorated with Christmas scenes, and nativity plays had been rehearsed and then staged throughout the county. I have always loved the weeks leading up to the year's most celebrated festival, both now and when I had been a child myself.

I was not aware of it at the time but, looking back, I realised I had had a charmed childhood and the very best life could offer—the combination of loving parents and dedicated teachers. I had assumed that all children, like myself, had parents who were, like the weather, always there—parents who never missed the opportunity of celebrating anything good that I did, however small; parents who told me stories and read to me every night; and parents who expected a great deal of me yet convinced me that I was as good as any of the other children. I think my parents believed that their first duty was to make me happy.

Of the many children I have met in the course of teaching and inspecting schools, some had been lucky and, like me, had had the very best; the world, to use one of Connie's expressions, was 'their lobster'. Some like Michael, with disabilities, had mountains to climb, but they often possessed the determination and strength of character to get to the top. Others like Miranda would feel the pressure of excessively self-assertive and overly ambitious parents who won't allow them to have a carefree and happy childhood. And then there were children like Terry—angry, lonely, mixed up, troublesome—who have a hard time of it growing up. Before he was taken into care, there was nothing in Terry's home except anger and unhappiness; there were no kind words of encouragement, no saving moments of fun; there was nothing to look forward to, nothing to strive for. He, of all children, deserved to have the very best teachers, teachers like Miss Bailey and Mr Hornchurch, who were enthusiastic, respectful, good-humoured, and who brought compassion, respect and laughter into the lives of the children they taught.

Wandering round Fettlesham on a cold, damp Saturday afternoon, a couple of weeks into my job as a school inspector, I had come on a second-hand bookshop down a narrow alleyway. I already had quite a collection of old books that I used to use in class when I was teaching—traditional fairy stories and fables, poetry anthologies, old-fashioned picture books, even defunct reading schemes. I had decided to go into the shop to see if there was anything of interest on the shelves.

The interior of the shop was as cold and damp as the world outside, and was deserted save for an elderly man who sat behind the counter, his nose in a small book. He looked up briefly at the sound of the tinkling bell but then returned to his reading and left me alone to browse. Some time later, I returned to the counter with the two books I had decided to buy.

The first book was a tattered specimen with a faded red leather binding but with what must have once been finely-tooled lettering; its pages were creased and discoloured. The book, written over a century before, by one Thomas Cobden-Sanderson, was about childhood. In it, I read later, he wrote of the qualities he hoped to inculcate in Richard, his five-year-old son. Of course, I never thought at the time that one day I would have a son of that name, too. The qualities that Thomas Cobden-Sanderson listed seemed to me to sum up what the good parent should endeavour to instil in the young: politeness, kindness, obedience, patience, unselfishness, fortitude, courage, truthfulness, self-control, application, modesty and reverence. I remember wondering at the time just what young Richard Cobden-Sanderson had made of himself in the world with such a start in life.

The proprietor handled the second tome with great reverence, stroking the covers with long fingers. It was clear he was reluctant to sell it. The book had a sturdy rust-coloured cover and was called *Dale Folk, Character Sketches in Prose and Verse* and had been written by Dorothy Una Ratcliffe over fifty years earlier. It was a treasure chest of anecdotes and stories, verses and memories and illustrated with detailed line drawings and delicate sketches.

'I shall be very sorry to see this one go,' he had told me sadly. 'I often used to take it off the shelf and read from it. And it's still in very good condition.' He had looked at me for a moment before adding, 'But I feel certain you will give it a good home.'

459

'How do you know that?' I'd asked, intrigued.

'Young man,' he'd said, 'you have spent the best part of an hour browsing the shelves, handling the books, turning the pages. You lost track of time. I can tell you are a lover of books.' Despite my protestations he would only take two pounds.

That night, in my cramped flat above The Rumbling Tum café, I had read *Dale Folk* from cover to cover, learning much about the people of the Dales who would soon become so special to me. It was a work of considerable poignancy and beauty, shrewdly observant, with a genuine flavour of the humour, plain-speaking, generosity and occasional dourness of this unspoilt rural people.

I had recently picked the book off the shelf at Peewit Cottage and re-read some of the chapters. Before shutting it, I had turned to the note printed near the front as a sort of dedication. 'The people in this book you will find anywhere so long as you really wish to meet them.' Having now spent over four years as a school inspector in the magnificent county of Yorkshire, I had indeed met a veritable cast of them: Harry Cotton, George Hemmings, Thomas Umpleby, Hezekiah Longton, Maurice Hinderwell, Lord Marrick, Andy—gamekeepers and gardeners, shepherds and lords of the manor, pest control officers and lollipop ladies, not to mention the many teachers and the wonderful children of the Dales.

*   *   *

It was a cold, overcast afternoon when I arrived at the final school I would visit that term. Backwatersthwaite Primary had been the very first

460

school I had visited on becoming a school inspector. I was now looking forward to renewing my acquaintance with the remarkable headteacher, Mr Lapping. Our paths had crossed on various occasions during the intervening years, and he had never failed to impress me.

I had got hopelessly lost on the way to that first visit and had, in fact, passed the school without realising it. There had been no traffic triangle warning of a school, no school board, no playground, nothing that would identify the austere building as an educational establishment. I formed the idea at the time that the window boxes, tubs of bright flowers, curtained windows and small carefully-tended garden in the front of the building were intended to disguise the fact that it was a school. Perhaps the headteacher had cleverly altered the appearance of the building to resemble a private dwelling to evade a visit from unwanted visitors, in particular anyone from the Education Department at County Hall.

I smiled now as I made my way up the narrow path towards the gaunt stone edifice with its shiny slate roof and high leaded windows. I recalled that first occasion when I had lifted the great iron knocker in the shape of a ram's head and let it fall with a resounding thump. The heavy black door had opened and I had been confronted by a thin, stooping man with frizzy greying hair like a tangle of wire wool and the complexion of a corpse. The figure appeared as though he had clambered up an embankment after a rail crash. He had had no policy documents, planning materials, schemes of work, lesson plans or curriculum guidelines. When I had asked to see his School Development Plan, he had run a hand through his hair and wrinkled his forehead into a frown. Then he had given a hollow laugh and had informed me frankly that he wouldn't recognise such a thing if it were to fly through the window. He had gone on to inform me that, in his book, education was not about paper and processes, procedures and documentation, it was about *teaching*. Then he had tapped his brow.

'It's all up here, Mr Phinn,' he had said.

He had told me, on that first meeting, that he reckoned it was the teacher who made the real difference in children's lives and that the teacher has an awesome power and a great responsibility. 'A teacher can inspire or deaden, challenge or bore, hurt or heal, develop a love of learning or kill it stone dead,' he had told me. 'Teaching is a vocation, Mr Phinn, not a job.'

Because of my late arrival, the children had in fact already gone home and so I had returned a month later for a proper visit. Despite the fact that there was still nothing written down or recorded, I had been highly impressed by everything I had seen and heard. Before I had left, a small nine-year-old with wide eyes and thick bracken-coloured hair had approached to inform me seriously that 'Mester Lapping's a reight good teacher, tha knaws.' He had then suggested that I ought to write it down in my little black book in case I should forget.

Mr Lapping was now retiring after forty years in a profession he described as the most influential of all. I was there that afternoon to wish him the very best in his new life. He was moving south to Canterbury to live nearer to his daughter and grandchildren. I knew he would miss Yorkshire

462

desperately and wondered if he would ever settle so far away from his beloved county. I had been invited to his farewell party, which was to take place later in the village hall, but sadly I had had to decline since it clashed with the nativity play at Hawksrill School. I had promised Christine I would be home in time to go to it with her.

Mr Lapping and I were sitting in his office, during the afternoon break. Through the window, I could see that snow had started to fall softly, and the deep valley, where a wide unhurried river flowed gently beneath the arches of a slender bridge, was speckled in white.

'This is for you, George,' I said, passing him a brightly wrapped present. 'As you browse through the pages, it's to help you remember your days in Yorkshire. It will perhaps remind you of the people of the Dales who have been so much a part of your life.'

'How very kind,' he replied. 'May I open it?'

'Of course.'

He stared at the book, then read from the binding: '*Dale Folk, Character Sketches in Prose and Verse* by Dorothy Una Ratcliffe. How wonderful. Thank you so much.'

'The final poem is a particular favourite of mine,' I told him. 'Perhaps I might read it to you and wish you all the very best in your retirement. It's called "The Yorkshire Blessing"—I expect you know it.' I turned to the very last page and read:

> To thi mind—Peace,
> To thi 'eart—Joy,
> To thi soul—
> Strength

463

And Courage.

In thine outgoings
Nowt amiss,
To thi 'ome comings
'Appiness.

'Thank you, Gervase,' he said quietly. 'I shall treasure it.' There were tears in his eyes.

He took a moment to compose himself, and then asked, 'You will stay for the final rehearsal of our nativity play, won't you? I am sure you will enjoy our very own Yorkshire version, which the children have written and produced themselves. They took the Bible story and re-wrote it in their own inimitable words. I suppose some might say it's not really appropriate to go tinkering about with the Good Book but, then again, it has been translated into a fair few languages in its time and I reckon God won't object if He hears it in dialect—especially since God is, of course, a Yorkshireman,' he added, with a twinkle in his eye.

I sat in at the back of the large room as the children performed their drama on the makeshift stage. Of all the nativity plays I had seen over the years, this was undoubtedly one of the most original and perhaps the most memorable. The cast had dispensed with the usual attire—sandals, dressing gowns, pasteboard crowns, coloured towels draped over heads (usually held in place by elastic belts with snake clasps), cottonwool beards, cloaks, cardboard wings and tinsel halos, and had opted for simple modern dress.

A large, fresh-faced girl with long flaxen hair and attired in black slacks and a white blouse stood at the side of the stage as two children, the boy dressed in jeans and denim jacket, the girl in a bright flowery dress, entered holding hands.

'And it came to pass,' said the narrator, 'that a decree went out from Caesar Augustus, the Emperor in Rome, that all the world should be taxed. Joseph, the carpenter, took Mary, his wife, who was having a baby, from Galilee to the city of David, which is called Bethlehem, in Judea from where his family came. They walked wearily along the hot and dusty road and into the town, which was crowded with people all there to be counted. Very soon Mary and Joseph, tired from their long journey, arrived at an inn looking for somewhere to stay.'

A boy wearing a blue and white striped apron stepped on to the stage, his hands on his hips.

'Innkeeper! Innkeeper! 'As thy any room?' asked Joseph.

'Nay, lad,' replied the Innkeeper. 'I've nowt left. We're full to burstin'. Place is chock-a-block wi' fowlk cum to pay their taxes.'

'That's a rum do. We've been on t'rooad all day,' Joseph told him, 'and both on us are fair fit to drop. We're fair fagged out!'

'Well, I'm reight sorry, lad, but there's nowt I can gi' thee. We're full up for t'neet.'

'I've got t'wife out 'ere,' announced Joseph. 'An' she's 'avin' a babby, tha knaas.'

'I'm reight sorry abaat that, an' all,' said the Innkeeper, 'but there's no room in t'inn, an' that's top an' bottom of it.'

'Nowt at all? Anythin' will do.'

'Theer's t'stable round t'back. Bit basic like, but it's warm an' dry enough. Tha can sleep theer if tha

465

wants.'

'It'll 'ave to do,' said Joseph. 'Come on, Mary.'

The narrator took up the story. 'And so Mary and Joseph had to sleep in the stable with the oxen and the asses, for there was no room in the inn that night.' The holy couple left the stage and two boys and a girl entered. They wore old jackets and flat caps, and carried crooks. 'Now far off, in a distant dale, on a dark, cold night, three shepherds were tending their sheep and watching over their flocks, when suddenly there appeared, in the dark sky, a great shining light.'

' 'Ey up!' said the first shepherd. 'Tek a look at that then!'

'Weer?' asked the second shepherd.

'Theer.'

'Weer?'

'Theer, up yonder in t'sky.'

'Wor is it?'

'I don't know but it's gerrin' brighter.'

A girl entered in a white blouse and skirt. ' 'Ey up, lads! Don't be frit. I'm not gunna 'urt thee. I'm Hangel o' Lord, 'ere wi' tidin's of gret joy.'

'What's that, then?' asked the third shepherd.

'There's a babby boy been booarn toneet, a reight special babby, who's liggin in a manger, wrapped up in swaddlin' bands, ovver in Bethle'em. God's own lad, Saviour o' World, Christ the Lord, the Messiah, an' does thy know what?'

'What?' asked the first shepherd.

' 'E's reight champion, that's what.'

'Way, 'appen we berrer gu an' see 'im then, sithee,' said the first shepherd.

'Wor abaat t'tups and yows?' asked the second.

466

'I'm not reight chuffed abaat leavin' 'em on their own, what wi' wolves.'

'Ne'er thee mither abaat tha sheep,' said the angel, 'I'll see to 'em fer thee.'

The narrator stepped forward and a group of children came on stage, dressed in white shirts, white trousers and white plimsolls. 'And suddenly the sky was filled with a host of heavenly angels.' The children sang lustily, 'Glory to God, Glory to God, Glory to God in the highest, and on Earth peace and goodwill toward all men.'

As the angels and shepherds left the stage, the Three Kings entered, wearing long red cloaks. 'Now far far away in a distant land, Three Kings, wise men of the East, saw a star high in the dark sky which foretold the birth of the newborn king.'

'Hey up!' said the first king. 'Tek a look at that, then!'

'Weer?' asked the second king.

'Theer.'

'Weer?'

'Theer, up yonder in t'sky.'

'Wor is it?'

'By the heck, it's a reight big star.'

'Tha knaas what that means, dunt tha?' said the third king.

'No,' chorused the other two.

'Tha does!'

'We doaan't.'

'Summat special's 'appenin', that's what. It's a sign from on 'igh. A new babby king's been born toneet. It were foretold. Come on, lads, let's follow yonder star an' see weer it teks us.'

' 'Old up,' said the second king. 'We shall 'ave to tek 'im a present.' The Three Kings left the stage,

467

picking up three brightly wrapped parcels on their way out.

'So the Three Kings set off to follow the star,' said the narrator, 'carrying their gifts of gold, frankincense and myrrh, and soon they arrived at a huge marble palace.' The Three Kings appeared back on stage. 'They knocked loudly on the great iron door and from inside came a voice. It was King Herod.'

'Clear off!'

'Oppen dooer!' shouted the first king. 'We're t'three kings from t'Orient.'

'I don't care who thy are or weer tha from. Clear off!'

'We've got gret news that a new babby king 'as been born this neet an' we're off to see 'im? Does tha want to come wi' us?'

On stage came a small boy with spiky hair and a brightly-coloured shirt. 'What's all this abaat a babby king, then?' he asked.

'I've just telled thee,' said the first king. 'See that theer star up in t'sky?'

'Weer?' asked Herod.

'Theer.'

'Weer?'

'Theer, up yonder in t'sky.'

'Wor abaat it?'

'Well, it's tekkin us to see this new babby king. Get tha cooat on an' tha can come wi' us.'

'Nay, I'll not bother,' replied Herod, 'but cum back this way, will tha, an' tell me weer this babby is and 'appen I'll go an' see 'im missen an' tek 'im a present.' He turned to the front and pulled a gruesome face. 'I'll tek 'im a present, all reight, and it'll not be wor 'e's hexpectin'. I'm not reight

468

chuffed abaat this at all. There's only gunna be one king around 'ere, sithee, an' that's gunna be me.' Herod stomped off.

The narrator continued as the stage filled with all the children, except Herod; they gathered around a small manger that had been brought onto the stage. 'And that night, in a stable in Bethlehem, Jesus Christ was born and the Three Kings and the humble shepherds, the angels and the beasts of the fields worshipped Him for He was the Son of God, the most wonderful, the King of all Kings and the Light of the World.'

'Glory be to God,' chorused the children.

'And all who saw the child marvelled,' said the narrator finally, 'but Mary, holding her newborn baby close to her breast, kept all these things to herself and pondered them in her heart.'

*   *   *

As I drove back to Hawksrill in the late afternoon sun, the light dusting of snow making the Dales look ethereal yet peaceful, I recalled the last words of the nativity play I had just seen—'Mary, holding her new born baby close to her breast',—and thought of my own beautiful wife and baby whom I should shortly see. How lucky I was!

The cottage looked welcoming as I parked the car on the track alongside the garden; there were lights behind the closed curtains, and a wisp of smoke curled up from the chimney into the frosty air. As I went through the back door and into the kitchen, the smell of something delicious cooking made me sniff the air appreciatively.

'Hello, darling,' said Christine, who was sitting

at the table, with Richard in his carrycot beside her.

I kissed them both. 'I was determined not to be late today,' I said. 'I really didn't want to miss the Hawksrill play. What time is your mother coming? It's good of her to baby-sit for us.'

'She rang about half an hour ago to say she was just leaving. And I can promise you, it's no hardship to her at all. She'll come any time and look after this little bundle for us.' The baby gurgled as if on cue.

I noticed there was a five-pound note on the table, and went to pick it up. 'Is this mine or yours?' I asked.

'It's mine—for the moment,' replied Christine. 'But it will be Andy's as soon as he calls round for it. I was expecting him earlier.'

'I don't understand,' I said. 'I paid Andy the other weekend all we owe him for the gardening.'

Christine laughed. 'This, I'm afraid, is for something quite different. It's for that bet you had with him—the red-tails are back!'

'What—here?' I asked. I had hoped I'd never see those wretched squirrels again.

'No, not here. You'd have heard about it long before if they were here. Andy called in to say that he had seen a flash of red tails down at Ted Poskitt's farm—and, incidentally, he said there's not much red on them any more. Apparently, they've taken up residence in the roof above an old tractor shed.' She stood up and crossed to stir something on the stove.

'I expect they'll be back here soon enough, then,' I said gloomily. 'The farm's not far away.'

'No,' said Christine, who appeared amazingly

calm about the return of the pesky creatures. 'Andy thinks that they will winter there now, hibernate, and in the spring they will be so busy thinking about babies that they will probably stay where they are.'

'Oh, good, that's that then', I said, mightily relieved.

'Well, don't forget you owe me for the fiver that's going to Andy,' she said.

'I won't forget,' I said, crossing the room to put my arms round her. 'Nor will I forget that I am married to the most enchanting girl in the world.'

Christine turned and nuzzled her face into my shoulder. 'And that we have a wonderful son in Richard,' she murmured, 'who would like at least two brothers and perhaps a little sister as well.'

And, in due course, that's just what happened.

A Dalesman to His Son

Well, lad,
I'll tell thee summat:
Life for me aint been no easy road to walk.
It's been a long hard journey—
Mostly uphill all the way.
At times it's been a hot and dusty trail,
Wi' potholes and sharp stones beneath mi feet
And a sweltering sun burning the back o' mi neck.
Sometimes it's been knee-deep wi' mud
And thick wi' snow and blocked wi' fallen trees,
With an icy wind blowing full in mi face.
There were times when it's been dark and
    dangerous
And I've been lonely and afraid and felt like
    turning back.
But all the time, lad,
I've kept plodding on,
And climbing stiles,
And scaling walls,
And seeing signposts,
And reaching milestones,
And making headway.
So, lad, don't you turn round,
Don't go back on the road
For I'm still walking,
I'm still walking,
And life for me aint been no easy road to walk.

CHIVERS
LARGE PRINT
–direct–

If you have enjoyed this Large Print book and would like to build up your own collection of Large Print books, please contact

Chivers Large Print Direct

Chivers Large Print Direct offers you a full service:

• Prompt mail order service

• Easy-to-read type

• The very best authors

• Special low prices

For further details either call Customer Services on (01225) 336552 or write to us at Chivers Large Print Direct, **FREEPOST**, Bath BA1 3ZZ

Telephone Orders: **FREEPHONE** 08081 72 74 75